Blackstc
Crime Invest
Handbook

Blackstone's Crime Investigators' Handbook

Third Edition

Steve Hibbitt, QPM
Gary Shaw, MBE

OXFORD
UNIVERSITY PRESS

OXFORD
UNIVERSITY PRESS

Great Clarendon Street, Oxford, OX2 6DP,
United Kingdom

Oxford University Press is a department of the University of Oxford.
It furthers the University's objective of excellence in research, scholarship, and education by publishing worldwide. Oxford is a registered trade mark of Oxford University Press in the UK and in certain other countries

First Edition published in 2013
Second Edition published in 2016
Third Edition published in 2023

Published in the United States of America by Oxford University Press
198 Madison Avenue, New York, NY 10016, United States of America

British Library Cataloguing in Publication Data

Data available

Library of Congress Control Number: 2022951047

ISBN 978–0–19–286789–6

DOI: 10.1093/oso/9780192867896.001.0001

Printed in the UK by
Ashford Colour Press Ltd, Gosport, Hampshire

Preface

This handbook is primarily aimed at police investigators and other persons or agencies involved in undertaking or studying criminal investigation. The contents follow the general principles of the National Occupational Standards for police investigations and wider law enforcement. The intention is to assist PIP Level 1 and PIP Level 2 investigators at the constable/investigator and sergeant/supervisor levels, including those returning or are new to role and those in training or working towards accreditation.

The overarching objective has been to compile a comprehensive handbook which contains concise practical advice and essential information for performing the duties of a criminal investigator. The book has been deliberately designed to be easily carried and is written in a straightforward style that enables the subject matter to be quickly located and referred to when required. It contains sufficient information to support investigative decision making and to apply appropriate procedures and processes when investigating various criminal offences. A series of checklists are included as guidance, and key points are summarised for easy reference. These are comprehensive but they are not definitive and investigators are encouraged to develop further approaches.

This handbook includes elements that relate to most of the fundamental aspects of investigation. The general investigative practice that applies to all investigations is included along with further considerations which apply to specific types of crime. The chapter sections and headings have been chosen to ensure that the most important topics are covered. These should reinforce and build upon knowledge available through the College of Policing *Authorised Professional Practice* (APP) and relevant other sources.

The subjects covered are those that mainstream investigators can expect to investigate or encounter at some point when performing their role. A handbook of this size can never cover all of the areas in extensive detail and that is not the intention. The depth of content has been developed to supply sufficient information to refer to as a starting point and to help develop an investigative strategy. Due to the nature and complexities involved with some of the subjects covered, this book could have easily developed into a more comprehensive volume containing additional detail and discussion. Had this been the case, the objective of producing a single 'reach for' handbook would have failed.

This is the third edition of the *Crime Investigators' Handbook* and the contributions of Tony Cook and Mick Hill, who previously co-authored the first edition (published in 2013) and the second edition (published in 2016), are rightfully and gratefully acknowledged. This third edition is now co-authored with the former National Investigative Interviewing Adviser Professor Gary Shaw, MBE.

Society continues to evolve and developments in investigation reflect this, including new and emerging crime types that require additional consideration. The impact of digital technology is significant, not just because of the investigative opportunities that are now available, but also because of the challenges of managing the disclosure of the high volume of mobile communications generated by many investigations. Technology is exploited by criminals and this has led to a significant use of the internet for criminal purposes and to commit online crime.

The demographic of the police workforce has changed, with a current national shortage of detectives. There are now direct entry routes into investigation and new to role investigators inevitably require training and development of their knowledge, skills and experience. Our intention

and wish are that investigators find this handbook both practical and convenient and it goes some way to assisting with performing their duties.

Steve Hibbitt
Gary Shaw

Contents

Abbreviations

5WH	Who? What? Where? When? Why? How?
AAIB	Air Accident Investigation Branch
ABC	Assume nothing, Believe nothing, Challenge/check everything
ABE	achieving best evidence
ACC	Assistant Chief Constable
ACPO	Association of Chief Police Officers
AFI	Accredited Financial Investigator
AFO	Authorised Firearms Officer
AG	Attorney General
AKA	also known as
ALTE	apparent life-threatening event
ANPR	Automatic Number Plate Recognition
AO	Authorising Officer
AOABH	assault occasioning actual bodily harm
APP	Authorised Professional Practice
AQ	Al-Qaeda
ATM	automatic telling machine
AV	audio visual
BCU	Basic Command Unit
BIA	Behavioural Investigative Adviser
BPA	blood pattern analysis
BT	British Telecom
BTP	British Transport Police
BWV	body worn video
CAA	Civil Aviation Authority
CACDP	Council for the Advancement of Communication with Deaf People
CAP	common approach path
CATCHEM	Centralised Analytical Team Collating Homicide Expertise and Management
CAU	Crime Analysis Unit
CBO	Criminal Behaviour Order

Abbreviations

CCRC	Criminal Cases Review Commission
CCTV	closed-circuit television
CDI	Communications Data Investigator
CDOP	Child Death Overview Panel
CDRP	Crime and Disorder Reduction Partnership
CEOP	Child Exploitation and Online Protection Centre
CFOA	Chief Fire Officers Association
CHIS	covert human intelligence source
CIA	Community Impact Assessment
CID	Criminal Investigation Department
CISO	Crime Investigative Support Officer
CJA	Criminal Justice Act 1967
CJPO	Criminal Justice and Public Order Act 1994
CLR	Criminal Law Review
COD	cause of death
CoP	College of Policing
COS	Crime Operational Support
CPA	crime pattern analysis
CPD	continuous professional development
CPIA	Criminal Procedure and Investigations Act 1996
CPS	Crown Prosecution Service
CQC	Care Quality Commission
CSC	Crime Scene Coordinator
CSE	Crime Scene Examiner or child sexual exploitation
CSI	Crime Scene Investigator
CSM	Crime Scene Manager
CT	counter-terrorism
CTC	counter-terrorism command
CTU	Counter-Terrorism Unit
CWB	Central Witness Bureau
DA	domestic abuse
DBIS	Department of Business Innovation and Skills
DCC	Deputy Chief Constable
DCS	Digital Case System

DDOS	Distributed Denial of Service
DHR	Domestic Homicide Review
DI	Detective Inspector
DIR	Dissident Irish Republican
DMD	disclosure management document
DMI	Digital Media Investigator
DNA	Deoxyribonucleic acid
DOS	Denial of Service
DPP	Director of Public Prosecutions
DSU	Dedicated Source Unit
DV	domestic violence
DVPN	Domestic Violence Protection Notice
DVPO	Domestic Violence Protection Order
EA	Environment Agency
EAW	European Arrest Warrant
ECHR	European Convention on Human Rights
EI	emotional intelligence
EIA	early investigative advice
ENQ	enquire (make enquiries)
EO	Exhibits Officer
ESDA	Electrostatic Document Apparatus
EWCA	England and Wales Court of Appeal
FCMH	Further Case Management Hearing
fDNA	familial DNA
FDR	firearms discharge residue
FLC	Family Liaison Coordinator
FLO	Family Liaison Officer
FME	Forensic Medical Examiner
FMPO	Forced Marriage Protection Order
FNO	Foreign National Offender
FOI	Freedom of Information Act 2000
FRA	Fire and Rescue Authority
FSID	Foundation for the Study of Infant Death
FSP	Forensic Service Provider
FSS	Forensic Science Service
GHB	Gamma Hydroxyburate
H2H	house-to-house enquiries
HBV	honour-based violence

HOLMES	Home Office Large Major Enquiry System
HP	high priority
HSE	Health and Safety Executive
HTA	Human Tissue Act 2004
ICC	International Coordination Centre
ICIDP	Initial Crime Investigators Development Programme
IED	improvised explosive device
IENCCU	Immigration Enforcement National Command and Control Unit
ILO	International Liaison Officer
ILOR	International Letter of Request
IMD	Investigation Management Document
IMEI	International Mobile Station Equipment Identity
IO	Investigating Officer
IOPC	Independent Office for Police Conduct
IP	internet protocol
IPLDP	Initial Police Learning and Development Programme
ISMDP	Investigative Supervisor and Manager Programme
ISP	Internet Service Provider or identify, secure and protect
JDLR	'just doesn't look right' principle
KCPO	Knife Crime Prevention Order
LA	local authorities
LKP	last known position
LCN	Low Copy Number
LP	low priority
LSCB	Local Safeguarding Children Board
LSD	lysergic acid diethylamide
LTDNA	low template DNA
MAIB	Marine Accident Investigation Branch
MAPPA	Multi-Agency Public Protection Arrangements
MAPPP	Multi-Agency Public Protection Panel
MARAC	Multi-Agency Risk Assessment Conference

MCA	Maritime and Coastguard Agency
MCIM	Major Crime Investigation Manual (2021)
MCIS	Major Crime Investigative Support (NCA)
MDMA	Methylenedioxy-Methamphetaminne (Ecstasy)
MHPRA	Medicines and Healthcare Products Regulation Authority
MIR	Major Incident Room
MIRSAP	Major Incident Room Standardised Administrative Procedures (2021)
MIT	Major Incident Team/Major Investigation Team
MLO	Media Liaison Officer
MLOE	main lines of enquiry
MO	modus operandi
MOD	manner of death
MoD	Ministry of Defence
MOSAVO	Management of Sexual or Violent Offenders
MP	medium priority
MPB	Missing Persons Bureau (UK)
MPS	Metropolitan Police Service
MtDNA	Mitochondrial DNA
NABIS	National Ballistics Intelligence Service
NCA	National Crime Agency
NCIS	National Criminal Intelligence Service
NCLCC	National County Lines Coordination Centre
NDM	National Decision Model
NDNAD	National DNA Database
NFIB	National Fraud Intelligence Bureau
NFRC	National Footwear Reference Collection
NID	National Injuries Database
NIM	National Intelligence Model
NIIS	National Investigative Interviewing Strategy
NOS	National Occupational Standards
NPCC	National Police Chiefs Council

NPIA	National Policing Improvement Agency
NPT	Neighbourhood Policing Team
NRM	National Referral Mechanism
NRPSI	National Register of Public Service Interpreters
NSA	National Search Adviser
NSPCC	National Society for the Prevention of Cruelty to Children
OBT	obtain
OCG	organised crime group
OIA	Operational Intelligence Assessment
OIC	Officer in Charge/Officer in Case
ONR	Office for Nuclear Regulation
OP	Observation Post
ORR	Office of Rail Regulation
OSC	Office of the Surveillance Commissioner
OSRI	Open Source Research of the Internet
PACE	Police and Criminal Evidence Act 1984
PAT	Problem Analysis Triangle
PCSO	Police Community Support Officer
PDF	Personal Descriptive Form or potentially dangerous person
PED	Police Elimination Database
PHA	Protection from Harassment Act 1997
PIB	pre-interview briefing
PII	Public Interest Immunity
PIP	Professionalising Investigations Programme
PNC	Police National Computer
PND	Police National Database
POCA	Proceeds of Crime Act 2002
POI	person of interest
PolSA	Police Search Adviser
PPE	personal protection equipment
PPO	persistent and priority offender
PST	Police Search Team
PTMH	Pre-Trial Management Hearing
PTPH	Plea and Trial Preparation Hearing

QBD	Queens Bench Division
QUEST	Query Using Enhanced Search Techniques
RA	responsible authority
RA	Regional Advisers (NCA)
RAIB	Rail Accident Investigation Branch
RARA	Remove, Avoid, Reduce, Accept
RASSO	Rape and Serious Sexual Offences
RAT	Routine Activity Theory
RI	reinterview
RIPA	Regulation of Investigatory Powers Act 2000
RMFHC	runaway and missing from home and care
ROVI	Record of Video Interview
RMP	Royal Military Police
RVP	rendezvous point
SARC	Sexual Assault Referral Centre
SCAS	Serious Crime Analysis Section
SCAIDIP	Specialist Child Abuse Investigator Development Programme
SCPO	Serious Crime Prevention Order
SHPO	Sexual Harm Prevention Order
SGM	Single Generation Multiplex
SIDS	Sudden Infant Death Syndrome
SIO	Senior Investigating Officer
SIODP	Senior Investigating Officer Development Programme
SOC	Specialist Operations Centre
SOCO	Scenes of Crime Officer
SOCPA	Serious Organised Crime and Police Act 2005
SOE	sequence of events
SOIT	Sexual Offence Investigation Trained
SOPO	Sexual Offence Prevention Order
SOS	Specialist Operational Support
SPoC	single point of contact
SRO	Sexual Risk Order
STPO	Slavery and Trafficking Prevention Order
STRO	Slavery and Trafficking Risk Order

SUDC	sudden and unexpected death of a child
SUDI	sudden unexpected death in infancy
SVRO	Serious Violence Reduction Order
SWIT	significant witness
SWOT	Strengths, Weaknesses, Opportunities and Threats
TACT	Terrorism Act
TCG	Tasking and Coordinating Group
TFS	Take Further Statement
TI	trace and interview
TIE	Trace, Investigate and Evaluate
TOR	The Onion Router
TRA	Travel Restriction Order
TST	take statement
TTL	threats to life
UF	unidentified female
UK	United Kingdom
UK-CRIS	UK Criminal Records Information System
UM	unidentified male
UU	unidentified unknown
UV	unidentified vehicle
VCCM	Volume Crime Management Model
VCSE	Volume Crime Scene Examiners
VEIC	video evidence-in-chief
ViCLAS	Violent Crime Linkage Analysis System
ViSOR	UK Violent and Sex Offenders Register
VPS	Victim Personal Statement
WOFD	Warrant of Further Detention
XRW	extreme right wing
YJCEA	Youth Justice and Criminal Evidence Act 1999
YOT	Youth Offending Team
Y-STR	Y Strand (DNA)

Chapter 1
Role of a Criminal Investigator

1.1 Introduction

Criminal investigation is a core police function that requires general and specific skills to be applied with an investigative mindset and sound professional judgement. To protect the public and build safer communities crimes need to be solved and offenders identified and processed. Investigative material must be located, obtained and evaluated to identify evidence that is admissible in a court, or that which could be used to inform and develop existing or further lines of enquiry. Victims and witnesses need supporting to give their best evidence whilst managing the potential impact that the crime or incident has had on them personally. Professional judgement and sound decision making are required which is capable of withstanding examination by the courts, if necessary, plus any internal and external scrutiny by others if required.

An effective investigator needs extensive knowledge to apply a wide range of existing and emerging legislation, policy, guidance and procedure which in some areas may be complex. This necessitates taking personal responsibility for continuous professional development to keep up to date with new developments, including advances in investigative and evidence gathering techniques, forensic science, technology, digital media and how these can be applied to investigation.

Blackstone's Crime Investigators' Handbook. Steve Hibbitt and Gary Shaw, Oxford University Press.
DOI: 10.1093/oso/9780192867896.003.0001

Contemporary issues impacting on the investigator include the rapid development of the internet and communications technology, which has led to the emergence of a parallel digital society. Keeping pace with criminals' exploitation of technology to commit new types of crime or assist in the commission of existing crime types is problematic and is likely to remain so. Crimes can be perpetrated in the United Kingdom by offenders who are located abroad by using sophisticated technology which present investigative, legislative and procedural challenges for investigators, and the demand for specialist resources is significant.

The continuing progress with technology has afforded unprecedented investigative opportunities which could have only been imagined previously. Whilst these are of enormous benefit to investigations, the application of digital media investigation requires careful consideration by investigators. Matters to consider include processing and managing the high volume of digital data now generated by investigations, whilst balancing the disclosure obligations required under Criminal Procedure and Investigations Act 1996. A contemporary issue, for example, is any necessity for the examination of sexual offence complainants' mobile phones and other devices and the extent and intrusion involved, including how this can be sensitively managed.

Public interest in criminal investigation remains high, supported by extensive and sometimes intrusive reporting, observation and comment through mainstream and social media. In addition to reporting on live cases there is an almost continuous supply of television documentaries, dramas, films, books and magazines. Perceived fact and fiction often have little resemblance to the reality of a modern investigator and can unrealistically raise public expectations, as with the Crime Scene Investigator (CSI) effect whereby the public believe some fictional techniques are real.

The manner in which crime is approached, investigated and prevented may include partnership or multiagency working and community involvement. Safeguarding vulnerable children and adults to identify and mitigate risks to them requires broad consideration beyond the actual investigation of any offences involved. Multi agency measures to tackle and prevent persistent offenders and target specific crime types such as adult and child sexual exploitation, county lines drug dealing and modern slavery through exploiting the vulnerable are all considerations. Regardless of rank, all investigators have a contribution to make in this respect. This may range from more senior officers developing policy and managing organisational relationships to officers conducting investigations and ensuring timely, accurate and actionable information and intelligence is submitted for assessment.

Investigators who adopt a thinking approach are required. Following existing processes and procedures is necessary to manage the volume of crime reported against the resources available to investigate it, including any financial constraints. However, using generic plans, tick boxes and drop down menus can only take an investigation so far regarding solvability factors.

Critical thinking and creativity are also required, to be applied with common sense and an investigative mindset to achieve the maximum chance of success. Being a crime investigator remains one of the most rewarding roles in policing. Considerable satisfaction can be gained from uncovering facts and evidence, identifying and arresting offenders, convicting the guilty in court and preventing further harm to others. So too is informing victims that their crime has been solved and helping them where possible to move on with their lives.

This handbook aims to provide practical suggestions, advice and help to those who are or intend to work in an investigative role. It seeks to minimise any complex concepts and act as a practical, straightforward guide for practitioners to quickly consult when required. It has been developed to logically follow the sequence of an investigation although inevitably these will overlap to a certain extent. It can also be used as a basis to encourage developing a deeper knowledge of the subjects involved so useful sources and references are included.

This first chapter begins by outlining various requirements and elements that make up a crime investigator's role and it is the foundation for the chapters that follow.

1.2 Criminal Investigation and the Investigator

1.2.1 Criminal investigation

Criminal investigations can be either reactive, proactive or investigations into 'crimes in action'. Reactive investigations are conducted after an offence has been committed, reported or discovered. Proactive investigations are often conducted before a crime has been committed, for example surveillance operations. A 'crime in action' investigation is conducted at the same time as the offence is being committed and is generally conducted covertly on a need to know basis until moving to a reactive phase. Examples of these usually include kidnap and extortion, blackmail and product contamination where ransom demands are made and a high risk of harm is involved. Other types of crime that might be committed over an extended time frame while the investigation is in progress could include computer ransomware attacks and perhaps romance fraud, but these do not fall strictly within the definition as they do not involve a threat to life.

Whatever type of investigation is being conducted, the emphasis should always be on the 'search for the truth' as opposed to the 'search for the proof' whereby investigative material and evidence is not properly considered or investigated if it does not support a point which could prove a prosecution case. A 'points to prove' approach presupposes that a crime or crimes has been committed whereas a 'search for the truth' approach could provide other possible outcomes, such as no crime having been committed or revealing a suspect to be innocent.

A general description of crime investigation could be as straightforward as 'gathering information, material and evidence to identify, apprehend and convict suspected offenders'. It is, however, much more complex than this and embraces a wide range of functions and responsibilities, the majority of which are contained in this handbook.

The statutory definition of a criminal investigation is contained in the Criminal Procedure and Investigations Act 1996 (CPIA) Code of Practice, Part II of which defines a criminal investigation as:

> An investigation conducted by police officers with a view to it being ascertained whether a person should be charged with an offence, or whether a person charged with an offence is guilty of it. This will include:
>
> - investigations into crimes that have been committed;
> - investigations whose purpose is to ascertain whether a crime has been committed with a view to possible institution of criminal proceedings; and
> - investigations which begin in the belief that a crime may be committed, for example when the police keep premises or individuals under observation for a period of time with a view to the possible institution of criminal proceedings.

It can be seen that the CPIA definition of a criminal investigation therefore includes reactive investigations, proactive investigations and investigations into crimes in action. Charging a person with an offence includes initiating a prosecution by way of summons or a requisition.

KEY POINT

Investigations may encounter challenges that need to be addressed, for example:

- lack of victim/offender close contact (eg online offences such as certain types of fraud and cybercrime)
- contaminated or disturbed crime scenes

- high risk and/or vulnerable victims
- absence of evidence or information from witnesses, forensic or other sources
- lack of cooperation and assistance from witnesses or others in the community
- multiple victims
- cases that attract widespread public/media attention
- drug-or gang-related crimes (eg so-called 'bad on bad' cases)
- absence of criminal indicators
- low or high volume of information and material to manage
- series of crimes
- critical incidents
- defined and demanding time scales for preparing case papers for trial (eg forensic reports and delayed tests, communications data enquiries and examination, passive data capture and viewing, obtaining expert evidence)
- crimes involving trans-European or international victims and offenders
- use of social networking sites, global communication, travel networks and 'virtual' communities to facilitate criminality
- lack of resources and funding
- managing competing demands
- changing public opinion, political overtones and investigative priorities

1.2.2 Criminal investigator

The term 'criminal investigator' tends to be a broad term that covers many activities and several types of specialists and professionals in law enforcement. It would include, for example, reactive detectives in traditional Criminal Investigation Departments (CID), Crime Scene Investigators (CSIs), Digital Media Investigators (DMIs), child protection specialists and external forensic experts and laboratory technicians. These examples are not exhaustive and perhaps the most obvious and visible is the police investigator who follows up enquiries and information about crimes, by developing leads, interviewing witnesses and suspects and preparing prosecution case files.

The *Oxford English Dictionary* defines the term 'investigate' as: 'To carry out a systematic or formal enquiry to discover and examine the facts of an incident or allegation so as to establish the truth …'; while an 'investigation' is defined as: 'The action of investigating something or someone by formal or systematic examination or research.' The same source defines a detective as: 'A person, especially a police officer whose occupation is to investigate and solve crimes'; 'detection' is: 'The action or process of identifying the presence of something concealed'; and the noun 'crime' is simply defined as: 'An action or omission which constitutes an offence and is punishable by law' (Soanes & Stevenson 2008).

In a policing context an investigator may be a police officer with powers of arrest but also a non-warranted police staff investigator with designated powers from their chief constable under the Policing and Crime Act 2017, Part 3, section 38. This amended the provisions of the Police Reform Act 2002 by replacing the categories of investigating officer, detention officer and escort officer into a single category of policing support officers. The powers that can be designated for police support officers in investigation roles include:

- applying for and executing search warrants
- seizing and retaining items and property including requesting information from a computer
- entry and search after arrest and general powers of seizure when lawfully on premises
- accessing and copying material
- extended powers of seizure (search and sift)
- access to excluded and special procedure material
- power to require arrested persons to account for certain matters

Police staff investigators must carry evidence of their designated powers and produce these on request. Their designated powers can also be exercised in another police force area where the chief constable includes this in the designation and they have the agreement of the other force identified.

In addition to the police there are also many other agencies that perform an investigative function including the National Crime Agency (NCA), the Health and Safety at Work Executive (HSE), the Royal Military Police (RMP) and the Inland Revenue and Trading Standards, amongst others.

Regardless of whether the investigator is a police officer or a police staff investigator, both have a duty to ensure any relevant material obtained or created by the investigation is recorded, retained and revealed in accordance with the disclosure obligations created by the CPIA. It is important that all investigators in whatever role they perform consider their approach to disclosure from the beginning of the investigation and not leave it until the end.

Part II of the CPIA Code of Practice defines the officer in charge of an investigation and their role within the Act as:

> the police officer responsible for directing a criminal investigation. They are also responsible for ensuring that proper procedures are in place for recording information and retaining records of information and material in the investigation.

The CPIA sets out duties for an investigator in relation to disclosure and also in respect of the investigation itself. Section 23 refers to the treatment and retention of material and information generated during such an investigation, and section 23(1)(a) contains a requirement for the police when conducting an investigation. It states:

> ... where a criminal investigation is conducted all reasonable steps are taken for the purposes of the investigation, and in particular all reasonable lines of enquiry are pursued.

Apart from satisfying the requirements of the CPIA for recording and retaining all potentially relevant information, crime investigators have many other duties and responsibilities, including:

Checklist—Duties of an investigator

- Establishing what happened through gathering facts and information
- Establishing what type and category of crime, if any, has been committed
- Gathering all available evidence
- Determining the objectives of the investigation
- Assessing what factors might impact positively or negatively on the investigation
- Planning and conducting an investigation
- Applying an investigative mindset to the circumstances of the case
- Critically questioning and scrutinising
- Briefing, tasking and debriefing others for the investigation
- Developing, prioritising and pursuing all reasonable lines of enquiry
- Identifying, securing and protecting crime scenes
- Establishing the identity of offenders and arresting, interviewing, processing and prosecuting those who have committed offences
- Developing hypotheses and theories and keeping them under review and updated
- Developing and implementing investigative strategies
- Locating and interviewing victims and witnesses and appropriately categorising them (eg significant, vulnerable, intimidated, reluctant or hostile)
- Acquiring intelligence and converting it into evidence
- Planning, organising and conducting crime scene and other searches

- Recovering stolen property or items of evidential value
- Collecting and accurately recording available information and material that may be relevant to the investigation
- Protecting the integrity of material or evidence gathered
- Identifying and obtaining the necessary resources including expert and specialist support wherever appropriate
- Developing and applying overt and covert and proactive tactics
- Keeping appropriate stakeholders, for example supervisory officers, victims, witnesses and communities, updated on progress
- Relaying to appropriate persons or departments any information or intelligence that may be relevant to other investigations
- Remaining accountable to police organisations, colleagues, the judicial process, victims and communities for the professional conduct of the investigation
- Assembling and submitting prosecution files, liaising with the Crown Prosecution Service (CPS),
- Assembling and submitting coroner's files regarding investigations into unexpected and/or unexplained death
- Presenting evidence in court and at other hearings
- Accurately recording all decisions and actions taken

KEY POINT

It cannot be overemphasised that one of the key roles of a crime investigator is to apply an investigative mindset to the evaluation of all information and material that is or becomes available during an investigation.

1.3 Investigative Skills and Knowledge Areas

Investigators need a combination of skills and knowledge, and there are added responsibilities for detective sergeants, detective inspectors and their police staff equivalents who perform a supervisory or management or role.

1.3.1 Investigative skills

- investigative ability (eg formulating lines of enquiry and decision making)
- strong problem solving skills
- competent and ethical decision making
- ability to appraise information (eg evaluating, interpreting and assimilating information, challenging assumptions, checking accuracy, reliability and relevance)
- adaptability and flexibility to react to changing circumstances
- strategic thinking and tactical awareness to recognise and understand the wider consequences of proposed actions and action taken
- innovativeness and creativity to achieve aims and objectives and solve problems
- effective communication skills (verbal and written)
- ability to manage time, prioritise and address competing demands
- ability to cope under pressure and uncertainty
- ability to work effectively as part of a team or as an individual
- ability to recognise and work with cultural diversity in an investigative context
- recognise wellbeing issues with others and themselves

1.3.2 Knowledge areas

- Knowledge of relevant law, procedure, policy and guidance and the context of its application

- Awareness of overt and covert tactics
- Theoretical knowledge. Investigators must maintain their continuous professional development (CPD) and conscientiously seek out, learn, appreciate and understand new knowledge and information applicable to their role. For example, current legislation including updates and changes, legal procedures, relevant powers and definitions of offences, points to prove, potential defences case law, rules of evidence, organisational and force policies and requirements for general criminal investigation and specific crime categories and types, authorised professional practice (College of Policing), national guidelines, manuals and doctrines, crime recording and processing methods, forensic procedures, investigative and technological advances, nationally and locally disseminated good practice and learning points, debrief reports, public and community awareness, organisational priorities and performance targets and indicators
- Critical thinking. Expanding and drawing upon the mental agility of self and colleagues, challenging existing knowledge and replacing it with improved information and process where this is proven and appropriate (eg looking at things from a different perspective to produce alternative methods and possibilities to achieve results)

KEY POINTS

- 'Critical thinking' involves looking at problems from different angles and different stakeholders' perspectives and identifying and questioning any assumptions. It tests the validity of theories, practice and process and explores whether there might be an alternative more effective approach or explanation.
- Creativity and ideas can come at any time (eg when off duty or the middle of the night) and may be triggered by unrelated activities and events. It is worthwhile having a means of noting them down so they can be recalled later and not forgotten.

- Investigative knowledge covers areas such as dealing with suspects, witnesses and TIE subjects (Trace, Investigate and Evaluate); awareness of forensic examination techniques and crime-scene examination; procedures relating to exhibit recovery, packaging, storage, examination and review; 'fast track' forensic tests; strategies for main lines of enquiry, such as developments in communications data, passive data collection and analysis, audio visual recordings from doorbell and vehicle dashboard cameras, cycle helmet recordings, train and bus onboard recordings as well as standard public authority, commercial and private CCTV footage; developments and updates with disclosure requirements, including investigation management documents
- Investigators need to be adept at communicating with a wide range of people and agencies at different levels and adapting to various styles; be able to speak, write and take notes quickly, coherently and intelligently, and to absorb information by active listening and accurately recalling facts and details.

1.4 Professionalising Investigations Programme

The Professionalising Investigations Programme (PIP) sets out a training and development structure to match the career pathway for police crime investigators (ACPO/NPIA 2005, 2013). It aims to embed investigative skills and development through recognised National Occupational Standards (NOS) against which performance can be assessed and accredited. There are defined core courses and training programmes under PIP which are summarised below in sections 1.4.1 and 1.4.2.

1.4.1 PIP core programmes

- Initial Police Learning and Development Programme (IPLDP)—PIP level 1

- Initial Crime Investigators Development Programme (ICIDP)—PIP level 2
- Investigative Supervisor and Manager Development Programme (ISMDP)—PIP Level 2. This is a combined course and programme for detective sergeants, detective inspectors and police staff equivalents
- Senior Investigating Officer Development Programme (SIODP)—PIP level 3
- Strategic Investigator—PIP level 4

1.4.2 Specialist training programmes

A full catalogue of crime investigation programmes and courses is available through the College of Policing. The following are some frequently encountered ones, but this is not an exhaustive list:

- Core Skills in Communications Data
- Digital Media Investigation
- Financial Investigation
- Specialist Child Abuse Investigator Development Programme (SCAIDIP)—PIP level 2 Specialist
- Specialist Witness Interviewer—PIP Level 2 Specialist
- Specialist Suspect Interviewer—PIP Level 2 Specialist
- Family Liaison Officer
- Home Office Large Major Enquiry System (HOLMES)
- Sexual Offence Investigation Trained (SOIT)
- Child Abuse/death Investigation

1.5 Motivation and Attitude

Personal motivation, confidence and optimism are assets for any criminal investigator. Motivated individuals are generally more productive due to their enthusiasm, commitment and conscientiousness. These positive attributes can rub off onto colleagues and also increase confidence in members of the public, including victims and witnesses. Visible and consistent motivation is especially important for supervisors and managers who should see themselves as role models for their teams and departments.

Positive thinking is a method of increasing confidence and ensuring any problems and obstacles are approached more favourably. Negative and pessimistic attitudes are not going to help and can almost become self-fulfilling. Optimistic attitudes allow tasks to be approached with greater vigour, energy and vitality; focusing on what can be achieved and not what cannot. Those who constantly raise problems about solutions, who play 'devil's advocate' and destroy rather than construct need to be challenged with balancing their negative views with positive ones.

The main benefits of motivation, confidence and optimism are their contribution to resilience in the face of setbacks. Staying positive and remaining confident about achieving successful outcomes and not becoming easily defeated is a consistent mental attitude in all top performers, not just crime investigators. Focusing on positives rather than negatives helps maintain morale and sustain interest, which is what victims expect from those who are representing their interests in the criminal justice system. This should be balanced against being realistic and managing expectations.

1.5.1 Managing expectations

Unrealistically high expectations risk becoming burdensome and difficult to manage. Communities, relatives and friends of victims, the media and internal supervision and management can place high demands and hopes on the individual and team performance of investigators. Personal morale and motivation levels can become adversely affected when under-delivering against highly expected, anticipated or promised results. Good results can become compromised when they fall short of what has been promised. Long-term failure to meet expectations will likely undermine an investigator's credibility and morale through loss of confidence and trust. It is therefore wiser to under-promise and over-deliver and be realistic without being negative. Only when certain and positive about a fact, piece of information or update should it be reported and made public. Predictions, estimates and speculative sometimes sympathetic promises to others should be avoided. Events or information should not be allowed to assume a greater significance or importance than their worth.

In some circumstances it can be tactically wise to temporarily withhold success stories or good news. This could prevent alerting suspects that vital evidence has been obtained or that they are to be arrested; or could avoid raising false hopes with victims or creating 'closed minds' from sources of information and/or communities from whom assistance is still required (including other investigators). In such circumstances, the reasons and justification for withholding the update and information would need to be recorded with the reasons so they can be explained at any later stage if necessary.

1.6 **Preparation**

In addition to knowledge and skills, physical and mental energy and stamina are also useful assets to have when performing an investigator's role, particularly when working long hours or on difficult and protracted enquiries under arduous conditions. At regular stages investigators need to refresh themselves to prepare for these challenges and be aware of their own wellbeing.

Effective and professional crime investigation requires adequate preparation in readiness for spontaneously having to attend and/or take charge of cases sometimes immediately if necessary.

Good routines are good practice. One worth getting used to is having the right materials and equipment ready and available for when needed. The maxim 'failing to plan is planning to fail' holds true, meaning the basic requirements can and should be prepared and ready to go. Essential items should be readily available and accessible.

Checklist—Crime investigator's basic kit

- A bag containing the essential items for attending a scene/incident
- A reliable timepiece for accurately recording the times that events occurred
- A 'daybook' or official notebook with reliable writing implements to record all information, details and decisions (or a digital equivalent)
- Weatherproof clipboard (or similar) to rest on with sufficient writing/drawing paper
- Essential documents, such as witness statement forms and crime scene logs
- Mobile phone (fully charged) and charger lead (and/or spare battery)
- List of important contact numbers (eg CSI, Duty Senior Investigating Officer (SIO), Duty Officer etc)
- A fully charged police airwave radio and list of channels
- Suitable and/or practical clothing (eg weatherproof and warm boots etc)
- Refreshments (food and drink)
- Maps (eg digital mapping or satellite navigation system)
- Torch/batteries
- Forensic gloves/overshoes
- Crime scene barrier tape and evidence bags/labels
- Suitable transport (if vehicle, sufficient fuel and notice to display saying whose it is)
- Money/loose change for emergencies
- Blackstone's Crime Investigators' Handbook

1.7 Specialist Assistance

Omni-competent and lone investigators have been replaced by those who have the advantage of being able to call upon a wide range of support, specialists and experts. It is accepted that one person alone cannot solve complex cases. There are specialist departments and units within the wider police family that assume responsibility for various elements of, or types of investigation, and in some cases may take overall responsibility. Units, squads and teams of various types and descriptions, such as Major Crime Units (e.g., homicide), Robbery, Burglary, Sexual Offences, Child Protection, Domestic Abuse, Public Protection, Protecting Vulnerable People, Drugs, Cyber Crime, Child Abuse Investigation, Financial Investigation and Serious and Organised Crime Teams, hold specific remits for particular investigations. They may also be able to offer advice or support, expertise, knowledge and specialist services even if not directly involved in the investigation.

Other supporting roles can be provided by tactical advisers, colleagues and outside experts who perform diverse roles and functions. A key skill is not only drawing on one's own personal experience and knowledge but also that which is available from others. This is useful not only for carrying out significant actions or activities but can also provide assistance and useful suggestions and solutions.

Specialist Crime Scene Managers (CSMs) and Crime Scene Investigators (CSIs) advise on scene preservation and forensic evidence recovery. Other specialists can also be called upon when required, such as specialist interview advisers, digital media investigators, Police Search Advisers (PolSA), ballistics experts, fire investigators, geographic and behavioural investigative profilers and advisers, trained analysts, media liaison officers, forensic specialists and advisers, community awareness and family liaison specialists. There are many 'ologists' to choose from depending on the circumstances, such as biologists, palynologists, entomologists, gastroenterologists, forensic anthropologists and so on.

Various units and departments within each force or agency, such as specialist firearms units or covert operations teams, can provide advice and guidance on a variety of techniques and tactical options. All these can at some stage form part of the investigation team.

KEY POINT

An important rule is not to step outside the boundaries of one's own training and expertise. It is better to seek assistance from those who have the necessary skills, ability and experience to perform a function than run the risk of making mistakes due to a lack of knowledge.

National assets can be worthwhile sources of advice, such as the National Crime Agency (NCA) Major Crime Investigative Support Team, Homicide Working Group, databases such as the Centralised Analytical Team Collating Homicide Expertise and Management (CATCHEM), the National Injuries Database (NID) and the Serious Crime Analysis Section (SCAS). These are resources worth knowing about and using, and they are usually provided without cost.

Several external statutory and other agencies and bodies now share responsibilities with the police and have obligations to mount investigations themselves or to assist certain crime investigations. Bodies such as local authorities, for instance, may be required to work in partnership with police investigators on cases involving safeguarding such as child neglect or cruelty. The Health and Safety Executive (HSE) are required to be involved in conducting investigations into deaths in a workplace. These agencies sometimes refer cases to the police for investigation, which may be the first time a police investigator becomes involved.

1.8 Welfare Management

It is essential, no matter how experienced or professional a person is, to be able to cope physically and mentally under pressure, sometimes when fatigued or even when stressed. Planning to avoid, identify or effectively manage the symptoms is important.

Stress is counterproductive and is to be distinguished from enthusiasm and energy. Stress is a personal thing and manifests itself in different ways, e.g., loss of patience, arguing or inappropriate behaviour. There is always a cause for irrational behaviour, and this should be remembered when the symptoms surface in oneself or colleagues to establish what may be causing the problem.

Emotional intelligence (EI) is the ability to identify, assess, manage and control the emotions of oneself, of others and of groups, and will help to make sense of and to survive a pressurised working environment. Coping mechanisms can include knowing one's own emotions, strengths, weaknesses, drives, values and goals and recognising their impact on others, using self-regulation to control impulses and adapting to changing circumstances. Demonstrating good social and teamworking skills is important.

Tiredness and taking on too much can cause problems, so adopting basic principles of being well organised and managing time become critical, because being unable to complete all necessary and urgent tasks leads to increased pressure and stress. Busy and conscientious crime investigators must be ruthlessly efficient at prioritising their workloads and getting the most out of their valuable time. Some issues and individuals conspire to commandeer valuable time, which is when it is necessary to be respectful but firm and polite, pointing out what any more pressing and urgent requirements in the overall case load. Planning and prioritising a working day and tasks are very important, whilst appreciating that events can and do change at a moment's notice.

It is important to be able to mentally 'switch off'. Sometimes it is difficult to concentrate on little else when engrossed in a challenging case or seeking to deliver a positive outcome for a vulnerable victim, but this carries a risk of developing compassion fatigue. Creating time to focus on unrelated matters and to pursue other interests can significantly help reduce mental anxiety and stress. A change of thought refreshes the mind and clears the head ready to refocus later. The national shortage of detectives which is evident at the time of writing has placed additional pressure on investigators. Police forces have their own occupational health procedures and resources, and advice and assistance are also available via the College of Policing's Wellbeing website page linking to the Blue Light Wellbeing Framework (containing learning from across the emergency services, Public Health England and academia) and the Oscar Kilo website.

KEY POINT

Creating time to sit quietly and enjoy personal space to think and gather thoughts without interruption counteracts fatigue and pressure. Putting something back into energy levels and the coping system by occasionally resting and concentrating on something completely different helps clear and refresh the mind and body.

1.9 Ethical Standards and Integrity

There are many legal rules, codes and guidelines that affect the work of a criminal investigator. There have been several high-profile cases of serious corruption and miscarriages of justice that placed questions of police ethics and integrity in the spotlight. Such high-profile cases have the potential to damage the reputation of the police, as do less serious, but more common, breakdowns in integrity that may impact negatively on service delivery and public perceptions. Ethical principles must prevail over any practices, preferences or other immoral external or internal cultures.

Fabricating information or evidence, conveniently ignoring material facts and evidence that don't fit with a convenient theory or showing preferential treatment towards a particular person or group for self-interest, personal convenience, profit or other extraneous motivation must never creep into an investigation or prosecution and should be challenged and reported if encountered.

Public trust and confidence in investigations depend on honesty, transparency and integrity. Statutory regulations such as the Human Rights Act 1998, the Police and Criminal Evidence Act 1984 (PACE) and its Code of Practice, the Code of Ethics (College of Policing 2014), the Code of Practice for Victims of Crime and bodies such as the Independent Office for Police Conduct (IOPC) have provided the public with ways of challenging police activities and actions. The media, through investigative journalism, make efforts to expose devious and unethical methods, and sometimes have their own creative ways of investigating public bodies. The TV documentary in 2003 entitled 'Secret Policeman' featured a BBC undercover journalist who infiltrated the police posing as a recruit to expose and covertly record racist behaviour. The Freedom of Information Act 2000 (FOI) and Criminal Procedure and Investigations Act 1996 (CPIA) also provide opportunities for hitherto protected material to be released upon request that may also reveal unprofessional and unethical processes.

Concepts known as 'tunnel vision' or 'closed mind syndrome' are unethical and must be avoided. Investigators should not focus on any individual (or individuals) or a particular line of enquiry at the exclusion of others without good reason. Any narrow-minded approach does not bode well for the integrity of the investigation and will always provide complications in the long term.

KEY POINT

In the 1970s and early 1980s, during the complex West Yorkshire Police 'Ripper' enquiry, the SIO fixated on letters and recorded messages from a person claiming to be the killer ('Wearside Jack'). Placing too much reliance on this individual led the team on a wild goose chase. Meanwhile, the real killer, Peter Sutcliffe, continued to murder more female victims. In March 2006, some 28 years after he had penned his first letter, hoaxer John Humble was convicted of perverting the course of justice and sentenced to eight years in prison. Similarly, between 2014 and 2016 the Metropolitan Police investigated allegations of historic sexual abuse made by Carl Beech against several high profile individuals. These allegations were automatically believed, and the investigation was subsequently severely criticised by a judge led review by Sir Richard Henriques. In 2019, Carl Beech was sentenced to 18 years imprisonment for offences including perverting the course of justice. These are just two high profile examples of a closed mind bias that are decades apart. There have been many others throughout the country.

Creativity and innovation from entrepreneurial detectives are one thing; deception of any kind that breaches the law is entirely another. This is to be distinguished from finding legal solutions to legal problems, which is a core skill of any good investigator who should seek to use the right methods to achieve the right result as demonstrated by the top left box in the integrity paradigm below.

Right Method **Right Result**	Right Method Wrong Result
Wrong Method Right Result	Wrong Method Wrong Result

Checklist—Role of a criminal investigator

- Detectives are expected to possess a wide range of knowledge, not just of legislative powers and statutory offences
- The emphasis is on a 'search for the truth' not 'search for the proof'
- Apply an investigative mindset using professional curiosity and appropriate scepticism to question and scrutinise material

- Be positive and optimistic
- Planning and preparation are highly advisable A wide range of specialists and experts are available for advice and support
- Don't step outside the boundaries of your own training and expertise
- Plan to avoid, identify and effectively manage the symptoms of stress
- Be well organised and efficient at getting the most out of valuable time
- Emotional intelligence helps survive a high pressure working environment
- 'Tunnel vision' or 'closed minds' are unethical and must be avoided

References

ACPO/NPIA *(2005,* 2013) *Practice Advice on Core Investigative Doctrine* (2nd edn)

College of Policing (2014) 'Code of Ethics: Principles and Standards of Professional Behaviour for the Policing Profession of England and Wales' available at <http://www.college.police.uk/what-we-do/Ethics/Documents/Code_of_Ethics.pdf> accessed 15 February 2022

Soanes C and Stevenson A (eds) (2008) *Oxford Dictionary of English* (2nd edn, OUP)

Chapter 2
Investigative Decision Making

2.1 Introduction

Making effective decisions and using sound judgement is a core skill and an essential attribute for an investigator. A decision is a choice between various alternatives and the person making the choice is the decision maker. Decisions can be made instantly and unconsciously but to be most effective investigative decisions should be conscious and methodical, involving an accurate assessment of the situation and structured analysis of information to identify options before making the selection. Many routine decisions are straightforward and do not require significant effort but more complex decisions demand more in-depth consideration. When time is critical, quick and sometimes bold, decisions may be necessary with less opportunity for assessment and planning, but these should never be 'gung ho'.

Regardless of the circumstances, investigators' decisions need to be justifiable, taking account of the circumstances in which they are made, and decisions taken or in some cases not taken need to be explainable to others. Potential scrutiny could come from colleagues, supervisors, the criminal courts, a coroner's court and in rarer more extreme cases possibly a judicial review or a public inquiry. Investigations and the decisions involved may be subject to formal internal or external reviews and could attract media scrutiny and interest from wider communities. It should

Blackstone's Crime Investigators' Handbook. Steve Hibbitt and Gary Shaw, Oxford University Press. © Oxford University Press 2023.
DOI: 10.1093/oso/9780192867896.003.0002

never be forgotten that decisions may need to be explained to victims and others affected by the crime or event and certain decisions may attract a victims right to review application. Failure to make effective decisions lead not only to failed investigations but potential miscarriages of justice.

This chapter outlines some fundamental processes, principles and approaches to investigative decision making and problem solving, including the application of what is known as the 'investigative mindset'. The content intends to demystify the complexities of effective decision making to help crime investigators consider and apply a logical approach to their thought processes.

2.2 Creating 'Slow Time'

A phrase often used by experienced and senior detectives describes how they like to *slow things down* when making decisions, particularly at incidents that are frantic with activity. This involves taking control and remaining calm and detached. It avoids the pitfall of allowing judgements to become clouded by making rash decisions and not thinking things through carefully. This takes nothing away from occasions when it is important to make bold decisions because they are time critical, such as arresting a suspect who is at large.

2.3 'ABC' Principle

Investigative decision making relies upon accurate and reliable information which must be carefully scrutinised, reviewed, assessed and evaluated. This involves testing the accuracy, reliability and relevance of any material that the decision is to rely upon. For many years, investigators have known this as the 'ABC' principle, and it was cited in numerous crime training courses and publications.

A — Assume nothing
B — Believe nothing
C — Challenge (& check) everything

An assumption is something that is automatically accepted as true without further investigation, and the history of investigation shows that assumption was the basis for many significant errors leading to failure. Whilst it is a mistake to automatically assume something is what it seems and accept it as correct at face value, this may not be as straightforward as the ABC principle sets out. Investigation has evolved and arguably the approach of assume nothing, believe nothing and challenge (and check) everything is now somewhat too simplistic and harsh and more careful consideration is required. Before placing too much reliance on it, investigators should always seek to corroborate, recheck, review and confirm facts by evaluating and testing material (including information) against what is already known to the investigation or what can reasonably be established. Care needs to be taken when evaluating victim and witness accounts, which should be neither automatically assumed to be correct nor automatically challenged or dismissed. The Home Office (2020) counting rules for recording crime state that when making a complaint victims should be believed for the purpose of recording a crime unless it is clear at that point that the incident did not happen. It must be emphasised that this applies at the point when the alleged crime is reported and recorded; it is not to say that a victim's interview should not be thorough, properly evaluated and appropriately, proportionately and sensitively investigated.

There are complex considerations around victim and witness memory and recall, and many factors can contribute to what on the surface could be seen as inaccuracy. Examples from many other considerations could involve perhaps vulnerabilities with the witness themselves, including how the event was or was not encoded in their memory, the impact of trauma and possible false memory syndrome. In some cases, however, it needs to be recognised that certain people may also be untruthful and have their own motivation for being so.

KEY POINT

Every account should be checked for inconsistency or conflict with other material. Investigators can be misled if they have not paid sufficient attention to detail. Prima facie assumptions should not be made, and material should never be accepted without questioning and applying an investigative mindset. Investigators should constantly seek corroboration.

An example might be when information is received from an intelligence source that has not been properly evaluated or graded. In these circumstances it is wise to check the accuracy and provenance of the information and reliability of the source prior to making decisions based upon the information. This is where the **investigative mindset** applies by not making decisions based on assumptions of the accuracy of material (including information) until checks have been made.

2.4 Investigative Mindset

Applying an investigative mindset is a frequently used phrase and it is important that investigators understand what this entails. It is a state of mind that an effective investigator needs to develop which assists with examining the material gathered throughout an investigation and on which decisions are made. It involves maintaining a professional curiosity, being receptive to other suggestions when approaching problem solving and decision making and keeping an open mind and looking for other explanations and not focusing on a single or small number of theories or hypotheses. Going beyond these general elements, applying an investigative mindset requires mental discipline and a structured approach. This involves understanding the material obtained by the investigation, planning how to obtain the material and approach its examination, how to record the examination, evaluate the results and review them in the context of how they apply to the investigation and their priority.

Not properly understanding the source material may lead to lost investigative opportunities, or in worst-case scenarios a complete failure of the investigation. A structured approach to applying the investigative mindset using a mnemonic of UPERE was first described in the *Core Investigative Doctrine* (2005), which was updated in 2013 (ACPO/NPIA 2013). This no longer features in the *Authorised Professional Practice* (APP) (College of Policing 2021) so is reproduced here as it is an effective investigative decision model:

- **U**nderstand
  - How was the source material obtained by the investigation?
  - How accurate and reliable is the material?
  - Has the material been evaluated and tested against what is already known or what can reasonably be ascertained?
  - What did any evaluation ascertain?
- **P**lanning and preparation
  - What are the objectives of the examination?
  - How will the material be examined?
  - If this is a physical item are there any forensic recovery priorities to be considered in sequence, e.g., swabbing for DNA before fingerprinting?
  - Should the examination be video recorded or photographed for evidence?
  - What is the interview strategy if the information is to be obtained from an interview?
- **E**xamination
  - Conduct the examination in accordance with the requirements identified from the planning and preparation.
  - Ensure the objectives of the examination are achieved.

- **R**ecord
  - Record the examination using the method of recording identified from the planning and preparation.
- **E**valuate
  - Evaluate the results of the examination against the identified objectives.
  - Evaluate how the results impact on the investigation.
    - Do they contribute to a current line of enquiry?
    - Have the identified new or further lines of enquiry?
    - Are any fast track actions required?
    - Evaluate whether the results could be admissible evidence to form part of a prosecution case as either direct or circumstantial evidence.
  - Evaluate whether the results would potentially undermine a prosecution case, assist or potentially be of interest to a defence.

This structured thought process should then be repeated and applied to all material gathered by the investigation.

KEY POINT

The investigative mindset can be broken down into the five following principles:

1. Understanding the source material
2. Planning and preparation
3. Examination
4. Recording and collation
5. Evaluation

KEY POINT

Effective decision making comes from:

- slowing things down, taking control and being calm and detached
- applying methodical thought processes
- being decisive when time is critical
- applying an investigative mindset

2.5 Problem Solving

Decision making involves an element of problem solving, and detective work requires a sequential and logical approach. There are useful techniques and methods aimed at applying a structured process. The aim is to develop a methodical collection and analysis of information and alternative solutions into a process that will help towards making well-informed decisions. A less structured approach is to jump to conclusions too quickly without proper thought and consideration. Effective problem-solving skills are an important part of decision making and will produce different options, leading to a more informed, rational choice and decision.

There are various problem-solving models, though most contain a similar structure. One recommended model contains a sequential process (also cited in Adair 2008). It involves choosing a course of action or decision only after collecting sufficient information, then analysing the pros and cons of alternative solutions before making a choice.

A good problem-solving model for investigators is shown in Figure 2.1.

An example of applying the model to making an arrest would be:

1. Determine the problem: X is suspected of a criminal offence and the objective is to make an arrest.
2. Gather 5WH information (Who? What? Where? When? Why? How?): What is the type and nature of the offence? What are the grounds for suspicion and necessity for the arrest? What powers, policies and legislation apply? What is the suspect's last known address? What is known about their current whereabouts? When were they last seen? What are the risks? What previous convictions and warning markers are there, for example violent, uses weapons, or drug abuser? What existing curfews or bail conditions are in place? Who or what

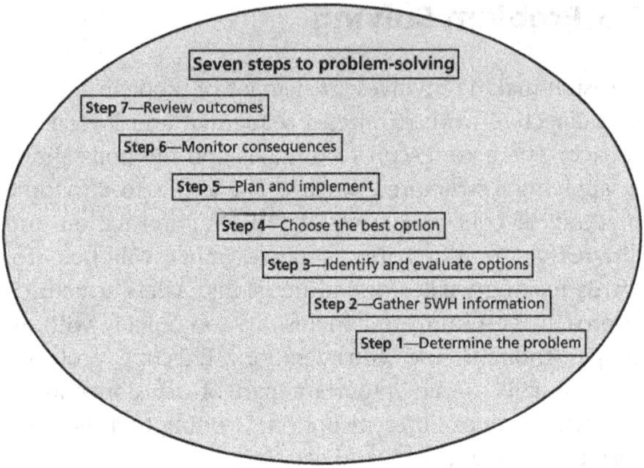

Figure 2.1 Seven steps to problem solving

else resides with them, such as criminal associates, young children, elderly residents and dangerous pets? What sort of property is it? How many entrances/exits are there? Where is the address and what other police activity has taken place there, for example searches or arrests? Why is it believed they will be at this address? What are the known movements and times that they are likely to be present? What method of entry will be required? What is the reliability of the information the decision is based upon?

3. Identify and evaluate options: Consider making the arrest early in the morning; conducting surveillance to confirm they are at the address; or arrest at another venue or place frequented; or delay until an intelligence source can place them at a location or address, such as using a Covert Human Intelligence Source—CHIS; or arrange for arrest by appointment through a legal representative.
4. Choose the best option: Decision: Arrest at current known home address in the early morning. Reason: this will increase likelihood of their presence and use an element of surprise to control risk, maximise evidence

collection opportunities, including forensic and physical evidence, and search of the premises. Not to arrest by appointment, as it is believed the suspect could abscond once they learn they are being sought by the police and may also destroy evidence or interfere with witnesses. No suitable intelligence sources or surveillance resources are available.

5. Plan and implement: Arrest will take place (time and date) with an operational order containing precise details of the arrest strategy, method, resources etc.
6. Monitor consequence: During the arrest operation, monitoring will be dynamic by the lead investigator, arrest supervisor and communications/radio operator.
7. Review outcomes: A debrief of the arrest and search will take place at (time, date and location) and the lead investigator will collate all relevant information, evidence for the investigation. Additionally, any learning points, good and bad practice, what went well, what didn't work, what should be done differently next time should be recorded for future intelligence.

KEY POINT

Crime investigators are accountable for their decisions and must be prepared to provide reasons for what they did and why. Therefore, any key decisions and their rationale should be properly and proportionately recorded.

2.6 Evaluating Options and Alternatives

The investigative mindset applies when considering alternative solutions and options for making decisions. The more alternatives considered, the greater the chance of selecting the best option or solution. One method of analysing the advantages and disadvantages of options is to examine the strengths, weaknesses, opportunities and threats (SWOT analysis). Using a SWOT analysis may assist decision making about pursuing investigative opportunities when balanced against the potential threat, harm and risk concerned and how to mitigate these.

2.6.1 'Do nothing', 'defer' or 'monitor' options

Sometimes a decision maker has to consider whether any action is necessary. It may, for example, be that cost outweighs gain. Therefore, there may be an option to do nothing and not take any further action, or to defer and postpone until later, or monitor the situation and wait and see. With the arrest example used in section 2.5 earlier, for example, if the suspect was in prison or ill in hospital this could provide an option to defer an arrest until it became feasible and such a decision would be monitored and remain under review.

KEY POINT

A decision to do nothing or defer a decision must be justifiable. Not making a decision is a decision itself, which needs to be for the right reasons, properly recorded and communicated clearly where necessary to supervisors, colleagues and maybe even victims.

2.7 The National Decision Model

In 2011 the then Association of Chief Police Officers (ACPO, now the National Police Chiefs Council) approved the adoption of a single National Decision Model (NDM) for the Police Service (see Figure 2.2). The ACPO Ethics Portfolio and the National Risk Coordination Group developed this to provide a structured framework across all levels of decision making in the police service.

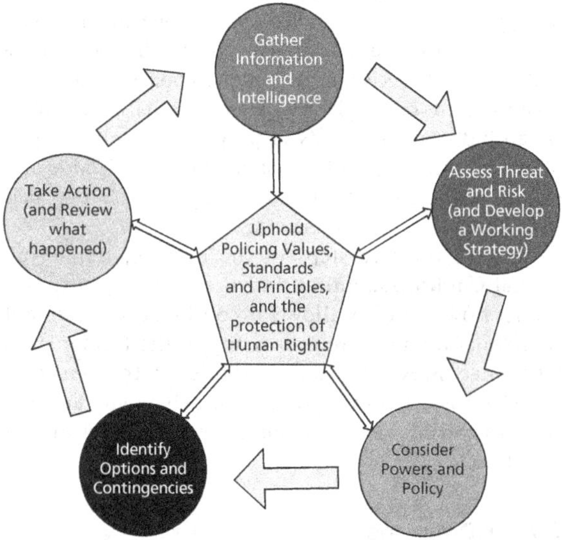

Source: *The National Decision Model* (College of Policing APP, 2014)

Figure 2.2 The National Decision Model (College of Policing 2021)

Adopting the NDM was part of a concerted drive to ensure a greater focus on delivering the mission of policing, acting in accordance with police values, enhancing the use of discretion, reducing risk aversion and supporting the appropriate allocation of limited resources.

In 2014 the NDM was amended by the National Police Chiefs Council (NPCC) who by then had replaced the ACPO. This revision placed the Code of Ethics at the centre of the NDM cycle and replaced the previous statement of mission and values (College of Policing 2014). This was in response to a series of controversial high-profile incidents that had emerged during the intervening years which had called police ethics into question and caused public concern.

Understanding the NDM will help investigators develop an appreciation of the professional judgement necessary to make effective decisions. The NDM is intended to be suitable for all decisions and can be applied to spontaneous incidents or pre-planned operations. It can be applied by an individual or teams of people, and to both operational and non-operational situations. The NDM is also similar and compatible in structure to decision models used by other emergency services.

Each of the five steps of the decision framework logically follows another and the cycle repeats. The model however does allow for continual reassessment of a situation and a return to any of the former steps when necessary. The Code of Ethics at the centre of the NDM is a reminder of ethical behaviours and the need to consider what the public would expect in that situation.

2.7.1 **NDM stages**

Throughout the situation, you should ask yourself:

- Is what I'm considering consistent with the Code of Ethics?
- What would the Police Service expect of me in this situation?
- What would any victim(s), the affected community and the wider public expect of me in this situation?

NDM Stage 1: INFORMATION: Gather Information and Intelligence

During this stage the decision maker assesses the situation to identify what is happening or has happened and clarifies matters relating to any initial information and intelligence. The investigative mindset should be applied to assess the accuracy and reliability of the sources which may be the basis for the decision.

- What is happening?
- What do I know so far?
- What do I need to know?
- Where does that information reside?
- What further information (or intelligence) do I want/ need?

NDM Stage 2: ASSESSMENT: Assess Threat and Risk and Develop a Working Strategy

This stage involves assessing the situation, including any specific threat, the risk of harm and the potential for benefits.

- Does action need to be taken immediately?
- Is more needed?
- What could go wrong and what could go well?
- What are the threats?
- What is the intent of any threat?
- What is the capability of carrying out the intention of any threat?
- What is the immediacy of any threat?
- What are the harms involved?
- What are the consequences of any harm?
- Who might suffer the consequences of any harm?
- How probable is the risk of harm?
- How serious would it be?
- What am I trying to achieve?
- Is that level of risk acceptable?
- Is this a situation for the police alone to deal with?
- Am I the appropriate person to deal with this?
- Develop a **working strategy** to guide subsequent stages (amongst other things consider community relations)

When assessing threat and risk and making associated decisions, it is worth considering the principles laid down by the Association of Police Officers and remain relevant (ACPO Risk Principles, 2010). Important points from these ten principles recognise that uncertainty is an inherent feature of operational decision making, and making decisions in an operational context is a form of risk taking. It is in the nature of risk taking that harm, including serious harm, will sometimes occur. Whilst risk offers the possibility of harm it also offers the chance of success and members of the police service must be willing to take risks and not avoid them. The police have a duty to confront risks and make risk decisions on behalf of the community. A good decision can have a poor outcome but that does not necessarily mean the decision was wrong and vice versa. The important point here is that such decisions are described as a duty and fear of being criticised should not detract from the duty to protect the public. Even though there is a duty to protect life, this duty is not absolute.

Risk takers should consider and compare the value of the likely benefits balanced with the possible harm of their proposed decision. Greater consideration and mitigating action should be directed at serious risks where the likelihood of harm is high and proportionate to the seriousness of the risks. Police officers and staff must, when taking risks, act reasonably.

NDM Stage 3: POWERS AND POLICY: Consider Policy and Powers

This stage involves considering what powers, policies and legislation might be applicable in this particular situation. In dynamic situations where a quick decision is necessary it is unlikely that time will be available to research any gaps in your knowledge. This emphasises the importance of investigators maintaining and developing their legislative and procedural knowledge.

- What legislation might apply?
- What police powers might be required?

- Is there any national guidance covering this type of situation?
- Do any local organisational policies or guidelines apply?
- If it is considered reasonable and necessary to act outside of existing policy there must be justifiable and documented reasons for doing so that could withstand scrutiny by others.

NDM Stage 4: OPTIONS: Identify Options and Contingencies

This stage involves considering the different ways to make a particular decision and resolve a situation with the least risk of harm.

Options:

- What options are available? (Consider the immediacy of any threat; the limits of the information to hand; the amount of time available; the resources and support required and available; the impact of potential actions on the situation and the public)
- Any contingencies required
- Consider what to do if things don't happen as anticipated
- Is the decision proportionate, legal, necessary, ethical and reasonable in the circumstances at that time?

NDM Stage 5: ACTION and REVIEW: Take Action and Review What Happened

This stage requires decision makers to make and implement appropriate decisions and to evaluate and review what happened once the incident is over.

Action

Respond:

- Implement the selected option.
- Does anyone else need to know what has been decided?

Record:

- If appropriate, record the decision and the reasons behind it.
- Monitor:
- What happened as a result of the decision?
- Did the expected result happen?

If the incident is continuing, go through the NDM again as necessary.

Review
If the incident is over, review the decision(s), using the NDM

- What lessons can be taken from how things turned out?
- What might be done next time?

2.8 '5WH' Method

Effective problem solving and decision making rely upon having sufficient accurate information and material upon which to base a decision. A decision is only a decision if there are choices, and asking the right questions is the best way to obtain the right answers. The more accurate the information, the greater the chance of making a correct decision. This is because more information provides a greater number of options and alternatives, resulting in informed decision making. Decisions should be recorded in decision logs or their electronic equivalent with what information was known and available at the time. This is so the decision can be explained, if necessary, including why a particular option was chosen and what information this was based upon.

The 5WH method is another effective mental process. It helps to generate information by structuring relevant questions. It also provides a means of achieving the requirements of Step 2 of the problem-solving model (as outlined earlier). The 5WH method stands for six strong leading interrogative pronouns (which can be used in any particular order):

WHO?
WHAT?
WHERE?
WHEN?
WHY?
HOW?

For example:

1. What happened? (incident information and details)
2. Who is the victim (victimology)
3. Where did the incident take place? (geographical parameters)
4. When did it take place? (time parameters)
5. How did it happen? (modus operandi/method)
6. How was the incident discovered?
7. Who reported the incident?
8. Why did it happen? (reason and motive)

These are just a small example of the many 5WH questions investigators should be asking others and themselves. The primary WH questions prompt supplementary ones to produce a quick, straightforward method that can be adapted to fit most circumstances. The following table provides examples of follow-up questions but is not exhaustive:

Primary questions	Supplementary questions
Who is the victim?	Why was the victim targeted? How was the victim(s) selected? What type of victim was targeted (their characteristics)? Were or are they a repeat victim? What risks are there of repeat victimisation? What 'victimology' information is available Who are their family, relatives and close friends? Where is the victim? What has the victim said happened? How is the victim's welfare being managed? What injuries have been received? What did the victim do after the offence? Who else has the victim spoken to since the offence? What protection measures for the victim are required?
Where did the crime take place?	Where is the primary crime scene? Where are any secondary scenes? How many scenes are there? Have they been sequentially numbered? What has been done to preserve and protect the crime scene(s)? Who is at the scene? Who has control of the scene? What has been done to avoid contamination? What has already been done at the scene(s)? What else needs to be done at the scene(s)? What is known about the location? What link is there between the location, victim and offender? Why was the location chosen by the offender? Was it a repeat location? How was the location chosen by the offender? How did offenders get to/from the crime scene? What type of property has been targeted? What/who else is in the locality that could be linked? What are the situational/economic/environmental factors?

Primary questions	Supplementary questions
What searches have taken place?	What type of searches have been conducted? Where has been searched? What were the geographical parameters of the search? Who conducted the search? How was the search conducted? What equipment or resources were used? What has been found? Where is any recovered material now? What has been done to preserve any recovered material for possible examination? What action was taken to prevent forensic contamination? What records of searches have been made? How long did the searches take? What H2H enquiries have been made? What CCTV has been recovered or is available? Where else needs to be searched? What needs to be revisited (if anything)?
When did the offence take place?	What is significant about the time and date? How have the time and date been confirmed? What else was taking place at the same time? What peak times, days, seasons or cyclical links are there? What are the frequency and intervals between any other offences? Has there been any increase in these types of offences?
When was the crime discovered?	Who discovered it and how? Why was the crime discovered? Who was it reported to and how? What actions did the person discovering the crime take at the scene?
How was the crime reported?	Who reported the crime? When was the crime reported? Where was the crime reported? Why was the crime reported? What was said by the person reporting the crime? What has been done to verify the information?

Primary questions	Supplementary questions
What exactly happened?	What crime has been committed? What crime category has taken place? What is currently known? What information gaps are there? What are the likely hypotheses? Who is known to carry out this type of crime? What other incident(s) may be linked to the crime? How many other similar crimes have there been? What is the risk of further offences being committed? What information has been given out?
What has been stolen?	What is the description and value? How much property has been stolen? Where might it be traded or disposed of? How could it be identified again? What is the rarity of the item(s)? What type of offender would steal the property? What does it indicate regarding choice of victim or location? What links are there to legitimate markets? What is the relationship with other criminality? Who are the handlers/receivers/buyers of such property? What quantities are being stolen elsewhere? What things were not stolen and why? Where was any property recovered (if applicable)?
How was the crime committed?	What was the precise modus operandi (MO)? What knowledge/skills were required by the offender? Was any weapon, tool or implement used? What tools, weapons or other equipment did the offender use to commit the offence? How would the offender's weapons, tools or equipment be obtained? How did the offender approach the scene? What route did the offender take to the scene? How did the offender leave the scene? What route did the offender take to leave the scene? What transport might have been required/used? What is unique about this crime? Have specific methods been used to evade capture? What evidence is there of any planning by the offender(s)?

Primary questions	Supplementary questions
Who are the witness(es)	Where are they now? How did they witness the event? What information have they provided? Why were they at that location? What has been done with them? What is their status (eg significant, vulnerable, intimidated)? How reliable and credible are their accounts? What current intelligence is available? What is the relationship between victim, offender and witness? Who are the witnesses' associates? Who else have they spoken to about the crime? What is the relationship to the location?
Who are the offender(s)?	Who are the suspects? How have they been identified? How can they be identified? What are the reasonable grounds for suspicion? What has been done to trace/arrest the offender(s)? Where is the offender now? What is known about the offender(s)? How many offenders were involved? What can the offender's behaviour tell us? What is the subject profile of the offender(s)? What is the description of offender(s)? How were/can the offenders be identified? What intelligence suggests possible offenders? Who has previously carried out this type of offence? Who has recently been released from prison?
What are the main lines of enquiry?	What are the solvability factors? What are the main lines of enquiry? What is the outcome of any completed enquiries? Who has conducted them? Where and how have the results been recorded? What are the supporting investigative strategies?
Why was the crime committed?	What was the motive? Personal/financial gain? Sexual gratification? Revenge? Jealousy? Concealment of other offences? Political motivation? Hate Crime, racially motivated? How was it committed—spontaneous or pre-planned? Was there any involvement of alcohol/drugs? Was it part of a series? Was it gang or OCG related?

Primary questions	Supplementary questions
What specialist resources are required?	What are they? What is required of them? What and whose authority is required? Where can they be obtained from? How can they be obtained? How much will they cost? Who will brief and manage them? Where and whom should they report to?
What forensic material is there?	Was any trace or forensic evidence left behind? What type of forensic examination is required? What type of evidence is it? How has it been preserved? What arrangements have been made to examine it? Who has been asked to examine it?
What exhibits are there?	What exhibits have been recovered? What has been done with the exhibits? Where are they stored? How have they been labelled and packaged? What is the strategy for examination? What needs to be fast tracked?

The same process can be used for other purposes. For example, when reviewing information and actions taken by others, the questions can be used to obtain (or provide) a structured briefing of the circumstances. It can also be used as a template to brief and debrief others and to avoid missing vital information through disjointed delivery, as each relevant 'topic' can be covered one at a time.

2.8.1 Information gaps

Not all 5WH questions are answerable immediately and some may highlight missing knowledge and information. By using a table or matrix these gaps are easier to identify and log. A gap analysis can be conducted by organising not only what information is known, but also what is not known; an added third column can prompt suggestions as to where the missing information can be obtained. For example:

5WH question	What is known?	What is not known?	Where can it be obtained from?
Who is the victim?	24-year-old male victim assaulted in the high street receiving wounds and bruising to head and body.	1. Motive. 2. Victim movements prior to attack. 3. Has he been attacked previously? 4. Are any other attacks likely? 5. Details of victim's family and associates 6. Previous incidents or convictions 7. Identity of offender(s).	1. Check victim's account, previous convictions, profile lifestyle and intelligence. 2. Reinterview victim and check witness accounts, CCTV, phone. 3. Check local hospitals, crime recording systems, family and associates. 4. Risk assessment and crime pattern analysis. 5. Victim interview and associates and intelligence records. 6. PNC/PND data, incident logs, local intelligence and partner agencies. 7. Investigation plan.

2.8.2 The 'what?' question

One of the first 5WH questions is 'What happened?' It is important to maintain an investigative mindset and not become overly influenced by the initial information, contact, accounts and statements or anyone else's scene assessment, which might already have their own interpretation.

2.8.3 The 'where?' question

The location where an offender commits a crime (the main crime scene) and surrounding geography can reveal information about them and their relationship to the victim. The Routine Activity Theory (RAT) developed by Cohen and Felson (1979) was based on the premise that offenders tend to commit crimes in areas they are familiar with, and in which they have had the opportunity to do so without someone or something being able to prevent them. Whilst this is relevant, it should also be considered that some offenders commute to commit crime or may frequent an area but not actually live there.

Examining the characteristics of the environment surrounding a crime scene, such as the local neighbourhood, usually provides a good perspective for the crime under investigation. It can provide insights and considerations that would not otherwise be identified or available. Although it is acknowledged that investigators will be busy with other matters, the importance and benefits of personally visiting and assessing a scene should not be underestimated or dismissed.

It is recommended that a scene assessment (which may be further or supplementary to the initial visit) is made at the same time and day on which the offence occurred. This makes it more realistic and informative and may reveal information that would not be available at other times of the day. A town or city centre location is likely to be very different in the daytime than it is in the early hours of the morning. It will be frequented by different types of people and different premises will be open and closed. Visiting a crime scene that would have been dark at the relevant time could gain an appreciation of what an offender, victim or witness has seen and experienced which might otherwise not be appreciated.

Two theoretical principles help with understanding the relevance of geography in decision making and crime investigation:

2.8.3.1 Rational Choice Theory

In summary, Rational Choice Theory espouses that when deciding whether to commit an offence or not (as opposed to having a need to offend), a rational offender makes a conscious decision by weighing up the potential rewards against the chances of being caught. Extensive criminology literature describe these factors as including the availability of a suitable victim, a motivated offender and the absence of a guardian capable of preventing the offence. Rational Choice Theory has been widely studied but one of the classical works is Cornish and Clarke (2008).

This theory is relevant to investigators because it links identifying offenders to using the 5WH questions to explore the characteristics of the victim (including people or premises) and the location of the offence. Depending on the type of crime committed, some locations provide better opportunities than others, and this may be the reason why a location and victim have been chosen and targeted over others. It should not be forgotten however, that not all offenders behave rationally, and some may be intoxicated through alcohol or drugs or have mental health issues.

2.8.3.2 Problem Analysis Triangle

A further theoretical dimension to the importance of geographic information at crime scenes is the *Problem Analysis Triangle* (PAT) (see Figure 2.3). This states that for a crime to occur, an offender and suitable target must come together in a specific location without an effective deterrent. The elements are also referred to as the coincidental elements of crime and sometimes presented in a Venn diagram format. The association between victim, location and offender can be considered when making decisions to identify an offender. These can include virtual as well as physical locations to take account of cyber enabled or facilitated offences.

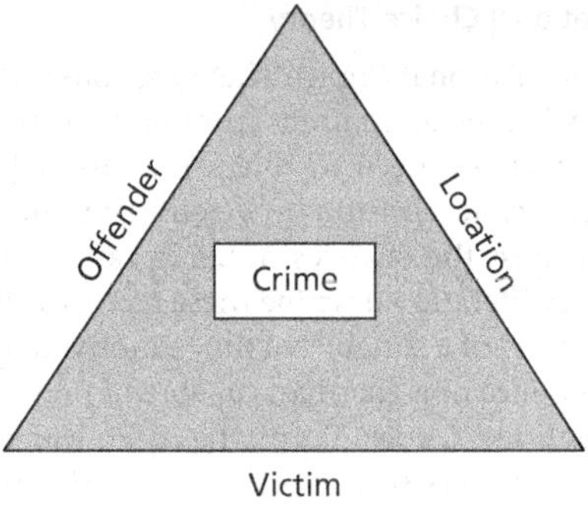

Figure 2.3 Problem Analysis Triangle

2.8.4 The 'when?' question

The time frames (temporal) for an offence are also significant. This links to making decisions around setting time parameters for potential sightings of suspects, elimination procedures and alibies, viewing times for passive data and CCTV, how and when proactive investigative strategies should occur, such as conducting observations for an offender returning to commit more crimes and ensuring resources are deployed at the most effective times and locations.

It is advised that when framing time parameters these are not just confined to when the offence was believed to have occurred. They should also include consideration of the offender's activity before and after the offence. Careful thought should be given to the time parameters for identifying relevant events that may have occurred before the event, such as offenders conducting reconnaissance for target acquisition, or to establish a victim's movements and routines and weaknesses and vulnerabilities with any security procedures of systems.

After the offence, consideration ought to be given to time parameters for offenders disposing of items used in the commission of the offence, and the disposing of and monetising of stolen property. The possibility of offenders returning to the scene to monitor police and emergency service activity should also be considered along with the possibility of returning for repeat victimisation.

An accurate time must be established for when an offence occurred. When recording times and dates from victims and witnesses, they must be carefully checked and reviewed for accuracy. People who are estimating times may be inaccurate, and others such as children may have different perspectives of times depending on their age and cognitive development. Corroboration should be sought where possible by comparing with an accurate time source (a digital device or by calling the BT speaking clock '123' service), or perhaps CCTV if the event or part of the event was recorded.

Also useful for comparison are the times certain television programmes were broadcast, or the times of sporting fixtures or other memorable events of note if these were relevant. The times of any events used for corroboration should be evidentially verified for the satisfaction of a court in case this time becomes relevant at any trial. Dates and times need to be reliably confirmed because cases can be lost if defendants are able to prove they were elsewhere due to a relevant time frame being inaccurate.

Investigators must also ensure they record their own times and dates accurately. For example, the time and date a decision was made, when they arrived at a crime scene and when they were told something. An accurate timepiece is an important accessory to possess and have readily available for use.

2.8.5 The 'why?' question

Establishing what cause, reason or motive induced an offender to commit a crime is a useful line of enquiry as it may help to identify the offender(s). It may also assist in linking incidents and matching modus operandi.

However, investigators need to be mindful that if a motive is wrongly introduced and publicly stated it may in some cases unfairly demonise a victim and/or the community with which they are associated. Some people with potential information or perhaps witnesses with stereotypical beliefs may feel less inclined and be discouraged from assisting the investigation. Examples might include, wrongly identifying the motive as hate crime or because of criminal rivalry or associating a victim with a particular activity such as being a sex worker, drug user or gang or organised crime member. This could potentially prevent investigators from accessing important sources of information.

Checklist—possible motives

- Gain (financial or otherwise)
- Revenge
- Personal cause
- Jealousy
- Criminal enterprise
- Gang-related (disputes over drugs, territory or power and respect)
- Hate crime (racism, homophobia or other prejudice)
- Anger or loss of control (rejection, argument, drug or alcohol induced etc)
- Crime concealment or witness elimination purposes
- To cover up another crime such as arson following a burglary
- Sexual or violence gratification
- Power, control
- Thrill and excitement
- Mental illness/personality disorders (eg psychopath, narcissism, paranoid, schizoid)
- Political/religious/ritualistic causes
- Terrorism related
- Noble cause, for example a mercy killing

2.9 Developing and Using Hypotheses

A hypothesis, according to the *Oxford Dictionary of English* (2005) is defined as 'a supposition or proposed explanation made on the basis of limited evidence as a starting point for further investigation'.

This means examining and evaluating the surrounding circumstances of a situation and devising plausible explanations or theories about the crime and/or elements within the crime which are based on the limited available evidence. These hypotheses can then be graded, prioritised and investigated further to prove or disprove them. When investigating competing hypotheses, the starting point for further investigation is to begin with the hypothesis considered most likely to have happened.

When posing 5WH questions (eg what happened?), the process of generating and building hypotheses is a useful investigative technique. It is also a means of populating Step 3 of the problem-solving model, by developing suggestions and options. Well-developed hypotheses are particularly useful when there is little or no information to go on. A good hypothesis though should make full use of all available information and material.

KEY POINT

Developing and applying hypotheses is a technique that establishes an explanation, theory or inference. Adhami and Browne (1996) referred to these inferences as a series of 'if-then' rules (involving a sentence that begins 'If ... ' closely followed by 'then ...'). As always when evaluating any material on which to base a hypothesis, an investigative mindset must be applied.

As always when evaluating information and other material on which to base a hypothesis, an investigative mindset must be applied. As more information becomes available to the investigation and developing facts emerge, any hypotheses need to be reviewed against any new or changed information. All hypotheses, therefore, should always remain *provisional,* meaning they can be changed at any time and can and should remain under regular review. Wherever possible it is worthwhile making a record of the information that was available at the precise time at which any hypotheses were made. As previously stated, this is an important part in any recording process linked to decision making (Cook 2020).

2.9.1 **Principle of Occam's Razor**

William of Occam (also spelt Ockham) was a fourteenth-century medieval logician, philosopher and Franciscan friar. Ockham was the village in the English county of Surrey where he was born. The rule of Occam's Razor (sometimes expressed in Latin as *lex parsimoniae,* meaning the law of parsimony economy or succinctness) is a principle recommending that, from among any competing hypotheses, the theory that makes the fewest complex assumptions is usually the correct one. In other words, when there are multiple competing theories, the simplest explanation is usually the most plausible and the best one to select first for further investigation.

Considering most crime investigations are characterised by missing or ambiguous information, decision making can be quite complex, which can encourage complicated theories and hypotheses. Investigators can get easily drawn into developing *overly* complex theories and hypotheses, causing errors in decision making and judgement. Remembering to apply the principle of Occam's Razor should help minimise this danger.

Checklist—hypotheses generation

- The use of theories or hypotheses can be useful when there is limited information available
- Apply an investigative mindset and do not become overly reliant on intuition and be open to multiple potential explanations.

- Ensure a thorough check of relevance and reliability for any material relied upon (wrong information = wrong conclusion)
- Identify what information gaps are linked to any hypothesis generated
- Hypotheses always remain provisional and kept under constant review
- Whenever possible use colleagues and specialists (eg analysts or a Behavioural Investigative Adviser) to assist formulating suggestions and hypotheses
- Apply the principle of Occam's Razor—the simplest explanation is possibly the right one

2.10 **Heuristics and Biases**

When there is limited information about what happened, experience, prior knowledge or memory are likely to be relied upon to help formulate hypotheses and apply intuitive decision making (or so-called 'gut feelings'). A problem arises, however, when this process becomes overly subjective and influenced by personal opinion and biases, rather than an objective assessment of facts.

Training, knowledge and experience inform and influence bold decision making in *fast time or critical* situations. In such circumstances more reliance may be placed on these, rather than on deliberate slower reasoning or analysis. Such mental shortcuts allow the current circumstances to be associated with similar past examples and experiences to help select options from which to make decisions and draw inferences. These can, in some circumstances, prove useful but the decision maker must be aware of the limitations and careful not to make decisions that could be based on or influenced by inherent bias in themselves and others.

The theory of 'heuristics' refers to the use of experience-based knowledge (or working rules) for problem solving when previous knowledge or experience is used to compare scenarios and draw similar conclusions, for example '... it looks like something I've dealt with or seen before so that is what it is'. However, this is not always totally reliable, as judgements can and do become unduly influenced by personal bias, such as perceptions of people, situations, locations or stereotypes (Kahneman 2011).

There may also be a lack of information or incorrect recall of the knowledge or experience being relied upon. Just because a course of action once worked in previous similar circumstances it does not mean it will automatically be effective in the current situation.

This may have an adverse impact on other important lines of enquiry if a preferred hypothesis based solely upon intuition is preferred at the expense of others. It may mean that decisions, evidence gathering and the selection of material are only geared towards supporting the chosen theory, rather than exploring other possible hypotheses. If the theory is thought to be correct, then investigators are more likely to believe unsound arguments that support it. This is known as 'verification' or 'confirmation bias'.

Wherever possible, the best option is to adopt a methodical and logical decision-making approach, as outlined earlier in this chapter, together with an investigative mindset that minimises any psychological bias inherent in more intuitive approaches to decision making.

2.11 **Decision Recording**

Maintaining accurate records throughout an investigation is important and is a requirement of the Criminal Procedure and Investigations Act 1996 (CPIA). This includes making and keeping records of the conduct of the investigation and the decisions that were made during various stages.

Decision makers are accountable for their decisions and must be prepared to provide a rationale for what they did and why. In some circumstances the need to record decisions is prescribed by statute or is required by organisational policies and local practices. A contemporary example of this is completing the Investigation Management Document. This is intended as a working document containing the ongoing rationale of the reasonable lines of enquiry and the disclosure strategy applied to an investigation (National Police Chiefs Council, 2020).

This document is required because of the updated *Attorney Generals Guidelines on Disclosure* which came into effect on 31 December 2020 (Attorney General's Office, 2020). The reality of why this was mandated was because of ongoing disclosure failures and a lack of decision recording by investigators to explain and justify their disclosure decisions.

Usually, whether to record a decision and what to record is left to the decision makers' own discretion. Whatever the circumstances, the police service recognises that it is impossible to record every single decision and that not all decisions need to be recorded (ACPO Risk Principle 7), however the caveat to this is that a record of decisions with their rationale will assist in ensuring decisions are defensible.

In most instances professional judgement should guide whether or not to record a decision as well as what to record and the extent of any explanation provided. A decision record should be proportionate to the seriousness of the situation or incident involved, particularly if the decision addresses an element of risk.

Records and audit trails are necessary for justifying taking, or sometimes not taking investigative decisions and actions. This safeguards information and provides a record of the reasons why certain decisions were made or not made. In serious, complex or major investigations, this process is known as maintaining a decision log or a policy file.

It is now recognised that decision records can be kept on electronic crime recording systems and is not confined to bound bespoke policy books with sequentially numbered pages as previously. Enquiry officers' investigation books might also be used but an important requirement is transparency and maintaining the integrity of the record keeping system, and entries must be in a permanent, legible and durable format.

Decision records should be recorded contemporaneously where possible and if this is not possible it must be in a timely manner. The date and time the decision was made should be documented, including by automatically generated electronic time stamps for digital records.

If the decision was not recorded at the time for pressing operational reasons, this should be reflected in the record and include the time the decision was made as well as the time the entry was made. The identity of the decision maker or their nominee should be clear, including signed paper records or a digital signature or audit trail.

Entries must accurately reflect key decisions made, whether they are of a strategic or tactical nature, over the course of an investigation. These include topics such as aims and objectives, main lines of enquiry and their supporting strategies and actions, such as scene examination, witness identification and their categorisation, house to house enquiries, searches conducted, digital media recovery and examination. This is by no means an exhaustive list of considerations and it is recommended that in all cases relevant objectives and parameters are recorded. Key decisions such as the grounds for suspicion when nominating a suspect for an offence require greater detail reflected in the decision recording.

Systematically recording decisions with their supporting rationale, based on information known at that time is an important skill to develop, practice and routinely use. Not only is this important for explaining decisions to others in future, if necessary, it also provides clarity when handing over cases to others and can be a useful aide memoire when reviewing one's own decisions and reviewing the progress of investigations. Good record keeping imposes self-discipline and aids structured and well-reasoned problem solving and decision making.

KEY POINTS

- Three important elements of decision logs and entries are: (1) the decision; (2) the reasoning behind it; (3) the information known, available and relied upon at the time the decision was made. All three should be linked together.
- In cases where sensitive information is involved care must be taken when decisions are recorded. It is good practice and strongly recommended that any sensitive decisions such as the use of sensitive tactics are recorded in a separate sensitive decision/policy log. This maintains operational security and assists with managing sensitive decisions and the associated material through the disclosure process.

Decision recording is best kept simple in a straightforward decision/reason format. The actual decision is clearly articulated in one paragraph with a paragraph below this containing the reasons for the decision and if necessary any other considerations. Two examples follow:

Example 1

Decision: *H2H enquiries to be conducted with the immediate neighbours and others in the vicinity in line of sight and hearing of 86 Longfellow Crescent (scene of a burglary dwelling). The objectives are to identify any witnesses to the offence, identify and recover material from any private CCTV systems and gather intelligence about any activity in the area that may be linked to the burglary.*

Reason: *H2H in this vicinity is a fast track action as the scene of the burglary is overlooked by neighbours.*

Example 2

Decision: *A male by the name of Ashley Simmons (date of birth 20.2.1986) has been declared a suspect for the burglary at 86 Longfellow Crescent and is to be arrested.*

Reason: *His DNA and fingerprints have been found at the scene of the burglary and he has no legitimate access to the premises. Arrest is necessary to progress an effective investigation including the search of premises connected to Simmons, gather evidence and interview him under PACE.*

KEY POINT

Part II of the CPIA Code of Practice states:

> All investigators have a responsibility for carrying out the duties imposed on them under this code, including in particular recording information and retaining records of information and other material.

This includes keeping records of the conduct of the investigation.

References

ACPO/NPIA (2005, 2013) *Practice Advice on Core Investigative Doctrine* (2nd edn)

Adair J (2008) *The Best of Adair on Leadership and Management* (Thorogood)

Adhami E and Browne DP (1996) 'Major Crime Enquiries: Improving Expert Support for Detectives' Police Research Group Special Interest Series, Paper 9 (Home Office)

Attorney General's Office (2020) *Attorney Generals Guidelines on Disclosure*

Cohen LE and Felson M (1979) 'Social Change and Crime Rate Trends: A Routine Activity Approach' 44 *American Sociological Review* 588–608

College of Policing (2021) *Authorised Professional Practice* (APP) available at <http://www.college.police.uk/

Chapter 3

General Investigative Practice

3.1 Introduction

Effective investigation management is necessary to achieve successful outcomes. This applies whether an investigator is working individually and in effect managing the investigation themselves, such as in volume crime cases, or whether they are part of a larger team working under the direction of a supervisor or other investigating officer. Investigators working on major incidents will be working to the direction of a Senior Investigating Officer (SIO) and completing enquiries to support their investigative strategy. Even if the offence under investigation is of a minor nature, effective management and administration of all the necessary processes remain equally important. Process management is necessary to meet the requirements of a thorough, methodical investigation, prosecution and appropriate case disposal.

Investigators must strive to demonstrate to victims, supervisors, the Crown Prosecution Service (CPS) and the courts that these responsibilities have been fulfilled and enquiries undertaken and completed with professionalism and rigour. This goes a long way towards establishing trust and confidence in the investigation and the investigator.

Blackstone's Crime Investigators' Handbook. Steve Hibbitt and Gary Shaw, Oxford University Press. © Oxford University Press 2023.
DOI: 10.1093/oso/9780192867896.003.0003

3.2 Stages of a Criminal Investigation

A well-known cliche states 'a chain is only as strong as its weakest link', and in criminal investigations several phases sequentially link together to complete the chain of the investigation process. Investigators should be mindful of the requirements in each of these phases from the beginning to the conclusion of the investigation. The stages for most reported crime is illustrated in Figure 3.1.

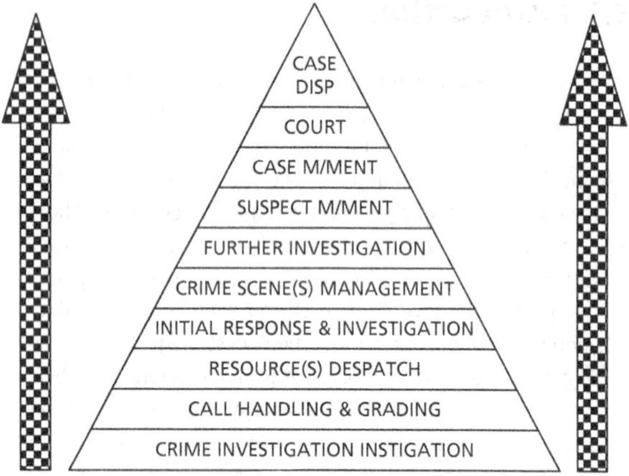

Figure 3.1 Pyramid of Investigation

In summary, these phases are:

1. Crime Investigation Instigation. This could be initiated by direct reports to the police from victims or other people on their behalf, by phone or online or in person at the police station or to patrolling officers. Some reports are referred to the police by other agencies and organisations. Intelligence gathering and proactive work also generates investigations as do the reviews of previously 'cold cases'. Delays in reporting can be detrimental, as offenders then have more time to conceal

or destroy evidence, concoct alibis, disappear to evade arrest, gain confidence and interfere with witnesses whose memories fade over time. Forensic evidence may be lost or contaminated and CCTV could be recorded over.

2. Call Handling and Grading. Communications room incident logs contain valuable information and a record of decisions made, which are important to the investigation. The manner in which a call is initially received and responded to, the quality of information gathered and the priority grading of the incident are significant.
3. Resource(s) Dispatch. Call takers/handlers are responsible for determining and arranging the resources required and the speed of deployment. Some minor and volume crimes are processed entirely by telephone or online due to the numbers reported balanced against the resources available to attend. It is self-evident therefore that no police enquiries will be conducted at the scene or in the vicinity. This could impact on investigators who may be allocated the crime in the future if further meaningful information or lines of enquiry comes to light, for example if stolen bank cards are used or stolen property is identified.
4. Initial Response. This includes confirmation of the initial incident report and grading and initial evaluation of the situation. This is the period when 'golden hour' tasks and fast track actions are needed, such as ensuring the safety and welfare of victims, identifying and preserving crime scenes, securing evidence, conducting hasty searches for suspects and obtaining initial witness accounts.
5. Crime Scene(s) Management. This encompasses identification, security and preservation of crime scenes and avoiding destruction and contamination of material. Processing the crime scene follows, involving recording, examination, searching and exhibit/material recovery. When this has been completed or when it is

forensically safe to do so, the scene is then available for the investigator to conduct a crime scene assessment.

6. Further Investigation. Lines of enquiry need to be identified or reviewed and investigative strategies and tactics considered and developed to progress the enquiry. This includes an evaluation of available evidence and identifying any information gaps. As previously emphasised, applying an investigative mindset is essential.
7. Suspect Management. This is a primary investigation objective and includes the decision to declare suspect status with the reasonable grounds for suspicion, locating the suspect, arrest, search, forensic and evidential processing, interview under caution and charge or other disposal decision including risk assessment and management.
8. Case Management. The importance of this phase should never be underestimated. Enquiries continue post charge to develop the prosecution case, or if bailed or released under investigation to support a prosecution decision or eliminate the suspect. Any results of specialist extraction of digital material and forensic submission results need evaluating for their context in the investigation. Disclosure obligations have to be completed, CPS requests fulfilled and a prosecution case file completed and submitted. Pre-trial time scales must be met which can be particularly demanding for defendants who are remanded in custody.
9. Court: The court process commences with the initial appearance followed by plea and case management and any pre-trial hearings. Before any trial, time scales are set for serving prosecution evidence and the provision of defence case statements to the CPS. Any defence case needs to be evaluated to identify if further enquiries are necessary. Special measures applications need to be made with supporting evidence if necessary. Importantly, victims and witnesses need to be updated

on the case progress and any witness management issues managed and addressed. If a guilty plea is entered and a sentencing hearing ensues, it is essential victims are informed in advance. If the case results in a trial all the necessary arrangements need to be made in advance, including ensuring the availability of witnesses and exhibits and the investigators own preparation for giving evidence if this is required.

10. Case Disposal. Depending on whether a prosecution ensued or the offence remains undetected, this includes considering the return, disposal, retention and archiving of exhibits and other relevant investigative material. For undetected offences this ought to include considering availability for possible future forensic examination as scientific techniques develop. Case papers and crime recording systems need finalising with the outcomes; victims, witnesses and stakeholders require updating.

3.3 Investigative Processes

Important processes that apply to the phases of an investigation are:

- enquiry management
- actions (including initial fast track actions)
- investigative strategies and main lines of enquiry
- information management
- resourcing
- health and safety and risk assessments
- internal and external communication
- exhibits management

3.4 Enquiry Management

Routinely applying and maintaining a high standard of methodical administration to enquiries provides the foundation for efficiency and effectiveness across all assigned investigations.

Most investigations do not merit the use of a Major Incident Room (MIR) unless it is a major or serious crime, but similar structured processes and principles can be adopted without using a Home Office Large Major Enquiry System (HOLMES). It is useful to know what these processes and procedures are as the principles can be applied to other methods of managing an investigations information flow.

3.4.1 Major Incident Room (MIR) and HOLMES

The computerised HOLMES database has multiple functions including an action management system. There are nationally standardised procedures which determine how an investigation using the HOLMES system is run, known as the Major Incident Standardised Administrative Procedures (MIRSAP). These processes are well established and have existed since around 1981. Before the advent of computers, the systems and processes were implemented by using paper and card index systems to cross reference information.

An MIR is the administration centre of an investigation. It is where the enquiry is controlled and managed, allowing information to be carefully scrutinised, evaluated, prioritised and 'actioned' for the benefit of the investigation. There are designated and titled roles such as Office Manager, Receiver, Document Reader, Indexer, Indexing Supervisor, Action Allocator, Action Manager, Analyst, Intelligence Research and Development Officer, Exhibits Officer, Disclosure Officer File Preparation Officer and other specialist roles. Each of these performs a distinct but linked function. UK detectives at some stage in their careers may become involved in an enquiry that is run on HOLMES and further information can be obtained from the manual, *Major Incident Room Standardised Administrative Procedures* (NPCC 2021) or Cook, 2019.

A scaled-down non-computerised version (sometimes referred to as a paper system) can also be an efficient way of managing an investigation as can developing and using appropriate excel type spreadsheets. If necessary, this allows enquiry details and information to be back-record converted and transferred later onto a computerised database if necessary. For example, if a victim of an assault later dies from their injuries or the case becomes part of a complex or larger linked series of investigations.

Being familiar with other MIR terms and abbreviations and using them regularly is suggested good practice.

TIE	trace/investigate/evaluate
TI	trace/interview
TST	take statement
TFS	take further statement
RI	reinterview
OBT	obtain
ENQ	make enquiries
NOMINAL	person or individual allocated a number (eg N14)
UF	unidentified female
UM	unidentified male
UU	unidentified unknown
UV	unidentified vehicle
PDF	personal descriptive form
M	message
D	document
X	exhibit
A	action
HP	high priority
MP	medium priority
LP	low priority

3.5 Actions

Actions are instructions to carry out an investigative activity or enquiry. They are generated from the evaluation of material, including information gathered by the investigation. Actions are likely to establish significant facts, preserve material or lead to the resolution of the incident.

Actions are recorded in a standard format and sequentially numbered. They are prioritised as high, medium or low for completion, depending on their importance to the investigation at that time.

Fast track actions are pursued immediately because they could secure evidence and material that might otherwise be lost, or they could lead to the resolution of the incident. These are usually to be completed within 24 hours or a time scale as instructed by the SIO. Examples of fast track actions are recovering CCTV before it is recorded over or preserving a possible crime scene.

Details on Actions include the sequential number (eg A8, A13), the instructions for what task (action) is required (such as, TST from witness N9 Collins), who the Action has been allocated to, time and date allocated, source/origin of the enquiry and the outcome.

Once completed, supervisors and/or lead investigators and MIR Receivers check the contents to decide whether the task has been completed satisfactorily or whether further enquiries are required before it is recorded as being completed.

A list, table or matrix of actions containing each number, a brief resumé, whether allocated or unallocated and who to, and its current status (allocated, resulted, pended or completed and filed) can be a useful aid.

3.6 Main Lines of Enquiry and Investigative Strategies

Main lines of Enquiry (MLOE) are specific to key aspects of an investigation, for example TI (trace and interview)

N18 (Nominal 18) who was seen on CCTV outside Scene 1 (S1) shortly before the UI suspected offender (N9) arrived at that location. Investigative strategies are developed and used to pursue the main lines of enquiry and progress the investigation.

Prioritised MLOE aimed at gathering particular types of evidence come from relatively standard sources from which core investigative strategies are developed such as:

- crime scene processing
- victims/witnesses (identifying, tracing, interviewing)
- suspects (identifying, tracing, interviewing)
- TIE subjects (trace, investigate, evaluate)
- forensic and contact trace evidence (scene(s), victim(s), suspect(s), other)
- searches
- house to house enquiries
- passive data, CCTV, ANPR, financial sources, etc)
- communications data
- digital media/hi tech investigation
- intelligence Collection
- analysis
- internal and external communications
- media appeals
- consequence management
- proactive and covert methods
- external specialist advisers and experts (National Crime Agency Major Crime Investigative Support)

Invariably there are changes in priorities as some lines of enquiry become less relevant and others more so. Effective control of an investigation can be maintained by (re)producing the MLOE in an overarching focused investigative strategy document which should be regularly reviewed and updated if necessary.

The selected investigative strategies should be developed to meet the circumstances and objectives of the specific investigation's main lines of enquiry. The strategies represent grouped activities that are likely to establish facts, find and preserve evidence and progress the investigation. Their purpose is to generate actions/tactical activities to achieve the objectives of the strategy and in doing so contribute to completing the main line of enquiry to which it is linked.

A strategy is not a checklist and to be effective it needs to have specific aims and objectives. It is based on agreed decisions and should be documented. There is no approved template for strategy documents but fundamentally they are briefing documents with the purpose of informing and instructing the investigators who are to execute the strategy.

A strategy document also serves as one of the records of the conduct of the investigation and therefore it is potentially disclosable to the defence under the Criminal Procedure and Investigations Act 1996 (CPIA). It ought to be recognised that a strategy is not a policy, and neither is it a plan. The documented strategy should be straightforward for investigators to understand and follow and be as concise as possible. It should not contain a list of thoughts and considerations, as these are more appropriately recorded in a decision log.

Before selecting which strategy to develop and use, the relevance, proportionality, necessity, feasibility, cost and resources needed to execute it need to be considered. Without the means of achieving the aim and objectives, it is a wish list and not a strategy. As an example, strategies, such as covert surveillance are resource intensive and costly and would not usually be justifiable for minor or less serious crimes. Force resource allocation policies and priorities are likely to influence the extent to which a strategy is feasible.

KEY POINTS

- Investigative strategies need aims and objectives and specific directions to achieve these.
- When determining MLOE, investigators are free to use any available information and investigative material (eg intelligence) and not just what might be admissible evidence.

3.7 Information

Reliable information is essential for any investigation, therefore an effective method of receiving, capturing, collecting, recording and evaluating information is important. Valuable time and opportunities can be lost if information is overlooked, ignored, misdirected or not understood. Willing sources of information such as potential witnesses and other members of the public can become frustrated or discouraged from assisting or contacting the investigation.

Regardless of the level of investigation, internal communications and systems of processing messages must be capable of receiving, identifying and notifying the lead investigator to pass on important messages or information. Investigators are advised to ensure a reliable channel of communication exists for when they are on or off duty such as having a nominated deputy who is aware of the case and can receive information and instigate appropriate urgent action if necessary.

HOLMES message recording forms are recognised green, self-carbonating documents (known as an MIR/6) and include all the details of the information, such as the originator, time, and date received and what is to be done with it. They are sequentially numbered, usually initially handwritten, and given a priority marking of high, medium or low. They are an effective method of recording information as opposed to using ad hoc pieces of paper, emails or scribbled notes. It is useful to have a ready supply of forms available and use them on a regular basis, as they are the prescribed national message recording method; their use makes any enquiry administration system more organised and professional.

KEY POINT

A public contact number for the investigation team or officer (other than a general non-emergency police number such as '101') may be distributed while conducting enquiries, during media appeals, making H2H visits etc and circulated internally to colleagues and staff. Arrangements must be in place to receive calls and/or check automated or electronic message systems, emails or mailboxes, particularly during periods of absence, leave and courses etc. Investigators need to be assured that messages and information will be forwarded to them without delay. Consideration may be needed for interpreting facilities for callers who may not understand or speak English.

3.8 Resources

Investigators should identify the resources required to conduct the investigative activity and use them to good advantage and manage them properly. Resources need to be proportionate to the level and type of offence under investigation, and much depends on whether they are necessary, justifiable and available, together with time and cost implications. Local policies, budgetary systems, authorisation and procurement regimes are decision-making factors.

KEY POINT

Resources that could be considered include;

1. **Human**—police officers, Police Community Support Officers (PCSOs) and police staff, Crime Scene Investigators (CSIs), fingerprint experts, hi-tech and Digital Media Investigators (DMIs), forensic providers, specialist interviewers, witness liaison, media liaison, search teams, proactive and covert assets, financial specialists, community advisory groups and outside experts and agencies.
2. **Financial**—costs for forensic submissions, instructing expert witnesses, specialist services, overtime, expenses and travel costs obtained from local budgets or applications for special funding from central funds.

3. **Physical**—office or desk space, vehicles, specialist equipment, interview facilities, exhibit storage facilities, computer access and printers, photocopiers and scanners.
4. **Communications**—telephones, radios, dedicated hotline number and recorded message facilities, media publicity, inter/intranet access, Bluetooth messaging, Twitter/Facebook and other social media accounts, useful contacts and conduits (eg Europol)
5. **Intelligence**—local and national intelligence systems, crime management systems, open source access, physical and technical surveillance assets and Covert Human Intelligence Sources (CHIS)
6. **Specialist**—National Crime Agency (NCA) Major Crime Investigative Support Team (MCIS), Serious Crime Analysis Section (SCAS), National Injuries Database (NID), external specialists and experts, interpreters, registered witness intermediaries

Local volume crime investigation protocols may direct that certain resources are dispatched as a matter of policy. Tactical tasking and coordinating processes and systems also determine what can or cannot be deployed and are guided and influenced by local and national policing priorities and objectives including the National Intelligence Model. Early consideration and planning in anticipation of making any necessary applications for resources is advised for to assist effective resource and asset procurement.

Additional staff, including experts and others brought in to assist the investigation, need to be briefed on the current situation and given specific objectives directing what is required of them. Added considerations to include are any logistical and technical matters, access to transport, health and safety considerations and any budgetary requirements and constraints such as overtime and expense claims.

Suggested good practice is to request or apply for any necessary resources as early as possible, particularly for investigations involving a high volume of potential material. This is to minimise the attrition of evidence and endeavour to capture and secure information and evidence as quickly as possible. Added staffing levels can be reassessed and reduced later when initial priorities may not be as time critical. It is worth being aware of what resources are available in advance, particularly if performing 'duty cover' duties in a rota.

With competing demands, investigators must prioritise the needs of an investigation against the available resources. Resources are always finite and operational decisions have to be balanced against their availability or non-availability. To ensure an accurate record of the conduct of the investigation is made, any requests and any refusals should be documented in a decision log. Time management is essential, along with maximising out of what is available. When staff are enthusiastic, motivated and willing, success, even with fewer numbers, is more likely.

3.9 **Resourcing Influences**

The type and category of crime under investigation will affect what resources are potentially available. Some other factors to consider are:

- seriousness of case, including the extent of victim harm or financial loss
- volume of work such as the number of victims, witnesses, crime scenes, suspects and communications data involved
- solvability factors such as potential forensic material, witnesses, identified suspects or passive data
- complexity, including the involvement of organised crime groups, linked crime and series crime
- levels of community impact and concern, public expectation, and media interest,
- political considerations such as local or national priorities or perhaps high-profile suspects
- economic constraints
- legalities

- competing demands from other significant events occurring at the same time
- organisational priorities and objectives
- a convincing or unconvincing business case or application

3.10 Specialist Support

Some of the most requested specialist support resources are:

- Crime Scene Investigators (CSI) and Crime Scene Managers (CSM)
- forensic service providers
- specialist Imaging and photography
- fingerprint experts
- specialist Police Search Teams (PST), including Police Search Advisers (PolSA)
- specialist interview advisers
- specialist witness interviewers, achieving best evidence (ABE) trained
- specialist suspect interviewers
- H2H teams
- digital media investigator (DMI)/communications data/ hi tech crime/computer examination specialists
- criminal intelligence hubs/units
- financial investigators
- family liaison officers (FLOs)
- covert operational support teams
- media liaison officers
- NCA Major Crime Investigative Support Team and Serious Crime Analysis Section (SCAS)

KEY POINT

The NCA Major Crime Investigative Support Team can be contacted via the Specialist Operations Centre on the national number **0845 000 5463**. The National Experts Database, witness intermediaries and other assets are also available through the same gateway.

3.11 Health and Safety and Risk Assessments

The Health and Safety at Work Act 1974 and Police (Health and Safety) Act 1997 state that due regard must be paid to the nature of activities and undertakings in order, so far as is reasonably practicable, to provide a safe and healthy working environment. The aim must be to prevent injuries and danger.

As some areas of crime investigation attract the potential risk of harm, activities must be properly assessed so appropriate arrangements to manage, mitigate and control any risks are in place. Everyone involved in crime investigation must ensure risks are recognised and managed by adhering to safety principles, such as wearing protective clothing, ensuring any equipment is properly used and that adequate welfare measures are adopted.

Any work activities posing significant risks to health and safety must be identified and documented risk assessments completed. A general requirement to conduct risk assessments is required under the Management of Health and Safety at Work Regulations 1999. The purpose is to identify measures necessary to comply with relevant statutory duties by taking steps to introduce control measures to manage risks. Risk assessments and control measures are generally generic, specific or dynamic:

1. **Generic**—produced for a variety of activities (eg executing search warrants) by identifying significant hazards that may be encountered and introducing suitable control measures aimed at reducing risks.
2. **Specific**—a systematic and detailed examination of a particular activity (eg arresting a suspect who has a Police National Computer (PNC) warning marker and intelligence for firearms and violence).
3. **Dynamic**—operational risk assessments may need to be revised quickly due to changing or unanticipated circumstances. This necessitates spontaneous decision

making concerning risks posed to self and others and their health and safety implications.

KEY POINTS

- Risk assessments help identify control measures and may involve a combination of generic, specific and dynamic risk assessments.
- Control measures are introduced to lower and counterbalance the degree of risk and its impact. For example, if a requirement to enter and search a loft of a house is a medium risk, a specific control measure may stipulate that only officers trained in ladder safety and searching in confined spaces, with the correct protective clothing and equipment, are to be used. This would then lower the risk from medium to 'low'.

3.12 Threat, Harm and Risk Control Models

In Chapter 2, assessing threat and risk and developing a working strategy was outlined in relation to the National Decision Model (NDM). Once a risk is identified a control strategy is required, and models exist to facilitate this.

There are basically four risk mitigation approaches from which strategies and tactics can be developed to inform decision making and address risks that need controlling. These are: to remove, avoid, reduce or accept the risk considering the acronym RARA, the contents of which should be self-evident:

R	Remove
A	Avoid
R	Reduce
A	Accept

Using whatever tactics are necessary, the intention is to remove, avoid or reduce the threat, harm and risk. Alternatively, some risks might be assessed as so negligible they can be accepted. When assessing risk, amongst the 5WH (Who? What? Where? Why? When? and How?) questions to consider are:

- What information is available to inform the risk assessment?
- How reliable is this information?
- What gaps are there in this information?
- How can any gaps be addressed?
- What are the limitations/gaps with the available information?
- What threat, harm and risk has been identified?
- What is the intent contained in any threat?
- What is the capability of carrying out any threat?
- What is the immediacy of any threat, harm and risk?
- Who owns the risk?
- Who owns the consequences of the risk?
- What is the urgency for the decision?
- What options to mitigate the risk are available?
- What (if any) of these options are contingent on other factors?
- What resources are required?
- What resources are available?
- Are there any other factors and considerations?

3.13 **Risk Assessment Scoring Matrix**

Models exist to assist decision making for structured risk assessments and one of these is the Risk Assessment Scoring Matrix. This is a scoring process which assesses threat and harm and their impact multiplied by the probability of this occurring. It uses the principle that the greatest risk is caused by a situation where the probability of a harm occurring and its impact are high. It follows that risks that have both a low impact and low probability of occurring are not great causes for concern.

Using this scoring matrix, a number is produced which indicates whether the risk is high, medium, low or negligible.

There is an element of subjective judgement on the part of the decision maker and accurate and reliable information is required to conduct an assessment that is as effective as possible.

The impact factors in the top column are multiplied by the probability likelihood in the left-hand column to produce a risk assessment score. As an example, if it is 'highly probable' (5) that arresting a suspect will meet strong resistance and violence, and if this occurs the impact would be very serious (4), the assessment score is calculated as 20 (5 × 4) making this high risk. However, the score can be reduced by introducing effective control measures, such as using a team of specially trained officers with protective equipment to conduct the arrest and staging the operation in the early hours of the morning by unannounced forced entry to the premises to add an element of surprise.

Using RARA, these risk reduction tactics can revise the risk assessment score. It can now be recalculated, as it is unlikely (2) the arrest will be resisted which produces a reduced score of 8 (2 × 4) making this a moderate risk.[1]

Using the matrix, a score of 12 to 25 equates to a high risk, a score of 6 to 10 equates to a moderate risk, a score of 2 to 5 equates to low risk and a score of 1 is a negligible risk.

Impact Probability	Catastrophic (5)	Very Serious (4)	Serious (3)	Moderate (2)	Minimal (1)
Highly Probable (5)	High (25)	High (20)	High (15)	Moderate (10)	Low (5)
Probable (4)	High (20)	High (16)	High (12)	Moderate (8)	Low (4)
Possible (3)	High (15)	High (12)	Moderate (9)	Moderate (6)	Low (3)
Unlikely (2)	Moderate (10)	Moderate (8)	Moderate (6)	Low (4)	Low (2)
Very Unlikely (1)	Low (5)	Low (4)	Low (3)	Low (2)	Negligible (1)

[1] There is further information about risk assessment and management available from the Health and Safety Executive (HSE) at <http://www.hse.gov.uk/> accessed 10 January 2022.

3.14 Communication

Communication can be separated into two types—internal and external. Internal communication refers to tactics and methods used to communicate, liaise, disseminate, brief and alert those within the police organisation. This might include conducting briefings and debriefings, circulating stolen property details or suspect descriptions, requesting information about sightings of vehicles, persons, suspects or victims, or writing updates or situation reports on the case under investigation.

External communication utilises outlets that are available within the public arena, including mainstream and social media. Whatever proposed external medium is to be used, it is strongly advised to seek advice from a media liaison officer.

There are legalities that must be complied with prior to releasing images or suspect details before charge. The impact on the wider investigation also needs careful consideration, for example ensuring any information supplied to the public links to the suspect interview strategy, including the pre-interview briefing to a legal adviser. There would be little point withholding information for the interview if this had already been released into the public domain by the investigation.

It should also be born in mind that depending on the matters in issue between a future prosecution and the defence, any media releases, and the responses to them could become relevant material for disclosure purposes under the CPIA. This could be highly likely if identity is disputed, and descriptions of suspects or images have been publicised. Furthermore, investigators should ensure that appropriate arrangements are in place to accurately capture any responses, and that any information is supplied to the investigating officer and properly managed.

Another consideration is the use of official social media accounts such as Twitter by officers not connected to the investigation. Many police forces encourage some officers and PCSOs to post updates about matters considered to be of potential interest as they go about their duties. If not properly controlled these have clear potential to impact on the content of information leaving the investigation.

If this is an issue of potential concern, the investigator should ensure all officers are quickly briefed not to post any information to social media without first seeking authority from the investigator.

3.15 **Briefings and Debriefings**

A briefing is a structured meeting to impart information and discuss matters of relevance to the investigation. This includes occasions when teams are briefed before conducting or mounting a pre-planned operation (College of Policing 2022).

Briefings play an important purpose in distributing instructions and information between a team and it is difficult to manage or control a team investigation without them. They are a means by which information is disseminated and shared; ideas, tactics and hypotheses are exchanged; progress is discussed; tasks are allocated; updates are provided and feedback is gained. Matters of interest and developments are discussed and pertinent issues raised.

Briefings are a tool for providing the communications link between colleagues, specialists, supervisors and managers. It is important that briefings are controlled and structured. Whilst valuing contributions from those present who are contributing relevant information, individuals should not be allowed to unnecessarily dominate the session nor deviate from the main topic(s).

Briefings are a means of motivating staff, as well as discussing the case, and they provide a good opportunity for collective discussions and use of the 5WH to identify and clarify information that is known and identify any gaps in the investigations knowledge. To conduct an effective briefing, it is advised that an approved structure such as IIMARCH or SAFCOM is used:

Information
Intention
Method
Administration
Risk assessment
Communication
Human rights and other legal issues
or
Situation
Aim
Factors
Choices
Option
Monitor

Hot debriefs are primarily used after the initial response phase of an incident by assembling all those who were involved to share and gather information. This includes gathering information about the golden hour response and the action taken thus far, including any witnesses identified and their initial accounts, any searches conducted and their extent and result, any exhibits and other investigative material recovered and their location, any suspects identified who have already been arrested, plus the circumstances of any suspects arrest including any significant comments or statements made.

The process involves discussing a chronological timeline of events as they occurred, identifying who did what, where, when, why and how (5WH). Post incident debriefs are an early opportunity to capture important information or evidence after an incident response. Everyone who was involved should be encouraged to attend and participate.

Debriefings contribute to identifying urgent actions and lines of enquiry, the gathering of intelligence and identifying information gaps. Investigators need to ensure that they evaluate any information they receive and material they recover or generate by applying an investigative mindset.

KEY POINTS

- So-called 'hot debriefs' form a useful conduit for information in the early stages when staff need to impart knowledge or information following 'golden hour(s)' tasks.
- Briefings and debriefings require some degree of structure and control to ensure the most is gained out of them.
- Any notes or records taken should be retained for disclosure purposes.

References

ACPO (2006), *Guidance on the National Briefing Model* (NCPE)
College of Policing, http://www.app.college.police.uk/briefings-and-debriefings accessed 22 October 2022
Cook T, *Blackstones Senior Investigating Officers Handbook* (5th edn, OUP)

Chapter 4

Initial Stages of an Investigation

4.1 Introduction

The initial stage of a reactive investigation begins after the discovery of the crime. This first contact could be a report to a call handling unit, a public enquiry desk, or reports to officers or other staff or agencies.

Many crimes can be quickly detected through prompt and decisive resourcing and dispatch for locating and arresting offenders, obtaining witnesses, seizing CCTV footage, finding and preserving forensic evidence, etc.

The actions taken, or perhaps not taken, during the initial stages of an investigation are critical success factors that can positively or negatively influence the outcome. This begins with how the initial report is handled, what information is obtained, how the incident is categorised and graded, and decisions on the level and timing of the initial response.

Key to most investigations is the early gathering and recording of accurate and detailed information, preserving scenes, securing evidence and taking necessary initial action. Initial assessments by attending officers with updates reported back to communications and control rooms should confirm the initial grading or revise the response in terms of seriousness, priority and resources. This period is often referred to as the 'golden hour(s)'.

This chapter contains practical considerations to trigger early investigative decisions during the initial response and

Blackstone's Crime Investigators' Handbook. Steve Hibbitt and Gary Shaw, Oxford University Press.
DOI: 10.1093/oso/9780192867896.003.0004

beyond. The suggestions are not exhaustive, and it must be stated that each case is unique. Over-reliance on fixed routines and checklists or tick boxes that are automatically followed can sometimes be detrimental to using initiative and maintaining an investigative mindset in which various hypotheses and alternative courses of action are considered.

For more serious crimes it is likely that a senior investigator at some point assumes overall command and responsibility for directing and controlling the enquiry. However, it is the actions taken during the initial stages before others become involved that are often critical to success. A key point for investigators, no matter what the seriousness of the crime is, is the importance of establishing exactly what has already been done, by whom, and to what level and standard. It may be necessary to quickly intervene to get things back on track if necessary. This is not possible without knowledge or an assessment of what others have done, should have done or should be doing.

It is acknowledged that some investigations are dealt with by not deploying officers at all and are conducted remotely using online crime reporting systems and the telephone and/or email. Others may fall outside an individual investigators level or area of responsibility or authority due to the type of offence or its seriousness.

Investigators need to be aware of the range of standard responses required for most types of crime and incidents, from volume and priority offences to the more serious and complex, such as serious injury assaults, rape and serious sexual offences, high-risk missing persons and threats to life. Knowledge and understanding of the required initial response will inform and assist effective decision making when the time comes.

4.2 **Golden Hour(s) Principle**

The 'golden hour(s)' principle originates from the medical world, where it is a basic premise in trauma cases that casualties need to be managed expeditiously to achieve the best chance of recovery and avoid future complications. The same principle applies to the initial police response to a reported crime. A prompt and effective initial response will have far-reaching benefits for the investigation that follows, and the converse is also true.

The golden hour(s) is a time when forensic evidence is freshest and easiest to detect before attrition begins. The longer time elapses before material with potential forensic value is identified, located and preserved, the greater the potential is for its contamination or degradation. Witnesses are likely to be at their most cooperative and their recollections more accurate the nearer to the event they are spoken to. Similar to crime scenes, a witness's memory can also become contaminated by external factors and their accounts distorted if there are delays before they are interviewed. Offenders are at their most vulnerable immediately following the offence, before potentially incriminating evidence can be disposed of and lies and alibis prepared. This is why it is important to maximise the available investigative opportunities during the golden hour(s) (ACPO/NPIA 2005, 2006).

4.3 Teamwork

Crime investigation, particularly in the initial stages or 'golden hour(s)', requires teamwork to achieve success. This is a combined effort between those who can use complementary skills and responsibilities to work towards a common goal. All members of the team contribute to the process of crime solving, whether it be the person who takes the initial report or the patrol officer who attends the scene. Each element has to fulfil their responsibilities to provide the optimum chance of success.

Crime investigators can contribute to creating a teamwork approach by coordinating all the work and activity. Various roles and resources in their team might include:

- call-handler/taker/resource dispatcher
- initial responders
- additional resources, such as traffic officers, dog handlers, police search teams, intelligence officers, air support unit
- specialist resources, like the Crime Scene Investigator (CSI), forensic service providers, communications data expert
- other colleagues, crime investigators and units/departments
- supervisors and line managers
- internal police stakeholders, for example neighbourhood panels/community policing teams)
- partner and external agencies and other interested parties such as the local authority
- Crown Prosecution Service
- coroner/coroner's officers/pathologists
- victim support network
- regional force resources

Momentum and progress need to be consolidated and maintained to provide the foundations for a well-coordinated investigation. This requires a shared sense of purpose, positive, professional attitudes and pooling of roles and skills. Effective teams acknowledge that those around them have complementary skills. Effective co-operation and communication skills with the sharing of information and knowledge will help crime investigators bring it all together.

KEY POINT

It is essential that everyone contributing to the response in whatever capacity is clear about what the objectives are for the activity they are undertaking. This needs to be accurately and clearly communicated and not just assumed.

4.4 'Five Building Block Principles'

The *Core Investigative Doctrine* (2005), updated in 2013 (ACPO/NPIA 2013) introduced the 'Five Building Block Principles' and they were replicated in the *Murder Investigation Manual* (ACPO/Centrex 2006). These publications have since been superceded by the *Authorised Professional Practice* (APP) (College of Policing 2021) and the *Major Crime Investigation Manual* (NPCC 2021), which also describe the same principles. These continue to underpin the response phase and the initial stages of most investigations.

Visually, the five building blocks have been made straightforward to recall when contemplating what action to take (see Figure 4.1). The headings contained within the building blocks are self-explanatory and are all covered within this handbook, particularly when considering the initial actions of the first responders to an incident.

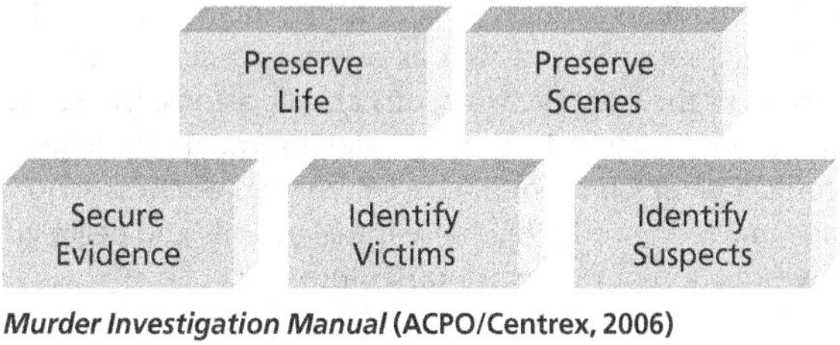

Figure 4.1 The Five Building Block Principles
(ACPO/Centrex, 2006)

4.5 Call Handling and Recording

The 'call taker' is also a member of the investigation team who can immediately influence the initial stages of the enquiry in a positive way. Their role in obtaining, receiving and recording vital information at the point of first delivery is extremely important. This is when a crime or incident is likely be at its freshest, and recollections and emotions at their highest level, immediately after the crime or incident has occurred.

If a call or report is handled effectively, important information can be obtained to launch and direct initial lines of enquiry. Depending on the circumstances, it is advisable to obtain a copy of any record or log made to review and scrutinise so that vital information is not missed. For example, when a witness contacts the police, the log is likely to contain their first account of what they have seen or heard, so this record needs to be scrutinised very closely. Information contained in telephone calls and recordings sometimes gets omitted from incident logs or is not passed on, and there may be an interim recording of emergency calls made before they are switched through to the police, which is also worth obtaining and scrutinising.

Incident logs can include running commentaries about crime incidents and reveal useful information about the person(s) reporting, as well as being a contemporaneous record of the call takers' actions and decisions, including resources dispatched, other agencies informed with names, contact details and times. This record is an essential source document from which to raise initial actions and begin an investigation or review enquiries initiated.

4.6 **Role of Call Takers/Call Handlers**

This role is now more proactive and investigative in nature. Call takers get inundated with vast numbers of routine calls and work in a high-pressure environment. By and large, they will differentiate those of a more urgent nature. Call handlers are not just a channel of communication;

they are trained to offer guidance on some aspects of the investigation, such as crime scene preservation.

Call handlers are expected to adopt an investigative mindset using open questions and the 5WH principles. A call may be the only opportunity to elicit crucial information from a caller, who may also be a victim, witness or offender. Most callers have a wealth of information of benefit to the investigation and need to be asked relevant questions to extract it.

KEY POINT

The exact words spoken by a person reporting a crime or incident may prove vital to the investigation. For this reason, the information given by the person making the report and any recording or logging mechanisms should be carefully checked. This includes details given to telephone exchange staff who transfer calls to the police and other emergency services.

4.7 Reports to Patrol Officers/ Public Enquiry Facilities

Crimes could also be reported to patrolling officers or at public enquiry desks. Similar principles that apply to call handlers will apply for extracting accurate details and information. Wherever possible, witnesses should be encouraged to remain with an officer until the full extent of what they have seen, heard or know is obtained (or arrangements made for a fuller interview).

If a person refuses to remain or to provide personal details, out of fear of intimidation or a reluctance to become involved for example, there is an option of recording observable information about them, such as their age, height, ethnicity, accent, unusual features, clothing worn, who they are in company with, vehicles used, direction of travel, etc. These details can later assist with establishing or confirming their identity and conducting follow-up enquiries.

Those reporting a crime could be involved in the crime themselves. If there are reasonable grounds to suspect their involvement, early consideration should be given to lawfully detaining them. It is not uncommon for offenders to speak to officers on cordons or to make reports at or near crime scenes, trying to look helpful, or they may return to crime scenes to observe what is taking place or offer themselves as witnesses. Sometimes they like to speak with journalists and reporters if present, for example Ian Huntley during the Soham murders investigation. This is why it is vital to record as much accurate detail as possible about and from such persons and for investigators to carefully debrief any officers and staff (and members of the public) who may have spoken with them.

4.8 **Initial Responders**

Not all of the following procedures apply to every case, but crime investigators should fully understand and appreciate the need to check, review and confirm what necessary tasks have or have not been completed. Early mistakes and errors happen which must be identified and rectified quickly. There must be a clear audit trail of any remedial action taken to demonstrate the core values of transparency, professionalism and honesty of purpose and compliance with disclosure rules, which should be considered from the outset of the investigation.

KEY POINT

When debriefing those involved in initial actions, it is best to encourage frankness and honesty about what has been done/not done. Mistakes cannot be rectified if they are withheld or unknown. Inevitably, some individuals may not comply with this rule, which is why it is important to ***check, check*** and ***recheck*** all information provided.

There are different procedures for responding to different types of incidents. The five building blocks mentioned earlier contain useful headings (preserve life and scenes, secure evidence, identify witnesses and suspects) from which to produce a quick guide of ten basic golden hour actions for first attendees at more serious crime incidents.

Checklist—First responders—10 x 'golden hour(s)' actions

1. Victims—Search for, identify, support and attend to any victims or casualties (administer first aid where necessary, summon medical assistance if required and preserve life).
2. Conduct an initial assessment and provide a situation report using the 5WH questions, such as: What happened? What resources are required? What officer/emergency services safety risks are there? Where? Who? When? Why? How?
3. Identify, secure and protect (ISP) crime scenes and any physical evidence, such as CCTV, weapons, mobile phones, clothing, blood marks, footprints, vehicles, escape routes.
4. Identify the entry/exit route to scene with one point of entry and designated common approach path (CAP) and rendezvous point (RVP). Mark out and protect the perimeter using barrier tape and cordons. Prevent unauthorised access and cross-contamination and commence incident scene log(s).
5. Identify the person(s) reporting the crime and potential witnesses; separate and obtain their first accounts. Ensure any 'first descriptions' provided are accurately recorded. Consider tactfully treating them as a scene and obtain their outer clothing.
6. Identify suspects and consider an early arrest. Identify their likely escape route/direction of travel

and means, including potentially public transport, car or on foot and conducting any hasty searches, including using a scent dog.

7. Check relevant locations and confirm the identity of those found nearby. Treat suspects as crime scenes.
8. Instigate and make initial enquiries, for example house-to-house (H2H) type, and record all details, including who was spoken to, what vehicles were present and anything that appears unusual at and around the scene. Include descriptions of people and clothing.
9. Intelligence. Seek and record all available wider investigative information that may be relevant.
10. Victim's family/community—establish their needs, concerns and expectations and keep them informed about the progress of the investigation.
11. Log the details and times of all activities, actions taken, when, why, how, where and by whom.

Important decisions and procedures rely on the effectiveness and professionalism of first responders. They are expected to apply their knowledge and practical and investigative skills to gain maximum advantage for the investigation. Aspects that seem irrelevant in the initial stages often gain significance later. All actions and information must be recorded and, if relevant, are always potentially disclosable.

The circumstances and environment may be simple and straightforward; alternatively, there could be challenges such as confrontational and difficult people to contend with in emotionally charged and volatile situations. Sometimes a crime scene is in a hazardous location or a difficult to reach location. Language and cultural barriers may present other difficulties, which may impact on responsibilities and investigative needs.

KEY POINTS

- Initial responders and resource dispatchers should consider what/where/how and when supporting resources can be put to best use, for example if suspects are making good their escape, covering possible exit routes instead of sending all resources to the scene.
- Hasty searches need to be systematic and methodical to swiftly identify and locate useful evidence, suspects or witnesses. Details should be recorded to assist fully managed searches later, including by CSI and forensic examiners.
- Public areas and transport links such as taxi ranks, buses, tram and train stations may need to be checked for offenders or witnesses, including local hospitals in violence cases.
- Scene preservation is important; so too is tracking offenders and pinpointing their direction of travel. Human scent dogs can prove useful but need to be deployed quickly.

4.9 **Preserving Crime Scenes**

One of the five building blocks is preserving crime scenes. This can be separated into three elements known as the 'ISP' principle:

I — IDENTIFY
S — SECURE
P — PROTECT

All areas relating to a crime scene(s), once identified, need to be sealed and secured. A key task of initial responders is to prevent disturbance and stop unauthorised persons entering and/or disturbing and contaminating crime scenes. This includes supervisory staff, unless there is an urgent operational need. These three procedures are outlined below and more fully explained in Chapter 5.

1. **Identify.** Depending on the circumstances, there may be more than one crime scene and the initial response may only identify and deal with just one of a number. The identification of all other potential crime scenes might originate from CCTV and witness observation or searching the area. If there is more than one scene each should be sequentially numbered, for example Scene (S1), Scene (S2) and so on. A list of what may constitute a crime scene, such as a location, victim, escape route, vehicle(s) used and possibly abandoned, attack sites, suspects, etc is contained in Chapter 5.
2. **Secure.** There are several ways to secure crime scenes and much depends on the circumstances and environment. In serious or complex cases, cordons are used with high visibility tape to mark out the sterile area and uniformed staff restricting and controlling access. Indoor scenes are generally easier to secure than outdoor locations, which need more resources to effectively keep sterile.
3. **Protect.** In addition to safety issues, officers should try to prevent any disturbance and interference from the public, media, weather, animals, etc. A common approach path (CAP) should be established for a single access and exit route, which needs to be the route least likely to have been used by the offender(s).

KEY POINT

An example of where there is more than one crime scene to identify, secure and protect (ISP) is a violent or sustained attack in an apartment block. Separate scenes may be identified such as an apartment, elevator, landing, interior stairwell, lobby and/or adjacent car park. Sufficient resources would be required to secure and protect these areas as quickly as possible to prevent contamination, for example from bona-fide visitors, residents or offenders.

Any item at a scene can be of evidential value and nothing should be touched or moved. If, however, something of a physical nature is in immediate danger of being lost, destroyed or contaminated, steps should be taken to protect or recover the item to preserve it. Removal should be conducted with minimum disturbance, carefully recording the exact position and location of the exhibit. If possible, it should be photographed in position (situ) first. This includes fragile material such as footprints, blood marks, footwear or tyre impressions in mud/soil which may be destroyed by the weather. Improvisation may be necessary to cover and protect items using available 'make-do' objects until the correct equipment arrives.

Once preserved and contained, nothing further needs to be done with a scene until a CSI arrives. Other pieces of evidence can be sought and collected including details such as eyewitness accounts, information offered, H2H and CCTV enquiries.

It is sometimes difficult to determine exact boundaries for scene cordons and preservation. If indoors, the task is much easier; outdoors, however, there are added complications such as the weather, general public, vehicular traffic, terrain and location, etc. Generally it is preferable to make cordons as wide as possible, using natural boundaries, as they can always be reduced later. This is not possible the other way around.

4.10 **Basic Crime Scene Kits**

Basic crime scene kits better equip staff to preserve evidence and minimise the chance of contamination. These should be carried by all operational personnel and as a minimum contain:

- cordon/barrier tape
- 2 × pairs of disposable overshoes
- 2 × pairs of disposable gloves
- major incident scene log forms
- exhibit bags and labels

- first-aid kit
- aide-memoire of actions

4.11 Emergency Responders

Ambulance crew, paramedics and fire crews attending scenes require debriefing soon afterwards as they may need to quickly redeploy or may have already been redeployed. The possibility of an emergency service vehicle being equipped with an on-board CCTV recording system should always be explored. The other 'blue light responders' often arrive at scenes before the police, particularly if notified via their own communication systems. Other services create and keep their own records of attendance and involvement, including the circumstances of what they find and are told upon arrival. Sometimes they may obtain or hear accounts from victims, witnesses and even suspects. In some instances, therefore, consideration may need to be given to treating them as significant witnesses, depending on the extent of what they have seen or heard.

Emergency services personnel are not trained investigators and therefore must be carefully debriefed for relevant information. Details to obtain include how they gained entry to the scene (indoors or outdoors), where they have been and what they have touched or moved. They should be asked questions along the lines of: Who was present? What did they see? What did the victim say? What medical intervention was made and what items were left behind at the scene? (ie the 5WH principles).

In some circumstances they take their own photographs or recordings which could contain relevant information about who was around the scene and its vicinity. The fire service may take photographs to assist their own assessment and investigation into a fire which could contain details of an arsonist, an associate or a significant witness. Some fire and ambulance service vehicles carry their own visual and audio recording equipment which investigators should make it a priority to obtain and examine.

KEY POINTS

- Medical personnel (paramedics) always have primacy at scenes until victims have been attended to and treated (preservation of life is the first priority).
- Medical teams can unavoidably disturb and/or contaminate potential evidence. This should be considered when interpreting a crime scene. Using resuscitation devices such as defibrillator pads causes injuries or marks which, together with any discarded medical equipment, needs accounting for.
- Sensible judgement should apply when recovering trace evidence from 'emergency services' personnel, clothing, footwear or vehicles, such as ambulances. Local agreements usually provide guidance on what should/should not be retained or impounded for forensic examination. Usually, samples can be taken without disrupting the ability of the emergency resources to continue providing a normal service. If ambulances and/or rapid response vehicles are located within a cordon, a path can be cleared for their release and tyre impressions, or photographs taken prior to their release or at some later stage for elimination purposes. Normally if victims are placed within ambulances, the only items that should be considered seizing are blankets; it is not sensible to seize equipment needed for other patients, such as defibrillators. Investigators may need to discuss with the Crime Scene Manager (CSM) how best to deal with such circumstances.

4.12 **Welfare Considerations**

The police and other agencies may have to deal with pressing emergencies at scenes, including spotting dangers and acting quickly. In extreme cases there may be a need to instinctively remove or avoid danger, to seize vital exhibits such as weapons or abandon or leave crime scenes because of imminent danger or the risks involved.

Potential threats to members of the public and/or police officers may present no alternative.

In some inner-city areas there can be distrust of the police, bitter gang feuds, high incidence of drug/alcohol abuse, firearms usage or hostile families and friends of victims. These added risks are the exception rather than the rule but add complications and, in some cases, frustrate or impede initial investigative requirements.

The health and safety of victims, witnesses, the general public and responders is at all times of paramount importance and non-negotiable. For the avoidance of doubt, if there is a conflict of interest between public safety and an investigation, the former takes precedence.

4.13 Crime Investigators Responsibilities

Investigators should aim for early attendance at crime scenes to assist with the commencement scene assessment and the handover of the investigation. When dealing with certain types of enquiries or serious crime, it may be force policy to deploy a supervisor or senior detective to assume the role of Investigating Officer (IO) or Senior Investigating Officer (SIO) and take command. The initial investigator will be expected to have commenced preliminary investigations, obtained and reviewed all the pertinent information and begun a list of enquiries that have been or need to be conducted. A crime investigator is often the person initially in overall charge of the investigation.

Initial assessments should decide whether to hand over to a more senior supervisor and/or SIO. Until such time it must be clearly recognised that it is they (the crime investigator) who are in charge of the investigation. This sometimes occurs when a sudden death is reported with uncertainties about the circumstances or in cases involving high-risk missing or vulnerable persons.

Appropriate administration and documentation should be used to begin a basic enquiry management system, such as statement forms, personal descriptive forms, crime scene tape, exhibit management logs, forensic labels and bags. These are the basis for implementing standardised administrative procedures.

The public often have different perceptions of plain-clothes (non-uniform) investigators than uniformed staff. They can therefore take full advantage of rummaging around and engaging with members of the public who could be sources of information but who may otherwise be reluctant to speak or to be seen speaking with uniform police officers.

Investigators should be skilled and adept at eliciting information from onlookers and getting amongst by-standers and passers-by to ask questions. Building rapport with those who may be useful as witnesses, sources of information and potential 'confidential sources', or informants (better known under the Regulation of Investigatory Powers Act 2000 (RIPA 2000) as covert human intelligence sources, or CHIS for short) is a core communication skill. Using intuition or a hunch that something 'just doesn't look right' (JDLR principle) and applying an investigative mindset is another.

A comprehensive and useful checklist containing a top 50 bank of initial considerations for crime investigators is contained in the Appendix. If any of the bank of actions are completed or are in progress, a lead investigator's role is to not only confirm this but apply a 5WH-type review process. Reviewing, checking, making decisions, accurately recording and directing the necessary process and taking ownership of the investigation that has begun.

KEY POINTS

- Investigators who are unable to attend a crime scene quickly need to confirm who at that time is in charge and make contact. They can then begin the process of finding answers to the 5WH questions.

- Verbal instructions can get misinterpreted, so they need to be given or received as clearly as possible, then repeated back and noted.
- The process of reviewing and updating fast track actions needs to commence quickly. High priority (HP) actions must be well founded, particularly if based upon uncorroborated information.
- Early assessments can trigger useful thoughts, such as what type or category of crime it is, what the motive might be, early investigative options, lines of enquiry and what resources may be required.
- Those nominated to protect crime scenes must be properly briefed regarding any contamination issues, preventing unauthorised entry and accurately recording details in scene logs.
- Staff should be reminded to look and appear professional and behave responsibly, and not to look bored or disinterested.
- Cordon officers must be aware that people approaching the cordon and asking questions about the investigation could be potential witnesses, or even possibly a suspect.

4.14 Contact Lists

One practical suggestion is to start and maintain a list and running log of important contact names and numbers rather than having to thumb through pages of notes to find details that have been written in amongst something else. A printed table attached to a clipboard or daybook is convenient and may be as simple as the one given here.

Name	Role	Contact Number
Sue Hayden	Crime Scene Investigator	07921 ******
Dawn Warren	Patrol Sergeant	07770 ******
Brendan O'Shea	Initial responder	Airwaves channel 34
Jason McClintic	Initial responder/PCSO	Channel 34
DC Javid Iqbal	Crime Investigator	07834 ******

4.15 **Attending Crime Scenes**

Crime scenes yield lots of information and potential evidence. Hearing and reading about an incident and crime scene is not the same as being there experiencing firsthand and getting a *feel* for the environment, contours, and layout of the location where the offence took place. This helps put everything into context and perspective and make sense of, for example, why a location or victim may have been chosen, perhaps for ease of access or availability of an escape route.

Geographical (spatial) and time (temporal) detail for most crimes are always significant. Looking around a location (preferably on foot) and scanning the environment from a three-dimensional (3D) perspective helps to develop knowledge about the crime and offender. It also relates to one of the primary 5WH questions, that is, 'Where?'. Clues stem from probing this fundamental question and raise supplementary queries such as was it:

Targeted victim?
or
Targeted location?
or
Opportunistic encounter?

Closely examining a scene and the surrounding location, geography and the social and demographic makeup of an area helps raise or answer 5WH questions. For example, who else may have been in the area or live nearby? What possible access and escape routes are there? Where are any buildings and places of interest? What are the distances between locations (if more than one crime scene or a series of offences) or the proximity of any key locations, events, or hot spots? Where are locations where key nominals live, frequent or have been seen?

A good map of the area helps greatly, together with someone with good local knowledge of the locality and community. Google images and street view may also be useful to give a general impression of the location but are no substitute for attending a scene in person. If it is an older or historic offence, checking to see if the layout has changed should also be completed.

4.16 **Detective Instinct**

Good awareness and instinct cannot be learnt solely from manuals, practical guides or in a classroom. They are qualities that are essential for those responding to reports of crime to ensure they notice important features or anything unusual or out of place. An inquisitive 'detective instinct' is and always has been something that can lead to taking quick and decisive action or finding the piece of evidence that solves the crime.

KEY POINT

A simple principle to follow when responding to reported crimes and making initial enquiries is to use all the senses and instincts to identify anything that '*Just Doesn't Look Right*' (JDLR)—a self-explanatory principle. The investigative mindset should always be applied in this situation.

4.17 **Victims and Witnesses**

Being a witness or victim of crime could be a distressing experience. Apart from physical trauma and injuries, there are potential emotional and psychological affects which may require support and welfare, either immediately or later. The effects of post-traumatic stress may not be initially obvious but can occur in the most hardened of people. In the initial stages of an investigation, welfare needs have to be identified, addressed sensibly and, if necessary, some appropriate support arranged.

Help and support includes practical assistance, such as arranging new security locks, completing compensation forms or arranging counselling. In some forces this may be triggered automatically and form part of the reporting and response mechanism.

Some crimes may require more specialist kinds of support, such as sexual assault, hate crime, stalking, harassment and child abuse. Force policy may stipulate how, when, where and what support should be provided, and it may be advisable to seek advice. Vulnerable or intimidated witnesses in particular require an enhanced level of support.

Some witnesses may be quite apprehensive about providing a testimony, attending court and giving evidence. In such cases support is likely to be required from one or other of the types of agencies available. Arranging support promptly (ie soon after the initial response) increases witness confidence and helps secure their cooperation.

Those who become affected through witnessing a crime, disorder or anti-social behaviour may be reluctant to engage with the police due to their perceived vulnerability. Specialist witness care and support units can be requested to offer moral and practical help. The range of available special measures may also need explaining, including how the judicial process works as part of the early witness encouragement and support process. Generally, the way in which people are first dealt with by the police influences their decision about assisting the investigation. First impressions always count.

4.18 Victims and Witnesses—Initial Actions

Victims and witnesses are invaluable assets who can provide evidence and fill information gaps. Steps must be taken to avoid them changing their intention to assist a police investigation or becoming discouraged by others. Witness testimony can also become contaminated and distorted if witnesses talk to or listen to others, watch or listen to news reports or speak directly to the media. It is a golden hour(s) task to seek and obtain initial accounts while an incident is still fresh in their minds. More detailed considerations regarding witnesses are covered in Chapter 8.

4.19 Initial Accounts

Initial accounts should be a focus of early investigative activity. It is not good practice to have different officers repeatedly asking the same witness for their account. Whereas if an officer obtains a witness account and records it, subsequent investigators can develop that information rather than asking a witness to repeat themselves all over again. To do otherwise may affect the integrity of the account provided and the entire interview and information collection process.

However, officers needn't be discouraged from seeking and obtaining *initial* accounts from victims and potential witnesses. There are guidelines in 'Achieving Best Evidence' on how and when certain categories of witnesses should be interviewed (eg visually recorded as vulnerable, intimidated or significant witnesses). This shouldn't detract from the importance of finding out what people have seen or heard, and without such information they cannot be classified. This information may be required to identify high-priority lines of enquiry, such as circulating the description of an offender or identifying a crime scene. If not obtained early, difficulty obtaining it later may be encountered if there is a change of mind about cooperating with the police.

Initial accounts can and should be taken without prompting, editing or correction and be accurately recorded. Relevant open questions should be used to signpost a witness to the investigative areas of significance and an accurate written record of the information (including the questions that elicited it) made. The notes should be accompanied by accurate details for identifying the individuals and recontacting them later. In certain circumstances it may be more appropriate (depending on the veracity of the evidence) to make arrangements for the witness to be formally interviewed (visually recorded) by trained officers. Sometimes there may also be welfare implications when it is more suitable to take witnesses to a place of safety such as a police station to conduct the interview.

KEY POINTS

- Details obtained from witnesses relayed to others must contain accurate information. These are recorded and if mistakes are made, particularly descriptions of offenders, they can undermine a prosecution case.
- Some witnesses need lots of encouragement and support to provide evidence and their first impressions of how they are treated and dealt will have an influence on their willingness to cooperate.

Witnesses can also be crime scenes, particularly if they are victims or have come into contact with offenders. There may be potential for the cross-transfer of trace evidence such as fibres, DNA, fingerprints or body fluids. Recovery may need tactful management so their cooperation is not adversely affected. Advice from a CSI about how to correctly seize any material should be obtained.

4.20 **Arrest of Suspects**

The arrest of an offender is a top priority when attending incidents, being mindful that suspects may still be present or could return. To reduce the risk of cross-contamination, wherever possible the arrest of a suspect should be conducted by an officer who has not been at the crime scene. However, the first officer(s) responding may be forced into taking spontaneous action. The lead investigator should take steps to reduce contamination and ensure every effort is made to reduce its possibility (such as using different custody suites or detention areas to other suspects in the same enquiry and using separate means of transportation).

Whenever there is an opportunity to be proactive and make an *early arrest* based on available information, then generally it should be made. The closer the detention to the time of the offence the more opportunity there is to prove culpability and recover evidence. Early arrest prevents offenders concocting alibis, intimidating witnesses, destroying, or disposing of evidence and committing further offences. It also reassures the victim and/or the community and limits the potential for 'taking the law into their own hands'.

KEY POINTS

- What suspects say and how they behave during and immediately after arrest can provide compelling evidence. These details must be recorded as soon after the event as practicable and a suspect given an early opportunity to sign any notes. Not many offenders offer 'no comment' when arrested and what they do say must be noted and brought to the attention of the interviewing officers (and lead investigator).
- Prompt action can lead to the identity and/or location of an offender. Initial police response should incorporate a search for suspects, such as the use of scent dogs. The checking of local hospitals in case offenders are injured is also worth considering.

4.21 Unsolicited Comments

If early arrests are made, then generally suspects should not be interviewed except at a police station (Police and

Criminal Evidence Act 1984 (PACE) Code C 11.1). An interview is defined as the 'questioning of a person regarding his/her suspected involvement in a criminal offence'. If, however, a suspect becomes talkative and spontaneously speaks about the offence without prompting or insists on providing unsolicited comments, once the caution has been administered those comments should be carefully recorded. Voluntary comments or 'significant statements may contain vital information or evidence about the offence under investigation. Denials also form part of the subsequent interview strategy when considered in the context of other evidence.

A *significant statement* includes anything which appears capable of being used in evidence against the suspect and in particular an admission of guilt (PACE Code C 11.4A). The term derives from Part III of the Criminal Justice and Public Order Act 1994:

> A significant statement or silence is one which appears capable of being used in evidence against the suspect in particular a direct admission of guilt or a failure or refusal to answer a question or to answer it satisfactorily which may give rise to an inference.

Suspects should be asked to sign an entry of any such statement after reading and agreeing it as an accurate and true record. Any refusal to sign should itself be recorded, together with the reasons, including any areas the suspect considers inaccurate. Significant statements should be incorporated into the subsequent interview plan to confirm and probe further during the interview under caution.

4.22 Identifications of Suspects by a Witness

The principal methods used to identify suspects connected to a criminal investigation and the requirement to keep records are contained under PACE Code D (revised on 1 August 2004), sections 60(1)(a), 60A (1) and 66(1) Codes of Practice A–G effective from 1 January 2006.

> A record shall be made of the suspect's description as first given by a potential witness. This record must:
>
> (a) be made and kept in a form which enables details of that description to be accurately produced from it, in a legible form, which can be given to the suspect or the suspect's solicitor in accordance with this code; and
> (b) unless otherwise specified be made before the witness takes part in any identification procedures under paragraphs 3.5–3.10, 3.21, or 3.23.
>
> A copy of the record shall where practicable, be given to the suspect or their solicitor before any procedures under paragraphs 3.5–3.10, 3.21, or 3.23 are carried out.

4.23 Transporting Suspects

Usually there are (force) guidelines on how to transport detainees to custody suites, but in exceptional cases they may have to travel in the rear of 'ordinary' police vehicles instead of custody vehicles. If so, this process needs managing carefully to:

1. avoid any potential accusation of encouraging conversations about the offence during the journey (with the exceptions of unsolicited comments/significant statements and provisions for 'urgent interviews', any questions about the case should be saved for the formal interview when the suspect's rights under PACE can be assured and proper legal representation arranged);
2. avoid cross-contamination; and
3. ensure safety.

If there is more than one detainee, separate vehicles/vans should be used. Separate custody offices should also be used wherever possible to avoid cross-contamination or contact between them. A CSI/CSM may advise that covers are placed on the internal surfaces of vehicles being used to transport detainees and in custody areas to capture any forensic material that may drop off them and eliminate possible secondary transfer.

4.24 Treating Suspects as Crime Scenes

Every suspect is a potential crime scene and source of evidence to prove or disprove their involvement in an offence. Depending on the offence, arrangements for the recovery of the suspect's clothing, footwear and other samples should be made quickly. Apart from samples such as fingerprints, DNA and recovery of clothing and footwear, detained suspects can provide a wealth of forensic evidence and trace evidence from hair, blood, semen, paint, soil, gunshot residue, glass fragments, fibres, pollen, etc.

Sometimes it is necessary to obtain samples or seize clothing at the point of arrest rather than waiting until arrival at the custody office. Firearms discharge or explosives residue, dust and glass, for example, need to be recovered as quickly as possible, and in some cases the covering of exposed areas, such as the suspect's hands, upon arrest is good for maximising success. Advice should be taken on all forensic recovery issues and contamination avoidance from a CSI/CSM or forensic specialist.

Once arrested suspects can, if necessary, be medically examined by a Force Doctor/Medical Examiner (FME) for injuries, marks, bruising, tattoos or unusual features for description purposes. These may help prove involvement in the offence, such as defensive scratch marks made by a victim. These should be photographed and mapped on a good drawing of the body. The doctor who performs the examination should be fully debriefed after the examination to establish what the suspect may have said to them.

4.25 Arrest Contingency Plans

The identity of a potential suspect may be known but their current whereabouts unknown, or an arrest for some reason cannot be immediate. If there is clear intention and investigative need to arrest the person(s) quickly, such as to protect the public or known individuals from serious harm, recover forensic evidence or prevent further offences being committed, details of the suspect and arrest requirement may need to be circulated.

It is often worthwhile having a pre-prepared contingency plan for if and when a suspect is arrested (including if they appear voluntarily), as this can occur when the lead investigator is unavailable or off duty. This plan needs to contain all necessary evidence, information and instructions for the arrest and detention of the suspect, for example details of the offence, what stolen property to search for, where to look, what forensic examination of the person is required, what to seize (vehicle, mobile phone, clothing), others they may be with who may also be implicated in the offence, details of any witness support once arrested, where all the case files and exhibits are stored (eg statements) and how and when to contact the victim. The case officer may also wish to include their contact details and availability.

4.26 Initial House-to-House Enquiries

Conducting house-to-house (H2H) enquiries is a tactic used to identify suspects and witnesses, gather local information and intelligence, recover CCTV and provide community reassurance or crime prevention advice. In a high number of cases a victim is known to the offender, who often resides or has connections within proximity of the crime scene. It is entirely feasible, therefore, that a police enquirer may encounter, uncover and/or interview the offender during the course of their H2H visits.

This tactic can be used during the initial stages of an investigation and golden hour(s) period. It is then sometimes referred to as an 'information seek' or 'hasty' H2H, rather than a fully coordinated H2H strategy. Even if no specific parameters have been drawn up, it can still be utilised as an initial means of seeking information and identifying early lines of enquiry. Accurate records should always be kept of all places visited and persons spoken to, including negative responses.

During the initial stages, H2H enquiries should concentrate on any premises located *within line of sight and/or hearing* of the primary crime scene, or within any other known locations of interest, such as escape routes, or at any linked scenes, for example abandoned vehicles. H2H enquiries are explained more fully in Chapter 6.

4.27 **Operational Debriefings**

Debriefings are conducted to capture information regarding initial actions taken and information obtained by those involved in the initial response. The objective is to identify what action has been taken, by whom, its result or progress, and to capture all possible evidence and information that may assist the investigation. This could include, for example, details of potential witnesses, useful observations or comments from bystanders, information and opinions regarding possible suspects, suspicious circumstances that may be linked, any persons or vehicles of interest and any possible intelligence.

A debriefing is a meeting aimed at clarifying the chronology of events and actions as they occurred, the people who did them, outcomes and learning points. Generally, they should be conducted as soon after the event as possible when recollections are strongest and the enquiry is in progress. Debriefings contribute to identifying urgent actions and potential lines of enquiry, and in developing useful intelligence. So-called 'hot debriefs' form a major source of information to investigators.

Relevant documents, statements and exhibits should be handed over to the lead investigator at this meeting together with material gathered and recorded for the purposes of disclosure rules (Criminal Procedure and Investigations Act 1996 (CPIA)).

KEY POINT

Section 5.1 of the CPIA Codes of Practice states:

> An investigator must retain material obtained in a criminal investigation which may be relevant to the investigation. This includes not only material coming into the possession of the investigator . . . but also material generated by him/ her (such as interview records).

Section 2.1 of the same Codes of Practice provides a definition of 'relevant material':

> Material may be relevant to an investigation if it appears to an investigator, or to the officer in charge of an investigation, or to the disclosure officer, that it has some bearing on any offence under investigation or any person being investigated, or on the surrounding circumstances of the case, unless it is incapable of having any impact on the case.

4.28 **Major and Critical Incidents**

A crime may form part of a large incident or contain elements that put it into either one or both of two categories known as 'critical' or 'major' incidents. This terminology is widely used in the UK, not only by the police but also by other emergency services and some public bodies. Although it would be very unusual for anyone other than a person of senior rank to make a decision to declare a major or critical incident, crime investigators should be familiar with the terms and what impact they may have on an enquiry.

The basic principle is geared towards getting the response right at every level in order to prevent incidents escalating into critical incidents or deteriorating if already identified as such. There is likely to be a force policy in existence explaining what is required should the need arise. Developing a proactive approach to victim support and community engagement following the discovery of certain types of crime will usually increase the public's trust and confidence in the police.

4.29 **Major Incidents**

Early diagnosis of this category of incident will help to facilitate the deployment of sufficient resources. Typically, this category relates to major disasters, mass casualties or fatalities and matters of very large proportions. A 'major incident' may be declared by any of the emergency services that consider the criteria to have been satisfied. There will often be large-scale and combined resources mobilised, either deployed or on a standby basis.

Once a 'major incident' has been declared, all those initially responding should in principle apply the same emergency procedures. This means, in theory at least, that there is a consistent approach to the initial response not just from all the emergency services, for example the fire and ambulance services, but any other relevant units and resources that become involved. It also means scene management and procedures are compatible, thus ensuring there is a clear approach to any incident so categorised.

The initial period of a major incident may be frantic, but in practice the police and other emergency services should quickly meet to discuss immediate priorities and implement an appropriate management or command structure as required for the incident. It is vitally important that crime investigators (moreover an appointed SIO/IO if the crime is of a serious nature) are involved in these meetings, discussions and decision-making processes to ensure the needs of the investigation are always considered, making sure all evidence recovery opportunities remain of utmost importance.

KEY POINT

The ACPO definition of a 'major incident' is:

> Any emergency that requires the implementation of special arrangements by one or all of the emergency services and including local authorities, for any large-scale incident involving a large number of people and/or casualties, enquiries (media), resources.

4.30 **Critical Incidents**

This term is used to describe any incident where police action may impact upon the confidence of victims, their relatives or the wider community. There are very few serious crimes that do not fall within the category of a 'critical incident'. Early recognition and declaration as such ensure that correct command and control procedures are quickly put into place. The term 'critical' may apply to a local area and/or the whole of a force or forces.

A key element of critical incident management is to give senior police management early notification of incidents that have escalated or have the potential to escalate into critical incidents. Good situational awareness should take into account the general feelings of vulnerability and insecurity and also the economic, political and social factors which impact on the community. Most forces have procedures to monitor and assess this, such as community impact assessments and the collection and analysis of community intelligence.

The decision to declare a critical incident can occur at any time during the various phases of an investigation. Identification may be as soon as the first telephone contact received by a call taker. It may also apply and be appropriate when an incident is being attended either by initial response officers or later by crime investigators. The process provides a means of focusing on all the 'critical' aspects of an incident and consequent decision making. For example, how family liaison support or community impact are to be addressed and managed effectively.

This special status has to be continuously monitored and it may be that as an investigation develops and more information becomes available, the decision to deem the incident 'critical' is reviewed. An example is when community confidence in the police response or the incident itself drops and becomes critical as the investigation develops. As a general rule, the case circumstances can become a 'critical incident' at any time, for example in the present, future or even past tense.

KEY POINT

The ACPO definition is:

> Any incident where the effectiveness of the police response is likely to have a significant impact on the confidence of the victim, their family, and/or the community.

4.31 Working Alongside Other Agencies

Emergency services and agencies often collaborate to form a team at various stages of an investigation. Working alongside the police might be paramedics, fire service, local authority, social care workers responsible for children and/or adults, the National Crime Agency (NCA), the Independent Office for Police Conduct (IOPC), Victim Support, community workers, etc. Representatives of these agencies may have priorities other than crime investigation and their roles may complement or conflict with the needs of the investigation. In some circumstances they may also be the lead agency.

Joint working agreements (Service Level Agreements, multi- or interagency working protocols) usually form part of the strategic objectives in most forces and are included in policy statements or policing plans. Protocols may stipulate matters such as primacy, roles and responsibilities and information sharing, which need to be clearly understood to ensure an effective collaborative (team) response. There can be benefits and challenges to collaborative working, and professional territories and responsibilities need to be respected for a team to be effective.

4.32 Initial Response to Crimes Involving Firearms

Crimes involving the use of firearms present different problems and challenges when, say, attending and dealing with crime scenes and the initial response.

It is likely that there is force policy, including a response plan, on how to deal with such incidents when they occur. Generally, with any incident involving the criminal use of firearms, only trained and authorised armed officers in protected vehicles should initially attend the scene. This is potentially the time when the public, the police and other emergency services are at greatest risk. First officers attending must make an immediate assessment of the situation from the information to hand.

Officers who attend should apply basic firearm tactics, known as the Six Cs (ACPO 2006):

1. Confirm	as far as possible the location of the suspect and that firearms are involved without unnecessarily exposing oneself to danger.
2. Cover	to be taken, if possible, behind substantial material. Brick walls are usually sufficient. Motor vehicle bodies or wooden fences do not stop bullets.
3. Contact	supervisors and convince them of the serious nature of the risk and call for suitable back-up.
4. Civilians	to be directed to a place of safety.
5. Colleagues	to be prevented from coming into possible danger areas.
6. Contain	the situation as far as practicable. Try to maintain observations on the suspect with an emphasis on safety.

The operational response to a firearms incident may initially be one of neutralising the scene and ensuring it is safe to deploy other resources, including ambulance personnel. This may not necessarily aid the successful securing of a crime scene for evidential potential but may be essential for safety reasons. It may still be possible to establish a rendezvous and forward control point, provided they are not so close as to be in danger from gunfire. Routes to and from the RVP must also be declared 'safe'.

The forensic recovery of firearms and ammunition, and the examination of scenes where firearms have been used, pose different requirements and procedures. The important points to stress for the initial considerations have already been covered in this section in terms of scene and exhibit preservation prior to a full and detailed examination and search, which are further discussed in Chapter 10.

References

ACPO (2006) *Manual of Guidance on Police Use of Firearms*
ACPO/Centrex (2006) *Murder Investigation Manual*

ACPO/NPIA (2005, 2013) *Practice Advice on Core Investigative Doctrine* (2nd edn)

College of Policing (2021) *Authorised Professional Practice* (APP) available at <http://www.college.police.uk/app> accessed 22 September 2022

NPCC (2021) *Major Crime Investigation Manual* , 2013

Chapter 5

Crime Scenes, Searches and Exhibits

5.1 Introduction

Processing a crime scene is an important element of an investigation and is the responsibility of the investigating officer in charge, working in conjunction with specialist and expert examiners. Activity and actions undertaken at crime scenes influences the amount and quality of evidential and investigative material gathered and its use and value in the context of the investigation. It is therefore important that crime investigators have a sound understanding of the roles, responsibilities and processes required and maintain their knowledge to take advantage of scientific developments in this area.

Most material gathered generally involves some form of search, recovery and examination, but the resources applied to these processes will depending on the nature of the incident and the policies and arrangements within individual police forces.

At crime scenes, investigators need to take charge, request and manage the resources required and available. At more serious and complex offences or major incidents a Senior Investigating Officer (SIO) takes overall command and control of the investigation, including crime scene decision making. However, a less senior crime investigator may have initial control in the early stages and ensure the scene is protected and preserved before any significant decisions are made. The importance and benefits

Blackstone's Crime Investigators' Handbook. Steve Hibbitt and Gary Shaw, Oxford University Press. © Oxford University Press 2023.
DOI: 10.1093/oso/9780192867896.003.0005

of investigators attending crime scenes should not be underestimated.

In addition to forensic material, there is potential for a variety of information to be gathered from crime scenes that could be useful for:

- identifying victims, suspects and witnesses
- background information on victims, suspects and witnesses
- evidential or intelligence material
- establishing modus operandi
- linking people to and from scenes
- linking objects to and from scenes
- corroboration of victim/witness/suspect accounts
- linkage to other offences as part of a series

5.2 Locard's Principle of Exchange

Locard's Principle of Exchange (Edmund Locard 1877–1966, a frequently quoted French criminologist) states that 'every contact leaves a trace'. This means everyone who enters a crime scene both takes something away and leaves something behind. This principle is used when seeking to connect people, including suspects to a crime scene or other location(s) and linking scenes together.

Locard's principle is the basis on which forensic examination is based because a transfer of material occurs when two objects come into contact with each other. It is used in the investigation of crime to try and establish links between people, locations, and objects. The types of material that can be transferred are infinite, but commonly include:

- DNA from biological materials
- blood
- fibres
- glass
- soil
- hair

- pollen
- drugs
- paint
- firearms discharge residue

The principle of exchange now also applies to digital connections and transfers between devices which provide investigative opportunities that could not have been imagined by Edmund Locard. In addition to physical scenes, modern detectives need to consider preserving and examining the digital scene including:

- digital communications devices/mobile phones
- computers
- digital notebooks
- wi-fi routers
- voice powered digital assistants such as Alexa, Siri, Cortana and others
- telematic data in motor vehicles

Preserving the digital crime scene is just as important as preserving the physical crime scene. Advice from a specialist Digital Media Investigator should be obtained if there is any doubt about how to approach this. It may be necessary for officers to switch off their own digital devices before attending a scene to ensure they do not contaminate the digital environment. If this is necessary, the consequences should be considered and addressed in any risk assessment including channels of communication to and from the scene.

5.2.1 Secondary transfer

This refers to the process that might occur if a person who has trace evidence on them transfers it to a secondary place or person (an intermediary), for example where a suspect has a victim's blood on their hands and physically connects with another person who transfers the blood onto something else. Other locations where blood is located may be worth considering for examining and designated as a crime scene.

5.3 Identifying Crime Scene Types

There are various types of crime scene and the sooner these are identified the better the chances are for preserving and recovering forensic material and potential evidence for further investigation (Beaufort-Moore 2015). It is relatively straightforward to identify and designate a location where an offence took place as a crime scene but there may also be opportunities to identify other potential scenes.

A location where an offence takes place, if this is known, is usually classified as the 'primary' crime scene, for example Scene (1). However, there may also be additional or 'satellite' scenes related to the incident to identify and consider.

Checklist—Crime scene examples (places/people/items)

- The location where an offence took place
- Any vehicle(s) connected to the enquiry
- The location where an object is suspected of being located
- Any victim (their body if deceased or body part)
- The place where a victim was last seen (eg if missing)
- The place where a victim has been deposited or moved from
- Any witness who has come into contact with a victim, offender or crime scene
- Suspects
- An attack site which does not form part of the 'primary' scene
- Anywhere there is trace or physical evidence, for example footprints, fingerprints or blood
- Any location where property and other material may have been disposed of
- Any articles connected to a victim(s), witness(es) or offender(s)

- Premises or places connected to an offender or suspect
- Access or escape routes taken by an offender
- A place where a crime has been planned or has significant connection to the enquiry

KEY POINT

It is important that any crime scenes such as those contained within this checklist are identified as quickly as possible so they can be secured and preserved to avoid contamination.

Crime scenes should be numbered sequentially, starting with the primary crime scene as Scene (1), and continuing, such as victim Scene (2), abandoned stolen vehicle Scene (3), suspect's address Scene (4) and so on. This is how they are referred to throughout the course of an investigation. It also makes it simpler to list what actions are required at each scene, such as when setting search or forensic strategies. To avoid any risk of confusion, it is important to ensure that everyone involved in the investigation is briefed and knows and uses the same scene numbers.

5.4 Health and Safety at Crime Scenes

It is the responsibility of all police personnel to ensure the health and safety of all persons present at crime scenes and also those who are likely to handle material and items present. General hazards need to be considered and these are often covered by generic operational risk assessments such as:

- slips
- trips
- falls

However, crime scenes can also contain specific hazards which require more dynamic, specific and continuous risk assessment such as:

- biological (body) fluids or tissue
- chemicals
- toxins
- bites from insects and other animals
- dangerous and unsafe premises or terrain
- drugs, drugs paraphernalia and needles
- sharp items
- firearms, ammunition, component parts and explosives
- dangerous terrain and environments
- areas where there are dangers from water or ice
- difficult weather conditions
- hostile environments or areas
- unsafe buildings, gas, electric or other utilities

There should also be an awareness and mitigation of potential risks, such as airborne infections, when items are recovered or moved at crime scenes. This should include the handling of exhibits, which, if potentially hazardous or dangerous, should be packaged and labelled in a manner that highlights the potential risks such as using:

- 'biohazard' tape for items bearing bodily fluids
- health hazard labels for items such as powdered drug residue
- flammable labels for items such as solvent and accelerants
- sharps tubes for pointed and bladed instruments
- distinct exhibit labels indicating a firearm has been 'made safe'

There is potential for any variety of hazard to be present within any given crime scene and the following sections contain some of these, but this is by no means an exhaustive list of considerations.

5.4.1 Blood-borne infections

The risk of infection from body fluids can be high, and protective clothing must be worn when handling material contaminated with body fluids or tissue. Dried blood can be as hazardous as wet blood and as blood dries small particles can become airborne and inhaled or ingested. Infection can cause medical and health problems including:

- Hepatitis B:
    - present in body fluids (blood, saliva, semen and vaginal fluid)
    - can be passed via open wounds
    - can be passed via needle stick injury
- Hepatitis C:
    - blood-borne viral infection
    - very rarely transmitted through other bodily fluids
    - transmitted when infected blood enters the bloodstream (usually through needle stick injuries)
- HIV:
    - spread through bodily fluids such as blood, semen and vaginal fluids
    - can be spread via open wounds
    - can be passed via needle stick injury

5.4.2 Wearing protective gloves

Wearing protective clothing assists with avoiding contamination by the mishandling of exhibits that are to be forensically examined. Protective gloves will protect both the material and the person when handling items of potential forensic value. There is a need to change gloves when handling and forensically recovering different/separate items. This is to prevent cross-contamination through secondary transfer between items. When handling certain items, it is necessary to wear two pairs of gloves (known as 'double gloving') due to the high possibility of transferability and the sensitivity of the forensic processes to be employed. This includes items that carry body fluids, drugs, firearm or explosive residue.

5.5 Legal Powers

Fortunately, the public usually support the police at crime scenes and cooperate during any cordon exclusion area and scene examination. There are legal powers conferred under sections 8, 18 and 32 of the Police and Criminal Evidence Act 1984 (PACE) to secure premises for the purpose of a search. However, sometimes there are doubts about police powers in relation to seizing and controlling crime scenes, particularly where private property is concerned.

5.5.1 Crime scenes

DPP v Morrison QBD, 4.4.03; is a relevant stated case for private property with a public right of way—consent can be assumed in the first instance.

It is confirmed that under common law police have power to erect a cordon to preserve the scene of a crime. The Divisional Court upheld this rule, given the importance of this function in investigating serious crime.

Rice v Connolly (1966) QB P414; reaffirmed the long-established principles that had not been challenged, confirming that police can take reasonable steps to keep the peace, prevent and detect crime and bring offenders to justice. Within these principles, police can secure scenes for examination and therefore also arrest for obstructing a police officer in the execution of their duty any person who obstructs, hinders or frustrates such a process.

It therefore follows that if anyone were to try and frustrate and obstruct the securing of a crime scene, they would commit an offence of obstructing a police officer in the execution of their duty. This would extend to any police staff with designated powers, such as a Crime Scene Investigator (CSI).

5.6 **Seizing Evidence**

When not under the power of a magistrate's search warrant (under section 8 of PACE which allows anything to be seized and retained for which the search is authorised), section 19 of PACE is relied upon for a power to seize *evidential* items which are *on premises*. This power extends to a constable or designated non-warranted investigating officer (under section 38 of the Police Reform Act 2002, Schedule 4, Part 2, paragraph 19(a)) provided:

(a) they are lawfully on premises; and
(b) there are reasonable grounds for believing:
 (i) that the item seized is either (1) a thing which has been obtained in consequence of the commission of an offence (section 19(2)): eg stolen items or the proceeds of crime); or (2) that it is evidence in relation to an offence under investigation or any other offence (section 19(3)); and
 (ii) that it is necessary to seize it in order to prevent it being concealed, lost, damaged, altered, or destroyed (section 19(2)(b) and (3)(b)); and
(c) the item is not one for which there are reasonable grounds for believing it to be subject to legal privilege (as defined in section 10 (section 19(6)).

The term 'premises for the purposes of this power under PACE is one that may be open to legal interpretation. However, the case of *Ghani v Jones* [1969] 3 All ER 1700 provides a ruling on the justification for taking articles where no one has been arrested or charged and is not restricted to being on 'premises'. This power should also extend to designated investigating officers under Schedule 4 to the Police Reform Act 2002. In summary, the ruling states there must be reasonable grounds for believing that:

(a) a serious crime has been committed.
(b) the article was either the fruit of the crime or the instrument by which it was committed or was material evidence to prove its commission.

(c) the person in possession of the article had committed the crime or was implicated in it;
(d) the police must not keep the article or prevent its removal for any longer than is reasonably necessary to complete the investigation or preserve it for evidence; and
(e) the lawfulness of the conduct of the police must be judged at the time and not by what happens afterwards.

There may be occasions when this case ruling may be useful, for example when dealing with persons who are potential 'scenes' but who are not under arrest or on premises and items are required from them for examination, such as clothing, personal effects or mobile phones.

5.7 Crime Scene Investigator

The title of this role may differ between police forces, and they might be known as a Scenes of Crime Officer (SOCO), Crime Scene Examiner (CSE) and Volume Crime Scene Examiner (VCSE). For the purpose of this handbook they will be referred to as Crime Scene Investigator (CSI).

In 1996 both the Association of Chief Police Officers (ACPO) and the Forensic Science Service recognised a key number of responsibilities for CSIs:

- photography and videoing of crime scenes
- location and recovery of potential physical evidence
- location and recovery of finger and palm marks at crime scenes
- packaging and storage of potential physical evidence
- recording and sharing of intelligence on modus operandi
- providing advice to investigators on scientific matters
- preparation of statements and providing evidence at court

The main function of the CSI is to support investigators in their enquiries by the recovery and preservation of physical evidence. Additionally, they should provide intelligence support regarding aspects of the crime scene, such as recurring footprints or glove marks at different scenes.

CSIs are an invaluable asset not only in performing their core role of collecting fingerprints, forensic material and photographic evidence, but also in ensuring exhibits are correctly packaged, sealed and labelled. They should also be able to identify links between crime scenes and modus operandi.

5.8 Crime Scene Manager

The role of CSI has developed further and occasionally they may perform the role of a Crime Scene Manager (CSM). When undertaking this role, they may oversee the examination of a scene where multiple CSIs are in attendance. They will usually supervise, prioritise and coordinate the examination strategy of a crime scene in consultation with the investigating officer.

5.9 Crime Scene Coordinator

A Crime Scene Coordinator (CSC) may be required if there are multiple crime scenes and they are needed to manage the scientific response to a serious crime on behalf of and in conjunction with an SIO. They will be tasked with ensuring that sufficient trained staff are allocated and available, and to monitor all activity at crime scenes to prevent potential contamination by staff who have dealt with one scene being sent to another. This includes maintaining a contamination matrix to record which officers have attended at which location and when.

5.10 Exhibits Officer

The Exhibits Officer (EO) when appointed during an investigation has a pivotal role. They are responsible for the collating, recording, logging and the safe storage of all exhibits gathered during the investigation. They take responsibility for ensuring the movements of all exhibits are accurately recorded, thus ensuring evidence of their handling, continuity and integrity during the investigation is maintained.

This role should ideally be carried out by an experienced detective or investigator trained in aspects of exhibit handling including, packaging, storage, documentation and using the HOLMES Exhibit Management System when required.

The EO usually performs this role for the duration of the investigation, which may include the case finalisation phase when exhibits must be disposed of, returned to their owners or retained by the investigation for future developments and use.

KEY POINT

The importance of maintaining the integrity of exhibits cannot be overstated. Even the strongest case can collapse if there is a breakdown in continuity of an exhibit or if it has been handled inappropriately, labelled incorrectly or the packaging is damaged or has been tampered with. This is a core responsibility of an EO and/ or crime investigator, if one has not been appointed separately.

5.11 Fingerprint Experts

Being able to identify a person from their fingerprints left at a crime scene is a fundamental requirement and a process in many police investigations. Once fingerprints have been obtained from crime scenes and/or from exhibits by either CSIs or forensic specialists, it is usual for a fingerprint bureau to undertake the comparison and identification of fingerprints using their own experts. They use the national database (IDENT1) to compare marks from scenes against the data held. The national database gives UK police power to identify people involved in cross-border crimes, and any prints submitted are automatically searched against unidentified marks. Fingerprint identification officers can give evidence to the courts and are deemed to be expert witnesses.

5.12 Chemical Development Laboratory

The title of this support differs from force to force, dependent upon responsibilities, but they usually offer support in the chemical development of fingerprints that the CSI was unable to recover at a scene, document examination, searching items for biological material or fibres, using forensic light sources, the location and recovery of blood, firearm residue and controlled drugs.

5.13 Forensic Scientist

The role of a forensic scientist is to examine and analyse material submitted from crime scenes in an impartial and methodical manner for the purpose of providing potential evidence in criminal investigations. They are qualified scientific disciplines, are afforded expert witness status and can offer statements of opinion and interpretation of evidence. They can also offer expert support and advice for and at crime scenes.

Since the Forensic Science Service was dissolved in 2012 due to national austerity measures, scientists are now obtained from a range of forensic service providers (FSP) who are accredited under the requirements of the Accreditation of Forensic Service Providers Regulations 2018. These usually analyse and examine items in a sterile laboratory, but can, in some instances, also attend crime scenes upon request. This can be a costly option and most forces have their own arrangements and processes for deploying scientists to scenes. It can be worth considering, as they may be able to offer additional specialist and expert advice and guidance that may not otherwise be available in the force.

The duties of a forensic scientist can range from examining items for blood, body fluids, DNA, hair, accelerants, weapons, fibres, footprints, blood pattern analysis, etc, to scientifically establishing links between materials on a suspect or item. They can help to identify and interpret a sequence of events and compare material gathered from different sources. Some of the specialist disciplines available from an FSP include:

- biology/DNA
- soil/pollen
- drugs and toxicology
- fibres
- glass
- footwear
- fire
- explosives
- firearms
- questioned documents
- crime scene attendance and interpretation

5.14 **Other Specialists and Experts**

There are many other experts and specialists, who, depending on the nature of the crime under investigation, may be able to assist at a crime scene. These include botanists and palynologists (the study of plant spores and pollen), ballistics experts, entomologists (the study of insects), forensic archaeologists and scene reproduction specialists. If there is a need for a specialism that is not usually provided by standard forensic providers, then an expert may have to be sourced externally. An important aspect is that there are added considerations to consider and extra financial implications for using their services, so it is always wise to seek advice before any external expert or specialist are asked to become involved in a case.

KEY POINT

The National Crime Agency (NCA) Major Crime Investigative Support Team maintains a national 'expert advisers database'. It is best practice to contact them for help and advice when considering employing the services of an external forensic specialist. They can be contacted on **0845 000 5463**.

5.15 Crime Scene Preservation

Actions taken at a crime scene must ensure investigators maximise all opportunities to gather material that may later prove vital to their investigation. Material gathered may later be used to identify suspects and witnesses, eliminate potential suspects and corroborate or refute allegations or versions of events as described by suspects, victims or witnesses. Not all material has to be used in court, but this does not mean it should not be collected.

Definition—Material

The Criminal Procedure and Investigations Act 1996 Code of Practice under Part II of the Act states:

> Material is material of any kind, including information and objects, which is obtained in the course of a criminal investigation and which may be relevant to the investigation; Material may be relevant to the investigation if it appears to an investigator, or to the officer in charge of an

investigation, or to the disclosure officer, that it has some bearing on any offence under investigation or any person being investigated, or on the surrounding circumstances of the case, unless it is incapable of having any impact on the case. Material can be used as evidence, intelligence or information or a combination of these.

It can be difficult at the outset of an investigation to identify what may become relevant and therefore investigators should err on the side of caution and recover all materials. The initial opportunity to recover these materials may also be the last and it is far better to collect something that is not considered important than to leave something behind that later becomes vital.

Crime investigators should be in close communication and liaison with the nominated CSI to ensure there is a clear understanding of what material they are searching for, preserving and subsequently recovering to exploit its evidential value.

Actions taken by responding officers can impact hugely on any subsequent forensic investigation. This is a time when destruction, contamination and transfer of material are most at risk of occurring. The initial attending officers have other things to consider when attending crime scenes, such as the five buildings blocks and 'golden hour(s)' principles and the ISP approach outlined in Chapter 4. The first of those principles is the preservation of life, which means the responding officer's and other emergency services actions could conflict with the requirement for forensic preservation and recovery of evidential material. However, once these tasks have been completed, the focus should return to identifying, securing and preserving crime scenes until scientific support arrives.

Initial responding officers should always make a record of the actions they have taken at the scene, including any items they may have moved or disturbed, and communicate this information to the CSI and the investigator. Failure to do so could lead to misinterpreting a crime scene assessment, causing difficulty to the enquiry. Investigators should proactively seek out and debrief the initial attending officers to obtain this information.

5.15.1 Scene security cordons

Properly controlled scene security cordons are an essential means of guarding and preserving the integrity of crime scenes by preventing unauthorised entry and potential contamination within the cordoned area. Cordons also protect the public, control sightseers and the media, facilitate a structured police and emergency services response and prevent potential interference by others, such as offenders returning to the scene.

Whilst arranging scene security as quickly as possible should always be a consideration, any action taken at a crime scene must be proportionate to the matter under investigation. Minor criminal offences, for example, would be unlikely to justify road closures to set up cordons but a proportionate level of scene preservation requires consideration and implementation. The nature and seriousness of the matter under investigation must therefore justify the necessary use of security cordons before they are implemented and maintained. Generally, indoor scenes are less resource intensive to secure and manage than outdoor scenes particularly if they cover an extensive area.

Cordon management begins with identifying the crime scene(s) and its size and parameters. In some cases, the location of a scene is obvious, such as a burglary at a house, but the extent of the scene may be larger than the premises and immediate vicinity. Investigators should consider access and exit routes used by offenders, victims and any witnesses. The parameters of the area to be cordoned must take account of such additional factors to enable a thorough and sterile examination.

It is helpful to obtain a good quality up-to-date map of the area from a reliable source such as Google Maps or Google Earth so that cordoned off areas can be clearly marked. This can be used as an aid to brief the CSI and any other resources attending the scene or be used elsewhere. Such an annotated scene map is also potentially a useful exhibit to evidence the arrangements that were put in place to protect the scene and support the decision making regarding mitigating any possible scene contamination. The officer producing the map and marking the scene parameters needs to formally produce it as an exhibit with a signed exhibit label and witness statement. Ultimately a case management decision will be made whether the map is an exhibit in a prosecution case or unused material for disclosure purposes.

Once a scene has been identified and the parameters set, it needs securing before any search or forensic examination begins. This means preventing anyone other than *authorised personnel* from entering the cordoned area. This is usually achieved using reflective barrier tape, marked police vehicles, police staff or the use of natural boundaries such as walls, fences, or streams.

Because they are relatively self-contained, indoor scenes are usually comparatively easier to secure by closing doors and placing officers at entry points. Outdoor scenes, particularly in rural settings, can have added complications, such as weather, traffic, people, and elevated observation point. These tend to be more resource-intensive to ensure people are unable to cross the cordon lines into the restricted zone.

KEY POINTS

- The size of a cordon is important to protect and preserve evidence. A cordon that is too big can always be reduced, whereas a cordon that is too small cannot be enlarged. As a precaution *always start big.*
- With firearms discharges, stray bullets can and do travel much further than the location of a target or a victim's location. This should be a factor when deciding on proposed search areas for bullet heads as it is likely the cordon parameters will need to be significantly extended.

- Cordons often attract sightseers and onlookers, so those engaged in scene security duties need to be reminded of what to say/not say if asked about the incident and investigation. For consistency and to control information emanating from the investigation it is advised that cordon officers are briefed on a corporate response.

Only the person in charge of the investigation or a CSI/CSM should permit access to a crime scene. This instruction needs clearly communicating to officers on cordon security duty and to all those in attendance (including sometimes interfering and curious supervisors). There is little point in having a cordon in place if there are no clear rules about who can and cannot cross the barrier. Accurate records need to be kept about who enters and leaves the scene.

5.15.2 Inner and outer cordons

In serious cases, two and sometimes even three or more cordons are required, which is standard practice at most murder or suspicious death scenes. Inner cordons are quite tight and set around the actual crime site, for example at the main attack site or where a victim was located. This is where the most thorough and detailed forensic examinations are likely to be conducted and usually where screening such as tents and covers are erected if it is in the open air.

Outer cordons are set with wider parameters to allow for physical searches whilst protecting the inner cordon and controlling overall access. Using two cordons allows for greater control of the crime scene and the use of two types of search and recovery strategies, such as a more thorough and detailed forensic examination and search of the area withing the inner cordon and a more general search of the outer cordon area. Once these two cordons have been established, the control of personnel and access to the scene can be maintained through rendezvous points located at the perimeter of the outer cordon as it will not be necessary for all personnel in attendance to enter the inner cordon.

5.15.3 Crime scene logs

Crime scene logs are a means of controlling and recording access to the areas inside cordons. They are a record of everyone who enters and exits a crime scene including the time they did so. This formal auditable record helps to prevent unauthorised access and preserve the integrity and sterility of a crime scene. Scene logs should be used at the earliest opportunity and most forces have specifically designed and printed books/forms for this purpose, which should be routinely carried by crime investigators to be readily available for use.

Checklist—Crime scene logs

- Pre-printed books/forms should be used or, if necessary because they are unavailable at that time, a legible record maintained in a pocket/day notebook or on blank paper.
- Scene logs become the exhibit of the person who starts them with all of those who subsequently take possession signing a continuity label.
- Minimum details to be recorded are:
  - o Identity of all those entering and leaving the scene
  - o Details of any protective clothing worn, for example overshoes, forensic overalls, protective gloves and masks
  - o Timings of entry and exit
  - o Purpose or role at the scene
  - o Full contact details
  - o Person's signature on entering and leaving the cordon
  - o Location of scene cordons
- It is advisable to document the weather conditions and any changes in the scene log. This is particularly important if a scene is open to the elements and

could be impacted by changes in the conditions. The correct spelling of names with their corresponding identification numbers is important and handovers between officers must be accurately recorded in the log.

5.15.4 Common approach paths

When using cordons, it is necessary to identify and designate a common approach path (CAP) to use as the best and only route in and out of a crime scene for those who need to enter, such as search and forensic teams. When required, a CAP should be established at the earliest opportunity and clearly marked out and used by *all* those entering and leaving the crime scene. To prevent potential disturbance and contamination this route should be one that is the least likely to have been used by the offender(s) or victims.

If preservation of life was a priority, the most direct route will have been used by initial responders to render first aid or check for life. Subsequent responders should also use the same route unless it is obvious the offenders have used it. All details of initial responders to an incident are required, and the CSI should be informed of the route they have used so any scene contamination and disturbance they have caused can be established and material such as footprints can be eliminated from that of the offenders.

KEY POINTS

- A common approach path (CAP) should be identified as the one *least likely to have been used by offenders or victims.*
- It needs to be of sufficient size so that a CSI and their equipment can operate effectively.
- At outdoor scenes, hard standing or compacted path areas are more suitable, as these can be searched and marked out far more easily than surfaces such as grassland.

5.16 **Releasing a Crime Scene**

A crime scene should not be released until there has been sufficient time and opportunity to complete all potential searches and examinations. This may have resourcing implications at some crime scenes and careful consideration should be given to the relevant circumstances of each individual investigation.

If a scene is released too early, problems may arise if new information surfaces that requires additional consideration and action regarding searches and forensic examination. A primary crime scene should not be released until all initial high priority main lines of enquiry have been completed, such as suspect interviews (where the suspect has been arrested early in the enquiry) and interviews with significant witnesses. These interviews may produce new information that may need to be contextualised at the crime scene whilst it is still secure and preserved. Once a scene has been released, its sterility and integrity are no longer maintained and effectively from then onwards have been lost. The principle to remember is *never release a scene too early.*

KEY POINTS

- Due to health and safety concerns and sensitivity to the victim and their families, some crime scenes may need extensive cleaning before they are released and reopened to the public.
- Always complete one final check of a crime scene before it is released, preferably with a CSI, to ensure that every investigative opportunity has been considered and all potential evidence has been recovered.

5.17 **Crime Scene Searches**

The primary objective for any crime scene search is to find victims or suspects and to locate and recover investigative and evidential material, information and intelligence items. Planning and preparation for conducting searches is the most effective way to achieve success. In time-critical situations however, it may be necessary to conduct 'flash' or 'hasty' searches during the golden hour phase of fast track actions. Looking for injured victims, escaping suspects or discarded weapons are three such examples.

Crime scene searches are not just limited to the recovery of forensic material such as blood, fingerprints and DNA, but also weapons, stolen property, discarded clothing, mobile phones and other digital devices or CCTV. The term 'search' can encompass different varieties of search, and in order to specify which type, it should be prefixed with another word describing it, such as *'suspect', 'forensic', 'physical', 'premises', 'vehicle'* or *'missing person'* ... search. A crime scene may require more than one type of search.

In some circumstances, one type of search may compromise another, for example if both forensic and physical searching is required. When determining which type of search should take precedence, the forensic search usually takes priority, unless there are concerns around preservation of life or an immediate search for a victim or suspect is required.

Searches can be linked to or be an element of other strategies, such as external communication and managing public reassurance. Conducting visible outdoor searching can provide reassurance to victims, families and communities, demonstrating that the police are conducting diligent enquiries. Images of these searches such as line searches or underwater search units are often used in the media, and care must be taken to control media access to ensure that they do not capture 'live' the recovery of any evidential finds. The potential for being photographed and recorded emphasises the importance for using correct processes when recovering and handling material at a crime scene, as evidence of bad practice undermines a case.

KEY POINTS

- The role of a search is to locate evidence, and the aim of a CSI or forensic specialist is to recover and examine anything found.
- Searches benefit from thorough planning, though 'flash' or 'hasty' searches for victims or suspects may be necessary and justified if time critical.
- Searches should be intelligence-led and based on facts that are available.
- As with any investigative strategy, searches must have clear objectives (eg to locate X and Y).

5.18 Police Search Advisers and Police Search Teams

Police Search Advisers (PolSAs) can be requested if the physical search is going to be complex or difficult, such as when searching large open spaces, difficult terrain, water, underground, premises, vehicles or vessels. A PolSA will:

- advise on most aspects of a search
- review any searches already conducted
- suggest parameters, methodology, techniques, search assets, health and safety aspects, logistical and technical constraints and limitations of the search
- plan, direct, manage, implement and record the searches as required by the investigator
- advise on and obtain technical resources or specialists
- lead and supervise a Police Search Team (PST)

Investigators need to ensure that the PolSA is fully briefed and provided with any relevant intelligence and information in relation to each search, including its aims and objectives. The PolSA requires this information to develop an appropriate search strategy and should ensure that a search policy/decision log is maintained together with comprehensive records of the search.

In addition to the PolSA, the members of the search team need a proper briefing about the matter under investigation, as it is not always possible to include an exhaustive list of things to look for. Investigators are more aware of the facts that are available and the investigative issues and are therefore able to recognise items of interest, whereas search teams depend heavily on the quality of the briefing provided to them. For this reason, it may be useful for the lead investigator or someone with a good knowledge of the case to be present when the search takes place.

Where it is evident that a search will be protracted, complex or that a large area has to be searched, the PolSA may suggest or require assistance from other agencies or specialists, such as blood/cadaver dogs, underwater search unit, air support unit, and height access or confined space teams.

PolSAs and their search teams are valuable assets, and they should not be left to work in isolation from the lead investigator and enquiry team. They are very much part of the investigation team and where practicable should be invited to attend team briefings and given access to information and material they may need, including updated and developing intelligence about the case under investigation. This specifically includes information and updates from witness and suspect(s) interviews that is relevant to the search locations and items being sought.

A PST works under the command and supervision of a PoLSA and comprises officers who are trained in specific search techniques used for searching for persons, vehicles, buildings, areas and routes and:

- are equipped and resourced to provide an effective search response
- produce appropriate documentation relevant to the search
- provide high levels of assurance that an effective search has been conducted

- raise the probability of achieving success
- have a heightened awareness of health and safety measures and dangerous materials

UK PSTs have established methods to systematically search vehicles and vessels which may be considered over and above what would be conventionally conducted by a crime scene examiner. Vehicles and vessels contain many voids which criminals can exploit to conceal evidential material including contraband. Before conducting a more invasive search of voided areas, the search strategy would consider moving proportionally from a non-invasive search. Techniques deployed might include using specialist equipment such as x-ray machines or using police scent detector dogs specialising in items such as drugs, explosives or cash.

When planning an extensive vehicle search, consideration should be given to whether any telematic information or evidence will be sought from the vehicles digital systems. Any search techniques employed need to ensure that the vehicle's digital information is not lost or contaminated and potential evidence compromised, altered or destroyed.

5.19 Searching Premises

It is likely during most investigations that some form of premises search will be required. These may or may not be a crime scene but should be treated as such until proven otherwise. These searches may form part of crime scene searches, general searches or part of an arrest phase or proactive strategy such as the search of a victim or suspect address.

Whatever type of premises are to be searched, the operation should be carefully and methodically planned and executed. These are opportunities to locate and recover evidence, and the more thought and effort that goes into them, the more chance there is of a successful outcome.

Checklist—Premises searching

- Careful planning and preparation are required beforehand
- Wherever possible make use of a PolSA and PST
- Consider what other specialists and resources may be required
- Arrange availability and use of a CSI
- Nominate a dedicated investigator to manage each search
- Appoint an Exhibits Officer for the search
- Arrange image recording facilities, such as photography/video or digital imaging
- Set defined objectives:
    - o specific to offence/scene/offender/victim etc, including the potential for hidden places
    - o state what is to be looked for
    - o state what else to look for, for example lifestyle, association, fetishes, signs of an attack site or disturbance, obvious added, new items or missing items, unknown keys
    - o what is to be seized/not seized, how, who by, why and when
    - o target specific areas such as bathrooms and kitchens that may be used to clean away forensic evidence (search baths, sinks, washing machines, shower traps, toilet cisterns and usage by offenders, etc)
    - o establish what other property is near to items seized to prove attribution and evidentially link the items to a person
- Include outbuildings, garages, sheds, gardens, roof spaces and vehicles
- Set criteria for specific recoveries:
    - o a clear policy on what should/should not be seized and how, for example footwear to be checked against images of crime scene impressions

- o examination and recovery strategy such as photograph the item in position before recovery, stipulate what type of photography and whether to forensically recover for fingerprints or DNA
- Produce a risk assessment
- Cater for dealing with persons and animals/pets that may be present
- Guard against cross-contamination and avoid the same staff going to two different search locations

A search may allow for added tactical opportunities such as communicating with people who could be useful sources of information and/or witnesses (eg disproving alibis). Some may be innocent third parties who become unfortunately tied into and affected by a search. If dealt with tactfully and sensitively they could provide relevant information and become useful assets. Neighbours and people visiting the property at the time of the search may also be sources of information.

When items are recovered in areas such as bedrooms, it may be necessary to look for evidence to link a person to that room, such as evidence of their personal belongings being present. The closer these items are to the recovered item the better.

Premises searching must take cognizance of modern digital media and communications technology that may be at the location and how best to locate, identify and recover it. Examples include smart phones, wi-fi routers, games consoles, digital assistants and other devices that are able to connect and transmit via the internet.

Data storage devices are becoming increasingly small and easy to conceal but have the capability to store huge volumes of data, images, documents, communications and other information. Consideration needs to be given to the potential impact that the search teams communication devices may have on some digital devices at the search location. If necessary, specialist advice from a Digital Media Investigator should be sought when planning the search, regarding recovery of devices and whether officers should turn off their smart phones and other devices when approaching the venue.

Important finds, whatever their type, should be photographed before being recovered. This helps indicate exactly where they were recovered, what condition they were in and what else was around them or nearby at the time. Photographs also allow investigators an opportunity to see exactly what an item looks like, which is more difficult once they are packaged and sent off to a laboratory. The images might also be useful to use during interviews with witnesses and suspects.

5.20 Open Area and Water Searches

These types of searches vary widely due to the environmental factors and are more likely to be encountered in major and serious crime and missing person investigations. More information can be found in Cook (2019).

In a complex open area or water-based search it is good practice for the crime investigator, CSI and the PolSA to visit the proposed search site together to consider, amongst other things:

- the extent of the area to be searched and the environment involved, such as in a public park perhaps searching only the paths and tracks and the areas adjacent to them that were potentially used by an offender for discarding items instead of searching the whole park
- logistical and technical costs, resources and constraints
- how the scene will be cordoned, contained and searched

Whenever a water-based search is required, specialist advice must always be sought.

5.21 National Search Adviser

The National Search Adviser (NSA) is a resource provided by the Crime Operational Support team within the NCA. They have a remit for providing operational support to forces in relation to complex searches. This includes advice for:

- homicides, no-body murders, missing persons, abductions and mass fatality disasters
- locating human remains, concealed, or otherwise disposed of
- reviewing previous search activity or strategies on critical or cold cases
- preparing and writing search strategies for SIOs and PolSAs and providing advice

The role includes acting as an independent adviser and facilitator to access specialists in relation to searches requiring geological (including geophysical, geochemical, hydrogeological, geomorphological) underwater and canine techniques. More information about the National Search Adviser can be obtained from the access number of 0845 000 5463.

Checklist—Searches general

- Plan each search methodically
- Determine power of entry or containment (PACE/warrant/common law)
- Ensure the search is intelligence-led (based on available information)
- Set clear objectives, including what is to be recovered/not recovered
- Designate what areas are to be searched and by whom, how, why, when, etc.
- Conduct a health and safety risk assessment, including any anticipated hazards and personal protective equipment required

- Plan for recovery of dangerous items such as syringes, sharp objects, firearms, weapons, chemicals
- Plan for areas and premises that need to be cleared for suspects or other dangers before the search
- Ensure there are suitable resources, equipment and specialists
- Ensure and check appropriate records and documentation are completed
- Plan for how any media or visiting/watching public are to be managed
- Mitigate potential contamination and integrity issues
- Use a search as an opportunity to speak with those present for information
- Plan for vulnerable third parties who may be affected by the search
- Remain vigilant for any digital media/communications devices and their usage
- Have mechanisms for reviewing/revising the strategy to take account of emerging information
- Remind staff to remember the 'just doesn't look right' (JDLR) principle!

5.22 Recovery and Preservation of Exhibits

Whenever possible forensic exhibits should be left in position for a CSI or forensic specialist to recover or provide advice. However, if the material is at risk of being lost or damaged then steps should be taken to protect it; any steps taken must be done carefully and only when it is necessary.

The weather may be a factor at outside scenes, as rain, snow or wind may interfere with recoverable evidence. If it is not feasible to protect them, then any items should be immediately seized and exhibited, noting the original position. When covering items, care should be taken to ensure that any improvised cover does not come into contact with the item itself, thus adding further contamination. Using items such as clothing or hats for cover should be avoided, as there is a danger of contaminating the item with someone else's trace evidence, such as DNA.

Occasionally it may be necessary to search a scene before it can be forensically examined. This should only be done after a risk assessment has been completed that considers the benefits of the search against the risks of contamination or destruction of material.

Checklist—Exhibit recovery

- Try to photograph items in position
- Record precisely and in detail the exact location items were located (and what was around them)
- Think contamination and always consider full forensic recovery
- Evidence that is fragile, could be easily lost or will only be available temporarily should be recovered first
- Fragile or sensitive exhibits should be stored and transported carefully to prevent damage or degradation
- Exhibits should be placed in appropriate containers/ bags and packaged/labelled correctly
- All those who handle an exhibit must sign the label
- Only one item per package/container
- Search documentation and witness statements must be completed
- *Always* ensure chain of continuity and custody of each item is adhered to

5.22.1 Continuity and integrity

An exhibit is a physical item that is recovered during the investigation of a crime. The process of demonstrating the continuity and integrity of the item begins when it is identified. Two key principles *must* be applied when dealing with items that are seized as potential evidence:

- continuity
- integrity

It is necessary to adhere to these principles to prove there has not been any mishandling or contamination of an evidential item and to ensure no damage, loss or degradation of potential evidence occurs. The microscopic nature of some forensic material means it is easily transferrable and at risk of cross-transference and contamination.

KEY POINT

Some key definition's.

Continuity:	A continuous, complete and accurate record of all handling and movements of evidential material from identification at a crime scene, recovery, transportation, examination, storage and any other investigative processes.
Integrity:	Handling, packaging and storage of evidential material that demonstrates beyond all doubt that there has been no interference, contamination, cross-transference, tampering, destruction or loss that could have occurred either intentionally or unintentionally.
Contamination:	When something is added to an evidential sample from another, either accidentally or intentionally.
Cross-transfer:	A process in which material from a location, person or item is transferred to another (eg, when an officer who has been to a crime scene arrests a suspect and transfers material from the scene onto the suspect).

5.22.2 Storage of exhibits

Recovered items need storing in a way that maximises the opportunity for the recovery of forensic evidence. It is always wise to seek advice if necessary about the correct packaging and storage of forensic exhibits to ensure that potential mistakes are eliminated. When storing materials that may be returned to their owners, they should be stored so they can be returned in the same condition as when they were seized. Extra consideration should be given when dealing with the return of contaminated items (eg bloodstained) to avoid health hazards or distress to victims or others.

5.22.3 Exhibit labels

Exhibit labels must be attached to all exhibits and contain important information about how they have been handled. The labels contain standard fields that need to be completed. Details entered onto the labels need to be accurately recorded to avoid giving legal defence teams an opportunity to question the professionalism of the processes adopted during the handling and management of the item. Where there is a key exhibit in a court case, there could be defence questions and allegations about the integrity of the exhibit or reliability of the police processes. Details to be included on an exhibits label include:

- an accurate description of the item:
  - identifying features (note: avoid stating measurements or assertions such as a stain is 'blood', instead use wording such as 'apparent blood' or 'presumed blood')
- time and date:
  - precise time and date the exhibit was originally seized
- location:
  - must include sufficient details, such as the precise location from where the item was seized, for example inside glove compartment of Ford Focus registered number AB12COP, or at 3 Henrietta Street, PE27 3RA main lounge on third shelf from bottom of display cabinet in right-hand corner of room
- person seizing:
  - include the exhibit reference number of person recovering the item using their initials plus a

sequential number, eg ABC/1 would be the first exhibit of Andrew Brian Collins and so on
- o signature and collar number of person finding
- o any persons subsequently handling the exhibit must also sign continuity field of label, including the relevant time and date

KEY POINTS

- Difficulties can be encountered when material is recovered and exhibited that is subsequently found to form part of a series of offences committed over an extended period of time. Although not known at the time of recovery these may become part of the same prosecution case or appear on different indictments in the same prosecution. In such cases it is highly likely that the same exhibit reference numbers will have been used but they will refer to different items (eg multiple instances of ABC/1 referring to different exhibits). This can become very confusing when building a case file and presenting the evidence in court. To mitigate this possibility, it can be good practice to include the date of recovery after the exhibit number, for example ABC/1/27.05.21. In this way a distinction can be made between items that are recovered on different days by the same person that are subsequently found to form part of a linked series or prosecution.
- A common mistake made with exhibit labels is when one of the continuity signatures is missing. This provides an opportunity for defence teams to place doubt over the integrity of an evidential item and ultimately the professionalism of the investigation.

5.22.4 **Sub-exhibiting**

This occurs when an exhibit contains multiple items, such as a backpack and its contents. When initially recording the seizure of such an item, it should be described as 'backpack and contents'. There is no requirement to list the individual items it contains at this point. However, if items are removed from the backpack (ABC/1), such as an iPad, then it needs to be exhibited sequentially as ABC/2—iPad recovered from backpack ABC/1.

5.22.5 **Principles for packaging exhibits**

Exhibits must be packed and sealed at the time and location of their seizure and recovery. Failure to do so may compromise forensic opportunities. Packaging and sealing at the time of seizure ensures the continuity and integrity of the exhibit is maintained. Advice should always be obtained from a CSI on the best methods of packaging exhibits.

References

Beaufort-Moore, D (2015) *Blackstones Crime Scene Management and Evidence Recovery* (OUP)

Cook, T (2019) *Blackstones Senior Investigating Officers Handbook* (5th edn, OUP)

Chapter 6
Forensic Investigation

6.1 Introduction

The term 'forensic' according to the *Oxford English Dictionary* (2008) means 'relating to or denoting the application of scientific methods and techniques to the investigation of crime'. Another definition from the *Oxford Dictionary of Law Enforcement* (2003) is 'of, or for use in a court of law. Frequently misused to apply narrowly to forensic science'.

Forensic investigation provides opportunities to scientifically link suspects, victims, witnesses and locations. The results may corroborate or refute other material gathered during the investigation, including accounts from witnesses and suspects, and can be compelling evidence.

Whatever forensic tactics and techniques are employed will depend on the needs and specific circumstances of the investigation. Some of these can be used not only to implicate persons as being responsible for a crime, but also to eliminate them. Obtaining fingerprints or buccal swabs from TIE subjects to compare against a crime scene stain or mark is something that may be included in an elimination strategy for example (see Chapter 7).

This is a highly specialised area of investigation involving scientists and other experts. This chapter merely aims to provide crime investigators with an awareness

Blackstone's Crime Investigators' Handbook. Steve Hibbitt and Gary Shaw, Oxford University Press. © Oxford University Press 2023.
DOI: 10.1093/oso/9780192867896.003.0006

and overview of some of the more common forensic techniques and opportunities that can be available to assist an investigation. It is always advisable to seek advice on any of the topics mentioned from a Crime Scene Investigator (CSI) or other relevant expert, as scientific techniques are constantly evolving and developing. The most well-known and obvious of them all has been around a long time and is the first to be outlined.

6.2 Fingerprints

Fingerprints (including palm prints), due to their unique nature, are a recognised means of identification and broadly fall into three categories.

6.2.1 Latent prints

These marks are not easily visible to the naked eye and are developed by using powders or other chemical development techniques on clean, dry and smooth surfaces. The mark is then 'lifted' from the surface using low tack adhesive tape and secured to a clear acetate sheet.

6.2.2 Visual marks

These are marks deposited in another substance on a surface, such as visible marks in paint, and blood. They are photographed and it is good practice to recover and exhibit the item the mark was left on/in.

6.2.3 Impressed marks

These are three-dimensional marks found in soft materials such as putty and wax. They are photographed and the item containing the mark should be recovered and exhibited if possible.

6.3 **IDENT1**

IDENT1 is the UK's central national database containing the fingerprints of all arrested persons and crime-scene marks. It compares:

- crime-scene marks with other crime-scene marks to establish links
- fingerprints with crime-scene marks to identify links
- marks from detained persons with those already on record to establish identity

6.4 **Footwear**

Footwear impressions are present when someone walks into and out of a location. They are not always visible and specialist lighting techniques may be required to locate them. Footwear comparison focuses on sole patterns and their unique characteristics through wear or damage to provisionally link the footwear to the mark. A conclusive match between a suspect's footwear and any scene marks is possible if sufficient detail is present, however the footwear that made the mark still needs attributing to the person wearing it at that time. Wear and damage patterns to the soles can change with continued use, so a comparison may only be valid for a limited period following the offence, depending on how often the footwear has been worn. To be used in evidence, any links must be confirmed by a forensic scientist. There are two types of footwear marks, namely:

- two-dimensional transfer marks, for example:
    - o on hard surfaces such as tiles, glass, laminate flooring
    - o substances transferred from the sole of the shoe to the surface leaving a two-dimensional impression, such as mud
- three-dimensional impressed marks, which are:

- indentations on soft surfaces such as mud, snow and on some types of carpet

Footwear impressions could also be found on a victim through the force of impact from a stamp or kick. Additionally, apart from leaving marks on surfaces, footwear may yield other forensic material to link to a scene, such as glass particles.

It is important to remember that although forensic investigation may place the footwear mark at a location, the suspect must also be linked to the footwear for it to have any evidential significance. In some circumstances, other forensic tests such as DNA will be required, or matching wear and tear of a shoe to a person's foot shape and walking style may be needed.

6.4.1 National Footwear Reference Collection

The National Footwear Reference Collection (NFRC) is provided free of charge to police forces and is a searchable library from which to identify different types of footwear from their sole patterns.

Identifying the make and model of the footwear which made a mark provides valuable intelligence when planning and conducting searches, circulating information about the offence and pursuing other lines of enquiry.

However, searching the NFRC may not provide a definitive answer when the mark for comparison is only partially complete.

6.4.2 Seizing footwear

The best method to seize footwear uses two sheets of paper. A person stands on one sheet and then steps onto the second sheet as they remove each shoe individually. This reduces the risk of the footwear collecting material from the floor.

Each shoe and the first sheet of paper are exhibited separately (one shoe per bag). If clothing is seized at the same time, the suspect should remain standing on the second sheet of paper until the process is complete. Gloves should always be worn when handling footwear due to potential risks from body fluids, glass shards, etc.

Footwear impressions may be taken without consent from persons in custody if they have been arrested, charged or reported for a recordable offence and they have not had a footwear impression taken in the course of the investigation; or, if one has previously been obtained, it needs retaking because it is incomplete or it is of insufficient quality to allow satisfactory analysis, comparison or matching (Police and Criminal Evidence Act 1984 (PACE), section 61A [3]). This is a useful proactive technique to employ in custody units where footwear impressions are usually obtained by using a footwear recovery pad or a dedicated flatbed scanner.

6.5 **Clothing**

Depending on the crime and its circumstances, recovering clothing and jewellery worn by a victim, suspect or witness at the time of the offence can provide various forensic opportunities, such as contact blood staining, fibre transfer, analysis of the distribution of blood patterns and gunshot residue.

A point to remember is the forensic potential of specific areas of clothing, such as pockets, turn ups, seams and stitching. These have often been found to contain forensic material not readily visible, even after the garment has been washed.

The recommended way to seize clothing is:

- stand the person on a sheet of paper
- remove the outermost layers first as opposed to any 'top to bottom' sequence
- as each item is removed place it into a separate sack
- note any areas of evidential interest, such as rips, marks, potential blood stains, and describe and record these on the exhibit label

- package items separately and seal them in the person's presence
- complete a witness statement (MG11) exhibiting the items and describing the process, including the method of packaging and continuity

Unsealed packages, bags or sacks should not be left near to each other. CCTV from custody areas could be used by defence teams to challenge the integrity of any items seized if not packaged and sealed correctly at the time. Advice should be sought from a CSI if the clothing is wet, including wet bloodstains.

KEY POINTS

- If clothing is to be placed immediately into exhibit bags, in some circumstances it may be worthwhile having it photographed beforehand to assist any identification process.
- If a suspect's belt is to be seized, where possible it is best not to remove it during the custody reception process in case material is trapped behind it which could be lost. In these circumstances, officer safety, including potential concealed weapons, must be considered together with the safety of the detainee who must not be left alone until the recovery process above has been completed.

6.6 Forensic Samples

Forensic considerations following the arrest of a suspect will depend on the crime under investigation and what proof is being sought. This could be as straightforward as checking with fluorescent light for the presence of Smartwater (a water-based theft deterrent), to full forensic processing in serious offences. The potential forensic yield from the suspect and their clothing should form part of any planned arrest strategy, including cross-contamination prevention measures.

6.6.1 Non-intimate samples

A non-intimate sample is:

- a sample of hair (other than pubic hair), including hair plucked with a root or cut
- a sample taken from a nail or from under a nail
- a mouth swab
- a swab from any other part of the body apart from body orifices or intimate areas
- saliva
- skin impressions from non-intimate areas

KEY POINTS

- Non-intimate samples can be taken at a hospital or any other place where the person is detained.
- Unlike intimate samples, a constable can use reasonable force if necessary if consent to obtain the sample is withheld by the suspect (PACE, section 63).

6.6.2 Intimate samples

An intimate sample is a:

- a dental impression
- a sample of blood, urine, pubic hair, semen or any other tissue or fluid
- a swab taken from any part of the person's genitals, or from a body orifice other than the mouth

KEY POINTS

- Intimate samples require written consent from the detainee and authority from an inspector or above. They cannot be taken by force, but adverse inferences may be drawn in any subsequent proceedings if consent is refused without good cause (PACE, section 62(10)).

- Except for urine, all intimate samples must be obtained by a registered medical practitioner or health care professional.
- A dental impression must be taken by a registered dentist.

6.7 Fingernail Samples

Fingernail samples may contain skin tissue/DNA from a victim or suspect from a scratch during an attack. Forensic recovery is by using an approved kit with the following methodology, always wearing gloves.

6.7.1 Nail clippings

Checklist—Nail clippings methodology

1. Place sterile paper on a clean bench
2. Place the suspect's hand over the paper and using the clippers provided clip all the nails of one hand (some clippers retain the samples inside their body)
3. Return the clippers to the container they were supplied in and place into a tamper evident bag
4. Fold the piece of paper inwards ensuring any deposited material is retained
5. Place into the same bag as the clippers
6. Seal and exhibit this bag then repeat the process for the other hand
7. Store in a freezer

6.7.2 Swabbing fingernails

Checklist—Swabbing fingernails methodology

1. Place the hand over a piece of sterile paper

2. Open the ampoule of water supplied with the kit and drip three to four drops onto the swab (do not use water from any other source)
3. Replace the swab in its tube and seal as *control swab* (ABC/1—control swab wetted)
4. Take a second swab and moisten with sterile water as above
5. Run the tip of the swab under each nail rim, the surface of the nail and around the cuticle using the edge of the swab as well as the tip to maximise its available surface area
6. Replace the swab into its tube and seal as *wet swab* (ABC/2—wet swab from right hand)
7. Take the third swab and, without wetting, run the tip of the swab under each nail rim, the surface of the nail and around the cuticle using the edge of the swab as well as the tip to maximise its available surface
8. Replace the swab into its tube and seal as *dry swab* (ABC/3—dry swab from right hand)
9. Place all three sealed tubes into a tamper evident bag with the folded piece of sterile paper and exhibit as one item using the initials of the person seizing and a sequential number (ABC/1—wet and dry samples from …)
10. Store in a freezer

6.8 **Hair Samples**

Hair might contain material such as glass and body fluids and can also be used for DNA comparison with hair at a scene shed by an offender or pulled out during a struggle. Hair can also potentially provide evidence of historical drug use and in some cases the racial origin of the donor.

There is always a risk of inadvertent secondary transfer of hair (and fibres), such as during transport in police vehicles. Records should be made of vehicles used to convey victims, witnesses and suspects, and cross-contamination prevention measures considered, such as using paper covers on vehicle seats or putting suspects in protective forensic suits at the point of arrest.

Any hair sample obtained should be no larger than necessary and the person should be given a choice where it is taken from. Forensic recovery is by using an approved kit.

Checklist—Hair samples

1. Place sterile paper on a bench and ensure the suspect's head is over the paper
2. Recover any visible evidence/foreign material using the tweezers provided or a gloved hand and place onto the paper
3. Comb through the hair using the comb provided or the fingers of a gloved hand to loosen any particles
4. Collect any material recovered onto the paper then fold inwards to retain it
5. Place the paper, comb/scissors and tweezers into the same tamper evident bag and exhibit
6. Exhibit the gloves worn separately

Hair comparison:

1. Cut a minimum of 25 hairs, as close to the scalp as possible, from different parts of the head
2. Do NOT use tweezers for comparison purposes as they may crush the recovered sample
3. Store in a dry store

6.9 **DNA Samples**

DNA samples (buccal swabs) are usually taken from cells lining the inside of a person's mouth using an approved kit.

Checklist—Buccal swabs

1. Ensure the person has not eaten or drunk for at least 20 minutes
2. Ensure swabs and containers are fully sealed and undamaged
3. Wear the disposable gloves provided and avoid coughing or talking over the samples
4. Take one sample making at least six scrapes of the inside of the mouth
5. Open a container and press down on the stem of the swab to eject the ridged swabbing tip into it
6. Seal the top of the receptacle containing the swab and place into the bag provided.
7. Repeat this process for the second sample
8. Seal the tamper evident bag in the presence of the donor
9. Complete the DNA sample form with the appropriate kit (evidential/elimination etc)
10. Place the completed form along with the bag containing the two samples into the larger tamper evident bag, seal and store in a freezer
11. Make an official notebook entry of the barcode and in the custody record if appropriate

6.10 Deoxyribonucleic Acid (DNA)

DNA is a complex molecule found in virtually every cell of the human body and in all living organisms. It carries genetic instructions in the form of a code (similar in appearance to a supermarket barcode), which can be used as a biological identification method. Except for identical siblings, each person's DNA is unique.

If saliva, blood, semen, skin or anything else containing cells is deposited by a person, it can be recovered, and a DNA profile obtained to search against records on the National DNA Database (NDNAD) and potentially identify the donor. The significance of DNA and its investigative and evidential potential cannot be overstated. Scientific developments have made possible opportunities to obtain DNA profiles from miniscule amounts of material. The sensitivity of the scientific techniques involved emphasises the importance of preventing cross-contamination even more.

6.10.1 Mixed DNA profiles

If two or more people's combined DNA is recovered from a location because they are mixed together this is known as a mixed profile, but a single profile might still be extracted. If the DNA of one of the people who has contributed to a mixed profile is known, it may be possible to remove it, leaving the DNA profile of the other person; for example, eliminating the DNA profile of a victim could identify a suspect. However, if neither person is known, it may be very difficult to separate the DNA of each person who has contributed to the mixed profile. Consequently, there are strict rules about placing a DNA profile on the NDNAD when it has been obtained from a mixture.

6.10.2 Incomplete DNA profiles

DNA may decompose over time, but the attrition rate of deterioration is very difficult to predict. Sometimes relatively fresh samples degrade quickly and at other times complete DNA profiles can be obtained from relatively old samples.

An incomplete DNA profile can still be used to establish a potential link between an individual and a crime scene. The statistical probability of any match reduces as the completeness of profile diminishes, but even very incomplete profiles can be used to conclusively eliminate a person from an investigation.

The following table is a summary of sample types and DNA potential recovery:

Sample type	Source of DNA	Comments
Blood	White blood cells	Good source of DNA
Semen	Sperm cells Non-sperm male cells	Good source of DNA Good source of DNA
Hair with roots	Hair follicle cells	Good source of DNA
Skin/dandruff	Skin cells (dead)	Not a good source for routine analysis
Shed hair shafts (dead)	Adhering dead skin/follicle cells	Not a good source for routine analysis Mitochondrial DNA (MtDNA) may be obtained
Sweat stains	Sloughed skin cells contained in fluid	Can be a good source
Vaginal fluids	Mainly fluid but may contain sloughed mucosal skin cells	Good source of DNA
Nasal secretions	Mainly fluid but may contain sloughed mucosal cells	Good source of DNA
Urine	Mainly fluid but may contain sloughed mucosal cells	Not routinely used as few cells generally present Seek advice in serious cases

6.10.3 Initial submission and analysis

Material bearing potential DNA is sent to a Forensic Service Provider (FSP) to extract and prepare a profile. The next stage depends on the objective to be achieved:

1. If the DNA profile is to be added to the NDNAD to identify the donor, for example from a discarded cigarette butt recovered from a scene, a straightforward one-page form is completed: Submission of Crime Stains (DNA) for the National Database (GF111).

2. If the DNA profile is to be compared with another sample, such as a crime scene stain requiring comparison with samples taken from a suspect, the more detailed form MG21 is submitted.

6.10.4 Low template DNA

Low Template DNA (LTDNA) is the term used to refer to what was previously called Low Copy Number DNA (LCN) or 'touch' DNA. This is an ultra-sensitive technique and is used when very few cells are available for analysis or they are partly degraded. The sample is analysed first using the standard SGM + technique and the results are amplified to provide sufficient material to obtain a DNA profile.

This process can produce a profile from extremely small samples, which means material previously analysed unsuccessfully using the standard process can be submitted for further testing. Due to its sensitivity, the risk of contamination and cross-transfer is high; however, results using LCN have the same discriminatory power as those produced by the standard process.

6.10.5 National DNA Database

The National DNA Database (NDNAD) contains the DNA profiles of persons who have been arrested, cautioned, convicted and charged for recordable offences. It is one of the largest databases of its kind in the world, containing over five million profiles. Each time a new crime scene sample is received it is entered onto the database and regularly cross-checked against the profiles of individuals.

The originating police force is notified when a link is made between profiles, including the strength of the reported match. This is expressed in the numerical probability of a match belonging to someone other than the identified person, for example one in a billion.

6.10.6 Police Elimination Database

The Police Elimination Database (PED) contains the DNA profiles of police officers and operational staff and sits within the same framework but separate to the suspect/crime stain database. It can only be searched on the authority of an SIO and is restricted to officers and staff who attended the scene or had access to exhibits for elimination purposes only. There must be genuine grounds to suspect that contamination has taken place between the officer and the crime stain, and profiles on the PED cannot be speculatively searched against the NDNAD.

6.10.7 Familial DNA searching

Familial DNA searching (fDNA) is based on the principle that DNA is inherited with family members sharing certain characteristics. Children share half their DNA with their father and half with their mother; the extent to which siblings share their DNA varies but tends to be larger than with unrelated people.

Familial enquiries are expensive and can be resource intensive, so they are only used for the more serious offences. The written authorisation of an ACPO officer from the requesting force is required together with agreement from the NDNAD Strategy Board. Early liaison with the NCA Major Crime Investigative Support Team is *mandatory* to advise on the complex issues surrounding potential filtering techniques.

A familial enquiry could be considered when a full DNA profile has been developed from a crime scene and searched against the NDNAD with a negative result. A familial search of the NDNAD would produce two lists (parent/child and siblings) that could contain relatives of the unidentified person.

The search is likely to present hundreds of DNA profiles of potential family members of the offender for further research and enquiries. These are filtered further using further discriminating forensic techniques and/or sophisticated calculations and analysis to prioritise the list based on a 'likelihood ratio' of success. The critical point to remember is that familial lists do not contain the offender; it is a list of people who might be related to the offender and requires considerable research.

6.10.8 Y-STR

Males have an X and a Y chromosome (XY) whereas females are characterised by two X but no Y chromosomes (XX). The Y strand (hence Y-STR) is inherited unaltered from father to son and can be used as an additional filter during a familial DNA search.

6.10.9 Mitochondrial DNA

Mitochondrial DNA (MtDNA) is only passed onto children through their mothers, so although males have MtDNA, only females can pass it on to their children. If a female appears in the results of a familial search as a possible parent or sibling of the offender, for that to be true her MtDNA must match the crime scene stain.[1] If it does not, all her siblings and children are eliminated as possible offenders. Her father, however, is not eliminated.

6.11 Blood Pattern Analysis

Blood pattern analysis (BPA) is the expert interpretation of blood distribution, such as at an attack site. This can establish a sequence of events, assist to develop hypotheses, reconstruct events and refute or corroborate the accounts of victims, suspects and witnesses.

BPA determines how blood staining and spatter was caused on clothing, weapons and at the scene of the

[1] It is not always possible to obtain a Y-STR or MtDNA profile from a crime scene stain.

crime. It can also establish the approximate positions of assailants and victims in the sequence of events. This is a complex process with many variables and is only undertaken by a scientist (usually a biologist) who specialises in the analysis of bloodstains.

The scientist's knowledge of the physical properties of blood and how it reacts in certain circumstances is used to examine and interpret the blood staining according to size, shape, location and quantity, including:

- passive bloodstains
- projected bloodstains
- transfer/contact bloodstains
- 'velocity' impact blood stains
- low/medium/high velocity impact blood spatter

BPA may also indicate blood from different sources and determine what samples are taken for DNA profiling. It is also possible to assess the degree to which the assailant would themselves become bloodstained during the attack. Blood distribution may not be visible, so CSI's and forensic scientists can use chemical development processes to locate even minute traces.

6.12 **Tyre Marks**

Tyre marks are useful when a pattern for comparison is clearly visible, as skid and scuff marks with no apparent detail cannot be linked. The recovery techniques for tyre marks are:

- photographs to show their position within the crime scene
- close-up photographs to show detail
- recovery of the entire mark if left on a portable surface

Tyre impressions should be recovered by a CSI or a forensic vehicle examiner.

- Tyres must not be removed from a vehicle; they must be photographed and either:
  - o the vehicle driven through a similar soft surface to recreate the mark or
  - o the vehicle rolled along a roll of paper for at least one full revolution of the tyre

If the vehicle is driven through a similar soft surface, a cast is taken of the mark to compare with the scene. If sufficient detail is present, the brand of tyre that made the mark can potentially be identified. If several tyre marks have been left by the same vehicle, it is sometimes possible to calculate the width of the wheelbase and use this information to establish the type of vehicle used.

When an examiner compares suspect tyres with marks at scenes, they seek to identify unique wear and damage, similar to the principles of footwear comparison.

6.13 **Tool Marks**

Any evidence of a 'tool' being used at the scene of a crime should be photographed and a cast is usually taken by a CSI for comparison with any tool/implement suspected of making the mark. This may link an offender to the scene by association. These marks normally fall into one of two categories.

6.13.1 **Lever marks**

These are created by tools like screwdrivers, crowbars and 'jemmys', used to force an entry. Any unique marks on the instrument caused by its manufacturing process or by damage during its use allow scientists to match a mark with the tool/implement that made it. Minute striations and imperfections in the mark have the most value, and ideally the item bearing the tool mark should be submitted for examination, for example the window frame section. If this is not possible, a cast showing the fine detail is required.

When lever marks are present in painted areas, it is possible the tool will have picked up some paint onto the blade. A paint sample should therefore be obtained for comparison.

6.13.2 Cutting marks

Cutting marks are left when items such as padlocks and chains have been cut through using tools like wire cutters and bolt croppers. Such implements may also carry striation marks and imperfections which can be used for comparison between the cut item and any tool recovered during the investigation.

6.14 Glass

When glass breaks it showers microscopic particles (not just forwards, but also backwards) which can adhere to the clothing and hair of the person responsible for breaking it and anyone else in close proximity. If suspects are identified quickly, this creates forensic opportunities as glass fragments recovered from a person can be compared with fragments from the crime scene to establish a forensic link.

Different types of glass have different properties and react differently when they are broken. For example, glass used in bottles differs from laminated and toughened glass. Depending on the type of glass, options for forensic comparison include:

- physical fit—no two pieces of glass break in the same way so it may be possible to match pieces together to establish if they came from the same source. It is vital their packaging prevents damage during transit
- Glass Refractive Index Measurement—this allows comparison between samples to identify if they came from

the same source by examining their refractive index. Several scene samples are needed as the refractive index can vary slightly from the same piece of glass
- comparing the colour, thickness and density of the glass
- comparing impurities present in the glass

Any forensic material transferred to a suspect will gradually be lost over time (this is known as persistence). The rate of loss for glass fragments depends on their size and the nature of the retaining surface; closely woven fabrics are not likely to retain much glass, but wool or fleece material will retain much more. Washing and wearing the item accelerates loss, but if clothing is not worn or washed after contact the glass could remain on it indefinitely. The type of clothing worn by a suspect and the time elapsed between the offence and clothing's seizure therefore influences the likelihood of glass remaining in place and its forensic potential.

Glass fragments can be trapped in hair, upper clothing, lower clothing and the uppers and soles of shoes. This should be considered when clothing and samples are recovered from suspects and selected for forensic examination. Initial interviews prior to forensic submission should seek to negate any plausible lie such as walking through already broken glass, as analysis may indicate how far the person was from the window when it was broken.

Samples of glass from broken windows should be taken from the actual window frame rather than being picked up from the ground to ensure its origin is not disputed.

6.15 **Paint**

Although paint is mass produced, its make-up has wide variation due to the processes and raw materials used.

Paint analysis can show transference between articles such as a crowbar and the point of entry in a burglary. Such transference can work both ways, with any paint already on a tool being transferred to the window frame while forcing entry.

The analysis of paint can show impact and force, such as when a person is struck by a vehicle. Any paint fragments embedded in clothing could have a distinctive appearance and provide evidence of impact, as opposed to light casual contact.

Paint samples analysed from scenes such as graffiti/hate crime may provide intelligence about the make and type of paint used. This could develop other lines of enquiry, such as identifying the location of sale, which in turn may lead to suspects. Any cans of spray paint recovered for comparison should be submitted as whole items to maintain the integrity of any sample taken from it later by a scientist.

6.15.1 **Vehicle paint**

Paint can be transferred when a vehicle collides with another vehicle or any other surface. The transferred samples may present themselves as smears, flakes or chips which can be analysed to establish any links.

Vehicles usually have four coats of paint, including pretreatment coating, primer, top coat and a clear coat. In some cases, it may be possible for a scientist to determine the make, model and age of a vehicle from paint samples left at the scene of an incident.

6.15.2 **Recovery of paint samples**

Paint samples for forensic analysis should be recovered by a CSI using clean scalpels to scrape areas of paint down to the bare surface. When visible flakes are found at a scene or on clothing, they can be collected into paper envelopes and sealed in tamper evident bags.

6.16 Soils

Analysis of soil provides a forensic opportunity to link soils attached to surfaces (such as footwear or vehicles) to a location. The composition of soil differs between areas, including potentially even neighbouring gardens, depending on what is grown there or the type of any fertiliser used. Soil sample analysis includes:

- visual observation of colour and texture
- microscopic examination of the soil structure, which may reveal the presence of man-made, plant or animal material
- determining any minerals and rock fragments
- determining the size and distribution of soil particles

The significance of any evidence obtained depends on the number of common factors between the two samples. The more common points of comparison, the stronger the evidential link will be. However, any link will not be conclusive unless there is something unique about the samples that only exist at that location.

Botanical evidence, such as comparable pollen and plant spores from the same flowers and foliage can also be obtained from soil samples; this is sometimes a preferred option and involves the use of a palynologist.

6.17 Fibres

Fibres fall into two broad categories of natural (wool, silk, cotton) and man-made (nylon, polyester). Their analysis can potentially provide evidence of the fibre type, colour, diameter, shape (cross-section), chemicals added during manufacture and comparison of dyes. Sometimes the origin of the fibre can be identified through pigments or dye contained in it.

Fibres may provide evidence of contact between people and surfaces, but the degree of any transfer depends on the nature of the item and the extent of the contact. Generally, closely woven material does not retain or shed fibres, whereas a fleecy type will.

As with glass, if the garment is washed or extensively worn after an incident the amount of available evidence will diminish, but if it is put to one side after the incident any fibres will be retained indefinitely.

The significance of fibre analysis depends on the circumstances of the offence and the number, combination and nature of the fibres recovered. The greater the number of comparable points, the higher the evidential value. Ideally fibres should be recovered by a CSI, but if this is not possible the same procedures as with recovering hair samples should be adopted.

6.18 Firearms and Ballistic Material

It is essential that every opportunity is taken to recover ballistic items (bullets, wadding and spent cartridges) from any incident where a firearm may have been discharged in suspicious or obviously criminal circumstances.

6.18.1 Firearms recovery

Any firearms found must be left in position to be made and certified safe by an Authorised Firearms Officer (AFO) or equivalent before any further action is taken. Weapons should always be treated as real and loaded until proven otherwise.

Once made safe, a CSI should undertake a forensic recovery for DNA and fingerprints, including taking photographs and noting the position of the safety catch or, in the case of a revolver, the position of the chamber and hammer.

Firearms should be secured in a protective box with a transparent window, which must be securely sealed and a 'made safe' certificate attached. Nothing should be pushed into the barrel of a firearm such as a pen or fingers; gloves must be worn during handling which should be retained, bagged and exhibited after the firearm has been securely sealed.

Wet firearms and components should be placed in boxes and sealed into paper evidence sacks. Plastic packaging MUST NOT be used as this encourages rust which can change the striations in the barrel and affect any test firing. This can also be detrimental to any subsequent court proceedings as by the time of the hearing the firearm may no longer be in the same condition as when it was recovered, for example it may no longer be capable of being fired.

Firearms and ammunition must not be stored, packaged or submitted for forensic analysis together. Care must be taken to ensure that the firearm and any related material is kept separate so that other exhibits, such as offender clothing, do not come into contact.

6.18.2 **Ballistic examination**

The ballistic examination of firearms can be split into three general areas, which can provide a picture of what occurred, enabling accounts to be corroborated or refuted.

- internal ballistics:
    - o what happens inside the weapon?
    - o imperfections transferred from the barrel onto the bullet or wadding
    - o establishing recoil and barrel pressures
- external ballistics:
    - o behaviour of projectiles in flight after discharge and before impact
    - o trajectory, maximum range and momentum of the bullet determined by mathematical principles
    - o aiding reconstruction of events such as position of victim(s) and offender when the weapon was fired, or the distance between firearm, offender and victim
- Terminal ballistics:
    - o behaviour of the projectile on its target

- o penetration potential—the ability to penetrate various materials
- o wound ballistics—the effect on living tissue

These examinations may also link ammunition to the firearm that discharged it and potentially forensically connect other incidents involving the same weapon.

6.18.3 Firearms discharge and explosive residue

Firearms discharge and explosive residue can be present on the hands, face, hair, clothing and jewellery of a person who has discharged a firearm or been in close proximity at the time. Places where a firearm or ammunition may have been stored, such as pockets and waistbands, should be checked for firearms discharge residue, as should places or items near to where a firearm may have been test fired.

Cross-contamination is a very real threat when dealing with microscopic nanograms of gunshot residue. For this reason, it may be necessary to use a specially prepared sterile custody escort vehicle and a custody suite, reception area and holding cell that has been deep cleansed and can be proven to be free from discharge residue brought in from elsewhere, perhaps from AFOs.

Checklist—Collecting firearms/explosives residue

1. Sampling kits MUST be sealed before use, NEVER use an unsealed kit
2. No one who has handled or been in the vicinity of firearms, ammunition or explosives within the previous seven days should recover samples or come into contact with them (AFOs)
3. Prevent secondary transfer through contact between the person taking the samples and any persons mentioned at 2
4. Do NOT use the kit if a regular user of firearms or explosives

5. Consider cross-contamination and transfer between multiple suspects and use multiple recovery officers at different locations
6. Thoroughly wash hands and forearms and wear a disposable overall before opening a kit
7. Only use the items from within the kit and make a note of the serial/batch number
8. Be aware that some cultures may forbid contact with alcohol (swabs)
9. Be aware that some medicinal treatments, such as for angina may contain nitroglycerine

6.18.4 Using a firearms and explosive sampling kit

Checklist—Sampling technique

1. Wear the gloves supplied with the kit
2. Take one swab and rub it over the front and back of the gloves you are wearing and place the swab back into its tube. Label this as control swab and seal in an exhibit bag
3. Using a second swab, rub it over the face and neck of the suspect including the eyebrows (take care not to get solvent into their eyes). Replace the swab in its tube and seal in an exhibit bag
4. Comb through the hair and any beard/moustache with the comb supplied with the kit. The comb has solvent material in it. If the suspect has no hair or it is difficult to comb, then run the comb across the head, ensuring that the solvent material makes contact. Place the comb back into the plastic bag it was supplied in and seal in the exhibit bag
5. Using a clean swab, rub the front and back of the suspect's right hand. Pay particular attention to the web of the thumb, between the fingers and under

any jewellery. Label as swab from right hand and seal in an exhibit bag

6. Repeat 5 for the left hand
7. Remove the nail scraper and gauze from its bag. Taking one finger at a time, hold the finger over the gauze and scrape the debris from the nail, wiping the scraper on the gauze after each nail. Replace the scraper and gauze into its bag and then seal in an exhibit bag
8. Ensure each item is properly sealed before sealing the exhibits bag
9. When sampling is complete, remove, bag and exhibit the gloves worn

6.18.5 National Ballistics Intelligence Service

The National Ballistics Intelligence Service (NABIS) manages a national database of recovered firearms and ballistics material. This provides a forensic capability to link offences where the same weapon or individuals are involved, including identifying persons concerned with importing, supplying, illegally adapting or converting firearms.

NABIS centres have facilities for test firing, analysing and linking firearms and ballistic material to items submitted from other incidents across the UK and are capable of linking bullets and cartridge cases to crime scenes and recovered weapons.

NABIS provides intelligence on submitted items, but does not develop this into evidence, which is delivered by forensic service providers. A firewall between intelligence and evidence is created with access to the NABIS database available to key staff in each police force. All recovered ballistic material should be submitted to NABIS for analysis via a force SPoC (single point of contact) as soon as practicable.

6.19 Documents and Handwriting

Documentary forensic evidence to assist investigations includes:

- handwriting and grammatical style analysis
- forged/altered document examination
- recovery of indented writing
- fingerprint recovery
- physical fit
- comparison of a printed document to a printer

6.19.1 Handwriting analysis

Forensic comparisons can be made between writing on a document (the questioned document) and samples obtained, such as from suspects. As writing and grammatical styles tend to be individual to the author and display their own characteristics, these comparisons may establish the 'author' of the writing, and/or whether a signature is forged or genuine. The same can be established with typed words and documents when checking for similar styles, punctuation, sentence length and grammar, etc. This could be useful when examining similarly produced documents that are found on a word processor, for example.

Comparison material can be written by the suspect on demand and under supervision ('on request' specimens), or be previous ordinary examples of their handwriting, such as letters, work documents or schoolwork correspondence that have been recovered (course of business writing).

The four general categories examined within handwriting samples are:

- capitals: all the letters are written in upper case. An analyst will examine the number and direction of pen strokes used to construct the letters

- cursive: all the letters of a word are 'joined up'. This is the most common form of adult handwriting with vast variations in individual styles
- disconnected: a variation on cursive and includes breaks between some letters. These breaks vary from person to person
- signatures: highly stylised and often illegible. Signatures are often written in a completely different style to a person's general handwriting and are therefore difficult to link to normal handwriting

6.19.2 Forged handwriting

It is difficult for a person to consistently forge their handwriting and invariably, although they will write slower than usual to try and disguise their usual style, they will often revert to normal, as letters are formed subconsciously. It is typical for a piece of forged handwriting to include lots of variations in the formation of letters and spacing etc.

When a case involves forged signatures, reference writing examples must be obtained from the loser/injured party. This allows the document examiner to exclude the signature holder and determine if the questioned signatures were made with any attempt at copying the genuine ones.

Checklist—Handwriting samples from suspects

- Should represent the suspect's usual handwriting
- Should contain sufficient writing to conduct an effective comparison
- Should be taken on a similar document to the questioned document, for example a blank cheque template, another appropriate form or alternatively plain or lined paper
- If the questioned document is written in capital letters, the suspect's sample should be written in capitals. The document examiner can only examine like

for like, including capitals versus capitals or lower case versus lower case. This should be specified in the request made to the suspect.

- Use the same sort of pen, preferably a well-used ballpoint
- Provide a suitable writing surface for the sample
- For signature comparison take at least 12 samples
- For cheque fraud take at least 12 signature simples and a further 6 handwriting samples
- Take samples at different times of the interview process
- Never show the suspect the original document as they may copy it
- Dictate to the suspect what is to be written at a reasonable pace allowing a natural writing style to be used
- Don't help the suspect with spelling or the layout of specimens (spelling mistakes may be a comparison factor)
- The suspect should sign and date each sample as it is completed
- Each sample should be taken on a separate piece of paper and removed from sight when completed to prevent the suspect copying it
- Sequentially number each sample with the time each was recorded
- Obtain samples of course of business writing of the suspect if possible

Note: If in any doubt it is advisable to obtain advice from a forensic examiner before taking the samples.

6.19.3 Indented impressions

Indentations caused by the pressure of writing can travel through several sheets of paper; the most common technique used to reveal these is a non-destructive technique called Electrostat Document Apparatus (ESDA). This is not routinely undertaken and if being considered it should be recognised that treating a document with chemicals (Ninhydrin) for fingerprint recovery first will render an ESDA test useless. Similarly, if the item to be examined has been subjected to wet conditions this can significantly reduce any indented impressions.

6.19.4 Printed documents

Document examiners may be able to establish if a document originated from a specific machine by comparing the printed item with defects produced by the machine. Some printers produce what is called a bitmap. This is not visible to the naked eye but can provide information about the type and model of machines involved in the production of the item.

6.19.5 Analysis of inks and paper/physical fit

Forensic examiners can compare inks on a document and compare different pieces of paper to determine if they are from the same source. They can also compare torn pieces of paper from a pad or a shredded document to determine the source through their physical fit.

Checklist—Recovering/preserving documents

- Always wear gloves
- If possible, photograph or photocopy the original, depending on the requirements of the case
- To preserve for indented writing or footwear impressions, place the item into a box before placing it into a paper or plastic evidence bag
- NEVER lean on the document whilst completing exhibit labels
- Paper or plastic evidence bags are suitable if no indented impressions are required
- Store documentary exhibits in cool dry surroundings

- DO NOT stick, staple or clip anything to the exhibit
- Undertake chemical examinations last in any sequence of tests

6.20 **Drugs and Illegal Substances**

To list all drugs that are taken for illegal recreational purposes would not be beneficial, however some common drugs of abuse likely to be encountered include:

- category A (the most harmful):
  - cocaine
  - crack
  - morphine diacetate (heroin)
  - opium (opioid mixture)
  - Ecstasy
  - Lysergic Acid Diethylamide (LSD, acid)
  - Psilocybin mushrooms (magic mushrooms)
  - Methadone
  - Phencyclidine (Angel dust)
- category B:
  - amphetamine (speed)
  - codeine
  - cannabis (weed, marijuana, hash, skunk) (reclassified from Class C to Class B in January 2009)
  - Methylphenidate
  - Ritalin (stimulant)
  - Pholcodine (opioid)
  - Methaqualone (Mandrake, Mandrax)
- category C:
  - some other tranquilisers, stimulants and sedatives
  - anabolic steroids (for building muscle tissue)
  - Diazepam (Valium)
  - Temazepam (becomes class A when prepared for injection)
  - Flunitrazepam (Rohypnol)

6.20.1 Types of drugs

6.20.1.1 Heroin

Heroin is derived from morphine extracted from the opium formed in the unripe pods of certain poppies. It is typically brown in colour and contains between 4 and 21 per cent morphine. The process of manufacture involves the morphine reacting with acetic anhydride or acetyl chloride. This produces a powdered substance that is soluble in water, allowing it to be injected.

Before sale, other substances are added or 'cut' into the heroin to increase the amount that is sold. These substances could include lactose, milk powders, and sugars, which therefore impact on the purity.

6.20.1.2 Cocaine

Cocaine is derived from the coca leaf; it is typically administered in powder form and can be sniffed, allowing it to be absorbed through the mucous membranes of the nose. Crack cocaine is manufactured by mixing cocaine with baking soda and water. This is then dried and broken into lumps known as rocks, which are normally smoked.

6.20.1.3 Amphetamine

Amphetamines provide stimulus to the user as they affect the nervous system, increasing alertness and activity. They are typically encountered in powder form and are most often inhaled by sniffing.

6.20.1.4 Club drugs

These are synthetically produced and include MDMA (Ecstasy), Gamma Hydroxyburate (GHB) and ketamine; they are typically found in tablet form.

6.20.1.5 Hallucinogens

LSD (lysergic acid diethylamide) is derived from certain types of grain fungus; a small amount causes auditory and visual hallucinations. It is typically taken by ingesting a small piece of impregnated blotting paper which has been soaked in a solvent containing dissolved LSD.

Psilocybin is similar to LSD but occurs naturally in a particular variety of mushroom known as 'magic mushrooms'.

6.20.1.6 Cannabis

Probably the most widely used drug in the world and now typically cultivated in the UK rather than imported. It comes in a variety of forms including:

- leaves/herbal
- skunk (produced from specific varieties of the plant)
- resin
- cannabis oil

6.20.2 Cannabis cultivation

It is common for large houses or disused warehouses to be used for cannabis cultivation, enabling high yields of the drug. This sort of crime is now routinely linked to both national and international Organised Crime Groups (OCGs). Investigators should be mindful of the indicators for this type of activity when conducting enquiries and searches. The issues for investigation when dealing with these incidents include:

- identifying the premises and equipment
- establishing the actual and possible/potential yield from the amount of plants
- quality of the plants
- linking the scene to other cultivation operations or supplied drugs and OCG activity
- identifying all those involved in the cultivation chain of command
- added health and safety risks when conducting searches

The growth cycle of the cannabis plants is regulated by exposure to daylight, and in natural conditions it grows quicker in summer than in autumn. Indoor cultivation requires growers to reproduce the effects of daylight by using large, powerful lighting systems which allow the flowering to be regulated. By reducing the plants' life cycle, more crops can be grown in the same time period. Plants grown in this manner are cultivated in pots or by a method known as hydroponics, which doesn't use soil, and the plants are grown in circulating water (including added nutrients).

Although the method may vary from scene to scene, certain common factors may be present (this list is not exhaustive):

- lighting systems using high-powered lamps
- walls and windows painted white or coated with reflective coverings to maximise the lighting effects
- air circulation systems to prevent fungal growth
- seedling nursery area
- documentation detailing growing schedules
- water tanks, trays and pumps
- stocks of plant nutrients
- an electricity source (possibly abstracted)
- added security at the premises where it is being cultivated

OCGs are often linked with the large-scale cultivation of cannabis. In some cases entire premises are obtained and occupied for this sole purpose.

6.20.2.1 Recovery of plants

Cannabis plant recovery depends on the scale and complexity of the cultivation operation and the evidence required for the charge in question. Guidance should be sought from FSPs regarding the volume of submission required for each specific case.

6.20.2.2 Packaging of samples

All plants and related vegetable matter should be packaged separately in paper evidence sacks (never plastic bags) and be submitted to the forensic laboratory as quickly as possible. Any cultivation equipment does not necessarily need to be submitted, but investigative opportunities for other forensic material such as DNA or fingerprints on these items should be considered.

The scene of the cultivation should be photographed by a CSI, including the use of a scale (ruler) to indicate the size of plants.

6.20.2.3 Health and safety at cultivation scenes

Premises used for cannabis cultivation are a hazardous environment with potential risks including:

- booby traps: check local intelligence systems to identify if this is a risk in the area
- electrical risks: installations at such scenes are often haphazard and poorly maintained with the mains supply bypassed. Calling out the electrical supplier to ensure the safety of staff present should be considered
- trip hazards
- heat from large lamps capable of burning exposed skin
- chemicals present which may be corrosive
- the odour from the plants can become overwhelming; staff should wear disposable masks

Always wear disposable over suits and gloves.

6.20.2.4 Forensic potential from drugs packaging

Potentially valuable evidence can be obtained from the material that drugs are wrapped or packaged in, such as pieces of tin foil, plastic cling film and paper. The initial analysis must always be to identify what the substance contained in the wrapping is and confirm it is a controlled drug. The substance must not be decanted into another container and should be submitted to the Forensic Service Provider in its still wrapped state.

The instructions for the examination need to include the details of what examination is required, which will be determined by the circumstances of the investigation and what the examination seeks to prove.

It may be possible to link the wrapping or bag to a single source, such as the roll that it came from, by comparing microscopic manufacturing marks. This is known as a 'batch match'. The roll that the wrap is suspected to come from would need recovering and submitting for comparison. If a 'batch match' is being contemplated, it would need completing before any fingerprint or DNA examination.

Adhesive tape can possibly be linked to a roll and could also be a source for fingerprint and DNA recovery.

6.21 **Illicit Laboratories**

Much of the information regarding illicit laboratories is restricted but can be accessed within forces. These laboratories may be involved in the manufacture of drugs or materials for use in terrorism offences. If an illicit laboratory is encountered while making unrelated enquiries, the following actions should be undertaken:

Checklist—Illicit laboratories

- Due to the high risk (fire/explosion/chemical contamination) any personnel in the vicinity must retreat to a safe distance
- Mobile phones and radios should not be used near to the scene (inform the control room when a safe distance away)
- Do not switch any power supply on or off at the scene
- Do not touch or open any bottles or containers
- Keep the scene under observation from a safe distance
- Use cordons and scene logs to manage the scene
- Only those properly trained and equipped for searching in hazardous environments should re-enter the scene
- Check local force policy and arrangements for any multi-agency protocols
- Be mindful these activities may be connected to terrorism or OCG activity

6.22 **Toxicology**

Forensic toxicology uses analytical chemistry, pharmacology and clinical chemistry to aid investigations into death, poisoning and drug use. Toxicology can be used in other types of cases, for example when proving or disproving drug or alcohol usage by offenders, victims or even witnesses. Typical samples that may be examined include:

- urine
- blood
- hair
- saliva (oral fluid)
- other samples, such as organs, other bodily fluids or gastric contents obtained during an autopsy

A forensic toxicologist will consider their analysis in the context of the investigation, looking at issues such as physical symptoms and evidence collected at the scene (tablet containers, powders, trace residue). By considering these along with the submitted samples, they will determine which toxic substances are present, in what concentrations and their probable effect on the person concerned.

6.22.1 **Forensic persistence**

Forensic persistence is the time it takes for a forensic sample to degrade to the point where it has limited, little or no investigative or evidential value. The following is a guide to forensic persistence when considering submitting samples for analysis. This is not exact; various factors can cause deviation. Generally, samples should always be obtained and specialist advice sought regarding the viability of examination:

- alcohol: up to 24 hours in urine
- drugs of abuse: up to 12 to 24 hours in urine, 48 hours in blood

- GHB: 4 hours in blood, up to 6 to 12 hours in urine
- Rohypnol: 18 hours in blood, 72 hours in urine

References

Oxford English Dictionary (2008) (OUP)
Oxford Dictionary of Law Enforcement (2003) (OUP)

Chapter 7

Core Investigative Strategies

7.1 Introduction

Core investigative strategies are the methods and tactical options available and used for progressing an investigation. A strategy is basically an overarching plan designed and developed to achieve a long-term aim and an investigative strategy contains:

- the overall objectives of the investigation
- the relevant time frames of the investigation, including during, before and after the offence or event
- the main lines of enquiry (MLOE) to be pursued to achieve the objectives
- the geographical parameters of the MLOE
- the relevant time parameters for relevant events at each of the MLOE
- the methods selected to pursue the lines of enquiry, which should be the most beneficial and efficient
- the necessary enquiries and actions within the selected methods required to gather investigative material and intelligence to achieve the objectives or generate further lines of enquiry
- the resources required to conduct the investigation

The initial assessment of the situation should identify the primary objectives of the investigation along with deciding on the main lines of enquiry and strategies needed to achieve them. These should not be treated as

Blackstone's Crime Investigators' Handbook. Steve Hibbitt and Gary Shaw, Oxford University Press. © Oxford University Press 2023.
DOI: 10.1093/oso/9780192867896.003.0007

fixed plans applicable to all investigations; they should be selected as being the most suitable and necessary for that individual enquiry and be proportionate and justifiable.

Generic considerations and aide memoires or checklists can be useful reminders to some extent, but ultimately careful consideration and decision making is required. Applying an investigative mindset is essential to understand the situation, evaluate the investigative material, identify available options and prioritise and pursue those options most likely to achieve a result for the specific investigation.

Resources are inevitably limited and must be used for the most productive investigative tasks and not just to follow checklists. A considered decision needs to be made based on the specific requirements of the individual investigation at that time. It is unlikely that everything can be done at the same time with the resources available. Investigators need to identify the most potentially productive lines of enquiry to follow and prioritise those.

If checklists are routinely followed rather than being used as a prompt, it is likely that the tasks at or near the top of the list will be pursued first. These may not be the most productive or appropriate for that situation because they are generic and are not based on the individual circumstances of that crime or incident. This could potentially lead to missed investigative opportunities that are available elsewhere and inefficient use of resources. Consideration must always be given to the legal and ethical aspects of any proposed action.

Most of the strategies described in this chapter also feature to varying degrees in the *Core Investigative Doctrine* (2005), which was updated in 2013 (ACPO/NPIA 2013) and preceded the *Authorised Professional Practice* (APP) (College of Policing 2021) and the *Major Crime Investigation Manual* (NPCC 2021). They are suitable for most investigations and not just serious crime. Investigators are strongly encouraged to read these sources and assimilate the content relevant to their role.

Checklist—Investigative strategies

- Suspect (identification, interviews and management)
- Witness (identification, interviews and management)
- Victim (interviews and management)
- Scene management (forensic examination, searching, recovery of evidence and recovery of wider investigative material)
- Searches
- H2H enquiries
- CCTV/Audio Visual (AV)
- Intelligence (gathering and development)
- Passive data generators
- Digital media investigation
- Communications data and social media
- Financial investigation
- Elimination enquiries (TIE)
- Media and communications
- Proactive enquiries*
- Covert enquiries*
- Family liaison
- Community liaison

7.2 Relevant Time Parameters

The importance of establishing accurate time parameters within which to focus the investigative activity cannot be overemphasised. In some cases, this may be relatively straight forward, such as when the crime has been captured on CCTV, or the victim or a witness can accurately describe where and when the offence was committed, such as a street robbery for example. In other cases, the time parameters within which the offence was committed may be more difficult to reliably establish and could be based on the time between certain events.

Using a dwelling burglary as an example, in such a case the timeframe would be between the time that the last occupant left the dwelling to the time the burglary was discovered.

Some of these times might be based on estimates because they involve routine activity such as a victim leaving their home address. The accuracy of such times can be established by questioning the victim or witness on what they were doing at the time. Examples could include going to work or to an appointment or another event that has a time linked, such as catching a bus.

In some cases, the time parameters may be more uncertain and rely on third party information which should be confirmed if possible. As an example, in missing person enquiries the accuracy of a last sighting will rely on whether the witness knew the person and the accuracy of their recognition. It will also rely on the time and location of the sighting, and the accuracy of the time will initially be dependent on the accuracy of the witness. It may be possible to verify the timing of a witness by external sources such as sightings recorded on CCTV.

The decision to conduct these further enquiries will likely depend on the nature of the offence, including its seriousness and the proportionality of the enquiries. However, in cases where the accuracy of the timeframe is significant, such corroboration enquiries should be conducted.

7.2.1 Before and after the offence/incident

The relevant timeframes for the investigation are not confined to the time of the offence or the times between which an offence was committed. To increase the chances of detection, consideration also needs to be given to what was happening before and after the commission of the offence and to identify their relevant timeframes for investigation.

The elements of the commission of the crime from the criminal's perspective should be assessed and considered from a temporal perspective. Before the offence, it is likely that some degree of planning will have been involved unless its commission was truly random.

Even in cases where the commission of the offence was apparently random, there will still have been some pre-offence activity by the offender which placed them at the scene. These provide investigative opportunities and they are relevant timeframes even though they are not within the timeframe for committing the offence.

For crimes that are not random, the preparation by the offender(s) will include elements such as travelling to the scene along with obtaining any means they intend to use to commit the crime, for example:

- tools
- weapons
- incapacitants such as cable ties and rope
- clothing, balaclavas, masks and disguises
- stolen vehicles for transport
- mobile phones acquired specifically to commit the crime

These examples are illustrative only, and there could be many others depending on the modus operandi (MO) of the offence.

The offender(s) activity before the commission of a crime will be outside the time parameters within which the offence was committed but it is nonetheless relevant and can present many potential investigative opportunities.

Establishing the relevant investigative timeframe for before the offence can be difficult to establish. This involves working backwards from the commission of the offence to identify any tangible points in time where there was criminal preparatory activity.

The first stage is to gather and analyse the investigative material gathered during the initial phase of the investigation. This could include, for example, witness accounts,

CCTV, items discarded or left behind by an offender, other passive data sources, information and intelligence.

The objective is to develop hypotheses in relation to the potential linked criminal activity before the primary offence was committed. It is important to be thorough and apply an investigative mindset. This process is known as developing a 'crime script' or crime script analysis.

It is likely that pre-offence and post-offence timeframes may have to be open ended unless a tangible cut off point can be established. Investigators should avoid selecting random times that are little more than guesses until there is an objective reason to establish any relevant time parameters. Any times should be considered to be provisional until they are accurately established with confirmation if this is available.

To some extent, establishing an element of a pre-offence timeframe might be reasonably straightforward in some cases. For example, if a stolen vehicle was used in the commission of the primary offence there will be a relevant timeframe between the taking of the vehicle and the commission of the primary offence.

A line of enquiry linked to this would therefore be to establish where the vehicle had been between the time it was taken and the commission of the primary offence. This would be a relevant investigative timeframe in its own right within which to conduct further enquiries.

The challenge for investigators' decision making in these circumstances is that following on from this, further consideration should be given to any preparatory criminal activity involved with taking the vehicle. This could then be designated as another relevant timeframe within which to conduct enquiries, and so on. The decision which needs to be taken is to what extent such time parameters need to be extended.

The pre-offence relevant timeframe can be more difficult to establish in the early part of the investigation in cases where there is little or no tangible investigative material to consider. For example, if weapons are used it is unlikely to be obvious at this stage where they originated from.

Potentially, any weapons could have been routinely kept in the offender's possession for a long time and be owned legitimately, such as a kitchen knife. Alternatively, they could have been stolen to commit the offence or perhaps purchased specifically to commit the crime. Each of these are reasonable hypotheses for further investigation but the timeframe is unlikely to be known initially.

The potential for criminals conducting reconnaissance of potential targets should not be overlooked when considering timeframes. This could include reconnaissance to identify a target person or premises, having identified a target to establish routines and behaviours to identify the optimum time to strike. This is highly relevant when considering targeted robbery such as cash in transit and deliveries or collections from premises.

For this reason, care should be taken when conducting enquiries at premises in the vicinity including CCTV recovery. There is clear potential for investigative opportunities to be overlooked if they are confined to considering only the timeframe for the commission of the offence.

Similar considerations should be given to the offenders' actions after the offence was committed. Using the stolen vehicle analogy again, a line of enquiry would be to establish where it has been between the commission of the primary offence and its recovery (if it is recovered). Again, this is a relevant post-offence timeframe within which to identify and pursue the investigative opportunities that may be available.

Like the relevant timeframe for pre-offence criminal preparatory activity, there will also be a post-offence timeframe to identify. This could include disposal of items used in the commission of the offence or the disposal or selling of stolen property. Where large amounts of cash were acquired by the offenders, the spending activity of any possible suspects should be considered.

7.3 House-to-House Enquiries

For major investigations SIOs may initiate a fully managed house-to-house (H2H) strategy. This is resource intensive and is unlikely to be proportionate for mainstream investigations. However, the principles of a fully managed H2H project are included in this section as they provide some useful considerations that can be adapted and implemented for more scaled down investigations.

H2H enquiries can be a useful tactic to support investigations and they do not necessarily have to be resource intensive. A small number of investigators and even a single officer can conduct effective enquiries in this manner provided they have a methodical approach.

The main reasons for conducting H2H enquiries are to identify suspects and witnesses, gather investigative material and seek information. With developments in technology and its wider availability there is an opportunity to locate and recover audio visual recordings from private CCTV systems and doorbell and vehicle cameras etc.

Conducting H2H also provides an opportunity to provide public reassurance offer general safety and crime prevention advice. This section provides an overview of how to develop and implement a full H2H strategy. Further guidance is provided in the *Major Crime Investigation Manual* (NPCC 2021).

7.3.1 Developing an H2H strategy

An effective, fully managed H2H strategy requires a methodical approach, including using a H2H coordinator to develop and implement the plan. Clear objectives are required including consideration of:

- identifying and stipulating the geographical parameters of the area to be canvassed
- preparing specific questions and subjects to be covered relevant to the investigation (questionnaires)

- completing documentation, such as questionnaires, Personal Descriptive Forms (PDFs) and occupancy forms
- timing of the enquiries
- resources required
- fast track information seeking
- 'no reply' and/or 'not at home' policies for revisits and follow-up enquiries so that no occupants are missed

Regardless of the scale of any H2H enquiries to be conducted, these points can be considered and adapted.

7.3.2 Location parameters

To ensure effective H2H enquiries are conducted in the investigations most relevant locations, the geographical parameters should be identified and recorded. Regardless of the type of investigation, it is best practice for the investigator to visit the scene and the surrounding area. This is necessary to identify and set the appropriate boundaries and objectives rather than relying on maps.

Images and maps from sources such as Google Earth are useful to quickly gain an initial impression of the location and the surrounding area, but they might not contain all the relevant detail; they are unlikely to accurately establish which premises are multi-occupancy buildings and are only a record of when the image was taken.

If such material is used in the absence of a scene visit it must be retained and revealed for disclosure purposes. This is even more significant if notes have been made or the image has been otherwise annotated, such as marking the geographical parameters of the H2H enquiries.

Walking the area and making careful observations is best practice. This is necessary to establish all the streets and premises of interest, including those that are not easy to identify by using plans or images, for example Number 14A, the small flat around the back of a house.

Walking the area is also the only way to identify relevant locations and objectives that cannot possibly be identified remotely. Examples include builders' skips and wheelie bins, which could be used by offenders to discard property or items connected to the crime. Similarly, apparently abandoned vehicles in the area that could also be connected will not appear on a map.

When setting location parameters, it is useful to use natural boundaries to create zones, such as streets, paths, rivers, railway lines and major roads.

7.3.3 Identifying suspects

When a suspect (or witness) is believed to live, work in or visit a particular area, H2H enquiries can be used to try to establish the identity and description of all such persons connected to the relevant geographical parameters.

If required in a major investigation, accounts might be obtained on all movements linked to the investigation's relevant time parameters. H2H enquiries are the only sure method of establishing this level of detail because no single source, such as voters records or other online databases, will contain all the required information. Any accounts of a person's movements should be verified against other sources. This is a process known as 'H2H verification' and might be conducted by a separate team of investigators allocated to complete the task.

This technique is particularly important in major investigations when an elimination project may be initiated or considered to identify a suspect, for example intelligence-led mass screening for DNA or fingerprints.

This could assist to identify and locate potential witnesses with relevant information, including investigative material such as dashboard camera footage. Such material and information might otherwise be lost if the person was not seen during an initial canvassing of the area.

It is self-evident that such a large-scale project is unfeasible for mainstream lesser-scale investigations, however the principle of establishing the identity of relevant people living in or frequenting the area close to a crime scene is potentially viable and achievable on a smaller scale if it assists the investigation.

7.3.4 Identifying witnesses

H2H can potentially identify witnesses to events (and sometimes additional victims) relevant to the investigation, such as:

- witnesses to the actual crime or event
- events connected to an incident such as the encounter, attack or disposal site
- sightings or information about a victim or offender before or after the event
- sightings or information regarding relevant items or vehicles
- sightings or information about potential witnesses (including identifying previously reported unidentified nominals)

In a fully managed H2H project the relevant information is obtained using questionnaires, which should be suitable for the circumstances of the incident under investigation. It may be necessary to produce a bespoke questionnaire so that questions asked during the H2H enquiries are relevant and consistent.

Closed questions with 'yes' or 'no' answers should be avoided. For example, the answer to the question, 'Do you own a white van?' might correctly be 'No', but the person might have access to someone else's vehicle. Open ended or closed specific questions are preferable rather than forced choice yest/no answers. Obtaining the support of an Interview Adviser to assist with formulating questionnaires is recommended.

In addition to questionnaires, another form used to support H2H enquiries is the Personal Descriptive Form (PDF). This is used to obtain comprehensive descriptive information from the person being spoken to. The completion of a PDF requires observation and attention to detail by the officer completing it. Information sought should never be guessed when completing a PDF as it is used for verification and cross-referencing with other material. The descriptive information obtained is used to potentially identify people who are relevant to the investigation whose descriptions are known but so far remain unidentified.

In a fully managed H2H project, when a decision is made to use the PDF by the SIO or the lead investigator, the type of occupants from whom they are to be obtained should be considered and be the subject of a decision log entry. For example, 'PDFs are to be obtained from all male occupants 10 years old and over'. The PDF descriptive parameters are a decision based on the requirements of the investigation.

7.3.5 General considerations for H2H enquiries

In major investigations it is usual for both suspect and witness H2H enquiries to be conducted simultaneously. This assists with not alerting potential suspects who may live in the area, and H2H can also be used to reassure the public and provide crime prevention and personal safety advice. This may include engaging with the local Neighbourhood Policing Team to assist with the H2H enquiries and/or community leaders to reassure residents.

Identifying and recovering CCTV footage (public and private), including doorbell cameras, dashcam and vehicle cameras and any relevant mobile phone recordings should be considered in conjunction with the H2H enquiries. This avoids duplication of effort and ensures any relevant footage is identified, preserved and recovered before it might otherwise be recoded over.

Care should be taken about using the phrase 'suspicious', because a person may have seen something they did not consider suspicious and not report it, but it could nevertheless be relevant to the investigation. If using a term such as 'suspicious', such as 'did you see anything suspicious/of interest/out of the ordinary/unusual?', define what is meant by 'suspicious' or 'of interest' etc. Avoid using two questions in the same sentence to ensure that the answers cannot be misunderstood.

Ensure ALL occupants/visitors during relevant dates/times are accounted for.

It is important that any information imparted by investigators during H2H enquiries is consistent from all officers and is also consistent with any information that has been or is intended to be released to the media.

Support options to consider when formulating an H2H strategy in complex investigations or locations could include:

- interview advisers to formulate questionnaires
- geographical profilers to assist with determining location parameters
- community leaders regarding language and cultural issues

Leaflet drops and using social media can also be effective methods of covering a large area to request public assistance. These leaflet or communications must include contact details for the investigation should a member of the public respond to the request, and could be multilingual depending on the demographics of the area.

7.3.6 **Fast track H2H**

For all levels of investigation, it could be productive to conduct fast track H2H enquiries at premises *within line of sight and/or hearing* of a particular location during the golden hour(s) period. These should not be confused with fully managed H2H enquiries and are more akin to information seeking. These are best supported by subsequent H2H enquiries if required to the extent that resources dictate is feasible.

An effective method of establishing what could be accomplished during fast track H2H is to concentrate on areas where an offender may have been and consider the following LEASH locations:

L — lain in wait
E — egress routes
A — access routes
S — line of sight
H — line of hearing

And LEAVERS for full H2H:

L — last sighting of victim
E — encounter site
A — attack site
V — victim frequented locations
E — evidence and dump sites
R — routes to and from any of the above
S — sites and proximities to witnesses

7.3.7 'No Reply' policy

At some premises there will inevitably be no response, so a consistent policy needs to be decided upon to manage this issue There are various options available, ranging from repeat visits (if so, how many and at what times of day and by whom?) or contact by other means such as by telephone or leaflet drop/calling card.

While there may be resource and time implications for making revisits, this is generally the best option as some might not appreciate that they have seen something significant. Such information may prove relevant to the enquiry.

Checklist—H2H enquiries

- When setting location parameters 'walk the route' to ensure all premises have been properly identified
- Questions should be worded carefully and avoid unproductive and multiple questions

- Use correct documentation, such as formal questionnaires, PDF, and house/premises occupancy forms which would be mandatory in major investigations
- Checks and requests for passive data such as CCTV, doorbell and dashboard cameras should be incorporated into H2H enquiries
- Have a 'no reply' policy for repeat visits, such as enquiries with neighbours or a letterbox drop

7.4 CCTV/Audio Visual (AV) Strategy

The recovery and analysis of CCTV/AV material is a routine line of enquiry in many investigations. Developing an AV strategy should contain specific objectives for the target of the strategy such as to:

- obtain a recording of the offence or incident
- identify specific people (witnesses or suspects) at the scene of the crime or other relevant location
- establish the actions of specific individuals (identified and unidentified) during the commission of the offence or the incident
- establish the movements of specific individuals (identified and unidentified) before the offence/incident, including their route to the location
- identify associations between relevant individuals before the offence/incident
- identify associations between relevant individuals after the offence/incident
- link people to locations (victim(s), suspect(s), witnesses, TIE subject(s), missing persons)
- establish the movements of specific individuals (identified and unidentified) after the offence/incident, including their route from the location
- identify any unidentified vehicles that are relevant to the investigation

- establish the movements of specific vehicles (identified and unidentified) before the offence/incident, including their route to the location
- establish the movements of specific vehicles (identified and unidentified) after the offence/incident, including their route away from the location

An effective AV strategy has three main elements:

1. Identify the locations of relevant AV material
2. Recovering AV material
3. Objectives for viewing the AV material

Geographical and time parameters relevant to the investigation need to be considered and set. The more specific elements of the strategy could then include suggestions such as:

- premises and areas to be checked for CCTV systems and doorbell cameras, including private residences, public and business premises
- the method of enquiry, for example a visual check or some form of H2H type enquiries to identify any hidden systems
- identification of bus routes and timings for possible onboard recordings to link to crime script analysis, including potential offenders travelling to and from a scene or other location
- method of recovery, including making a record of times and dates displayed on the recording system for accuracy against the speaking clock before removing the data
- enquiring if a maintenance policy exists for checking when the time was last reset
- noting camera angles, numbers, position, type of recording equipment (time-lapse or continuous), and locations captured in the image with the surrounding terrain to identify blind spots
- completing CCTV recovery forms and schedules, outlining precise locations and details of all systems and data recovered

- completing CCTV viewing records including the objectives of the viewing, the methodology employed and the circumstances of any recognition made of people, vehicles and other activity captured on the recording

KEY POINTS

- Not all CCTV is of reliable quality due to poor images or equipment. Dates and times and the integrity of captured material needs to be checked for accuracy before being relied upon. The investigative mindset is applicable once more.
- Public appeals for private CCTV systems within a defined area can be made as part of a communication/media strategy, together with requests for personal recordings such as that captured on mobile phones, helmet cameras and vehicle dashboard cameras
- Setting parameters and fast track actions for the early retrieval of CCTV are essential. Systems are generally used continuously and record over old material, sometimes on a 24-hour loop.
- If important CCTV cannot be recovered quickly enough, finding a way of recording it with another device (such as a smart phone camera) as secondary evidence might be a less optimum last resort option if the material will be deleted anyway.

7.5 **Conducting Searches**

Searching premises is a routine activity for warranted and non-warranted investigators. This section provides general practical guidance on the application process, planning and executing search warrants.

Section 18 and 32 PACE searches are routinely conducted after arrests for indictable offences, but intelligence may also identify premises where criminal activity is suspected prior to the arrest phase. Search warrants are applied for under various Acts of Parliament, but there are three general types, allowing some flexibility when planning a search:

1. A 'specific premises warrant' to enter one premises on one occasion.
2. An 'all premises warrant' to enter more than one premises, such as where it is suspected there is evidence of an offence or a wanted person at more than one location.
3. A 'multiple entry warrant' allowing entry to premises (or more than one premises) on more than one occasion, for example where it is suspected a significant amount of material may be found which will take multiple visits to recover.

7.5.1 Search warrant application process

The grounds to apply for search warrants often rely on information provided by third parties including covert human intelligence sources (CHIS). Reasonable steps must be taken to check this information is accurate; an application may not be made based on anonymous information unless corroboration has been sought from elsewhere.

An Inspector or above must provide written authority before an application to the magistrates' court is made. In urgent cases where they are not readily available the senior officer on duty may authorise the application.

Different provisions apply to applications under the Terrorism Act 2000, which are made to a judge and require the authority of a Superintendent or above.

When making an application there is no requirement to disclose the identity of any CHIS, but care should be taken when drafting the documentation to ensure a covert source is not compromised. Occupiers of premises are entitled to a copy of the warrant, and supporting documentation is subject to disclosure rules under the Criminal Procedure and Investigations Act 1996 (CPIA).

Applications are made in person to the magistrate's court, but in urgent cases out-of-hours applications to a magistrate (often at their home address) may be made. Whatever the circumstances, the constable must be in possession of the written authority for the application.

Applicants will be required to state on oath and can be questioned on:

- the grounds for the application
- the enactment under which the warrant would be issued
- if the application is for a 'multiple entry warrant', the reason why this is necessary and whether an unlimited number of entries are required or whether a maximum number is desired
- the identity of the premises, including the grounds for making an 'all premises' application if this is relevant
- in so far as is practical, the articles or persons that are sought
- the identity of the person occupying or in control of the premises; reasonable enquiries must be made to establish if anything is known about them
- the nature of the premises, including whether they have been searched previously, and if so, how recently

A search warrant is valid for three months, but if refused no further application can be made unless additional grounds are found.

A warrant to enter and search may be executed by any constable, but non-warranted investigators (with powers under Part 4 of the Police Reform Act 2002) must be in the company of, and under the supervision of a constable. An Inspector or above may direct a designated Investigating Officer not to wear a uniform for a specific operation.

7.5.2 Planning the search

Many searches are straightforward, but others require detailed planning and more complex risk assessment, particularly if dealing with a specialist method of entry to mitigate violent occupants who could possibly be armed, dangerous animals, or if the search has community impact issues necessitating management of the consequences.

7.5.3 Before the search

- PACE requires an officer to be designated as being in charge of the search (OIC); they may be a supervisor or the most senior officer present but can be delegated to a lower rank more conversant with the case and the requirements of the search if this is more appropriate.
- The OIC should consult the local police/Community Liaison Officer if there is reason to believe the search may have an adverse impact on the community. In urgent cases consultation can be as soon as practicable after the search.
- Identify the specific objectives of the search, including items sought based on the requirements of the investigation and intelligence.
- Conduct intelligence checks on the occupier, the premises, the location of the search and any associated persons to identify any risk factors and possible links to other offences, including any outstanding stolen property/other evidence.
- Identify measures to mitigate any risks.
- Brief others involved in the search, including:
    - o powers to be exercised
    - o items being searched for (with descriptions); consider also the Proceeds of Crime Act 2002 (POCA) and possible other linked offences where property may be seized if lawfully on premises
    - o individual responsibilities of the search team
    - o details of Exhibits Officer (EO)
    - o extent and limits of the search
    - o specialist resources, such as using a Digital Media Investigator, Police Search Adviser (PolSA) and Police Search Team (PST) and drugs/firearms dogs
    - o identified warnings/risks and mitigation measures
    - o It is good practice to sequentially number any briefing documents and ensure they are returned

after the briefing, as there have been occasions when briefing materials have been left at the subject premises

- Obtain any necessary equipment (this is not an exhaustive list):
  - o keys from a detainee's property to gain entry
  - o method of entry tools
  - o exhibit bags and packaging of assorted sizes
  - o exhibit labels
  - o ladders/steps
  - o torch/lighting/search equipment
  - o exhibits register
- Inform the control room/communications centre of the location and timing of the search in case urgent assistance is required
- Consider CSI attending to photograph items in position, assist with any forensic recovery and visually record the conduct of the search, including any damage caused (or not caused)
- Consider a Digital Media Investigator attending to advise on and assist with the recovery of any digital devices. If one is not available seek advice in advance or remotely
- Obtain the next consecutive number from the premises searched register

7.5.4 Conducting the search

- Searches should be made at a reasonable hour unless this would frustrate the purpose of the search; departure from this rarely causes difficulty with justification but should be documented. The number of officers involved in the search should be determined by what is reasonable and necessary in the circumstances.
- Reasonable and proportionate force may be used if necessary to gain entry where entry is refused, it is impossible to communicate with a person entitled to grant access or alerting them would frustrate the object of the search or endanger others.

- The OIC should first try to communicate with the occupier or person entitled to grant entry unless they are not present, the premises are unoccupied or alerting them would frustrate the objects of the search or endanger others (including the search team).
- The OIC should identify themselves and accompanying officers, producing identification if not in uniform and state the purpose and grounds of the search.
- The extent of the search is dictated by the offence under investigation and what is sought. If the extent or complexity of the search indicates it is likely to take some time, including the volume of material to be examined, the OIC may consider using seize and sift powers.
- Anything may be seized where there are reasonable grounds for believing it is evidence or has been obtained by or through the commission of an offence if it is necessary to prevent the items being concealed, lost, disposed of, altered, damaged, destroyed or tampered with. No item can be seized if it is believed to be subject of legal privilege.
- Premises may be searched only to the extent necessary to achieve the purpose having regard to the size and nature of things sought. A search may not continue once the objective of the search has been achieved or once the OIC is satisfied that whatever is sought is not on the premises.
- A friend, neighbour or other person must be allowed to witness the search if the occupier wishes, unless the OIC reasonably believes their presence would seriously hinder the investigation or endanger other people. A search need not be unreasonably delayed for this purpose.
- Searches also provide opportunities to speak with any people on the premises, any visitors and neighbours to gain information that might be useful to the enquiry.

7.5.5 After the search

- The occupier shall be supplied with a copy of the search warrant and Notice of Powers and Rights unless this is impractical. If they are not present the documents should be endorsed and left in a prominent place.

- If the premises have been entered by force, the OIC must ensure they are secured by arranging for the occupier or their agent to be present or any other appropriate means, but do not enter into discussions regarding compensation for damage.
- On arrival at the police station the officer in charge of the search shall make or have a record made of the search in the search register maintained at each subdivision or equivalent, including:
  - o address searched
  - o date, time and duration of the search
  - o authority used for the search
  - o name of the officer in charge of the search
  - o names of all other officers involved in the search
  - o names of any people on the premises
  - o grounds for refusing an occupier's request to have someone present during the search
  - o list of articles seized
  - o grounds for seizure
  - o whether force was used and the reason
  - o details of any damage caused and the circumstances
  - o location of the Notice of Powers and Rights, including who it was given to
- o Debrief the search, including:
  - o the result of the search and items seized (if any) and who by
  - o the location of seized items
  - o identifying wider investigative or evidential material
  - o identifying stolen property for identification
  - o identifying items for forensic examination and development
  - o checking the continuity of all items has been maintained and properly documented
  - o identifying material for suspect interview, including any special warning material
  - o securely secure material in accordance with local procedures

KEY POINT

Some evidential items may need attributing to individuals to avoid potential defences of lack of connection, knowledge or contact. It is important to evidentially link suspects not only to the premises but also to the items and the places they were found, for example by evidencing the presence of other personal items or belongings located nearby.

7.5.6 Seize and sift

Sections 50 and 51 of the Criminal Justice and Police Act 2001 allow for the seizure and removal of property found on premises or on a person where it is not reasonably practicable to complete a process of examination, searching or separation at the scene.

Section 52 includes a legal obligation to provide a written notice to the person from whom the property was seized; this includes a description of what has been taken and an application for any person with an interest in the property to attend the examination. All reasonable steps must be attempted to accommodate them subject to the need to prevent harm to, interference with or unreasonable delay to the investigation.

Although not specifically written into the Act when it was drafted, what is often overlooked is that seize and sift also applies to computer, tablet and wi-fi equipment examination and latterly to other digital storage devices and mobile phones, which in many cases now are basically small mobile computers. These will probably contain material not connected with the offence under investigation so serving a section 52 notice on the person from whom it was seized should be considered.

KEY POINTS

- An example of seize and sift might be where a large number of documents are recovered and it is impractical to examine them at the location of the search, or where a computer is seized for subsequent specialist examination.

- Officers must be careful only to exercise seize and sift powers if it is essential and not to remove any more material than is necessary. Removal of large amounts of material, particularly if it is obviously not relevant to the investigation may have serious implications for the owners, especially if it concerns their business activity.

7.6 **Passive Data Generators**

The broad term 'passive data' covers all *automated* systems which gather and collate information. This *automated* passive data material is not necessarily produced for the purpose of investigation. It is produced for various commercial and proprietary reasons but the data that it generates has potential investigative and evidential value. This includes recovering, evaluating and analysing automated data from, for example:

- CCTV systems (not monitored)
- billing systems
- voice recording systems
- access/entry systems
- customer information, such as subscriber details, fuel and loyalty cards.
- ANPR (Automatic Number Plate Recognition)
- satellite navigation systems
- speed camera systems
- images and data, such as recorded on digital cameras and/or mobile smart phones and tablets
- electronic (offender) tagging systems

These systems can generate large amounts of data which is periodically downloaded, archived or deleted. It is therefore important to recover any material while it is still available and, if it is to be used in evidence, demonstrate how the material was generated and prove its integrity and accuracy. The data generated can assist investigations with general or specific material. The disclosure implications of processing large volumes of data of this type require considering at the outset.

From an investigative perspective it is necessary to formulate specific objectives for the recovery. These could include, for example, placing a suspect at an identified location and potentially performing an activity related to the investigation. Establishing relevant time parameters for the recovery and analysis of passive data is important due to the volume of data that will be recovered.

Any requests will need to be justified and be for a specific investigative objective and not be merely speculative. Passive data contains personal information and the wider the recovery parameters involved are set, the greater the collateral intrusion involved. The product and personal data from passive data needs careful management and handling.

As always, the decisions taken should be properly recorded along with the justification and any relevant considerations.

7.6.1 General investigative material

This includes material from systems such as CCTV and ANPR which can be used to locate, gather and view images to identify relevant people (witnesses or suspects) and vehicles.

7.6.2 Specific material

Specific material is material sought to achieve specified investigative objectives such as:

- identifying the presence and activities of victims, witnesses, suspects or vehicles at particular locations and the times they were there

- relationships, associations and contact between individuals
- dates and times of contact between individuals
- lifestyles of individuals
- routes taken and directions of travel

A Passive Data Strategy should consider the:

- objectives to be achieved
- what value the material will add to the investigation and a potential prosecution
- legalities of access (Data Protection Act, RIPA and PACE)
- proportionality of the request
- volume of data to be obtained
- use to be made of the material
- format of material produced
- length of time needed to find, collect and view
- resources required to process the material including human, technological, analytical and financial
- storage and preventing unauthorised access
- arrangements for maintaining the integrity and continuity of material
- fulfilling the disclosure obligations concerning the material

7.7 Digital Media Investigation and Communications Data

The technological advances in what is now a digital age provides many investigative opportunities that were previously unavailable. Most people in their everyday lives leave some form of digital footprint which can be used to:

- identify offences committed
- identify suspects, witnesses, victims, missing persons
- analyse what is being discussed about incidents and crimes
- prove association with others

- establish travel patterns and links to places and premises
- provide historical and live location data on a person's movements
- establish use of services and amenities
- identify motives including planning offences and researching defences
- obtain lifestyle intelligence and 'victimology'

This list is by no means exhaustive, and it is routine to recover and analyse digital data from many everyday devices including:

- mobile phones (smart phones) with applications that record location data
- computers
- netbooks
- tablets
- online gaming devices, such as PlayStation and X-Box
- wireless routers that connect to and record connections to phones, computers and other Bluetooth devices
- MiFi
- data storage devices (some of which are very small in size)
- satellite navigation systems
- internet-enabled televisions
- digital assistants such as Alexa and Siri

Data that is likely to be recovered includes:

- internet history logs
- links between devices (a digital 'handshake')
- emails
- instant messaging logs
- media files
- text documents
- spreadsheets
- video/still images
- image location metadata
- text messages
- location of use data

This list is not exhaustive and rapid technological advances inevitably mean a chapter such as this may soon be out of date. This type of digital information and evidence must be considered in most, if not all, investigations, including during searching of persons, premises and vehicles.

In all cases it is important to remember that digital material and evidence is subject to the same rules and laws that apply to documentary material and evidence. The onus is on the prosecution to show to the court that the evidence produced is no more and no less than when it was first recovered.

Any digital media, communications data and social media strategy should ensure that any action taken by law enforcement agencies or their agents should not change the data held on a digital media device which may subsequently be relied upon in court.

In circumstances where a person finds it necessary to access original data held on a computer or on a storage media, that person must be competent to do so. They must be able to give evidence explaining the relevance of their actions and the implications.

An audit trail or other record of all the processes applied must be created and preserved. An independent third party should be able to examine those processes and replicate the results of the examination using the same techniques.

The person in charge of the investigation (the case officer) has overall responsibility for ensuring that the law and these principles are adhered to.

7.8 Financial Investigation

Financial investigation is not just directed at offences with obvious links to money and assets. Neither is it a tool just to recover criminal assets during investigations. Financial investigation can provide intelligence and evidence to exploit for all types of investigation.

Virtually everyone in the UK leaves some kind of financial footprint in their daily life, which is increasing as the use of cash diminishes. Such sources can be followed to:

- identify offences committed (including money laundering)
- locate and/or identify suspects, witnesses, victims, missing persons
- prove association with others and/or links to places and premises
- provide information around a person's location and movements
- establish use of services such as phones, transport and other amenities
- identify motives
- identify a person's lifestyle

Financial data may indicate motive, such as personal gain, debt or perhaps domestic abuse linked to financial stress. Productive lines of enquiry can be developed by identifying a credit card used to top up a mobile phone or examining till receipts in retail premises, or the use of automatic telling machines (ATMs) to see who was at or near a crime scene (as suspect or witness).

A 'financial footprint' may put people in the same place together, such as a victim and offender in the same premises or other location, plus any third parties who may be witnesses. This financial intelligence can be cross-referenced with CCTV and other location data from the specific location and wider area to identify individuals and develop further lines of enquiry.

Searches of premises or vehicles should include checks for financial information that may help build a picture of a person's lifestyle or generate additional lines of enquiry such as identifying sudden or unusual withdrawals and deposits into or out of a bank account.

There is a vast amount of information available in the financial world, but investigators must have clear objectives when seeking it which are appropriate and beneficial to the enquiry. Vague and non-specific requests, such as 'obtain a financial profile', are not practical or advisable.

Accredited Financial Investigators (AFI under the POCA 2002) are permitted to make pre-order enquiries to financial institutions under the Tournier Rules (*Tournier v National Provincial and Union Bank of England* [1924] 1 KB 461). These permit disclosure of information to law enforcement agencies that would otherwise be a breach of contract between the institution and their customers. Financial data may therefore be disclosed in the following circumstances:

- to protect the public
- to protect the institution's own interests
- under compulsion by law
- with the consent of the owner

This material is gathered by AFIs and is supplied for intelligence purposes only; if it is to be adduced into the evidential chain (including questioning during interview) a production order is required, hence the term 'pre-order enquiries'.

7.9 **Intelligence**

Intelligence is information concerning people, incidents, events, locations, etc that has been subjected to a system of processing in which it has been evaluated against other material, including data and background knowledge. Intelligence is used to predict what might happen in the future and to assist directing and prioritising the use of resources to their best effect and managing risk. From a crime investigators perspective, the conversion of intelligence into evidence that is admissible in a court of law is an important decision-making factor.

The collection and management of intelligence is comprehensively covered in the relevant 'Authorised Professional Practice' (College of Policing 2021) and only the key points are outlined here with some additions. Regardless of the seriousness of the crime involved, most investigations require information and intelligence to be generated, evaluated and analysed to identify and fill any investigative and evidential gaps and to inform their decision making. Intelligence generated may also be relevant to other hitherto unconnected investigations.

For most crime investigations the intelligence strategy is derived from the National Intelligence Model (NIM). This was developed in 1992 and adopted by all police forces as a commonly accepted standard by 2004. Its implementation is subject to a statutory code of practice that came into effect on 12 January 2005.

The NIM is a structured framework through which information is processed to generate intelligence that can be acted on to set strategic direction, make decisions about priorities, allocate resources, develop tactical plans and task and coordinate activity.

The NIM process has subsequently been adopted by other investigative agencies wider than the police and is in common use in Crime and Disorder Reduction Partnerships (CDRP). Whatever their location and area of activity, investigators are likely to find themselves working in accordance with priorities that have been through an NIM type process to meet their force or organisational priorities. The NIM works at three levels:

- Level 1: Local/Basic Command Unit level for volume crime and local problems
- Level 2: Regional or force level which involves neighbouring forces and more than one basic command unit
- Level 3: Serious and organised crime which is on a national and international scale

7.9.1 Internet intelligence sources

Many sources of information are readily available, including Open Source Research of the Internet (OSRI). These 'open' sources are accessible to anyone using internet search engines, including law enforcement agencies. Generally, no prior authorisation is needed, but depending on the circumstances (and potential breaches of privacy), prior authorisation under the Regulation of Investigatory Powers Act 2000 (RIPA 2000) might be required.

Accessing such resources, including using specialist researchers, therefore depends on the complexity of the investigation and the necessity and proportionality of exploiting the activity used. Local policies need to be adhered to, including only using computers that are not on a police network to conduct targeted OSRI research. This is to prevent the subjects of the research potentially becoming aware of police activity by identifying the researcher's computer IP address.

Open internet sources, which are also known as 'surface web' activities, includes anything that is publicly available using standard internet search engines such as Google, MS Edge and Bing. This represents only a small proportion of available internet information.

The next level is known as the 'deep web', which is below the surface and regarded as the largest portion of the internet. Deep web sources are often corporate, governmental, financial, educational, organisational and other industry networks. These require allocation of a bespoke password and individual account subscriptions for a user to be allowed access. They are not publicly accessible through a search engine but typically an organisation will have a public facing web presence.

Further below this is the 'dark net' in which dark websites reside which are inaccessible using standard search engines and browsers. Accessing these sites requires a special web browser known as The Onion Router (TOR), named because of its complex routing connectivity using multiple servers.

KEY POINT

Open source information may not be accurate and should not be automatically accepted as reliable. Care must be taken to corroborate the accuracy of such information when considering basing action on it.

7.9.2 Intelligence evaluation

All intelligence must be evaluated by the officer submitting it to assess reliability before being recorded in intelligence systems. It is important that personal feelings do not influence any evaluation, which should always be based on professional judgement and not exaggerated so that action is taken in respect of the information.

Investigators are responsible for evaluating any intelligence they submit, ensuring it is an accurate and unbiased evaluation based on their knowledge of the prevailing circumstances existing at the time. The 3 × 5 × 2 system should be used for evaluation, and it should be remembered that intelligence is subject to the disclosure rules under CPIA.

7.10 Analytical Support

A trained analyst can assess and interpret the intelligence collected during an investigation. They can identify information gaps, draw inferences and identify any material requiring further corroboration. This process assists with developing an intelligence strategy and enables continual review of the progress of the investigation including:

- assessing the progress of lines of enquiry

- identifying new lines of enquiry
- identifying specific elements of an enquiry which could be developed further

Analysts are a scarce resource and obtaining their services is usually difficult except for major inquiries and the most complex serious investigations. Out of necessity this can be mitigated to a significant extent by investigators applying an investigative mindset to the material gathered by the investigation and understanding its investigative and evidential context.

7.10.1 Standard analytical products

To task an analyst effectively (if one can be obtained), a basic understanding of their techniques and the analytical products that could be produced is required. These products depend on the initial tasking of the analyst and use standardised analytical techniques. These are not unique to the police; they are used by organisations and industries to support their business objectives. Some of the techniques are described in the NIM and the College of Policing Analysis APP including:

- crime pattern analysis (CPA) to identify the nature and scale of an emerging trend or current issue such as:
    - o hotspot identification
    - o crime/incident trend identification
    - o common characteristics of offenders/offending behaviour
    - o crime/incident series identification
- demographic/social trends analysis, which examines how demographic and social changes in an area or demographic group affect levels of crime/disorder
- comparative case analysis to identify whether similar crimes or incidents are part of a series which is likely to have been committed by one offender or a group of offenders. Likely links are made through similar modus

operandi, signature behaviour, intelligence or linked forensic material
- hypothesis testing and analysis of competing hypotheses to establish whether or not valid interpretations have been made
- network analysis, which provides an understanding of the nature and significance of links between people, locations, telephones, finances, etc
- market profiles, which aim to identify the criminal market around a commodity or service, for example drug distribution. It can provide an insight into the level of criminal activity, including the availability and price of the commodity or service
- criminal business analysis profiles, which help to develop an understanding of how a criminal activity or business operates. These explain the methods used and the flow of commodities, an understanding of the business structure and describes the roles and responsibilities in the business in the wider context of the market
- risk analysis, which is an assessment of threat and risk with the impact and probability of something occurring
- case/incident analysis, which examines an incident or a series of incidents to support the investigation of serious crime and it is often associated with major incidents
- operational Intelligence Assessment (OIA), which is a method of ensuring that the investigation remains focused on its original objectives. An OIA identifies if any departure from the agreed objective is occurring
- generating and evaluating scenarios to consider how a situation or area might look in the future after a given length of time. These assist in developing a range of plans should a situation change or develop
- results analysis, which evaluates the effectiveness of policing and partnership activity in relation to crime and disorder

Checklist—Intelligence strategy

- Consider internal and external intelligence sources and dissemination (Force Intelligence Bureau, other forces/agencies)
- Circulation bulletins
- Neighbourhood policing officers and community intelligence
- Analytical tools and products
- Research suspects, their history, family and associates
- Research victims, their history, family, associations and lifestyles, habits and routines (victimology)
- Research relevant locations including previous incidents
- Obtain intelligence from briefings and debriefings
- Source Management Units and use of CHIS
- Research intelligence systems and databases—PND/PNC/local intelligence systems/HOLMES/COMPACT/VISOR/NSPIS, custody records/QUEST/Niche
- Communications data and social media sites
- Covert tactics and resources are good sources of intelligence
- Information from other agencies

7.11 Elimination Enquiries, Trace/Investigate/Evaluate (TIE)

The use of elimination enquiries is a resource intensive activity that tends to be used in major investigations where a suspect has not been readily identified. The principles are included in this section for information, but they could be adapted to a much lesser extent for inquiries on a smaller scale if the circumstances were suitable. It is suggested that advice be sought from a suitable supervisor if this is contemplated.

The term trace, investigate and evaluate (TIE) is explained in detail within the Major Crime Investigation Manual and Major Incident Room Standardised Administrative Procedures (MIRSAP). This was previously referred to as 'trace, implicate and eliminate', but was revised to be consistent with the investigative mindset and reflect the objectivity of elimination as opposed to implication.

This is a strategy which identifies and investigates groups of people which could possibly include an offender, such as visitors to the scene of a crime within relevant time parameters. Subsequent enquiries into these groups can then eliminate those who cannot be the offender and allows investigators to focus enquiries on those who are potentially implicated.

TIE strategies can be resource intensive and must be carefully managed; if not carried out correctly, the process could wrongly eliminate an offender.

7.11.1 Constructing TIE categories

A TIE category is a group of people who share a common characteristic with the likely offender. The common characteristic will depend on the circumstances of the crime but could typically include:

- had access to the scene at the time of the offence
- resides in or is associated with a certain geographical area
- associated, linked or related to the victim
- previous convictions for a similar offence (usually referred to as 'modus operandi (MO) subjects')
- physical characteristics similar to the offender (where a description is available)
- access to certain types of vehicles
- named as being of interest
- registered sexual or dangerous offenders

This is not an exhaustive TIE category list, and it can include anyone at the investigator's discretion. The more that is known about the circumstances of the crime, the greater the prospect of constructing an accurate TIE category.

7.11.2 Populating TIE categories

Once a decision has been reached on which groups could include the offender, thought must be given to how many members of each group can be identified. Sometimes this is easily achieved with a certain degree of accuracy; for example, if the offence took place within a work place a check of company records identifying all employees would create a TIE category of those employed in the named premises. On other occasions it is more difficult, for example those visiting a public place within the relevant time. Useful ways of populating TIE categories are:

- using information generated by the investigation
- using official records (electoral rolls, membership lists, payrolls)
- police intelligence databases (PNC, PND, ViCLAS, etc)
- public appeals and witness information
- 'snowballing', where interviewing members of a TIE category leads to identifying other members of the group

7.11.3 Prioritising TIE categories

The number of subjects in a TIE category can sometimes be large, making it difficult to complete enquiries on all the listed nominals. A decision then needs to be made on how to prioritise the list. One method is to apply further filters, such as:

- geography, for example their proximity to the scene
- the date of last conviction for MO subjects
- age (where age of the offender is unknown, priority can be given to those who fall in the most likely age range for that type of offender)
- gender

7.11.4 TIE elimination criteria

The purpose of the TIE process is to eliminate people from a category. The criteria and level of elimination must therefore be determined. This includes forensic or fingerprint evidence, description, independent witness accounts or other material to verify an alibi.

A person eliminated or not eliminated from a TIE category is just that, and their potential elimination should be tested vigorously against all available material and revisited when new information comes to light. They have NOT necessarily been implicated or eliminated from being the offender.

Members of TIE categories may also be potential witnesses, and this should be considered when conducting TIE enquiries.

As a result of TIE enquiries, a member of a category may be elevated from being a 'subject' to being a 'suspect', but only when there are objective grounds or evidence for doing so, such as matching their DNA to the crime scene, or their alibi is proved to be false.

KEY POINTS

- Some forces have replaced or supplemented the term TIE with POI (meaning 'persons of interest'). This terminology has crept into the police environment and is often heard in television dramas, but it has no place in a TIE strategy.
- A person is a TIE 'subject' or, if the circumstances change, a witness or a suspect. The term 'person of interest' is none of these, so if it is used then an explanation needs to be recorded which establishes what is precisely meant by this term so that they can be investigated in the most appropriate manner. As an example, an explanation may be required for a court as to why a 'POI' was not afforded the recognised status as a witness or given their lawful rights under PACE as a suspect when they were interviewed.

7.11.5 Suspect parameters

These are the known characteristics of an offender or person suspected of committing the offence. They are used to implicate or eliminate persons/subjects from within a TIE category including:

- sex
- age
- physical characteristics
- fingerprints
- material for forensic comparison such as DNA and fingerprints
- ownership or wearing of particular clothing for forensic comparison, such as footwear marks and fibres
- ownership or use of vehicles, including the make and colour for comparison with tyre marks and material left at or taken from the scene

The value of these characteristics varies. Knowing only the sex of an offender has limited value; but DNA or fingerprint evidence at a scene is likely to eliminate everyone except for the offender (unless there were multiple offenders and only one left trace evidence behind).

It is usually valuable and advised to set the elimination parameters a little wider than those suggested by the material gathered during the investigation. This allows for a degree of error in, for example, descriptions provided by witnesses or victims.

7.11.6 Elimination time parameters

Accurate time parameters are useful for eliminating subjects from a TIE category provided they are confirmed as accurate. When the exact time of an offence is unknown, the relevant time parameters should be based on the earliest and latest times that the offence could have been committed.

7.11.7 HOLMES elimination criteria

There is a tried and tested numerical coding system on the HOLMES database which provides a hierarchy of reliability for the elimination criteria when applied to subjects in a TIE category. This coding system can be considered and used when conducting TIE enquiries regardless of whether HOLMES is being utilised or not and is:

1. Forensic elimination: such as DNA, footwear, fingerprints
2. Description of suspect(s)
3. Independent alibi witness
4. Associate or relative (alibi)
5. Spouse or partner relationship (alibi)
6. Not eliminated

7.12 Victim Liaison

An important area of any investigation is liaising with the victim, family and community. Policing is heavily dependent on the consent and trust of the public. Investigators rely on the cooperation of people to report crimes and incidents, provide evidence or information, assist in the identification of offenders and act as a measure of local and national tensions resulting from criminal and policing activity.

Victims depend on the police to bring offenders to justice and to help them by arranging appropriate support. They may also need added support if they are required as a witness and provide evidence against defendants in court.

Having a point of contact for regular updates on the progress of the investigation is what victims need, in addition to a professional response and investigation of their crime. A poor service may have lasting negative affects when their assistance is required for something else at a later stage or another occasion. A lack of contact from the investigation and not receiving important updates is an often-expressed frustration from victims and witnesses.

Developing and maintaining trust and confidence in the police and the criminal justice system from victims, their relatives, close friends and local communities is important regardless of the outcome of any investigation. There are a number of agencies who also work to support victims of crime and are useful contacts for referral.

Checklist—Victim support groups

Victim Support	National charity which helps people affected by crime by providing free and confidential support <http://www.victimsupport.org.uk>
Suzy Lamplugh Trust	UK charity devoted to providing practical support and personal safety guidance <http://www.suzylamplugh.org>
Refuge	Charity that provides temporary and emergency accommodation for women and children escaping from domestic violence <http://www.refuge.org.uk>
NSPCC	National Society for the Prevention of Cruelty to Children <http://www.nspcc.org.uk>
The Samaritans	Provide confidential emotional support for people who are experiencing feelings of distress or despair <http://www.samaritans.org>
Criminal Justice System Online	Information about the Criminal Justice process for victims and witnesses <www.gov.uk/browse/justice>
Crown Prosecution Service	The CPS website contains useful information. <http://www.cps.gov.uk>

7.13 Community Impact and Public Reassurance

The potential impact that an investigation or a series of linked inquiries may have on a local community should be considered. Members of the public may be concerned or anxious by the seriousness of the offence whether this is real or perceived. Any increased police activity might cause disruption to normal life however minor, for example maintaining crime scene cordons or closing premises. What investigators might perceive to be a minor intrusion or inconvenience could be significant to a member of the public or the community in general.

It should not be forgotten that the public will be unaware of the circumstances of the investigation, including how long any disruption to normal life may last. This applies to all investigations and is not confined to major or serious incidents. Whilst working to achieve the aim of an inquiry, an objective for investigators should include facilitating a return to normality as soon as possible. This is especially important if there is any disruption to the normal pattern of life or the potential to raise community tension.

From an investigative perspective, communities are not confined just to people living in a particular geographical area. A community includes groups of people that share relevant characteristics that might be impacted. This could include, but is not solely confined to, the personal protected characteristics of groups according to race, gender, sexuality, religion or disability etc. A community for investigative consideration could also be defined as groups such as sex workers, business holders and people who frequent certain premises or areas who may be impacted by the crime or the investigation, these are just examples to illustrate.

Ultimately measures of success include:

- the conviction of those guilty of a crime or crimes
- establishing the confidence of the victim in the investigation
- establishing and maintaining the confidence and co-operation of affected communities in the investigation
- lowering of tensions within those connected to the investigation

- a return to normality for the community concerned

Levels of community involvement vary from case to case. Most often this is confined to family members, other relatives, close friends and associates or members of a specific community. However, in larger investigations this may increase to the wider community.

In more serious cases the police might conduct a Community Impact Assessment (CIA), the purpose of which is to consider and manage the impact of the incident, particularly on minority or vulnerable communities by:

- enhancing investigative effectiveness
- protecting vulnerable individuals and groups
- developing community intelligence
- promoting community confidence

Producing a CIA if one is required should be the responsibility of the local Neighbourhood Policing Team who are best placed to understand their local communities.

7.14 **Family Liaison Officers**

Deploying a Family Liaison Officer (FLO) is not restricted to homicide investigations, and an FLO strategy can be considered at the outset of any serious and complex investigation. The primary role of the FLO is as an investigator as well as providing support and information to families. They are likely to be invaluable for obtaining information and intelligence from the family and developing victimology.

Victims and/or their close family and friends are reliant on the officer in charge of the investigation (through the FLO) providing them with accurate and regular information. This is extremely important, otherwise they may listen to rumours and gossip, which may not be accurate. It is extremely important that the information flow is controlled by the officer in charge and therefore regular communication between them and the FLO is required. The FLO should not disclose any information to the family that has not been previously agreed.

Advice and support from a local Family Liaison Coordinator (FLC) should be sought to ensure the most suitably trained FLO is appointed to the enquiry. The role is difficult and demanding and the FLO's position in any investigation should never be underestimated. They are not involved to solely comfort relatives of a victim; FLOs are investigators and for this reason should be PIP level 2 accredited.

7.15 **Media and Communications**

The purpose of a communications strategy is to disseminate or receive information to assist the investigation. This can be done internally with colleagues or partners within the criminal justice system, or externally through the media or other outlets including social media.

Advice should be sought internally and externally, especially when dealing with the media, community impact, equality, diversity, legal or human rights issues. This ensures an appropriate level of information exchange is established. Sources of advice may include:

- Force Press Officers or other similar titles such as Media Liaison Officers or Corporate Communications
- Community Equality or Engagement Advisers
- Crime Reduction Advisers
- local community leaders and councillors
- community groups or forums
- diversity support associations
- youth leaders and social service departments
- neighbourhood policing teams
- partner agencies

7.15.1 Internal communications

Investigators should look to utilise the following as internal communication methods:

- internal briefing tools, intranet, SharePoint, MS Teams
- operational briefings and debriefings
- daily or extended briefing parades
- local, regional and national intelligence bulletins and publications
- digital briefing systems and email systems
- posters and notice boards

Individual verbal briefings to:

- supervisors
- senior officers
- community officers
- MOSAVO officers
- local intelligence departments
- custody staff

This enables information and material to be shared and requested and obtained about likely suspects, modus operandi, identification of vehicles, information about a victim, relevant intelligence, etc.

The use of more formal briefings and debriefings supports this exchange of information and will be utilised on major and serious crime investigations. Such briefings may also benefit other investigations depending on the size of the investigation team. Any briefings should be planned and structured to provide opportunities for the investigation team to contribute information and obtain clear direction about the progress of the investigation. If conducting a formal briefing, investigators should consider:

- location
- notifications, including who should attend
- facilities and equipment
- record keeping and disclosure obligations under CPIA
- objectives of the briefing

- structure (use of an agenda and recognised briefing model)
- removing distractions, silencing mobile telephones, etc
- briefing models

To conduct an effective briefing, a recognised briefing model should be used such as IIMARCH or SAFCOM. This enables information to be relayed in a structured way that can easily be understood by others.

IIMARCH	SAFCOM
Information	**S**ituation
Intention	**A**im
Method	**F**actors
Information	**C**hoices
Risk Assessment	**M**onitor
Communication	
Human Rights Issues	

7.15.2 External communications

The use of the media in an investigation will be influenced by the enquiry itself. High-profile cases attract lots of media interest, but the media can be just as useful in volume crime investigations if managed correctly. The following are reasons to utilise the media:

- appealing for information
- appealing for material such as mobile phone and dashboard camera footage
- identifying offenders
- locating suspects
- identifying victims
- appealing for witnesses
- identifying or locating property
- public reassurance

All media activity surrounding a case should be monitored and all material released to the media should be retained for disclosure purposes in accordance with CPIA. Before making an appeal for mobile phone and other camera footage, advice should be sought from a Media Liaison Officer regarding the process of receiving the material and how this will be managed. Considerations should include whether any recordings are to be downloaded by the public to a common platform or drop box, or whether the investigator is to be informed of the recording's existence for collection.

If releasing an image of a named suspect is being considered before their arrest a supervisor must be consulted in the first instance. The authority of a senior officer is required and there may be implications for future identification procedures that require CPS consultation.

7.15.3 Media holding statements

Releasing a holding statement can be considered early in the investigation to deal with incoming enquiries from the media. The information released should be limited to:

- confirmation that the police are dealing with an incident
- the location of the incident
- what the incident is being treated as
- appeals for information
- any reassurance messages
- contact details for the enquiry team/officer in charge

The media will invariably want more information following the issue of a holding statement. Consideration should then be given to what further information can be released and the timing to benefit and not prejudice the investigation. Another important consideration is the impact of any material released to the media on the victim, their family or friends. It is best practice to inform the victim in advance of any releases for publication.

Consideration should also be given to mitigating the impact of the media making their own enquiries into the incident. This includes information readily available to them, such as victim information (including photographs) from social networking sites.

7.15.4 **Identifying a suspect**

Tactics aimed at identifying suspects by publicising e-fits, CCTV images, photographs, etc should always be cognisant of any identification issues to ensure compliance with the Police and Criminal Evidence Act 1984 (PACE) Code D. Further guidance regarding the use of photographs and CCTV can be found in the *Facial Identification Guidance* (ACPO/NPIA 2009) and the *Authorised Professional Practice* (College of Policing 2021) which succeeded this.

7.15.5 **Locating a suspect**

If a suspect has been identified during the investigation but their location is unknown, and a media appeal is being considered to locate and arrest them, a supervisor must always be consulted in the first instance.

The authority of a senior officer will be required, and the integrity of the suspect's evidential identification must not be compromised by such an appeal. Advice should be sought in advance from the CPS, a Media Liaison Officer and the force solicitor. It will be necessary to complete a risk assessment prior to releasing any images and ensure a clear message is delivered to the public about what action is requested of them, including not approaching the suspect. Staff who may receive reports of sightings should be briefed on the action required of them, including establishing the confidence of the caller in their identification and the prioritisation of possible multiple responses.

7.15.6 **Witness appeals**

These appeals should be focused to ensure potential witnesses are identified by targeting areas and sections of the community who are most likely to have information to offer. These will include people who have witnessed the offence, or another important event connected to it. Considerations used to target witnesses could include their residence, employment, places frequented and leisure activities.

7.15.7 Public reassurance

The power of the media is very strong in the eyes of the public, especially at times of concern. A careful balance needs to be struck between reassurance and warning the public of potential future risks; especially when offenders are still at large following serious assaults or sexual offences. The opportunity to offer general crime prevention advice as well as seeking information should be utilised.

7.15.8 Press conferences

Conducting media conferences should only be considered after consulting a Media Liaison Officer and should be fronted by more experienced investigators who have received media training. Police forces will have their own policies regarding individual officers' engagement with the media which will need to be followed.

7.15.9 Appeals for information

There are many and various opportunities available to carry out appeals to the public such as:

- social media platforms, such as Twitter, Facebook and others
- newspapers
- television and radio
- force websites
- crimestoppers
- posters and electronic display screens
- trade journals
- internet
- wi-fi hotspots

- hotlines
- sporting events
- using prominent public figures

The important consideration when using any of these as part of an investigation is to ensure there are sufficient resources available to deal with the response. Depending on the profile of the investigation this could be significant and demanding.

7.16 Specialist Support

Specialist advice and support in relation to major crime and vulnerable and intimidated witnesses is available from the Major Crime Investigative Support (MCIS) team who are located within the National Crime Agency (NCA). The MCIS is staffed by a mixture of NCA and police officers and are a single point of contact for police and other law enforcement agencies.

The MCIS offers a range of services including the Witness Intermediary Team who provide support to police officers and prosecutors in the use of registered intermediaries. Advice is provided on complex interview strategies for vulnerable victims and witnesses to enable them to provide their best evidence.

Other services include the access to the National Experts Database, the National Interview Adviser, the National Vulnerable Witness Adviser, the National Search Adviser, the National FLO Adviser, Crime Advisers and Digital Media Specialists, the Crime Team and National SIO Advisers, Crime Investigative Support Officers, Geographic Profilers, Behavioural Investigative Advisers, National Forensic Specialist Advisers, the National Injuries Database and the Specialist Research Team.

Although these national resources support major investigations, they may be available to other investigations should resources allow. Investigators in the first instance should consult a supervisor and in force specialists depending on the seriousness of the offence or the complexity of the matter they require advice for.

References

ACPO/NPIA (2009) *Facial Identification Guidance*

ACPO/NPIA (2013) *Practice Advice on Core Investigative Doctrine* (2nd edn)

College of Policing (2021) *Authorised Professional Practice* (APP) available at <http://www.college.police.uk/app> accessed 22 September 2022

NPCC (2021) *Major Crime Investigation Manual*

NPCC (2021) *Major Incident Room Standardised Administrative Procedures*

Chapter 8

Managing Witnesses

8.1 Introduction

Gathering accurate and reliable information from victims and witnesses significantly influences the positive or negative outcome of an investigation. Properly conducted interviews enable investigators to understand what has occurred and allows them to focus on the relevant time parameters of the incident to identify and support other lines of enquiry. Public confidence in the police and their investigative techniques is heavily influenced by witness contact.

The aim of the investigator is to try and obtain the most accurate and reliable account in the first instance.

Having to repeat accounts several times by being passed from officer to officer and unnecessary delays in conducting the interview often leave witnesses with a very negative perception. This may also result in valuable investigative material being lost or overlooked.

The accurate recording of what has been gathered is also essential in whatever means is appropriate in the circumstances.

The success of an investigation may well be influenced by the standards that are employed in obtaining the first witness account.

Blackstone's Crime Investigators' Handbook. Steve Hibbitt and Gary Shaw, Oxford University Press. © Oxford University Press 2023.
DOI: 10.1093/oso/9780192867896.003.0008

8.2 Witness Identification

Identifying and locating witnesses is a main line of enquiry. Some are self-evident, such as those who remain at a scene and identify themselves to responding officers or those who present themselves at cordons or who contact the police by some other means.

Other witnesses require some investigative activity to locate. This could be for any number of reasons, such as being unaware they are in possession of information relevant to the investigation or being reluctant to engage in or being hostile to the enquiry. Experience has shown that witnesses are more willing to cooperate whilst events are still fresh in their minds.

It is essential to identify and deal with witnesses before they are influenced by external factors, as their memory may become contaminated by talking with others (including other witnesses) or following media reports.

Each case differs depending on the nature and geography of the area and the timing of the incident. Offences occurring during the night might be witnessed by people who are not present at other times and vice versa. For example, potential witnesses such as taxi drivers, fast food vendors, delivery persons, night clubbers and night workers, shop and office workers.

The search for witnesses should not be confined to the scene of the event.

The establishment of the relevant time parameters in which the incident took place will assist in developing the required lines of enquiry that need to be conducted.

8.3 Principles of Investigative Interviewing

In 1992 the Home Office produced seven principles of investigative interviewing applicable to victims, witnesses and suspects. These were revised in 2007 and are reproduced below:

1. The aim of investigative interviewing is to obtain accurate and reliable accounts from victims, witnesses or suspects about matters under police investigation.
2. Investigators must act fairly when questioning victims, witnesses or suspects. Vulnerable people must be treated with particular consideration at all times.
3. Investigative interviewing should be approached with an investigative mindset. Accounts obtained from the person being interviewed should always be tested against what the interviewer already knows or what can reasonably be established.
4. When conducting an interview investigators are free to ask a wide range of questions in order to obtain material which may assist an investigation.
5. Investigators should recognise the positive impact of an early admission in the context of the criminal justice system.
6. Investigators are not bound to accept the first answer given. Questioning is not unfair merely because it is persistent.
7. Even when the right of silence is exercised by a suspect, investigators have a responsibility to put questions to them.

These principles underpin the nature of investigative interviewing and should assist the investigator in understanding their role when interviewing victims and witnesses. In essence, how the information is obtained from an individual may well be tested by those operating within the Criminal Justice System and must be able to stand scrutiny.

8.4 'PEACE' and Achieving Best Evidence

PEACE remains the recognised framework for police interviews with victims, witnesses and suspects and is compatible with the phased approach described in

Achieving Best Evidence (ABE) and illustrated in the following table.

Achieving Best Evidence	PEACE
Planning and Preparation	**P**lanning and Preparation
Establishing Rapport	**E**ngage and Explain
Initiating and supporting a free narrative account	**A**ccount, clarification and challenge
Questioning	
Closing the interview	**C**losure
Evaluation	**E**valuation

Extracted from the National Investigative Interviewing Strategy (NPIA/ACPO, 2009)

The interviewing of all categories of witness is governed by the Achieving Best Evidence guidelines. This is so whether the witness interview is digitally recorded or transferred into a signed written statement.

All investigators should have a comprehensive understanding of ABE in respect of their role and be able to outline the relevant parts of the guidance if required to do so.

8.5 **Planning Witness Interviews**

Planning is essential to conducting an effective interview that meets the needs of the investigation whilst supporting the witness to give their best evidence in court. Each interview is different; the planning requirements depend on the circumstances of the witness and/or the complexity of the interview, which must have specific aims and objectives to accomplish.

The first stage of planning is to assess the witness, including any initial account they have already provided. Depending on the circumstances, the witness may themselves be a 'scene' requiring forensic recovery avoiding cross-contamination (see Chapter 6). The timing of the formal interview may be influenced by any medical attention required or forensic examination/recovery, which should be prioritised.

The perfect situation is for interviewers to have extensive information about the witness but minimal information about the event, apart from its nature, location, timeframe and how it was reported. In these circumstances the interviewer is unlikely to inadvertently influence the witness account. However, this is rarely possible due to interviewers also being engaged in other aspects of the investigation.

KEY POINT

Utilising specialist interview advisers (PIP Level 2, previously known as Tier 5) is not confined to suspects. Advice is available on all aspects of witness interviews and should be sought as early as possible in investigations involving complex witness issues.

In all cases, a written record of the planning process should be maintained and an interview plan produced containing clear aims and objectives.

The following checklist covers some generic planning considerations:

Checklist—Initial considerations

- Identify if the witness is significant, vulnerable or intimidated
- Assess the witness to identify and address any issues impacting on the interview, for example personal circumstances, age, gender, physical/mental disorder or learning disability, cultural/religious considerations, first language, injury, trauma, medication taken, any current or previous contact with the police or other agencies, any relationship or contact with the alleged offender
- Identify any consent issues that may impact on their participation in the interview

- Assess the extent of any reluctance or hostility
- Based on what is already known, assess what the witness is likely to have seen, heard or otherwise experienced concerning the matter under investigation
- Decide on the method of recording (video, audio or MG11 with no recording)
- Identify any special measures to be applied for
- Set specific achievable objectives for the interview and identify topics to support them
- Obtain appropriate advice if necessary
- Obtain the resources to conduct the interview
- Prepare an interview plan
- Conduct a risk assessment to establish the extent, if any, to which the witness may be at risk of intimidation, and take action to mitigate

8.6 Witness Assessment and Classification

A witness should be 'classified' as early as possible to identify if they are 'significant', 'vulnerable' or 'intimidated'. This influences the method of recording and the presentation of their evidence in court, including any special measures applications required.

These classifications should not be applied too rigidly as some witnesses may cross over categories. Their circumstances could also change during the investigation, such as by becoming a victim of intimidation when none was present before or at the time of their interview.

Definition—Significant witness (ineligible for 'special measures)

- Significant witnesses (SWIT also referred to as 'key' witnesses) are those who:

- Have or claim to have witnessed, visually or otherwise, an indictable offence, part of such an offence or events closely connected with it (including any incriminating comments made by the suspected offender either before or after the offence) and/or
- Have a particular relationship to the victim or have a central position in an investigation into an indictable offence.[1]

Where practicable a SWIT should be interviewed on video (including DVD) unless they do not consent, in which case the interview should be audio recorded. If the witness does not consent to audio recording, a statement may be obtained directly. In each of these cases the reason for not consenting to video or audio recording should be included in the MG11.

With multiple witnesses, it may be necessary to limit the numbers who are video or audio recorded according to the resources available. A written record should be made of this decision with the selection criteria, for example the witnesses who are most evidentially valuable and factors such as their proximity and line of sight to the event, sobriety/intoxication at the time, availability and willingness to assist the enquiry.

When assessing the information that has been obtained from a SWIT, it is important to understand how they came into the enquiry and their relationship (if any) to the victim, other witnesses or indeed the suspect.

This may well assist in making sense of what has been provided before deciding on the next stage of the investigation, especially if it is contradictory to other information.

There is no statutory provision for significant witness interviews to be played to the court as their evidence-in-chief by the prosecution. The defence may ask permission

[1] *Achieving Best Evidence in Criminal Proceedings, Guidance on Interviewing Victims and witnesses, and guidance on using special measures* (Ministry of Justice, 2022) [ABE] and the *Major Crime Investigation Manual* (NPCC, 2021).

to play some or all of the recording to support their case, particularly if they intend to challenge the manner of questioning.

8.7 Informed Consent

The *Code of Practice for the Victims of Crime* (Ministry of Justice 2020) and the *Witness Charter* (Ministry of Justice 2013) require witnesses to be given sufficient information to make an informed decision on whether to consent to the interview. This means explaining the purpose of the interview, including the witness potentially attending court.

Definition—Vulnerable witness

Vulnerable witnesses are:

- All child witnesses (under 18 years); and
- Any witness whose quality of evidence is likely to be diminished because they:
- are suffering from a mental disorder (as defined by the Mental Health Act 1983) or
- have a significant impairment of intelligence or social functioning or
- have a physical disability or are suffering from a physical disorder.[2]

8.8 Child Witnesses

Before the implementation of the Coroners and Justice Act 2009, child witnesses were aged under 17 years and classified as being of two types:

[2] Section 16 of the YJCEA, amended by section 101 of the Coroners and Justice Act 2009.

1. those in need of special protection concerning sexual or violent offences
2. children giving evidence in all other types of case

This distinction no longer applies, so all child witnesses are treated the same regardless of the offence.

The presumption is that child witnesses will give their evidence-in-chief by video recorded interview, and any further evidence by live TV link unless the court is satisfied this would not improve the quality of their evidence. However, with the agreement of the court, they may opt out of giving their evidence by video recorded interview or by live link, or both. If they do this, there is a presumption the child witness will give evidence from behind a screen unless they also choose to opt out of this special measure and the court agrees.

Where a video recorded interview is made before a child witness's 18th birthday, they are still eligible for video recorded evidence-in-chief and live TV link after they turn 18.

KEY POINTS

- When deciding whether or not to allow a child witness to 'opt out', the court must be satisfied that the quality of their evidence will not be diminished. This decision is taken on a case-by-case basis and does not mean the interview should not be visually recorded during the investigation stage.
- The staged process of explaining the opt-out process to the child or their carer where capacity is an issue is described in *Achieving Best Evidence* (Ministry of Justice 2022), paragraphs 2.50 to 2.60.

8.8.1 Fraser guidelines

A child can consent in their own right provided they can understand the implications of the interview, including the use to which it is to be put, but the consent of a parent or guardian is required if they cannot understand. This follows Lord Fraser's judgment in the 1985 case of *Gillick v*

West Norfolk and Wisbech AHA[3] and is often referred to by the term 'Fraser' or 'Gillick' competent.

Informing the child's parents or guardian of the interview and consent are separate issues; however, except in exceptional circumstances, they should be informed even where the child has the capacity to consent to the interview themselves.

8.9 Mental and/or Physical Disability

Witnesses with a mental and/or physical disability are only eligible for special measures if the quality of their evidence is likely to be diminished by reason of their disorder or disability (section 16(1) of the YJCEA). This means the 'completeness, coherence and accuracy' of their evidence and the witness's ability to provide answers which address the questions put to them that can be understood individually and collectively by others. A physical disability which does not affect the ability to communicate does not classify the witness as vulnerable.

8.10 Identifying Vulnerability

In principle everyone, whatever their age, is competent to give evidence, unless the court finds they are unable to understand the questions put to them, or they are unable to give answers which can be understood (section 53 of the YJCEA).

The court must consider the special measures that are available to assist the witness, so identifying an

[3] 3 All ER 402.

individual's abilities as well as disabilities is important during the planning phase of the interview.

Historically the police have found identifying vulnerability difficult, particularly when the indicators are not easily recognised, such as limited speech and understanding. Hidden factors to consider could include a witness's inability to read or write, responding inappropriately or inconsistently to questions, focusing on small points or the irrelevant rather than the important issues, a short attention span, being eager to please, becoming withdrawn or over exuberant.

Apart from visible behaviour, other indicators of vulnerability include:

- receiving Disability Living Allowance
- resident at a group/residential home or institution
- employed in a sheltered workplace
- attending a specialist day service
- possessing certain prescription medicine
- receiving support from a carer
- receiving support from a social worker or community psychiatric nurse

8.11 Mental Capacity Act

The Mental Capacity Act 2005 applies to anyone over 16 who lacks mental capacity, and a decision needs to be made concerning them. It establishes a principle that everyone is assumed to have capacity unless established otherwise and provides an obligation on the police to try and communicate with people where mental capacity is an issue; including modifying the language used when providing information, enabling it to be understood.

Where mental capacity is an issue, the overriding principle is to act in the best interests of the individual, which may involve consulting widely with persons known to them and, in the interview context, may be relevant to witnesses over 16 where consent to a visually recorded interview is required.

Definition—Intimidated witnesses

Intimidated witnesses are those whose quality of evidence is likely to be diminished by reason of fear or distress in relation to testifying in the case.[4]

When deciding whether a witness is intimidated, the court considers the nature and alleged circumstances of the offence, the age of the witness and where relevant:

- their social and cultural background and ethnic origins
- their domestic and employment circumstances
- any religious beliefs or political opinions
- any behaviour towards the witness by the accused, members of the accused's family or associates or any other person who is likely to be either an accused person or a witness in the proceedings

KEY POINTS

- The *Code of Practice for Victims of Crime* (Ministry of Justice 2020) indicates that the families of homicide victims fall into this category and are entitled to an enhanced service from the police.
- The police have a responsibility to identify vulnerable and intimidated victims and ensure this information is passed to other organisations with responsibilities under the Code.

8.12 Complainants in Cases of Sexual Assault

Complainants in cases of sexual assault automatically fall into the intimidated category. However, there is now a

[4] Section 17(4) YJCEA.

rebuttable presumption that video evidence-in-chief will maximise the quality of their evidence so they may opt out. This must be decided on a case-by-case basis and is the complainant's decision, provided they give their informed consent.

Opting out of video evidence-in-chief does not mean the interview should not be visually recorded; it means it is not played to the court as the complainant's statement, and an MG11 witness statement is taken and used instead.

KEY POINT

Not all complainants need or want to use their visually recorded interview as their evidence in court. Some victims, on realising the defendant can see them on the live link screen, have preferred to give their evidence from behind a screen; others may prefer to see the alleged offender in court and give their evidence without screens. This is decided on a case-by-case basis.

8.13 Witnesses to Gun and Knife Offences

Witnesses to specified gun and knife crime also automatically fall into the intimidated category unless they opt out. The offences included in the definition of gun and knife crime are extensive and contained in the legislation concerning:

- murder and manslaughter
- Offences Against the Person Act 1861
- Prevention of Crime Act 1953
- Firearms Act 1968
- Criminal Justice Act 1988
- Violent Crime Reduction Act 2006

Offence—Witness intimidation

Witness intimidation is an offence in its own right under section 51 of the Criminal Justice and Public Order Act 1994; it can be committed before the crime has been reported, during the investigation or after the case has been heard at court.

8.14 Special Measures

A range of special measures are available under the YJCEA to help vulnerable and intimidated witnesses give their best evidence in court; they apply to prosecution and defence witnesses but not to defendants who give evidence.

Special measures are granted by the court if it is agreed any or a combination of them would improve the quality of the witness's evidence, including:

- screens to shield the witness from the defendant when giving evidence
- live TV link allowing the witness to give evidence from outside the court room
- giving evidence in private (limited to sexual offences and those involving intimidation by someone other than the accused)
- removal of wigs and gowns by judges and barristers in the Crown Court
- use of video recorded interviews (visually recorded statements) as evidence-in-chief
- video recorded cross-examinations

Vulnerable (not intimidated) witnesses are also eligible for:

- using an intermediary who specialises in helping those with communication difficulties
- special communication aids, for example an Alphabet Board

8.14.1 Early special measures meetings

Any of the special measures (or a combination of them) that would help a witness give their best evidence should be identified and communicated to the Crown Prosecution Service (CPS) as early as possible, either by recording on the case file (MG2) or through an early special measures discussion/meeting.

Unless it is impracticable to do so, a pre-interview early special measures meeting takes place where there is any doubt as to whether or not to video record the interview, where an intermediary or aids to communication are involved or where there might be an issue regarding an interview supporter.

The police are responsible for calling early special measures meetings during the investigation where necessary and the CPS can call a meeting after reviewing the case file. In practice, these meetings are usually telephone discussions with decisions recorded on form MG2.

Special measures are not automatically granted, and prosecutors must have sufficient information and evidence to support the application. Witnesses should not be promised or misled into believing that they are guaranteed to be granted any special measures.

8.15 Registered Intermediaries

A registered intermediary is a communications specialist accredited by the Ministry of Justice. They can provide assistance when interviewing people with communications difficulties. This includes witnesses with learning disabilities and very young children.

The intermediary conducts a pre-interview assessment and provides advice on conducting the interview, including questioning techniques. During the interview, the intermediary is allowed to explain questions and answers so far as is necessary to enable them to be understood by the witness or the questioner, without changing the substance of the evidence.

Approval for the admission of evidence obtained through an intermediary is applied for retrospectively to the court, who may also appoint an intermediary to assist the witness in giving evidence.

Police forces have different internal processes for obtaining a registered intermediary, and advice is available from the NCA Specialist Operations Centre.

8.16 Interview Supporters

An interview supporter's role is to provide emotional support to the witness, not to facilitate communication. They are not appropriate adults, who are no longer referred to in the Police and Criminal Evidence Act 1984 (PACE) regarding witness interviews.

The views of the witness should be sought before the interview on the identity of any interview supporter. They cannot be another witness or potential witness in the case, people allegedly involved in the offence in some way, interpreters or intermediaries.

With the permission of the court, an interview supporter may now accompany the witness in the live TV link room while they give evidence.

8.17 Interpreters

When English is not a witness's first language it may be necessary to conduct the interview with an interpreter, depending on the wishes of the witness if they have sufficient understanding of English.

Interpreters should be briefed before the interview to explain the questioning techniques to be used and how they may impact on their interpretation, for example by not filling pauses when used deliberately to allow the witness to focus, and accurately translating what has been said.

Questions should be directed to the witness for the interpreter to translate. A common mistake is interviewing the interpreter and not the witness.

8.18 Reluctant Witnesses

Reluctant witnesses are those who have the ability to provide testimony but are unwilling to do so. This could be due to fear of the offender, not trusting the police/criminal justice system, or their personal circumstances and the perceived consequences of giving evidence.

There is no single tactic to overcome reluctance. The first stage is to identify the reason(s) and mitigate them. Gaining the witness's trust is crucial, so the timing, location and method of any approach needs careful consideration to prevent the witness being compromised and caused difficulty.

Reasonable steps should be taken to address their concerns, and depending on the reasons for their reluctance the witness could be categorised as intimidated and be eligible for special measures. Other options include additional security measures and referral to support from the Victim Support Service and Witness Care Units. No false promises should be made or pressure put on the witness to give evidence.

Checklist—Security and protection measures

- Providing a 'HomeLink' alarm system
- Providing a portable personal attack alarm
- Upgrading security at the home address
- Installing temporary CCTV
- Entries on briefing and intelligence systems
- Critical Address Register entry to prioritise any police attendance

- Temporary relocation
- Using an agreed codeword when making contact

Where life-threatening intimidation is involved, if certain criteria are met full witness protection is a consideration. This has life-changing consequences for the witness and significant resource and financial implications. Witness protection is a protected tactic, and any further advice should be sought from local or regional People Protection Units or SIOs.

8.19 Witness Summonses

Paragraph 4 of Schedule 3 to the Crime and Disorder Act 1998 provides a power to bring a relevant witness before a magistrates' court, either by summons or warrant, to make a deposition before the court. This should only be considered in exceptional circumstances if:

1. A person is already charged with the offence in question.
2. The witness has provided information which is of value to the prosecution but has refused to provide a written statement.
3. The procedure would not place them at unacceptable risk if the evidence is produced, which cannot be mitigated by special measures (screens, anonymity).

8.20 Hostile Witnesses

Hostile witnesses are people who are believed to have witnessed an offence, part of an offence or events closely connected with it, but who are opposed to the investigation process (ABE 2022, paragraph 2.164). This could be due to their lifestyle, their own criminality, a close relationship with the alleged offender and/or intending to appear as a defence witness.

Some hostile witnesses simply refuse to cooperate with the police, whilst others may provide false information intended to support an alleged offender's account.

Where a hostile witness consents to be interviewed, it should be visually recorded in accordance with the significant witness guidance; any refusal to visually or audio record the interview should be dealt with in the same manner.

KEY POINT

Where a hostile witness claims not to have any information to assist the investigation, every effort should be made to record this in a witness statement. These 'negative statements' are useful if the person intends to appear or later appears at court as a defence witness.

8.21 **Witness Anonymity**

Open justice is a fundamental principle enshrined in Article 6(1) of the European Convention on Human Rights (ECHR). This underpins the requirement for prosecution witnesses to be identifiable to the defendant and the open court, and to support the defence when presenting their case by cross-examining the witnesses.

Sometimes this principle acts as a barrier to successful prosecution, particularly in cases of homicide, organised crime, and gang and gun offences, where revealing the witness's identity would put them and their family/friends at risk of serious harm.

Potential witnesses also have rights under Article 2 of the ECHR (right to life) which the police have a positive obligation to protect.

8.22 Investigation Anonymity Orders

The Coroners and Justice Act 2003 (sections 74 to 83) created Investigation Anonymity Orders to reassure people with information in gang-related gun and knife murder that their identity will be protected throughout the investigation and permanently afterwards.

The qualifying criteria are:

- the offence must be murder or manslaughter
- the person likely to have committed the offence is aged between 11 and 30 years and
- is a member of a gang where the majority of its members are aged between 11 and 30 years
- the informant has reasonable grounds to fear intimidation or harm if identified
- the informant must have information that will assist the investigation and without an order would probably not provide the information

The application is made by a Superintendent on behalf of the Chief Officer of Police to a Justice of the Peace.

At the time of writing the Secretary of State is to review the use of Investigation Anonymity Orders.

KEY POINT

A separate Witness Anonymity Order must be applied for if the investigation proceeds to trial.

8.23 Witness Anonymity Orders

An Investigation Anonymity Order does not guarantee the witness anonymity at trial, so a separate application must be made for a Witness Anonymity Order (sections 86 to 90 Coroners and Justice Act 2009).

An order made by the court requires appropriate specified measures be taken to ensure the identity of the witness is not disclosed in, or in connection with, the proceedings. These include:

- their name and other identifying details being withheld and removed from any material disclosed to any party to the proceedings
- using a pseudonym
- the witness not being asked questions that might lead to their identification
- use of screens
- the witness's voice being modulated/distorted
- the order will not allow a witness to be screened so they cannot be seen by the judge or other members of the court (if any) or the jury (if there is one)

KEY POINT

Witness anonymity including information security requires careful management to prevent compromise. Anonymous witness interviews must be meticulously planned and executed, so engaging an interview adviser in the process is essential.

The Act and the Guidance apply to all witnesses, including undercover police officers and test purchase officers. Applications must be authorised by Heads of CPS Complex Casework Units or Heads of Division.

8.24 Interview Resources

The resources required for an interview will reflect the needs of the witness, such as the requirement for any interview supporter, interpreter or intermediary. Interviewers should always ensure they are properly equipped to conduct the interview as follows:

Checklist—Equipment and resources

- interview suite
- suitable location if the interview is not being conducted in a dedicated suite
- recording equipment, including portable equipment and a background screen if required
- aids to communication if required
- interview plan
- note-taking material
- paper for the witness to produce a sketch or plan
- exhibit labels
- maps, plans or diagrams which may be required for the witness to mark locations of significance during the interview
- exhibits or copy exhibits to be shown to the witness during the interview if required

8.25 Contingencies

Planning the response to possible contingencies may prevent a future legal challenge to the interview process.

Researching and evaluating the witness assists in identifying potential issues which can be anticipated and planned for, for example an assessment of their lifestyle may provide indicators of potential admissions to criminality.

8.25.1 Witness involvement in offences

Witnesses could admit criminal offences during the interview and this contingency should be planned for. Such admissions fall into two categories:

1. Admissions concerning or linked to the offence under investigation, such as assisting an offender.

2. Admissions to offences unconnected to the offence under investigation, for example a witness to a serious assault admitting taking drugs shortly before.

Admissions to other offences should take into account the seriousness of the crime under investigation, measured against the seriousness of the offence admitted by the witness.

Where the priority is to obtain evidence from the person as a witness, the interview can proceed (ABE 2022, paragraph 3.165). However, if during the interview it is considered the evidence of the witness as a suspect is highly relevant to a particular case, the interview should be terminated (taking care not to close it abruptly) and the witness told they may be interviewed later about the matter they have made incriminating admissions to.

Decisions on witness admissions to offences should be made by the officer in charge of the investigation in consultation with the CPS if necessary. Promises of immunity from prosecution should never be made or offered during the interview.

8.25.2 Witnesses who become suspects

Where there is no objective reason to suspect a person is involved in the offence under investigation they should be treated as a witness, or be a subject in a trace, investigate, evaluate (TIE) process (see Chapter 7).

If, however, during interview a 'witness' admits involvement in the offence, they should be allowed to finish what they are saying but must not be asked any further questions. At this point any further questioning must be conducted under caution with access to legal advice.

The interview should be closed and the officer responsible for the investigation informed immediately to decide whether to caution and arrest the person whose status has now changed from witness to suspect due to self-incrimination.

As outlined above, if the witness admits an offence which is not part of the current investigation (depending on its severity) the person can be continued to be interviewed in relation to the current investigation as a witness and the 'new' offence can be dealt with at a later time.

8.25.3 Suspects who become witnesses

Not every person interviewed under caution for an offence is prosecuted; they may be eliminated and released, or disposed of by other means, such as cautioning.

Before a person who was previously a suspect is interviewed as a witness they must be released from any obligations as a suspect, meaning they must be unconditionally released. A person cannot be on bail to return to the police station and simultaneously be treated as a witness in the same case.

The interview recording(s) and associated material produced when the person was a suspect are unused material. The defence may compare any account given by the witness with their interview under caution, so it is important to identify and explain any omissions, anomalies or changes of information between the person's witness and suspect interviews.

A different situation arises when a suspect is charged with an offence connected to the crime under investigation but is willing to provide evidence against any accomplices or co-accused.

In these circumstances, the person responsible for the investigation must consult the CPS. An option (with CPS agreement) is for the person to enter an early guilty plea, be interviewed as a significant witness and then provide evidence before they are sentenced.

8.26 Serious Organised Crime and Police Act 2005

Sections 71 to 75 of the Serious Organised Crime and Police Act 2005 (SOCPA) provide opportunities for criminals (including convicted persons) to give evidence for the prosecution against accomplices in return for reductions in sentence and even immunity from prosecution.

The options in such circumstances are:

- granting conditional immunity from prosecution for assistance (section 71)
- providing a 'restricted use undertaking' for any information the individual provides for a prosecution or investigation (section 72)
- powers available to the court when sentencing persons who plead guilty to take account of their undertaking to assist an investigation or prosecution (section 73)
- powers for a person sentenced to be referred back to court for their sentence to be discounted when they assist an investigation or prosecution (section 74)
- when sentencing people under section 74, courts can exclude people from the court or impose reporting restrictions

This tactic is used for offenders who could provide evidence against the higher echelons of serious organised crime and terrorist groups. Interviews with these 'assisting offenders' is a highly specialised area involving high-level CPS authorisation, risk assessment, resource and cost implications and detailed planning.

8.27 Interview Objectives and Structure

Whatever recording medium is used (if any), and whatever the circumstances of the witness, it is essential to plan and structure the interview with clear objectives to achieve, supported by relevant and properly sequenced topics.

Common criticisms of visually recorded interviews are they are overly long, often containing confusing, repetitive and unnecessary detail, create ambiguity rather than clarity and can even undermine the witness due to the manner of questioning.

Review processes consistently identify the reason for these issues as failure to plan. It cannot be over-emphasised that planning is not a luxury to sacrifice in the belief that it wastes time; effective planning actually saves time by producing more focused and timely interviews which meet the needs of the courts and the investigation.

Investigative interviews are not confined to the evidential account of the event experienced by the witness; they also support the investigation by obtaining information to identify and support lines of enquiry which themselves may not be relevant to the court. For this reason structure is important.

The structure of a witness interview is summarised in the table that follows.

Phase 1	Rapport
Phase 2	Witness's free narrative account of the incident(s)
Phase 3	a) Topic division and probing of the witness's account of the incident
	b) Topic division and probing of case-specific information important to the investigation
Phase 4	Closure

Extracted from ABE 2022 (paragraph 3.46, Figure 3.2)

It is beyond the scope of this chapter to describe in any great detail how to conduct the interview. Detailed guidance is contained in Chapter 3 of ABE 2022 and other approved professional practice.

The four-phased structure applies to all witness interviews, but a key point to highlight is the importance of getting to the purpose of the interview (eg the event) at the beginning in Phase 2. After covering any necessary rapport, Phase 2 of the interview deals with the witness's description of the incident by obtaining their uninterrupted account of the event.

This is followed by Phase 3 where the *account of the event* is divided into topics, then probed and expanded for further information. Phase 3 separates into areas of (a) *general investigative practice* and (b) *wider investigative material* which reflect the differing needs of the court and the investigation.

Depending on the complexity of the interview, the circumstances of the witness and/or volume of material to be covered, it may be necessary to conduct a series of interviews with a distinct break between phases 3(a) and 3(b).

8.28 General Investigative Practice

General investigative practice applies to all witness interviews and includes subjects such as:

- points to prove the offence
- any statutory or likely defences
- other people present at the time, including if they are known to the witness and their description (using the ADVOKATE mnemonic)[5]
- anything said by the witness to a third party after the incident, for example evidence of first complaint
- assessing any identification evidence provided by the witness using the ADVOKATE mnemonic

A—Amount of time the person/event was under observation by the witness.
D—Distance from the witness to the person/event.
V—Visibility—including lighting conditions at the time, does the witness wear spectacles and were they worn at the material time.
O—Obstructions—obscuring the witness's view.

[5] The ADVOKATE mnemonic is from *R v Turnbull and Camelo* (1976) 3 All ER 54.

K—Known or seen before—does the witness know or have they seen the person before and in what circumstances.
A—Any reason to remember—anything specific that made the person/incident memorable to the witness.
T—Time elapsed—how long since the witness last saw the person prior to the incident.
E—Errors—or discrepancies in the witness's description.

8.29 Wider Investigative Material

Wider Investigative material is specific to the witness and differs from case to case and witness to witness; it links to the *investigative areas* or identified topics to be covered. This information may be revealed during the witness's free recall of the event or during earlier questioning, but this is the phase of the interview where the topic needs expanding. However, if the material has not been mentioned by the witness in the earlier phases it should then be introduced by the interviewer.

Such material includes investigative areas such as:

- background information relevant to the witness's account
- relevant lifestyle information
- access to mobile phones and other digital equipment
- relevant financial transactions
- if the witness has knowledge of others (victim/witness or suspect) an exploration of relevant contact and background history pertinent to the investigation
- any relevant activity after the incident up to the interview
- risk assessment factors

Wider investigative topics should link the interview to other lines of enquiry, for example obtaining information relevant to the strategies for forensic evidence, identification, media, CCTV, search, passive data, victimology, intelligence and arrest.

8.30 Post-interview Responsibilities

8.30.1 Evaluating the interview

The witness interview should be evaluated to establish:

- what any information provided says about the alleged event
- whether any new lines of enquiry have been identified
- whether any fast track actions/urgent lines of enquiry have been identified that need communicating immediately to the enquiry team
- any gaps or omissions in the witness's account when compared with other material available to the enquiry
- any inconsistencies in the witness's account when compared with other material already gathered and assessed
- any welfare issues requiring post-interview support for the witness, for example experiencing an unexpected traumatic reaction

KEY POINT

Evaluating a witness interview should be an objective assessment of the information they have provided and not their behaviour whilst revealing it, which could be tainted by the interviewer's opinion on the veracity of the witness.

8.31 Supplementary Interviews

Effective planning should reduce the need to conduct further interviews with the witness. However, evaluation or developments in the investigation may necessitate a supplementary interview, such as:

- a further interview to address any identified relevant inconsistencies or omission
- the witness indicates to a third party that they have significant new information which they did not disclose during the initial interview, but they now wish to tell the investigation team
- the initial interview identifies new lines of enquiry (or wider allegations) which cannot be satisfactorily explored in the time available
- when preparing their defence an accused raises matters not covered in the initial interview
- significant new information emerges from other witnesses or other sources

In such circumstances, a supplementary interview should be planned and recorded in the same medium as the original. Consideration should be given as to whether a supplementary interview is also in the best interests of the victim/witness and a record made of the decision.

8.32 **Interview Products**

8.32.1 Significant witnesses

Apart from exceptional cases, the evidence of a 'significant witness' is adduced in a Criminal Justice Act 1967 witness statement (MG11) compiled by reviewing the recording as soon as possible after the interview. The witness does not need to be present at this point.

The witness is asked to read the statement, indicate any alterations or additions they consider necessary and sign it, having agreed the statement's content.

There is no requirement to visually record the statement signing unless the witness reveals significant new or changed information whilst checking it. In this case, a supplementary visually recorded interview should be conducted to provenance and preserve the integrity of the additional or changed information.

The witness statement is submitted as evidence with the case papers, and the recordings with any notes and other material are unused material.

KEY POINT

In exceptional cases it may be appropriate to take a brief written statement from the witness introducing the recording, then produce a transcript of the interview instead of a section 9 CJA (Criminal Justice Act 1967) statement. In these rare circumstances, prior agreement from the CPS is essential.

8.32.2 Statement chronology and content

Generally, evidence written in a statement should be direct evidence reflecting the first-hand knowledge of what the witness saw, heard, felt or otherwise experienced, otherwise it is likely to be hearsay and inadmissible in court.

Hearsay is an extensive subject and the rules have never been absolute. If there is any doubt about the information's relevance or otherwise, particularly in complex cases, the hearsay should be included. It is then open to the CPS to either edit the hearsay or request a further statement to be obtained omitting it.

Written statements are the product of the earlier investigative interview. The better structured the interview is and the quality of investigative material that is obtained should reflect in the production of a quality statement. Written statements should adopt the following chronology:

1. Introduction
    - Set and describe the scene
2. Circumstances

- Describe the incident/event in chronological order, explaining the physical and verbal actions of the persons present
- Record the event first before moving on to background material

3. Descriptions
   - Description of offender(s) in as much detail as possible
   - Names or descriptions of relevant others at the scene
   - Use the ADVOKATE mnemonic
4. Objects
   - Detailed description of objects involved, for example any vehicle, weapon, stolen property (including where stolen from)
   - Identify any objects produced as exhibits with an exhibit number
   - Chronologically list any exhibits
5. Other issues
   - Information that links to the case-specific information if relevant, for example antecedents and victimology, personal relationships, movements

8.32.2.1 Victim personal statement

If including a victim personal statement (VPS) about the impact of the offence on the victim, underline after the main body of the statement and record the VPS in the victim's own words or consider recording in a separate statement.

8.32.2.2 General rules and practice

- if applicable, the opening paragraph explains the interview was visually (or audio) recorded
- the witness's own words should not be converted into police jargon
- anything said by an accused should be recorded in direct speech (as far as the witness remembers it)

- errors should be crossed out with a single line and initialled by the witness at the time the statement is made
- the address or telephone number of a witness should not be included in the body of the statement unless it is relevant to the enquiry, for example a burglary victim
- all surnames should be in capital letters
- if a witness is under 18 state their exact age
- signatures are required on each page and the declaration on page one

KEY POINTS

- Witness statements should represent the chronological order of the events which may not be in the same order that the witness revealed the information when interviewed. When preparing the statement, it is permissible to organise the information to structure the statement.
- The previous point should not be mistaken for permission to edit the witness's account. All information about the event must be included in the statement to prevent accusations of being selective.

8.32.3 **Investigative summaries**

Witnesses rarely provide all their information in a chronological order at the first time of asking. Some witnesses provide comprehensive information during the interview with key details revealed at different points in their account or during the questioning phase.

It could be essential for others involved in the investigation to have a clear understanding of the information provided by the witness, but it may be impractical for them to view the video recording. This often occurs during major investigations where decision makers are not directly involved with conducting the interview but require the information before a witness statement is prepared.

Upon completion of an interview, the compiling of an accurate chronological 'investigative summary' of the information should be considered. This differs from a Record of Video Interview (ROVI) in that the chronology of the document reflects the alleged incident and not the order that the witness recalled the information during their interview. In other words, the information about the account and each relevant topic is all in one place within the document.

Chronological investigative summaries assist others, including the officer responsible for the investigation, when making decisions about further lines of enquiry. They can also help the interviewers of any suspects with their interview plans and decisions concerning the content of pre-interview briefings with legal representatives.

Investigative summaries also inform any early special measures discussions with the CPS and any later special measures applications.

8.32.3.1 Record of video interview (ROVI)

A ROVI should be compiled in every case where a vulnerable or significant witness is interviewed, and a visual recording made. As far as possible they should provide a chronological summary of the conduct of the interview (unlike an investigative summary which chronologically describes the event) and be as succinct as possible. A ROVI is different from any notes made during the interview.

Checklist—ROVI content

- Identify that a rapport phase took place (more detail may be required concerning some vulnerable witness interviews)
- Identification issues, including descriptions and the ADVOKATE points
- Location of the event(s) witnessed
- Points to prove

- Time, frequency, dates, locations and those present when the offence occurred
- Injuries
- Threats and admissions made
- Key statements made by the witness, other witnesses, the suspect
- Anything negating a potential defence
- Any aggravating factors
- Any issues undermining the prosecution or assisting the defence case
- A short summary of a VPS if made on the same recording
- Background material of no apparent relevance should be summarised in general terms

Checklist—ROVI completion

- ROVIs should always be recorded on a form MG15 and be typed if possible
- Include timings recorded in hours, minutes and seconds using the clock shown on the video and speakers
- Identify speakers against the relevant entry

KEY POINTS

Although prepared from the same interview:

- a ROVI is a chronological record of the interview
- an investigative summary is a chronological record of the event

A ROVI is different from a ROTI with a suspect and is not:

- a statement
- a transcript
- a replacement for the video or
- an exhibit
- a chronological investigative summary

8.33 Photographs, E-Fits and Identity Procedures

If a witness is to view photographs or an identification procedure, their witness statement containing the first description of the suspect should be recorded before the viewing.

Additionally, where a visually recorded interview has been conducted, the production of facial composites using E-Fit or other systems or producing an artist's impression should also be visually recorded. This enables the court to hear the evidence from the witness in the same medium as their main evidence-in-chief and may reduce the need for them to give additional evidence by showing how the E-Fit/sketch was obtained.

Staff compiling images with witnesses using these procedures should be trained to the appropriate level to record the interview.

8.34 Refreshing the Memory of a Witness whose Evidence is Visually Recorded

Witnesses are entitled to see a copy of their statement before giving evidence and, unless it has been ruled inadmissible, a visually recorded interview may also be shown to the witness before the trial to refresh their memory.

How, when and where this viewing is done is decided on a case-by-case basis. The aim is to enable the witness to give their best evidence in court. It is a police responsibility to arrange for prosecution witnesses to view their video recorded interviews; the CPS should be consulted about where this should take place and who should be present.

Police forces have their own policies and procedures for facilitating the viewing. In some areas Witness Care Units or support staff are responsible and in others it is for the officer in charge of the investigation to organise.

In all cases, the purpose should be explained to the witness and their views sought; a record must be kept of anything said during the viewing. To maximise the benefit, the timing should take account of the witness's needs, ability to concentrate and the date of the trial, for example it is generally bad practice to rush a viewing on the morning the witness is due to give evidence. However, if the witness is scheduled to give evidence that afternoon, a morning viewing may be beneficial.

Issues such as providing support to the witness while they refresh their memory and any implications of this at trial should be raised for a decision at a Pre Trial Hearing (PTMH) stage.

8.35 **Defence Witness Interviews**

Accused persons in all Crown Court trials are required to submit a statement before the trial setting out the nature of their defence and the details of any alibi witnesses they intend to call. These are generally referred to as defence statements and are compiled by the legal representative and signed by the defendant; they are not section 9 CJA statements and should not be confused with such.

Since 1 May 2010 the accused is also required to provide details to the prosecution of anyone they intend to call as a defence witness at the trial (other than the defendant). This notification allows an opportunity for the police to interview them before the trial unless they have already obtained a statement from them during the investigation.

The defence witness must be asked whether they consent to be interviewed and informed:

- the interview is requested following their identification by the accused as a proposed witness either for an alibi or as a defence witness
- they are not obliged to attend the proposed interview
- they are entitled to be accompanied by a solicitor (at their own expense)
- a record will be made of the interview, and they will be supplied with a copy

If the witness consents to the interview they must be asked:

- whether they wish to have a solicitor present
- whether they consent to a solicitor attending the interview as an observer on behalf of the accused
- whether they consent to a copy of the record of interview being sent to the accused
- even if they do not consent, the disclosure obligations under the Criminal Procedure and Investigations Act 1996 (CPIA) may nevertheless require the prosecution to disclose the record of interview to the accused (and any co-accused)

The accused or their legal representative should be informed before the interview that:

- an interview has been requested with the witness
- whether the witness consented to the interview or not
- if the witness consented, whether they also consented to a solicitor attending the interview as an observer on behalf of the accused
- if the accused is not legally represented and if the witness consents to a solicitor attending the interview as an observer on their behalf, the accused must be offered the opportunity to appoint a solicitor to attend before the interview is held
- a reasonable date, time and venue for the interview must be nominated (with notification of any changes)
- with consent of the witness, the accused's solicitor must be given reasonable notice of the arrangements and be invited to observe the interview

Conducting the interview:

- an accurate record must be made, whether the interview takes place at a police station or elsewhere
- the record must, where practicable, be a visual recording with sound, or audio recording, or a section 9 CJA statement (MG11)
- any witness statement must be completed during the interview and timed and signed by the maker
- a copy of the MG11 and recording (if made) must be served on the witness, and, if the witness consents, provided to the accused or the accused's solicitor

KEY POINTS

- A defence witness is not under any legal obligation to be interviewed or make a statement to the police. If they refuse, an official notebook entry should be completed and an MG11 produced by the officer describing the full circumstances.
- Provided the accused's solicitor was given reasonable notice of the interview taking place, the fact that they are not present does not prevent the interview being conducted.
- If the witness withdraws consent to the accused's solicitor being present, the interview may continue without them.
- If the witness intends to appoint a solicitor for the interview, they must be permitted to attend.
- The MG11 must be completed whilst the interview is in progress; this means it is not prepared later by reviewing the recording, as with a significant witness interview.
- The interview will always be unused material and will need listing and describing on the MG6C.

8.36 Witness Charter

The *Witness Charter* (Criminal Justice System 2009) applies to all witnesses regardless of whether they are a victim.

It sets out what help can be expected from the police by witnesses to a crime or incident and the standards of service from other criminal justice agencies and lawyers if the witness is asked to give evidence for the prosecution or the defence in criminal proceedings.

The Charter outlines 34 standards on the level of service a witness should expect at every stage in the criminal justice process and intends to ensure every witness receives a level of service that meets their individual needs.

References

College of Policing (2021) *Major Crime Investigation Manual*

Ministry of Justice (2022) *Achieving Best Evidence in Criminal Proceedings, Guidance on Interviewing Victims and Witnesses, and Guidance on Using Special Measures*

Ministry of Justice (2020) *Code of Practice for the Victims of Crime*

Ministry of Justice (2013) *Witness Charter*

NPIA/ACPO (2009) *National Investigative Interviewing Strategy 2009*

Chapter 9
Managing Suspects

9.1 Introduction

Having identified that a crime has been committed, the next objective is usually to identify the offender(s). Suspects can emerge from any of the 'golden hour' actions and main lines of enquiry described in previous chapters. Managing suspects requires management of risk and community impact and exploitation of evidence-gathering opportunities available, from arrest and forensic recovery through to detention management and interviewing. Generally, suspect status should only be declared when:

- tangible investigative material exists to directly link a person to involvement in the offence, for example physical/forensic evidence, eyewitness testimony, CCTV, or
- circumstantial investigative material exists of sufficient strength to provide reasonable objective grounds for suspicion based on known facts or information (as opposed to merely a hunch), or
- there is a strong intelligence case supported by properly graded and evaluated material

Nominating a 'suspect' is a significant phase in an investigation and needs careful consideration, with the rationale and justification being recorded, usually in a policy file/decision log. The term 'suspect' implies there are reasonable grounds to suspect a person's involvement in an offence. It affords them protection and rights under the Police and Criminal Evidence Act 1984 (PACE), including legal advice and being cautioned before questioning.

Blackstone's Crime Investigators' Handbook. Steve Hibbitt and Gary Shaw, Oxford University Press. © Oxford University Press 2023.
DOI: 10.1093/oso/9780192867896.003.0009

It is important not only to declare suspect status when appropriate (as there needs to be justification for doing so), but also in some circumstances to justify why a person was not nominated as a suspect before they were interviewed. This may be necessary to defend against possible future accusations that a person's rights were deliberately circumvented.

The investigative interviewing of a suspect is a vitally important part of the process in any investigation. The interview allows the suspect to establish their position in relation to the investigation, the investigator to develop further lines of enquiry and provides an opportunity to present the gathered investigative material to the suspect.

When planning and preparing for an interview the investigator should be cognisant of the need to try and create a conducive environment that affords the suspect an opportunity to provide an account if they choose to do so.

In those circumstances where a guilty person admits their involvement, it enables the investigator to probe for the required detail that allows the correct means of case disposal to be taken. Additionally, there are many added benefits associated with a properly obtained admission. A professionally conducted interview also allows the innocent person to be identified by means of appropriate questioning and approach.

KEY POINT

The term 'suspect' should not be confused with the term 'subject' which is often used during investigations. The two terms can become confused not only in police circles but also by the media and sometimes even lawyers, so any misunderstandings need to be corrected quickly.

9.2 Powers of Arrest

The amendments to PACE by the Serious Organised Crime and Police Act 2005 (SOCPA) mean arrests can be made for any offence provided certain conditions apply. For an arrest to be lawful the arresting officer must have:

(1) Reasonable grounds to *suspect* an offence has been committed, and the person committed it, or they were in the act of committing, or were about to commit the offence; AND
(2) Reasonable grounds to *believe* arrest is necessary for one or more of the specified reasons (known as the necessity test) to:
   a. ascertain the person's name
   b. ascertain the person's address
   c. prevent the person causing physical harm to themselves or suffering physical injury
   d. prevent loss of or damage to property
   e. prevent an offence against public decency
   f. prevent an unlawful obstruction of the highway
   g. protect a child or vulnerable person
   h. prevent any prosecution being hindered by the disappearance of the person in question
   i. allow a prompt and effective investigation of the offence or of the conduct of the person in question

The prompt and effective investigation condition may be satisfied if there are grounds to believe that the person:

- has made false statements or statements that cannot be easily verified
- may steal or destroy evidence
- may intimidate, threaten or make contact with witnesses
- it is necessary to obtain evidence by interviewing

Where the suspected offence is *indictable*, this condition may justify arrest if there is a need to:

- enter and search premises occupied or controlled by the person
- search the person
- prevent contact with others or take fingerprints, footwear impressions, samples or photographs for comparison purposes

On 12 November 2012 a revision of PACE (Code G) was implemented demanding more detailed consideration of the necessity test by arresting officers than was previously required. Arresting officers must consider facts and information tending to indicate the person's innocence as well as their guilt (including whether any use of force was lawful and reasonable), and consider practical alternatives to arrest, such as street bail or conducting a voluntary interview with the suspect.

Each case must be decided on a case-by-case basis according to the circumstances existing at the time, using professional judgement and discretion concerning the necessity and proportionality of arrest. The importance of documenting decision making for future scrutiny cannot be underestimated.

9.3 Voluntary Interviews

Necessity to arrest and necessity to interview are two separate issues, therefore if arrest is not considered necessary a suspect could be interviewed voluntarily under caution.

Code G now clarifies the situation of what to do if a 'volunteer' leaves the interview before its conclusion having been told (under Code C) they are not under arrest and are free to leave at any time. Leaving the interview could now justify arrest (under Code G) if there is a necessity to continue questioning, but this must be judged on the circumstances of the individual case existing at the time.

Necessity to arrest should be kept under continuous review during the interview. Circumstances could change making arrest necessary, for example threats made to others necessitating arrest to prevent physical harm, or denials requiring corroboration necessitating detention for a prompt and effective investigation (these are not exhaustive examples).

Voluntary interviews should be planned and conducted as thoroughly as for a person under arrest. Attendees should not be treated with any less consideration than an arrested person. It is the interviewer's responsibility to ensure any vulnerability is identified and appropriate safeguards are in place, including any requirement for an appropriate adult, interpreter etc. Voluntary attendees also have an absolute right to outside communication and legal advice.

KEY POINTS

- Special Warnings under sections 36 and 37 of the Criminal Justice and Public Order Act 1994 (CJPO) only apply to suspects under arrest; therefore, they do not apply to voluntary interviews. Planning to deliver special warnings may therefore justify necessity to arrest.
- Adverse inferences from silence may apply when a person is interviewed voluntarily as they can access legal advice if they wish.

9.4 Planning and Conducting Arrests

Arrest plans depend on the nature of the offence and what is known about the suspect. The primary objective is to gather as much evidence as possible from the arrest whilst minimising any identified risks. Generic considerations include:

- the timing and location of arrest
- recording significant statements
- searching suspects and premises
- transporting suspects
- preventing forensic cross-contamination
- location of detention
- briefing Custody Officers
- checking personal property and seizing relevant items (eg mobile phones)

- physical and forensic medical examination and evidential samples
- photographing injuries
- considering urgent or emergency interviews
- holding incommunicado
- fitness to interview
- appropriate adults
- interpreters
- interview strategies
- fast track actions and forensic submissions etc
- researching the suspect and the likely place of arrest, including who or what may be present to inform the risk assessment.

Although each case differs, some generic intelligence requirements include the following:

Checklist—Suspect intelligence profile

- Name, age, date of birth
- Other names used or known by
- Full physical description
- Known intelligence (including any medical conditions/vulnerabilities, habitual drug use etc)
- Recent photograph
- Current residence
- Details and layout of the location of arrest (owner of the premises, other occupants, risks and hazards such as children, pets, likely substance abuse, hiding places, outbuildings and gardens, access and exit points, previous police visits and outcomes, local community/neighbourhood details, etc)
- Vehicles owned, used or accessed
- Other premises and places frequented
- Known associates and their profiles including descriptions
- Criminal history including modus operandi and behaviour on arrest
- Current intelligence

- Warning markers, such as use of violence, weapons or access to firearms
- Previous responses in police interviews

9.4.1 Timing of arrests

The best time to arrest a suspect is ideally as soon as possible after the offence has been committed during the 'golden hour' period. This reduces the loss of material and is always in the public's best interest.

The timing of an arrest should meet the needs of the investigation whilst being balanced against the risk posed by the suspect to the victim, witnesses, the public and the arresting officers. Additionally, any likelihood of further offences being committed or evidence being concealed, destroyed or falsified requires consideration. The circumstances must be kept under continuous review should circumstances change.

Reasons to delay arrest could include pursuing other lines of enquiry, using covert tactics, coordinating the simultaneous arrest of multiple suspects, gathering further evidence to conduct a more effective interview and reducing the possibility of using pre-charge bail. A record should be maintained outlining the reasons with justification for the delay.

KEY POINT

Any decision to delay arresting an identified suspect must be fully justified. If they commit further preventable offences, it may be difficult to defend the decision, so it is extremely important to make a record of the decision and its rationale.

9.4.2 Location of arrest

The arrest location is influenced by its timing, including whether the suspect is likely to be at home or at another location during a particular time of day. In some sensitive areas the impact of the arrest on the wider community needs consideration and consultation in advance with the Community Cohesion Officer or Neighbourhood Policing Team Inspector to manage the consequences.

Juveniles should generally not be arrested at their place of education unless it is unavoidable, in which case the principal or their nominee must be informed (PACE Code C, 11E).

9.4.3 Powers of entry

Excluding entry under a search warrant, powers to enter and search premises to arrest for an indictable offence are available under section 17 of PACE. Reasonable force may be used, if necessary, where there are reasonable grounds to believe the person sought is on the premises. Searches must only be to the extent reasonably required to locate the suspect.

Powers of entry are available for certain non-indictable offences, namely:

- prohibition of uniforms in connection with political objectives, section 1 of the Public Order Act 1936
- offences relating to entering and remaining on property, sections 6 to 8 or 10 of the Criminal Law Act 1967
- fear or provocation of violence, section 4 of the Public Order Act 1986
- driving under the influence of drink or drugs, section 4 of the Road Traffic Act 1988
- failure to stop when required by a constable in uniform, section 163 of the Road Traffic Act 1988
- offences involving transport system workers being over the prescribed alcohol limit, section 27 of the Transport and Works Act 1992
- failure to comply with an interim possession order, section 76 of the Criminal Justice and Public Order Act 1994

- certain offences relating to prevention of harm to animals, Animal Welfare Act 2006

Premises can also be entered and searched for a suspected person with the written permission of a person able to provide consent (PACE, Code B, 5.1 to 5.4), and to capture persons unlawfully at large, save life and limb or prevent serious damage to property (section 17 of PACE).

9.4.4 Arresting officers

There are no rigid rules on the most appropriate person to conduct an arrest, for example an interviewing officer or someone not involved in the interview process, and there are advantages and disadvantages to each. Whoever is tasked must be fully briefed, ensuring they form their own opinion of the grounds and necessity; otherwise the arrest may be unlawful.

In order to record the exact nature of what takes place at the arrest the use of Body Worn Video (BWV) should be considered.

9.5 Significant Statements/Silence

Significant statements and unsolicited comments have been discussed in Chapter 4 and do not require further elaboration, except to say that when planning arrests an officer should be nominated to record in writing/video all significant statements and unsolicited comments, and to maintain a contemporaneous record until the suspect has been booked into custody. They are of tremendous value to the subsequent interview, and even denials when arrested can form the basis of a challenge when presented later.

9.6 Urgent Interviews

Arrested persons must not be interviewed except at a police station or other authorised place of detention, unless delay would be likely to lead to interference with or harm to evidence connected with an offence, interference with or physical harm to other people, serious loss of or damage to property, alerting other suspects not yet arrested or hindering the recovery of property obtained as a consequence of an offence.

If any of these criteria is satisfied, an 'urgent interview' can be conducted, such as questioning to locate and recover a firearm discarded by a suspect before anyone finding it is caused harm. Critically, questioning must cease once the relevant risk has been averted or the necessary questions have been put (PACE, Code C, 11.1). Urgent interviews should therefore not be used to ask evidential questions about other lines of enquiry.

When planning arrests involving urgent interviews, consideration must be given to practicalities, including the method of recording, such as contemporaneous notes or portable visual recording/audio equipment.

9.6.1 Interviews before requested legal advice at a police station

When a detainee requests legal advice at the police station, they cannot be interviewed until they have received it, unless the grounds above apply and authorisation has been provided by a Superintendent or above (not necessarily independent of the investigation).

KEY POINTS

- Should the criteria apply, PACE allows urgent interviews to be conducted away from the police station, such as at the location of arrest. There is no reference in the Act to any authority being required in such circumstances.

- At the police station, after legal advice has been requested, urgent interviews need to be authorised by a Superintendent (or above) and use the caution *'You don't have to say anything but anything you do say may be given in evidence'*. This means adverse inferences cannot be drawn from the interview.
- Urgent interviews are infrequently used except in missing persons, kidnap, abduction and terrorism cases and are likely to be closely scrutinised by the courts.

9.7 **Searches**

Searching detainees and their premises and vehicles is a routine activity requiring little expansion here. Searches are an opportunity to gather investigative material linking suspects to alleged offences, and although it seems obvious, when planning arrests, full details of items sought should be supplied to the search team. Specific tasks and responsibilities should be designated to individuals ensuring nothing is overlooked and opportunities missed through wrongful assumptions and misunderstandings.

9.8 **Location of Detention**

Suspect arrest planning includes considering the location of detention if multiple suspects are to be arrested simultaneously. Ideally, detention should be at different locations to prevent collusion and forensic cross-contamination. If this is impracticable and the same location is used, the Custody Officer should be briefed in advance to prevent the investigation being disadvantaged.

Particular facilities and resources may be required, which is worth considering as part of the arrest strategy. Forensic kits and cells that are not regularly used may be ideal when it is necessary to maximise forensic examination opportunities. Access to interviewing facilities with downstream monitoring capability may also be a consideration.

9.9 Pre-briefing the Custody Officer

In pre-planned operations the Custody Officer and their staff should be briefed in advance, including the grounds for arrest, to prevent unnecessary information being asked for and revealed in the presence and hearing of the suspect.

A Custody Officer briefing is an opportunity to raise issues concerning the detention, such as managing multiple suspects, availability of cells including 'dry cells', forensic considerations, welfare and risk management.

9.10 Arrest Team Briefing

All personnel involved in the arrest operation, including any specialist resources such as Crime Scene Investigators (CSIs) and others if involved should be briefed by the officer responsible for the investigation or their nominee. An operational 'order' or briefing document is often prepared using a recognised structure such as IIMARCH or SAFCOM.

Effective briefings can have a positive or negative impact on success. Questions about roles and responsibilities should be encouraged and dealt with at the briefing.

Documents and records are subject to disclosure rules, and care must be taken to ensure no briefing material is inadvertently left at the subject premises (which has embarrassingly happened in the past).

Checklist—Arrest and Search Team Briefing Agenda

- Introductions
- Operational objectives
- Details of the investigation
- Current situation
- Details of suspect(s) to be arrested, including recent photograph(s)
- Background details on persons expected to be at an address
- Powers of arrest and the grounds
- Powers of entry
- Precise wording for arresting officer(s)
- Search strategy and parameters (if applicable)
- Details of items sought and how they are to be dealt with
- Documentation including any warrants and search record numbers
- Roles and responsibilities
- Risks and control measures
- Communications including Airwave channels and contact telephone numbers
- Arrangements for collecting material under the Criminal Procedure and Investigations Act 1996 (CPIA)
- Debriefing location and time

The control room/command centre for the relevant area should be informed in advance should assistance be required. The local policing team manager should be informed and any local community issues considered.

9.11 Arrest and Search Team Debriefing

A structured debriefing of staff involved in the arrest operation ensures all evidential opportunities have been maximised and relevant information disseminated:

Checklist—Debriefing agenda

- Any significant statements
- Other persons present
- Potential witnesses spoken to
- Search results
- Details and location of any items seized
- Fast track actions identified
- Other investigative material identified
- Potential special warning material identified
- Completing and collating evidential statements
- Completing the Premises Searched Record
- Intelligence gathered
- Other relevant information, such as callers to the address and spoken to
- Handover and collection of any relevant material under CPIA
- Welfare/health and safety issues
- Local community impact information

KEY POINT

Arrests and searches provide opportunities to conduct other enquiries, including speaking to other people at the address who could be witnesses or potential intelligence sources. Neighbours and any visitors can be spoken to at the same time to see if they have any useful information about the detained person, such as movements, habits, associates and vehicles used. Conducting house-to-house (H2H) enquiries with neighbours can be useful for the same purpose.

9.12 Proactive Hunts for Suspects

Often swiftly locating and arresting a known suspect(s) is paramount due to the risk they present to the safety of the public. These cases can attract significant public and media attention and involve substantial resources, particularly if firearms are involved.

The offence under investigation could be a 'crime in action', meaning the offender is or may be continuing to commit the offence or further crimes whilst the investigation is in progress, such as an abduction where a victim's whereabouts are unknown, or there is reason to believe there may be further victims, or the same victim remains at risk of further harm.

The priority consideration is potentially increasing the risk to others by generating publicity and identifying the suspect. Additionally, there are consequences for the investigation, including the impact on any subsequent identification procedures and obtaining and coordinating the necessary resources.

Any high-impact 'person or manhunts' are potential critical incidents and are usually the responsibility of a Senior Investigating Officer (SIO) involving the Crown Prosecution Service (CPS) and Association of Chief Police Officers (ACPO) level consultation in a Gold Commander role.

9.13 Detention Management

9.13.1 Custody Officer briefing

Whilst recognising the Custody Officer's obligations when authorising detention, the content of the custody record (which is available for inspection by legal representatives) should be managed to prevent it having a negative impact on any subsequent pre-interview briefing of a suspect's legal adviser. PACE Code G, Note 3 now specifically states:

> An arrested person must be given sufficient information to enable them to understand they have been deprived of their liberty and the reason they have been arrested, as soon as practicable after their arrest, e.g., when a person is arrested on suspicion of committing an offence they must be informed of the nature of the suspected offence and when and where it was committed. The suspect must also be informed of the reason or reasons why arrest is considered necessary. Vague or technical language should be avoided. When explaining why one or more of the arrest criteria apply, it is not necessary to disclose any specific details that might undermine or otherwise adversely affect any investigative processes. An example might be the conduct of a formal interview when prior disclosure of such details might give the suspect an opportunity to fabricate an innocent explanation or to otherwise conceal lies from the interviewer.

When briefing the Custody Officer, any information which could impact on the investigation should not be supplied within hearing of the suspect. Additionally, other matters affecting the suspect's detention should be included in the briefing.

Checklist—Custody Officer briefing

- Nature of offence
- When and where committed
- Significant statement(s) made by the suspect
- Welfare, vulnerability, risk assessment and any requirement for:
  - o appropriate adult
  - o interpreter
  - o strip search
  - o intimate search
  - o delayed intimation
  - o delayed access to legal advice

- o conducting an urgent interview
- o forensic considerations (such as intimate and non-intimate samples, medical examination, photographing injuries or identifying features)

It is helpful (as well as courteous) to provide a contact number for custody staff to contact the lead investigator if necessary.

9.13.2 **Strip searches**

A strip search is the removal of more than a person's outer clothing. It is authorised by the Custody Officer when considered necessary to remove an article which the detainee would not be allowed to keep because it may present a danger to themselves or others, might be used to assist escape or be evidence relating to an offence. The conduct of strip searches is covered by PACE Code C, Annex A.

9.13.3 **Intimate searches**

Intimate searches are the physical examination of a person's body orifices (other than the mouth). They are authorised by an Inspector or above with reasonable grounds for believing the detained person may have concealed on them anything they could and might use to cause physical harm to themselves or another, or a Class A drug which they intended to supply to another or export.

There must be reasonable grounds for believing an intimate search is the only way of removing the item(s), and the detainee must be told before the search that it has been authorised, along with the grounds.

If the intimate search is for drugs, before being asked to consent, the detainee must be warned that refusal without good cause may harm their case if it comes to trial, and their consent must be provided in writing.

KEY POINTS

- Intimate searches seeking items the detainee might use to cause harm may only be conducted by a registered medical practitioner or registered nurse, unless an Inspector or above is satisfied *as a last resort* that the risks associated with allowing the item to remain with the detainee outweigh the risks associated with removing it and it is not practicable for a doctor or nurse to conduct the search. In such cases an officer of the same sex as the detainee may carry out the search.
- A drugs search can only be conducted at a hospital, surgery or other medical premises by a healthcare professional.

9.13.4 Delaying intimation/incommunicado

Detainees may have one friend, relative or other person known to them or interested in their welfare informed of the location of their detention as soon as practicable. This can be delayed when the offence is *indictable* and an Inspector or above believes communicating the information is likely to lead to interference with or harm to evidence or other people, alerting others suspected of committing the offence but not yet arrested or hindering the recovery of stolen property.

The officer may also authorise delay where they have reasonable grounds for believing the detained person has benefited from their criminal conduct, and the recovery of the value of the property constituting the benefit will be hindered by telling the named person of their arrest.

Intimations must not be delayed for more than 36 hours and cannot be delayed once the grounds have ceased.

KEY POINT

With arrested juveniles, the person responsible for their welfare must be informed of their detention.

9.13.5 Right to legal advice

Delaying legal advice is only permitted if the detainee is in police detention for an *indictable offence* and authorisation has been provided by a Superintendent or above. Reasonable grounds are required to believe delay might lead to interference with or harm to evidence connected with an indictable offence, interference with or physical harm to other people, serious loss of or damage to property, alerting other people suspected of having committed such an offence but not yet arrested for it or hindering the recovery of property obtained in consequence of the commission of such an offence.

The officer may also authorise delay if they have reasonable grounds to believe the person detained for the indictable offence has benefited from their criminal conduct, and the recovery of the value of the property constituting the benefit will be hindered by allowing access to legal advice.

Once sufficient information to avert the risk has been obtained, questioning must cease until the detainee has received legal advice.

KEY POINT

Where legal advice has been requested but denied, adverse inferences from silence cannot be drawn. The interview must be conducted using the shortened caution, 'You do not have to say anything but anything you do say may be given in evidence'.

Where a solicitor nominated or selected by the detainee cannot be contacted or has previously indicated they do not wish to be contacted or, having been contacted, has declined to attend, and the detainee has been advised of the duty solicitor scheme but has declined to ask for the duty solicitor, an Inspector or above may authorise the interview to proceed. Adverse inferences may be drawn in these circumstances because legal advice is not being denied.

Where a detainee who has requested legal advice changes their mind, the interview may be started or continued without delay, provided they agree in writing or on the interview record and an Inspector or above has enquired about the reasons and authorises the interview to proceed. Confirmation of the detainee's agreement, the reasons (if any) for changing their mind and the name of the authorising officer shall be recorded in the interview record. Adverse inferences may be drawn because legal advice is not being denied.

KEY POINT

If a solicitor arrives at the station to see a particular person, that person must be informed of their arrival and asked if they would like to see the solicitor, whether they are being interviewed or not (unless Annex B applies). This applies even if the detainee has declined legal advice, or if, having previously requested legal advice, they have agreed to be interviewed without it. The solicitor's attendance and the detainee's decision must be noted in the custody record.

9.14 **Forensic Strategy**

Depending on the requirements of the investigation, a forensic strategy to prove or disprove a suspect's involvement in the offence may be required. Any necessary authorities should be planned for in advance and the attendance and briefing of a forensic medical examiner and CSI coordinated. All requirements should be made clear to fully exploit any opportunities.[1]

[1] Recovering forensic evidence from people including suspects is described in Chapter 6.

Checklist—Suspect forensic considerations

- Forensic material available, for example clothing, jewellery, trace evidence through swabbing for blood or fibres
- Relevant authorities required
- Cross-contamination control plan
- Coordinate attendance and brief/debrief FME and/or CSI (if required)
- Full body examination (body mapping) noting marks, scars or injuries
- Record descriptions of any tattoos or other identifying marks
- Describe any injuries using conventional medical terms and layman's language in brackets
- Measure and photograph all injuries with a scale
- General body photographs of detainee's front, back, hands, feet, legs, head, including full length images
- Medical staff to record the detainee's height, weight and build
- Sample of blood/urine for evidence of intoxication or misuse of substances relevant to the investigation
- Buccal swab
- Firearms discharge/explosive residue swabs
- Swabs from palms and backs of both hands
- Fingernail scrapings
- Fingernail cuttings
- Combed head hair
- Plucked head hair
- Cut head hair
- Swabs from body sites suspected of being connected to an assault
- Body impression
- Dental impression
- Continuity and storage of exhibits

9.15 **Managing Legal Advisers**

The solicitor's role in the police station is to protect and advance the legal rights of their client. On occasion this may require giving advice which has the effect of avoiding their client giving evidence which strengthens the prosecution case (PACE, Code C).

In fulfilling their obligations, solicitors probe the evidence and actively enquire into the investigation, including the police conduct towards their client. They assess their client's vulnerability (if any) and ability to communicate during interview and identify the safest defence. This could be to answer questions, produce a prepared statement or remain silent.

Furthermore, the solicitor will attempt to gain the most favourable disposal by influencing the police not to charge, or obtaining the most favourable alternative, for example a caution. If their client is charged, they will seek the most favourable position, such as granting bail.

9.15.1 **Pre-interview briefings**

Solicitors will seek as much information as possible about the case from all sources including custody staff, investigators and the suspect. Custody Officers should only provide information on the *grounds* for detention and matters relating to the custody record. Any requests for further information should be referred to the investigating officer for consideration of the pre-interview briefing (PIB).

A PIB is the meeting between an investigator and the legal representative before the interview. This is when the reason(s) for arrest and the purpose of the interview are outlined.

This briefing should be conducted in a suitable location like an office or interview room, where it can be held in private without interruption. Discussions at custody desks in full view and hearing of others with surrounding distractions are not good practice.

The content of the briefing should be contained in a typed or written document, a copy of which is provided to the legal representative and signed by all parties present. Best practice is to audio record the process so an accurate record is available for future scrutiny if necessary. This may be impractical for all cases due to resource restrictions (particularly in volume crime investigations), but as a minimum a written briefing should be provided.

A record of the PIB including any information provided or withheld with the reasons should be recorded on form MG6a and submitted with any prosecution file.

Although there is no legal obligation to provide any information about the *investigation* prior to interview, it may be beneficial to disclose certain material so the solicitor can provide realistic informed advice to the suspect.

The content of the briefing is therefore a matter of professional judgement, decided on a case-by-case basis considering:

- the material available or likely to become available to the investigation
- The impact on the interview of disclosing the information
- what the suspect already knows about the investigation, in which case there is probably limited value in withholding this information
- the material gathered by the investigation which the suspect is unaware of, in which case the decision is when and how to reveal this information
- if the suspect is vulnerable, this may influence the amount of information provided to prevent allegations of confusing them
- with multiple suspects a common pre-interview briefing strategy may be initially required
- the content and timing of any media releases may impact on the content of the PIB and timing of the interview
- whether phased disclosure over a series of interviews is an appropriate tactic to use

- care must be taken not to mislead the solicitor or to overstate the importance of any evidence disclosed

KEY POINTS

- A balance must be drawn between providing sufficient information for a solicitor to provide realistic advice whilst preventing a suspect fabricating a defence based on the information disclosed.
- Solicitors are aware the police are not legally obliged to provide further information but often press for further disclosure and question the strength of the evidence. Such requests should be politely and professionally resisted.

9.15.2 Pre-interview disclosure to unrepresented suspects

Providing a form of pre-interview briefing to suspects who are not legally represented has generated some debate. The National Police Chiefs Council (NPCC) position is that providing disclosure to unrepresented suspects is not recommended. Legal advisers are experts in law and can therefore properly advise their clients on the strength and significance of any evidence revealed. Unrepresented suspects could misunderstand the content of a PIB and its significance for the interview; they may have questions on the information provided which in themselves risk becoming an interview.

9.15.3 Legal advice during interview

Solicitors may intervene during interview to seek clarification, challenge improper questions (or the manner in which they were put), advise their clients not to reply to particular questions or to provide further legal advice. Their role is clear and does not include questioning the interviewer on the conduct of the investigation or the content of the PIB.

9.15.4 Exclusion from interview

Solicitors can only be required to leave an interview if their approach or conduct prevents or unreasonably obstructs proper questions being put to the suspect or their response being recorded. Examples of unacceptable conduct include answering questions on the suspect's behalf or providing written replies to quote (this does not include introducing a prepared statement).

If this happens the interview should be stopped and a Superintendent or above consulted if readily available, or if not an officer not below Inspector and not connected with the investigation. After speaking with the solicitor, the officer consulted decides if the interview should continue with that solicitor present. If it is decided to exclude them, the suspect is allowed to consult another solicitor and have them present during interview.

Removing a solicitor from interview is a rare and serious step; a court may need to be satisfied that the decision was properly made. The officer making the decision may therefore need to witness the solicitor's conduct by listening to a recording of the interview.

9.16 Interviewing Suspects

Interviewing is a constantly evolving discipline and beyond the scope of this section to cover in more than cursory detail. As with victims and witnesses, the PEACE framework and principles of investigative interviewing described in Chapter 8 also apply to suspects.

9.16.1 Planning suspect interviews

All interviews must be properly planned with achievable topic-based objectives to meet the needs of the investigation. Planning should never be sacrificed or dismissed as too time consuming (which it is not).

The following checklist contains some generic planning considerations but is not exhaustive:

Checklist—Interview planning

- Review available material/facts already established
- Review the suspect's antecedents/background information to identify:
  - o evidence of bad character
  - o any vulnerability which may impact on the interview
  - o age
  - o gender
  - o domestic circumstances
  - o educational attainment/intellectual ability
  - o physical and mental health
  - o trauma
  - o intelligence linking the suspect to other offences
  - o previous contact with the police and responses when interviewed
- Examine the custody record
- Establish fitness to interview
- Review detainee's property for relevance to investigation
- Review detainee's physical description for relevance to investigation
- Identify any injuries/marks for potential special warning
- Review detainee's clothing for relevance to investigation
- Identify significant statements/silences
- Identify special warning material
- Visit the scene
- Identify all possible offences
- Determine points to prove
- Consider possible defences
- Identify interview objectives/facts to be determined:
  - o significant statement/silence
  - o suspect's account of the event
  - o victim

- scene
- time parameters (movements/alibi)
- introducing evidence suggesting involvement in the offence
- introducing forensic evidence
- introducing exhibits
- other investigative areas
- other information required from the suspect, for example mobile phone numbers, PIN codes and passwords, medical release permissions, authority to examine financial records, consent to identification procedures, handwriting samples

- Consider innocent/reasonable explanation
- Identify exhibits required for the interview
- Consider the suspect's potential responses and how to respond:
  - admissions
  - denials
  - no comment
  - production of a prepared statement
  - reasonable/innocent explanation
- Prepare an interview plan
- Pre-interview briefing:
  - method of recording
  - information disclosed
  - information withheld
  - handling requests for further information
- Resources and practical arrangements:
  - interview room
  - recording equipment
  - timing of the interview
  - sequence of multiple suspect interviews
  - exhibits
  - photographs
  - notepaper
  - exhibit labels
- Coordinate others required:
  - appropriate adult

  - o interpreter
  - o solicitor
- Roles and responsibilities:
  - o lead interviewer
  - o co-interviewer
  - o downstream monitor(s)

9.16.2 Conducting suspect interviews

The structure of the suspect interview should have been considered and planned by the investigator taking into account its relationship between the pre-interviewing briefing (legal adviser) and the investigative strategy.

The *Principles of Investigative Interviewing* and PACE underpin what is required from the interviewer when conducting the suspect interview. It is important that the interviewer has a clear aim and has identified the relevant investigative topics that will help them to achieve their aim.

In accordance with the PEACE framework, the first aim should be to establish the suspects position in relation to the offence that they are suspected of committing. Therefore, questioning the suspect about their involvement in the suspected offence concerning their movements during the identified relevant time parameters should be the focus of the first phase of the interview. How the interview will progress will then be determined by the response from the suspect.

The second phase of the interview should then focus on relevant investigative topics in relation to the actions of the suspect both before and after the offence was committed. These are areas that have not been covered during the first phase of the interview. It must be remembered that an investigative interview is being conducted where the overall objective is to gather relevant investigative material which may assist in determining a person's involvement or non-involvement in an offence under investigation.

The final phase of the suspect interview is the challenge section where the investigator presents the relevant investigative material that has been gathered during the investigation.

The earlier planning of the interview will have determined when the respective phases of the interview were to be conducted. It is important that the interviewer maintains a professional role throughout and recognises their role in respect of gathering investigative material if the suspect chooses to waive their right to silence.

9.16.3 Juveniles/mentally disordered or otherwise mentally vulnerable people

Vulnerable suspects should be treated as being at some risk during the interview and given special consideration. Although often capable of providing reliable evidence, they may without knowing or wishing to do so also provide information that is unreliable, misleading or self-incriminating.

An appropriate adult must be involved where there is any doubt about a person's age, mental state or capacity. Their role is not passive; they are present to ensure the interview is conducted fairly and to facilitate communication.

If the appropriate adult is present at the police station during the reception process, the rights and entitlements must be completed in their presence. If they are not present, the process provisions must be completed again when they arrive.

Fitness to interview is the responsibility of the Custody Officer, in consultation with the officer in charge of the investigation and appropriate health care professionals as necessary. This includes identifying any safeguards required to allow the interview to take place.

9.16.4 Foreign languages

Unless authority to conduct an urgent interview has been granted, a person must not be interviewed without an interpreter if they have difficulty understanding English, the interviewer cannot speak the person's own language or the person wants an interpreter present.

KEY POINT

Where possible, interpreters should be obtained from the National Register of Public Service Interpreters (NRPSI) or the Council for the Advancement of Communication with Deaf People (CACDP), Directory of British Sign Language/English Interpreters.

9.16.5 Significant statements/silences

At the beginning of the interview after caution, any significant statement or silence which occurred in the presence and hearing of a police officer or other police staff before the start of the interview should be put to the suspect (unless put in a previous interview). The suspect should be asked to confirm or deny the statement/silence and if they want to add or dispute anything. This may also be expanded on later in the interview.

9.16.6 Special warnings

Some evidence has more significance than other elements of the investigation when an explanation is requested during interview. These areas may be the subject of special warnings under the CJPO.

When a suspect who is interviewed *after arrest* fails or refuses to answer such questions or fails to answer them satisfactorily after being given due warning, a court or jury may draw a proper inference.

Section 36 applies when a person is arrested by a constable and there is found:

1. on their person, in or on their clothing or footwear, or otherwise in their possession, or in the place where they were arrested, any objects marks or substances or marks on such objects,
2. which a constable investigating the case reasonably believes may be attributable to the person participating in an offence specified by the constable, and
3. the person fails or refuses to account for the objects, marks or substances found when requested to do so by a constable who informs them of their belief.

Section 37 applies when an arrested person was found by a constable:

1. at a place at or about the time the offence for which he was arrested is alleged to have been committed, and
2. a constable investigating the offence reasonably believes their presence at that place at that time may be attributable to their participation in the offence, and
3. the constable informs the person of their belief, and the person fails or refuses to account for their presence at that place when requested to do so.

For an inference to be drawn, the suspect must be informed by the interviewing officer using ordinary clear nontechnical language:

- the OFFENCE under investigation
- what FACT the suspect is being asked to account for
- the belief this FACT may be due to the suspect taking part in the commission of the offence
- a court may draw a proper INFERENCE if the suspect fails or refuses to account for that fact
- the interview is being RECORDED and may be given in evidence if the case goes to trial

KEY POINTS

- The arresting officer and person giving the special warning do not have to be the same person.

- Special warnings do not apply to suspects who are not under arrest so cannot be used in voluntary interviews.
- Under the Police Reform Act 2002, designated non-warranted investigators can administer special warnings.
- Situations where a suspect's DNA is found on the victim's clothing was clarified in the case of *R v Abbas* (CLR 2010) where the court of appeal directed this did not fall within the definition of section 36 and therefore a special warning should not be given in these circumstances.
- The delivery of any special warnings and any suspect response should be highlighted in the record of interview and brought to the attention of the CPS on the form MG6.

9.16.7 **Bad character evidence**

Evidence of bad character is discussed in more detail in Chapter 13 so is only outlined here in relation to interviews with suspects.

Bad character is defined by section 98 of the Criminal Justice Act 2003 as 'evidence of, or a disposition towards misconduct'; this is not restricted to previous convictions and includes other reprehensible conduct. Supporting evidence is available from many sources, such as employment/disciplinary records, previous arrests which did not result in charges, previous charges and acquittals, and other information which demonstrates a propensity to be untruthful.

There are seven gateways through which a defendant's bad character may be introduced into evidence depending on the matter in issue:

1. All parties agree to it being admissible.
2. It is adduced from the defendant himself or is given in answer to a question asked by him in cross-examination and intended to elicit it.
3. It is important explanatory evidence without which the fact finders could not reasonably be expected to understand the background to the case.

4. It is relevant to an important matter in issue between the defendant and the prosecution.
5. It has substantial probative value in relation to an important matter in issue between the defendant and another co-defendant.
6. It is evidence to correct a false impression given by the defendant.
7. The defendant has made an attack on another person's character.

KEY POINTS

- Consider where the most appropriate place in the interview is to raise bad character.
- When framing questions, the relevance of the bad character material when compared with the subject of the interview should be pointed out and comment invited. There is little value in merely reading out lists of previous convictions, which generally attract a 'no comment' response.
- Bad character information is recorded and supplied to the CPS on form MG16.

9.16.8 Prepared statements

If a prepared statement is tendered and read out by the suspect or solicitor at the start of the interview (although they may be introduced at any stage) it should be dealt with as follows:

- accept the prepared statement, or copy (although solicitors cannot be forced to supply it)
- confirm the statement was made by the suspect
- if not already signed, ask the suspect to sign it (although they cannot be forced to do so)
- the statement should be exhibited by the interviewer
- conclude the interview informing the solicitor that the statement and the need for further interview will be considered

- analyse the statement, identifying any missing information, gaps and anomalies and revise the interview plan
- conduct a further interview based on the revised interview plan

KEY POINT

Prepared statements are rarely sufficiently detailed to answer all relevant questions. The interview should continue despite any indication that no further comment will be made. The threshold for ceasing questioning is when it is reasonably believed there is sufficient evidence for a realistic prospect of conviction. This is wider than the previous threshold of sufficient evidence to charge.

9.16.9 Refusal to be interviewed

A suspect may choose not to answer questions, but the police do not require their consent or agreement to be interviewed (PACE, Code C, 12.5).

If a suspect attempts to prevent questioning by leaving the interview room or refusing to leave their cell, they should be advised that their consent or agreement is not required. They should be cautioned and informed that if they fail or refuse to cooperate, the interview may take place in the cell and their failure or refusal to cooperate may be given in evidence. If they continue to be uncooperative, they should be interviewed in the cell using portable recording equipment. If this is not an option, a contemporaneous record of questions and answers should be recorded on form MG15.

KEY POINT

If a suspect refuses to be interviewed, it is still necessary to put relevant questions to them and provide an opportunity to answer for adverse inference applications to be made at court.

9.17 Detention Times

Generally, a detainee's relevant time is calculated from their time of arrival at the police station (section 41 of PACE). Exceptions are when a person wanted in one police force area is arrested and detained in another; their relevant time would start from the time of their arrival at the first police station in the area where they are wanted, or 24 hours after their arrest, whichever is earlier.

A different situation arises when a person is arrested for an offence in one police force area and found to be wanted for a different offence in another force area. In these circumstances, provided they are not interviewed about the second offence whilst in the first police area (or in transit), a fresh detention clock commences and their relevant time starts when they arrive at the first police station in the second force area, or 24 hours after they leave the station in the first police force area, whichever is the sooner.

KEY POINT

'Relevant time' should not be confused with 'authorised time' which is the time the Custody Officer authorises the detention of an arrested person and is the point from which periodic review times are calculated.

9.18 Detention Reviews

Periodic reviews of detention must be conducted:

- no later than six hours after detention was first authorised (the first review), then
- no later than nine hours after the first review (the second review), and
- subsequently at intervals of not more than nine hours

Where the detainee has not been charged, the review officer is an Inspector or above not directly involved in the investigation; but after charge, reviews are the Custody Officer's responsibility. The state of investigations should be communicated regularly to review officers to allow them to effectively discharge their responsibilities.

9.19 Extensions of Detention

Some investigations may require detention without charge beyond 24 hours for enquiries and interviews to be progressed.

Any time after the second review has been conducted (so no later than 15 hours) a Superintendent or above with responsibility for the police station holding the detainee may authorise extended detention without charge for up to a further 12 hours, where they have reasonable grounds for believing:

- an offence for which the detainee has been arrested is an indictable offence and
- further detention without charge is necessary to secure and preserve evidence or to obtain evidence by questioning and
- the investigation is being conducted diligently and expeditiously.

Detaining a juvenile or mentally vulnerable person longer than 24 hours depends on the circumstances of the case and additional consideration of the person's vulnerability, any representations made on their behalf (including the views of the appropriate adult) and any alternatives to police custody.

Review officers must conduct extensions of detention in person, including considering any representations, and should be briefed in a timely manner on the progress and conduct of the investigation. This includes what further enquiries and interviews are considered necessary whilst the suspect is in custody and the timescales involved. This briefing may include providing information with a request that it is not revealed to the detainee or their legal representative.

KEY POINTS

- The maximum extension that can be granted is 12 hours (total detention time 36 hours), but shorter periods may be authorised depending on the circumstances of the case.
- Reviewing officers need sufficient time to consider requests and attend the custody office in person, which needs advance planning. Police forces have their own arrangements, particularly outside office hours when a Superintendent or above could provide PACE cover for the entire force area and have conflicting demands to manage.
- An extension of detention cannot be authorised beyond 24 hours purely to obtain a charging decision.

9.20 Warrants of Further Detention

A person can only be detained without charge beyond 36 hours for an indictable offence under the authority of a Warrant of Further Detention (WOFD) issued by a Magistrates Court (sections 43 and 44 of PACE), who must be satisfied there are reasonable grounds for believing further detention is justified because all three of the following criteria are met:

1. An offence for which the person is under arrest is indictable.
2. Detention without charge is necessary to secure or preserve evidence relating to an offence for which the person is under arrest or to obtain such evidence by questioning them.

3. The investigation is being conducted diligently and expeditiously.

A WOFD can be issued for such a period as the court thinks fit (not automatically 36 hours) and should relate to what the police intend to do to progress the investigation.

If there are sufficient grounds, further applications can be made up to an overall maximum detention period of 96 hours from the relevant time.

9.20.1 Court procedure

Applications are made by a constable (or other rank) on oath and supported by information.

- A court cannot hear an application unless the detained person has been supplied with a copy of the information and has been brought before the hearing.
- The detained person is entitled to legal representation at the hearing.

  An application may be made:
  - o at any time before the expiry of 36 hours from the relevant time; or
  - o where:
    - (a) it is not practicable for the court hearing the application to sit at the expiry of 36 hours after the relevant time; but
    - (b) the court will sit during the 6 hours following the end of that 36-hour period; the application may be made before the 6 hours have expired.
    - (c) if an application is made after the 36 hours have expired (but within the additional 6 hours) and it appears to the court that it would have been reasonable for the police to have made the application within 36 hours from the relevant time, the court shall dismiss the application.
- Applications should be made between 1000 hours and 2100 hours and if possible during normal court hours.
- If it appears a special sitting is required outside normal court hours but between 1000 hours and 2100 hours,

the justice's clerk should be notified of this possibility, while the court is sitting if possible.

- It will not usually be practicable to arrange a special court sitting outside 1000 hours and 2100 hours.

9.20.2 Information supplied

The information supplied to the court and the detainee includes:

- the nature of the offence
- the general nature of the evidence on which the person was arrested
- enquiries relating to the offence that have been made and what further enquiries are proposed
- the reasons why continued detention is believed necessary to conduct further enquiries

A general summary outlining what the investigation has achieved so far and what needs to be completed within the timeframe of the proposed extension is necessary to support the application. This includes any time scales for results such as forensic tests or hi-tech examinations that will be available for further interviews. The information supplied to the court needs careful consideration as it may impact on future pre-interview disclosure.

The term 'diligently and expeditiously' may have to be justified under cross-examination and means enquiries are being conducted as quickly as possible in an industrious manner. This could involve explaining how several areas of investigative activity are being conducted simultaneously and investigators are working extended tours of duty to facilitate this.

The following checklist provides some suggestions but is not exhaustive:

Checklist—WOFD supporting information

- Whether the investigation was pre-planned or a spontaneous incident

- The number of investigators and other resources engaged on the enquiry
- Extensive forensic examinations and testing is being conducted
- CSIs are dedicated to the incident
- Forensic scientists have been deployed to the scene(s)
- A postmortem examination is to be/has been conducted
- Witness testimony from significant/key witnesses has been/is being recorded in accordance with ABE (Ministry of Justice 2021)
-
- H2H enquiries have/are being conducted with extensive parameters
- CCTV identification, recovery and analysis is in progress
- Checking of fingerprints
- Checking detainee's replies against other material
- Correlating information obtained from other detainees in the same case
- Checking alibis
- Communicating with other police forces (in the UK or abroad)
- Obtaining interpreters to conduct interviews with witnesses and suspects
- Translating documents

KEY POINTS

- The application is made at the time an officer is sworn in to give evidence. This is important when managing applications involving multiple suspects who are appearing separately, to ensure their detention time does not expire before their application commences.
- If granted, the time of the WOFD commences when it is signed by the magistrate.

- Planning a WOFD should consider the logistics and timeframes involved; it is often prudent to make early applications, taking account of the court's availability.
- Police forces will have their own documentation to supply the required information for an application which has to be authorised by a Superintendent or above.
- As a contingency it is advisable to conduct a 'wash up' interview with the suspect(s) before the application to ensure all critical questions have been put, in case further detention is not authorised.

9.21 **Intelligence Interviews**

An 'intelligence interview' with a person in police detention is voluntary. The objective is to obtain information about criminal activity other than the offence(s) for which they have been arrested. They, therefore, do not fall within the PACE definition of an interview and are not conducted under caution or recorded.

Police forces have individual policies balancing the integrity of the investigation in progress whilst exploiting the opportunity to obtain potentially actionable information from an intelligence interview. Considerations include not conducting the interview until after the investigation phase has concluded, using officers not connected to the investigation (usually Intelligence Bureau or Dedicated Source Unit staff) and managing the content of the custody record so the safety of a detainee who agrees to an intelligence interview is not compromised.

KEY POINT

Interview advisers (PIP 2, Specialists) can provide assistance with all aspects of interview strategies and should be consulted as early as possible in complex investigations.

9.22 **Coronavirus Arrangements**

If suspect interviews are being conducted during any present or future pandemic, consideration should be given to the content of the Joint Interim Interview Protocol between the NPCC, the CPS, the Law Society, the Criminal Law Solicitors' Association and the London Criminal Courts Solicitors' Association (JIIP) (Crown Prosecution Service 2020). This guidance was initially formulated in April 2020 and was intended to assist investigators and prosecutors in deciding whether suspects should be interviewed as part of a police investigation during the Covid-19 pandemic.

This guidance has been reviewed regularly since its inception and continues to be kept under review as it is only intended for use during the period of the Covid-19 pandemic. The latest edition circulated in October 2021 (version 4).

If interviews are scheduled to be held within a period in which the Protocol is active, then the investigator should ensure that they are fully aware of the latest guidance covering the factors that are highlighted within the document.

9.23 **Sentencing Guidelines**

The Sentencing Council was set up in April 2010 with its primary role to issue guidelines on sentencing to the courts. In December 2020 the Sentencing Code came into effect and incorporated within it all previous Sentencing Guidelines.

The guidelines cover some of the most serious offences, and amongst its overarching principles is the need for the court to take account of the aggravating and mitigating factors that were present when the offence was committed.

During a suspect interview many of the factors could form part of the interview plan around the topic that may impact upon increasing the seriousness of the offence. Topics such as motivation, planning the offence, reasons for the selection of vulnerable victims, the level of violence if relevant to the offence can be explored within the interview.

Similarly, factors that reduce seriousness should be explored within a structured way within a suspect interview. The suspect may have been coerced into committing the crime, the offence may have been spontaneous or there may be vulnerability issues that impacted on the commission of the crime.

In planning and preparing to conduct a suspect interview an investigator should make themselves aware of the guidance that covers the crime that they are investigating in order that they can ensure that the best possible understanding of what has taken place is presented before the court.

9.24 Pre-charge Engagement

Annex B of the *Attorney General's Guidelines on Disclosure* (Attorney General's Office 2020) details the scope of pre-charge engagement which in essence focus on discussions that can take place with investigators, suspects and their legal advisers about an investigation any time following the first PACE interview.

The document outlines what the purpose of pre-charge engagement is and when it is appropriate. If an investigator is to conduct a discussion of this nature then they must make themselves aware of Annex B and any other relevant national guidance that is in existence.

References

Ministry of Justice (2021) *Achieving Best Evidence in Criminal Proceedings: guidance on interviewing victims and witnesses, and using special measures*

Attorney General's Office (2020) *Attorney General's Guidelines on Disclosure* (HM Government)
(Crown Prosecution Service, 2020) *Joint Interim Interview Protocol between the National Police Chiefs Council, Crown Prosecution Service, Law Society, the Criminal Law Solicitors' Association and the London Criminal Courts Solicitors' Association (JIIP)*(Crown Prosecution Service)

Chapter 10

Crime Types and their Investigation

10.1 Introduction

The basic principles of general investigative practice, decision making and the initial response to the report or discovery of a crime outlined in earlier chapters are the foundation for all enquiries. Crime, however, is diverse and evolves, requiring some investigations to develop approaches and follow processes and policies which do not apply to others. This chapter outlines some considerations for specific types of criminal investigation.

10.2 Volume Crime

Volume crime is 'any crime which through its sheer volume has a significant impact on the community and the ability of the local police to tackle it'. Offences include acquisitive crime such as burglary, theft and street robbery, and other 'volume' offences such as criminal damage and assault. The definition can also be extended to include anti-social behaviour. Volume crime is managed and investigated using the principles in the Volume Crime Management Model 2009 (VCMM) (NPIA 2009) which is cited in the *Authorised Professional Practice* (APP) (College of Policing 2021).

Blackstone's Crime Investigators' Handbook. Steve Hibbitt and Gary Shaw, Oxford University Press. © Oxford University Press 2023.
DOI: 10.1093/oso/9780192867896.003.0010

The VCMM links to the National Intelligence Model (NIM)(NCIS 2000) where a Tasking and Coordination Group (TCG) identifies local volume crime priorities and allocates resources to tackle them. It is designed to improve performance by ensuring everyone involved in the process knows what is expected of them, including minimum standards of investigation and supervision.

An investigator's role in the VCMM depends on whether they are deployed in primary and/or secondary investigation, processing suspects or a combination of these. Reported crimes are assessed against a range of 'solvability factors' which inform decisions on allocation and further investigation. These factors include whether any of the following are immediately available to link a suspect to the offence:

- forensic material
- identifiable property stolen or recovered
- material left at the scene by the offender(s) which could lead to their identification
- a witness who may identify the offender(s) by viewing photographs or describes them in sufficient detail to compile an E-Fit
- the suspect is known, or their identity is likely to become apparent, or a suspect's vehicle is located, described or identified
- a linked series of offences is identified, including repeat victims
- CCTV or other digital or passive data sources to identify suspects are available

Crime reports with limited solvability factors not requiring resources to attend may be allocated for 'primary investigation', including telephone investigation to identify potential lines of enquiry, repeat victims and other possible linked offences. An investigation plan is then recorded before allocation for secondary investigation with suggested disposal options and, where a suspect is known, evidence collated, and an arrest package prepared.

Individual force policy may allocate certain crimes for secondary investigation where there are no solvability factors, such as those which impact on public confidence and satisfaction like dwelling burglary, hate crime and repeat victimisation.

Crime reports allocated for secondary investigation should contain an investigation plan documented in a simple format describing what further enquiries should be conducted before finalisation and be flexible to develop as the enquiry progresses. Typical plans for acquisitive crime are likely to contain actions concerning the scene and stolen property, such as:

- preserve and assess the point of entry for forensic and physical evidence and Crime Scene Investigator (CSI) examination
- establish with the victim anything the offender has touched, moved or brought to the scene and preserve any forensic opportunities
- identify the approach/egress routes and search for footwear marks, blood, tools brought to the scene and articles removed or discarded by the offender
- search possible locations where stolen property could be concealed for later collection, such as wheelie bins
- house-to-house (H2H) enquiries in line of sight of the scene, the immediate area and potential route taken by the offender.
- if available, obtain a detailed description of any suspect(s) from witnesses.
- obtain comprehensive details of stolen property including serial numbers and unique identifying marks (including photographs if available)

Following initial attendance:

- with the complainant, review and update the crime reports stolen property list (where applicable) with details of further missing property, items located that were previously believed stolen and any additional descriptions not previously available

- circulate property details ensuring a Police National Computer (PNC) record is created for any stolen plant (agricultural and construction), engines, trailers, firearms, marine craft (including jet skis and rigid inflatables) and animals (which are registered with a marking company)
- attempt to locate stolen property by enquiring at outlets such as second-hand dealers, pawnbrokers, Cash Converters and similar outlets, antique dealers, car boot sales, classified advertisements, eBay/other internet sites, trade journals, trade auctions, jewellers, markets, auction rooms, scrap metal dealers and convicted/suspected handlers
- preserve any recovered stolen property for CSI examination
- circulate details of distinctive stolen property in the local media
- check property registers, including the systems of neighbouring Basic Command Units (BCU) or forces where appropriate
- update crime reports concerning any recovered property and amend the investigation plan as a result of new solvability factors and lines of enquiry identified
- if stolen property is recovered, obtain an identification statement from the owner specifically containing how they can identify the item (serial numbers, identifying marks).

10.3 Violent Crime

Violent crime may form part of a control strategy within the VCMM and, regardless of the severity of injury, is broadly divided into three types:

1. Stranger attacks where the alleged offender and victim do not know each other.
2. Acquaintance assaults where the alleged offender is known to the victim but is not a relative or intimate partner.

3. Domestic Abuse (DA); referred to as domestic violence in the 2009 publication.

Identifying these broad circumstances helps prioritise lines of enquiry for each case, for example identifying the suspect in a stranger attack compared to dealing with a reluctant victim of domestic abuse where the suspect has been immediately arrested.

The core investigative and forensic strategies should always be considered, ensuring the following are completed wherever possible:

- treat the victim as a crime scene, including collecting any available forensic evidence such as clothing
- obtain early injury photographs
- obtain evidence of a victim's injury from a CSI or attending police officer
- obtain a statement of complaint from the victim as soon as possible after the incident
- obtain an initial account if the victim is unable to provide a statement at the time
- obtain statements from any witnesses to the incident
- obtain evidence from a health care professional describing the victim's injuries, any treatment provided and their prognosis
- submit all intelligence, including locations of violence to identify 'hot spots', for the tasking and coordination process, and assist in developing multi-agency solutions for violent crime reduction

10.4 Domestic Abuse

Domestic abuse (DA) is now defined by the Domestic Abuse Act 2021 (section 1) which states that for the purpose of this Act the behaviour of a person (A) towards another person (B) is 'domestic abuse' if they are both aged 16 or over and are personally connected to each other and the behaviour is abusive, which consists of any of the following:

- physical or sexual abuse
- violent or threatening behaviour
- controlling or coercive behaviour
- economic abuse, meaning any behaviour that has a substantial adverse effect on the person's ability to acquire, use or maintain money or other property, or obtain goods or services
- psychological, emotional or other abuse

The behaviour of A may be behaviour towards B despite the fact that it consists of conduct directed at another person, for example B's child. For the purposes of this Act two people are personally connected if any of the following applies:

- they are or have been married to each other
- they are or have been civil partners of each other
- they have agreed to marry one another (whether or not the agreement has been terminated)
- they have entered into a civil partnership agreement (whether or not the agreement has been terminated)
- they are or have been in an intimate personal relationship with each other
- they each have, or there has been a time when they each have had, a parental relationship in relation to the same child. A person has a parental relationship if they are the parent of a child or have parental responsibility for a child under the age of 18 years
- they are relatives (under the same meaning of the Family Law Act 1996)

Where the behaviour of a person (A) towards another person (B) is domestic abuse, any reference to a victim of domestic abuse includes reference to a child (under 18 years) who sees, hears or experiences the effects of the abuse and is related to A or B, as the person is a parent of or has parental responsibility for the child, or the child and the person are relatives.

KEY POINTS

- Under the Domestic Abuse Act 2021 the legal definition of who could be a victim of domestic abuse is broad and builds on the previous ACPO (now NPCC) definition of domestic violence which was:

  Any incident of threatening behaviour, violence or abuse (psychological, physical, sexual, financial or emotional) between adults, aged 18 years and over, who are or have been intimate partners or family members, regardless of gender and sexuality.

- Family members include a mother, father, son, daughter, brother, sister and grandparents whether they are directly related, in laws or stepfamily.
- Domestic abuse is not confined to acts of physical violence and extends to wider patterns of behaviour over a more extended timeframe than a single incident. Investigators need to consider this when conducting DA investigations and gather evidence from a variety of sources in addition to the victim.

The priority of the police when responding to DA is to protect the lives of both adults and children at risk, investigate all reports, facilitate effective action to hold offenders to account and adopt a proactive multi-agency approach to prevention and reduction.

As well as identifying and mitigating risks faced by the victim and any children in the family and safeguarding, challenges may include overcoming the victim's reluctance to prosecute, which is particularly relevant as initial responding officers have an obligation to take positive action in all DA cases and exercise a power of arrest where one exists.

Sufficient evidence to prosecute may have to be obtained from other sources to support an evidence-based prosecution if a victim does not wish to support a prosecution. Forensic material may have limited value if the suspect and victim are living together, and other sources of admissible evidence for a court should be sought.

Checklist—DA potential sources of evidence

- Attending officers (including head/body-worn cameras)
- Photograph/video of disturbance at the scene
- Recordings of 999/101 calls
- Injury photographs including further photographs when injuries are more apparent
- Recovery of torn/damaged/bloodstained clothing
- Analysis of blood pattern distribution to corroborate a physical assault
- Recovery of potential weapons (which may be ordinary domestic items) and forensically linking to the suspect, recognising this may have limited evidential value if the item is in common use
- Linking suspected weapons to victim injuries by means of bloodstaining or injury comparison through the National Injuries Database
- Evidence of previous violent incidents, such as records of previous calls to the police, including those with prior partners
- Police intelligence systems
- Incidents of sexual violence not previously disclosed
- Incidents witnessed by children
- Incidents witnessed by other family members, friends or colleagues
- H2H enquiries
- Incidents outside the home or occurring in public
- CCTV/passive data recordings
- Child contact agreements or disputes
- Previous civil injunctions
- Medical information that may constitute evidence
- Evidence of social isolation, such as lack of contact between the victim and their family, friends, neighbours or schools, medical appointments that have not been made, or made but not kept, or where the suspect accompanied the victim (to maintain control and prevent them disclosing information)
- Evidence held by other agencies

- Evidence of the offender's bad character, such as other similar reprehensible behaviour including previous victims held on any data source

Conflicting accounts and counter-allegations where each party claims to be the victim may be presented. Dual arrests should be avoided without conducting a full investigation, which should include a separate evaluation of the claims to establish if justifiable force was used in self defence. An attempt should be made to identify the primary aggressor, including recording:

- the severity of any injuries inflicted by either party
- whether either party has made threats to another party, child, or other family/household member
- whether either party has a prior history of violence
- whether either party has made previous counter-allegations
- whether either party acted defensively to protect themselves or a third person from injury

KEY POINTS

- Specialist Domestic Abuse Officers and/or Police Domestic Abuse Coordinators can provide DA investigation advice, including identifying, categorising and monitoring risk and safety measures, engaging in the tasking and coordination process to address high-risk and persistent offenders and appropriately sharing information with partner agencies/organisations.
- All DA cases fall within the pre-charge Crown Prosecution Service (CPS) advice scheme even when a guilty plea is likely. CPS will also decide whether there is sufficient evidence to proceed without the support of the victim so all available material should be collected.
- DA is frequently repeated, making homicide potentially preventable. Any precursor incidents including police action and decisions will be closely scrutinised by a Domestic Homicide Review which are obligatory under section 9 of the Domestic Violence, Crime and Victims Act 2004.

10.5 Protection from Harassment Act 1997

The Protection from Harassment Act 1997 (PHA) can be used to address harassment or fear of violence caused to a victim on at least two occasions. Harassment is not defined, but causing alarm or distress are elements; therefore if a suspect's behaviour does not involve specific threats but causes the victim harassment the offence is committed, for example silent telephone phone calls or following the victim around.

KEY POINT

Where a person's actions amount to an offence under the Offences Against the Person Act 1861, the Public Order Act 1984 or the Criminal Damage Act 1971, proceedings should not be instigated under the PHA.

10.6 Hate Crime

A hate crime is any criminal offence which is perceived by the victim or any other person to be motivated by hostility or prejudice based on a person's race or perceived race; religion or perceived religion; sexual orientation or perceived sexual orientation; disability or perceived disability and any crime motivated by hostility or prejudice against a person who is transgender or perceived to be transgender.

Currently, an allegation from any party (not just a victim) is sufficient for a hate *incident* to be recorded; however, an incident must only be recorded as a *crime* where there is evidence that an offence has been committed or attempted etc. At the time of writing there is a legal challenge in the High Court to the recording of hate incidents.

Hate incidents/crimes are potential critical incidents, particularly where repeat victimisation is involved, and whilst making enquiries to identify the offender the investigation should also:

- identify repeat victimisation and/or linked incidents ensuring all necessary steps are taken to prevent a reoccurrence
- identify any risks to the victim, their family or community as a whole
- allay the fears of the victim and mitigate any identified risks with protective measures where appropriate, such as covert monitoring measures, personal attack alarms and overt tactics such as high visibility patrols
- where appropriate visually record the victim's interview
- not question victims of homophobia about their sexuality and not disclose this information to their family/friends without permission in case they are unaware of the victim's sexual orientation
- identify and report any concern about community tension
- update the victim on an ongoing basis
- submit any information into the intelligence system using the 3 ×5 × 2 grading system
- refer any crime which involves an element of hate to the CPS for the charging decision

10.7 Rape and Serious Sexual Offences (RASSO)

Generally serious sexual offences fall into one of six types which influence the investigation strategy when prioritising lines of enquiry:

1. Stranger—where the victim has no previous knowledge of the suspect, has not met them before the offence

and is unable to name them or provide information about their identity or whereabouts.

2. Acquaintance—where the victim is able to identify the suspect as a person known to them.
3. Domestic—committed by people who are, or who have been intimate partners or family members of the victim.
4. Drug-assisted—where alcohol and/or drugs are intentionally administered to the victim before committing the offence, including offending against an incapacitated victim who does not have the capacity to consent.
5. Child victim under 18 years old.
6. Multiple offenders—involving more than one offender, either in the actual offence or the commissioning of the offence.

These categories do not have any separate legal status but are useful to consider when prioritising enquiries, for example the priority in stranger offences is to identify the unidentified suspect, so forensic recovery from the victim and fast track analysis should be a high priority. With acquaintance offences, the identity of the offender is probably known at the time of the initial report or is likely to be straightforward to ascertain. Forensic recovery from the victim would be completed in such cases but fast track submission may not be as productive as other lines of enquiry, such as obtaining evidence of early complaint and investigating the background of a suspect including any relevant bad character material.

The investigation plan should include whichever of the core investigative strategies are appropriate, and depending on the individual case, the following checklists may provide further considerations.[1]

The investigation of a sexual offence committed by a stranger could be led by a Senior Investigating Officer (PIP3), or an appropriately experienced and senior

[1] While these have been separated into groups for ease of reference, there may be overlaps.

detective depending on the local force crime allocation policy. Investigators may therefore be working as part of a larger team and not be the primary decision makers when the following suggestions are considered.

Checklists—Serious sexual offences investigation

Checklist 1—Stranger (unconnected and unknown) offender

- Obtain DNA samples from the victim and scene and submit to obtain a profile and cross match with the National DNA Database (NDNAD)
- Examine and check for any fingerprints, finger marks and other physical trace evidence at the crime location and on victim
- Conduct a 'Query Using Enhanced Search Techniques' (QUEST) or postcode search on the Police National Computer (PNC) for offenders within a relevant defined area
- Assess any suspect connections to and targeting of the crime scene(s) or victim by considering the coincidental elements of crime and the 'problem analysis triangle 'or the coincidental elements of crime (see Chapter 2)
- Research any links, such as targeting by victim type, location and time of the offence, prowlers, indecent exposures, suspicious activities
- Establish if time and date of the offence is significant or coincides with something else such as activity at local pubs/nightclub activities, other premises and any special events in the area
- Check if there are any sex workers operating nearby who may have knowledge of a suspect including a possible encounter
- Consider the mode of transport of the offender to commit the offence, including motor vehicles, taxis, public transport, cycle or foot. Check nearby car parks and stolen/abandoned vehicles around relevant times

- Liaise with MOSAVO and Public Protection Teams to identify possible suspects or associates of a suspect. Pay particular attention to any similar modus operandi including any unique or unusual signature behaviour by the suspect
- Consider producing and circulating E-Fits of the offender, forensic drawings or photographs of relevant matching items such as a suspects clothing, tattoos, unusual marks, peculiarities, hairstyles and vehicles used
- Search intelligence databases, particularly the Police National Database (PND)
- Map the scene including routes in and out as used by the victim and believed to have been used by the suspect. Identify relevant features and nearby premises and areas to be searched
- Produce a sequence of events (SOE) chart and timeline, including the chronology of events as described by the victim. Update the SOE to include relevant information from witnesses and other sources. The provenance should be established for any times supplied by victims and witnesses and where possible these should be corroborated by reliable external sources. Consider the relevance of any parallel or sequential significant events for the SOE and include any suspect account if they have been identified and interviewed
- Revisit the scene of the offence and other significant locations at times relevant to the investigation. Conduct stop checks to identify witnesses who routinely frequent the area during the relevant times.
- Consider conducting and publicising reconstructions at relevant times, dates and anniversaries relating to the original offence to identify witnesses and generate information
- Consider conducting covert activity/surveillance to identify a suspect potentially returning to the scene or offenders conducting reconnaissance to locate and identify possible future victims and their

routines and habits. Be aware that any pre-offence activity and preparation by an offender may be conducted in plain sight and might not necessarily attract suspicion

- Search for any objects reported missing by the victim
- Distribute details of any missing items in local and force circulations and particularly ensure specialist burglary investigators are made aware
- Develop a suspect priority matrix and a trace, investigate and evaluate (TIE) strategy based on known information
- Consider intelligence-led DNA screening (if no match on NDNAD)
- Consider familial DNA (fDNA) analysis (if no match on NDNAD)
- Assess the possibility of the suspect being employed locally, including possibly on a temporary contract and subsequently relocating and changing employment due to police investigation
- Consider the possibility of the suspect having a legitimate reason to be in the area such as commuter, delivery persons, HGV drivers and taxi drivers.
- Research databases to identify any similar offences in a possible linked series. Conduct a comparable case analysis for reports with similar modus operandi to identify any common denominators
- Consult outside experts and specialist resources—National Crime Agency (NCA) Crime Operations Support Team, Serious Crime Analysis Section (SCAS), Child Exploitation and Online Protection Centre (CEOP, an NCA command), Behavioural Investigative Adviser (BIA), forensic clinical psychologist or geographic profiler

Checklist 2—Acquaintance offender

- Investigate the circumstances of how victim met the offender

- Check for evidence of targeting of the victim by the offender
- Examine the offender's method of contacting the victim, for example internet dating sites, singles clubs, evening classes
- Consider attempts to contact the victim post-offence (possibly justifying or minimising their actions or acting as if nothing untoward had happened)
- Seek behavioural information from the suspect's current or previous partners to identify relevant reprehensible conduct. Investigate and develop bad character material that could be potentially admissible evidence in court and relevant to a prosecution decision
- Gather and evaluate information about the suspect's routines, employment, hobbies, financial transactions, telephone records, internet access, social media usage, social habits and fetishes
- Formulate a digital communications strategy including relevant time parameters for pre-offence and post-offence contact and messages.
- Examine and evaluate the content of any messages between the suspect, victim and relevant others.
- Identify and evaluate communications that could potentially support a prosecution or be relevant or of interest to a defence.
- Consider any pattern in the frequency and timings of any contact and any departures from these.
- Check other force areas via the PND where the offender may have come to notice for similar offences or behaviour

Checklist 3—Domestic-related

- Identify any children, relatives, friends and neighbours who could be potential witnesses to a pattern of abusive behaviour between the suspect and the victim

- Link the history of any reported domestic abuse to the offence under investigation
- Investigate any history of violence and abuse not reported to the police which could be corroborated by records from other agencies, such as GP medical records (obtain the necessary consent)
- Trace and interview witnesses to any previous offences or relevant incidents
- Identify other family members (including children) who the suspect has had close access to, both currently and in the past and interview for any relevant information
- Obtain information from previous partners about their relationship and specifically sexual behaviour, including changes in sexual behaviour that may develop into potential evidence of bad character
- Research any previous allegations against the suspect which have been withdrawn or discontinued and, depending on the circumstances, evaluate their relevance to the current investigation.
- Prepare a sensitive contact and management plan if a previous complainant is to be approached and consider the impact on them
- Seek assistance from any other useful partner agencies that might be involved in connected areas of DA, family, relationship problems, health or education

Checklist 4—Drug-assisted

- Use an early evidence kit to secure samples at the earliest opportunity
- Use a forensic physician to examine the victim at a Sexual Assault Referral Centre (SARC) and identify any symptoms of drug ingestion. Obtain toxicology samples and submit to a forensic service provider for analysis
- Preserve and consider forensically examining the victim's and suspect's (if identified) clothing for

traces of drugs used for intoxication (blood and hair samples also)

- Seek evidence of the offence(s) being photographed or recorded by the suspect using mobile phone, digital camera or other recording device
- Develop sequence of events to account for lost time that cannot be recalled. Evaluate and use CCTV, other passive data sources and mobile phone records. Establish whether periods of any device activity or inactivity are relevant to the sequence of events for lost time. Note that drugs tend to take 15 to 20 minutes to take effect
- Identify any associated offence(s) such as abduction, kidnap or sexual exploitation
- Investigate possible serial offending by checking records for any similar offences or attempts
- Look for possible links to other serious sexual assaults (seek SCAS assistance)
- Identify any theft of non-valuable items from the victim and check property records
- Check any suspects use of internet sites related to supplying drugs and advice about their use and effectiveness
- Identify and interview any suspect's current or previous partners for relevant information
- Examine the suspect's connections to internet pornography and any relevance to the offence under investigation
- Check any suspect's internet and credit card purchases for drugs or other items potentially connected to the offence

Checklist 5—Multiple offender serious sexual offences

- Obtain and attempt to cross-match DNA samples from the victim's forensic medical examination with the NDNAD

- Cross-match any unidentified fingerprints, finger marks and other physical trace evidence
- Examine the possibility of the offence being drug-assisted
- Consider the possibility of several scenes
- Examine any possible links between TIE's or suspects
- Identify any similar modus operandi (not necessarily multiple offenders based)
- Seek intelligence about any sexual exploitation group which might be linked
- Identify any vehicles or premises used
- Identify the primary or dominant suspect (usually the first to commit a serious sexual offence on the victim)
- Investigate the possibility that the dominant suspect has a previous conviction for a sexual offence against an individual victim
- Identify any suspect who appears to have been coerced into committing the offence and interview them first, where possible

10.7.1 Common assumptions and rape myths

Investigators need to be aware of some common assumptions that sometimes manifest themselves in rape investigations.

Within the criminal justice system there is now a greater understanding of the complex issues concerning victims of rape and other sexual offences, but assumptions still sometimes persist. It is important to challenge any of these 'rape myths' wherever they may arise to ensure that do not have a negative impact on the investigation such as not pursuing potentially relevant lines of inquiry or pursuing lines of inquiry but without the necessary thoroughness.

Victims should never be judged because of the way they present themselves through either their behaviour or the information they provide. Every investigation should be conducted without bias towards the victim (or anyone else involved) and without pre-judging what the possible outcome may be. The common assumptions and myths include:

- Rape victims will have sustained internal injuries because of the offence: this is not true as most victims do not suffer any internal injury.
- The victim did not put up a fight so therefore they did not object: this is not true. Rape trauma affects victims in different ways and in a significant number of cases the reaction is for self-preservation which might include acting passively and not fighting back.
- The offender did not use violence so it cannot have been a sexual assault: this is not true as the issue in most cases is a lack of consent not violence used. In some cases, other forms of non-violent abuse such as duress and coercion may be used.
- Victims should be able to recall exactly what happened: this is not true as recall might be inhibited by the shock and trauma of the offence and be difficult or take some time to recollect. This is why conducting detailed victim interviews is perhaps best delayed until they are ready and able to participate.
- Without forensic material or witnesses there is no chance of proving the offence: this is not true because corroboration might be obtained from other sources regarding relevant events during, before and after the offence.
- The victim has previously had sex with the suspect so there is little chance of a conviction: this is not true; all allegations should be investigated on their own merit and sexual assault does occur within relationships.
- Most allegations are false: this is not true and there is no statistical support for this belief.

The investigative approach requirements to each investigation should be considered on its own merits depending on the circumstances. All allegations should be treated seriously and investigated by applying an investigative mindset. Some enquiry options are listed below as suggestions to consider but they are not exhaustive:

- Physical material
  - o physical injuries apparent (complainant)
  - o injuries identified during forensic medical examination (complainant)
  - o physical injuries apparent (suspect)
  - o injuries identified during forensic medical examination (suspect)
  - o forensic samples obtained (complainant and suspect)
  - o level of intoxication complainant if any (early evidence kit)
  - o toxicology (complainant)
  - o level of intoxication of suspect (toxicology samples)
  - o condition of complainants clothing/damaged/disturbed/rearranged
  - o condition of suspects clothing/damaged/disturbed/rearranged
  - o clothing missing
  - o medical records (suspect)
  - o recovery and examination of bedding (scene)
- Crime scene assessment
  - o layout of the area and geographical characteristics of the location of the offence
  - o outdoors and overlooked
  - o outdoors secluded
  - o indoors, shared occupancy dwelling
  - o indoors, single occupancy dwelling
  - o neighbours
  - o potential access and egress routes
  - o method of opening doors and windows (if inside)
  - o opportunities to leave or escape
  - o items disturbed at the scene
  - o digital media recovery
- Victim
  - o initial/first account
  - o interview (video evidence-in-chief unless opts out)

  - evidence of early complaint
  - mobile phone/communications devices
  - medical records (complainant)
- Suspect
  - interview under caution
  - mobile phone/communications devices
  - search of home address
  - digital media recovery
  - search of vehicle(s)
  - search of other relevant locations
  - medical records
- Witnesses
  - early complaint
  - complainants' demeanor
  - suspects demeanor
  - knowledge of pre-offence movements and behaviour (suspect and complainant)
  - noises heard
  - knowledge of post-offence movements and demeanor (suspect and complainant)
  - communications with complainant
  - communications with suspect
  - expert evidence
- Intelligence requirements
  - suspects previous convictions
  - suspects subject profile and intelligence
  - location/venue off first encounter between complainant and suspect/investigative opportunities at venue/any previous similar incidents
  - crime profile of the area of the offence/any precursor incidents (not necessarily reports of sexual assault)
  - any similar incidents reported to other agencies

10.7.2 Investigating consent

Statistics show that in the majority of reported offences of rape and serious sexual assault, the suspect is likely to claim that the complainant consented to the sexual act that is the subject of the allegation.

This may be reasonably straightforward for a prosecution to rebut if the offence is a stranger rape, due to the attendant circumstances. This could include factors such as the location of the attack, injuries sustained by the victim, damage to clothing, an early complaint being made and the absence of any contact between the victim and the offender before and after the offence.

The situation is significantly more challenging to investigate and prove beyond reasonable doubt where a complainant and suspect are known to each other and the matter in issue is whether the alleged sexual act was or was not with consent. It does not matter how well a suspect and the complainant knew each other.

Rape can be committed by an offender who has just encountered a victim and hardly knows them, through to people who know each other well, including where the victim and the offender are in a long-term relationship. A person can now be convicted of raping their spouse, and consent can be withdrawn during the sexual act itself. Also, it is plausible that both parties have a different interpretation of the same events that have led to a different belief regarding consent. There could have been many obvious or subtle behaviours before, during and after a sexual act that contributed to the different beliefs about consent on the part of the complainant or suspect.

According to the Sexual Offences Act 2003 (section 74) a person consents if they agree by choice and have the freedom and capacity to consent. A noteworthy case to consider on this issue is *R v Bree*,[2] which concerned the state of intoxication of a complainant and defendant and involved the issue of consent. This case demonstrates the complexity of investigating alleged offences of this type when the appeal court judge ruled:

> When someone who has had a lot to drink is in fact consenting to intercourse, then that is what she is doing, consenting: equally, if after taking drink, she is not consenting,

[2] (2007) EWCA Crim 256

then by definition intercourse is taking place without her consent.

Investigators need to examine and investigate the specific facts of each case to determine whether consent could be deemed to have been given or not. This includes the mental state and capacity of the complainant and the suspect at the time of the sexual act. In essence, where a person loses their capacity to consent due to intoxication, they cannot consent. However, it is possible for a person to be heavily intoxicated, having voluntarily consumed a large quantity of alcohol or other intoxicants, but still be able to consent.

10.7.3 Involuntary intoxication

A main line of inquiry in consent cases should be to investigate whether the complainant had the freedom and capacity to make an informed choice and whether any impairment of their capacity was voluntary. This is a significant point when considering and investigating whether the complainant was provided with intoxicants in quantities that they were unaware of or perhaps has been the victim of drink spiking or was drugged using a syringe (a needle spike), which caused memory loss and thus a lack of capacity to consent.

The location of the 'spiking' and the location of the sexual offence are likely to be different locations. It will be necessary to establish the relevant timeframes for the offence to build a detailed timeline of the complainant's movements and activities. Due to the complainant's possible memory loss, it is advisable to divide the timeline into phases, and establish timeframes for movements before, during and after the alleged offence, to be determined by the circumstances of the offence.

As a rough guide it is suggested that the time period that the complainant is unable to account for would logically be the period where any sexual act was committed. A pre-offence timeframe would work backwards from the last memory of the complainant; the starting point would be determined by whatever they were doing earlier and its relevance. It should be noted that this could be a period where any intoxicant or substance was administered to take account of the time required for it to take effect.

The final timeframe would be from the complainants restored recollection to the time they reported the alleged offence.

Within these timeframes, the investigative opportunities described in previous chapters can be exploited. These could include, as suggestions, obtaining accounts from witnesses who were in the company of the complainant, recovering and reviewing CCTV from premises visited and other passive data opportunities such as payment data, identifying transport used including taxis and other public transport and recovering and reviewing public and private CCTV from routes taken by the complainant. This is not an exhaustive list by any means and enquiries will need to be prioritised depending on the circumstances of the case.

Examining the complainant's mobile phone or similar device in these circumstances could be considered a necessary and justifiable enquiry that could support a prosecution or assist a defence. This is not a disclosure exercise as evidence of no communications activity during the timeframe that cannot be accounted for could be supporting prosecution evidence, particularly if this was not consistent with the complainant's normal pattern of use.

Likewise, any communications data during this period is investigative material showing phone use. The content and timing of this could potentially assist a prosecution or a defence but cannot be established until the data has been extracted from the device and evaluated in the context of other material gathered by the investigation.

10.7.4 Examination of communications devices

The examination of mobile communications devices is a relevant reasonable line of enquiry to consider depending on the context of the case (CPS 2018). Such examinations are also discussed in Chapter 13 in relation to case management and disclosure. That content is not repeated here and should be cross-referenced to, as the investigation and disclosure aspects of examining a device overlap.

10.7.5 Bad character evidence

Bad character evidence has been briefly summarised in Chapter 9 in the context of interviews under caution with a suspect. It is expanded upon here because investigating the bad character of a suspect is a relevant line of inquiry in all investigations, but it has the potential to be particularly significant for investigating rape and other sexual offences where consent to the sexual act is disputed. It should go without saying that the suspect's bad character should be at the centre of the criminal investigation and not the character of the complainant.

Bad character is defined by the Criminal Justice Act 2003 (section 98) as 'evidence of, or a disposition towards misconduct' and such evidence can be admitted into a criminal trial in certain circumstances through one of seven gateways.

Misconduct is defined as either the commission of an offence or other reprehensible behaviour. Evidence of the commission of an offence could be another offence on the indictment, a relevant previous conviction, an allegation of an offence that was never prosecuted or an offence for which a defendant was acquitted. The legal test for what might be determined by the court to be 'other reprehensible behaviour' comes from the stated case *R v Renda*[3] and is determined by whether the conduct of the defendant expressed 'some element of culpability or blameworthiness'.

Developing investigative material to potentially form part of a prosecution case under a bad character gateway is a legitimate tactic that should be exploited by investigators. The seven gateways are also briefly summarised

[3] (2005) 1 Cr App R 24

in Chapter 9 because they may be relevant to a suspect's interview under caution.

A suspect's bad character and its potential to be relevant prosecution evidence should be considered when police supervisors and CPS prosecutors make a Full Code Test or Threshold Test. Certain offences are challenging to prove beyond reasonable doubt and the character, credibility and truthfulness of the suspect(s), along with any similar or relevant reprehensible behaviour could be the main matter in issue between a potential prosecution and a defence.

Rape and serious sexual offence investigations are cases in point. For example, where identifying and investigating any bad character of a suspect ought to be considered a potential main line of inquiry. Similarly bad character evidence could enhance the prosecution of domestic abuse and assist to prove a pattern of behaviour on the part of the suspect. This could be particularly important where the victim does not proceed with the complaint, perhaps because of fear, and an evidence led prosecution is being built.

The circumstances of each allegation should be thoroughly investigated, including exploring the potential bad character of the accused. In sexual cases where consent is the main issue between the complainant and the suspect, it is likely that forensic contact material is of limited evidential value for a prosecution in the context of the allegation.

For a suspect to advance a defence that the complainant consented to the sexual act under investigation it is likely they will have answered questions during their interview under caution. Failure to mention or raise consent during interview would put the suspect at risk of attracting an adverse inference direction should a prosecution ensue. Any account a suspect provided needs to be explored in detail and not accepted at face value. This includes the potential for any answers provided by a suspect to open any of the bad character gateways.

Potential bad character that ought to be identified and investigated could include any similar allegations made by other complainants that were not prosecuted at the time. This could have been due to evidential difficulties, the complainant withdrawing their support for the prosecution or any other issue.

The suspect's relationship history should also be considered as a line of enquiry to identify any other similar relevant reprehensible behaviour that occurred within those relationships which perhaps was not reported to the police.

Converting the investigative material relating to bad character into admissible evidence for a court could be the tipping point when decisions are taken about whether to initiate a prosecution or not. Under the Criminal Justice Act 2003 (section 101), evidence of a defendant's bad character is admissible if, and only if:

Gateway A—All parties to the proceedings agree to the evidence being admissible (section 101(1)(a)).

This gateway may be used by either the prosecution or the defence and through it bad character evidence of the defendant could be admitted where the prosecution and the defendant (and any co-defendant) agree to this.

Gateway B—The evidence is adduced by the defendant themselves or is given in answer to a question by them in cross-examination and intended to elicit it (section 101(1)(b)).

Evidence can be admitted through this gateway either by the defendant as part of their case or following examination. It will only be admitted through cross-examination if the question asked was intended to elicit evidence of bad character. Therefore, if a witness provides information about bad character that was not expected, it will not be admissible through this gateway.

Gateway C—Important explanatory evidence (section 101 (1)(c)).

Evidence is important explanatory evidence if without it, the court or jury would find it impossible or difficult to properly understand other evidence in the case, and its value for understanding the case is substantial. To enter through this gateway, the bad character evidence must need to be adduced only because it explains other evidence in the case. It should not be admitted through this gateway if, for example, the evidence is used for another purpose.

Gateway D—It is relevant to an important matter in issue between the defendant and the prosecution (section 101(1)(d)).

Only the prosecution can admit evidence of the defendant's bad character through this gateway. A 'matter in issue' relates to any evidence which goes to the defendant's propensity to offend or their propensity to tell the truth. An 'important matter in issue' is a matter of substantial importance to the case as a whole.

Evidence will only be admitted through this gateway where it is relevant to one or more of the matters in issue. This includes elements of the offence under investigation and/or any available defences. The evidence adduced under through this gateway must also have 'substantial probative value', which suggests that for bad character evidence to pass this test it should have a higher degree of relevance.

Gateway D—Could be the main route to admit a defendant's bad character into evidence when investigating and prosecuting sexual offences if disputed consent to the sexual act is the important matter in issue between the prosecution and the defence. Any previous convictions for sexual offences, or a history of similar sexual allegations involving consent, or a pattern of similar behaviour established by the investigation could be admissible in court depending on the circumstances.

Gateway E—It has substantial probative value in relation to an important matter in issue between the defendant and a co-defendant (section 101(1)(e)).

Through this gateway, evidence of the defendant's bad character can only be adduced by a co-defendant (not the prosecution). In these circumstances, such evidence must relate to an important matter in issue between the defendant and a co-defendant. The matters in issue may include facts in issue in the case, together with any issues relating to credibility.

The evidence must have substantial probative value and there is no power to exclude the evidence once it is admitted through this gateway. This is the case even if it prejudicial to a co-defendant. Basically, this is bad character evidence in relation to an important matter in issue between defendants when a 'cut-throat' defence is being put forward.

Gateway F—It is evidence to correct a false impression given by the defendant (section 101(1)(f)).

Where it appears that a defendant seeks to give an impression or assertion about themselves which is false or misleading, the court may treat a defendant as having given a false impression. Only the prosecution can adduce bad character evidence through this gateway.

The legislation refers to 'express or implied' assertions. An implied assertion includes the conduct of a defendant. An express assertion could include a false assertion made by the defendant during a police interview. This is particularly important when gathering investigative material to convert into bad character evidence in the context of the suspect's interview under caution.

For sexual offences where consent is the matter in issue, any answers to questions in which the suspect seeks to create a false impression about themselves could potentially open this gateway to admit the bad character evidence. Examples of such answers could include claiming innocence and never being accused of anything similar before or claiming to be of good character when relevant previous convictions exist. In straightforward terms, these could be described as 'I'm not like that' explanations.

Merely denying the alleged offence cannot be treated as a false impression given by the defendant. Neither can unspecific and insubstantial remarks that do not amount to assertions of fact.

If a defendant withdraws an assertion or disassociates themself from it, they will not be treated as being responsible for making the assertion. For bad character evidence to be admissible through this gateway, it must be capable of rebutting a false impression given by the defendant.

For the purposes of this gateway a defendant is treated as having made an assertion where the assertion is made:

- by the defendant in the proceedings
- by the defendant upon being questioned under caution and before charge about the offence with which they are charged, and evidence of the assertion is given in the proceedings
- by the defendant on being charged, and evidence of the assertion is given in proceedings
- by a defence witness
- by a witness in cross-examination in response to a question asked by the defendant that was intended to elicit it, or was likely to do so, or
- by a person out of court, and the defendant adduces evidence of it in proceedings

Gateway G—The defendant has made an attack on another person's character (section 101(1)(g)).

Evidence of a defendant's bad character can only be admitted through this gateway by the prosecution. Evidence of 'attacking another person's character' means evidence that the other person has committed an offence, or has behaved, or is disposed to behave in a reprehensible way. The purpose of this is to assist the jury in deciding whether an attack made by the defendant on another's character should be believed.

In the context of investigation of sexual offences where consent is the matter in issue, this could potentially include where a suspect claims a complainant has fabricated the allegation. Making a false allegation of rape or sexual assault could reasonably be construed as reprehensible behaviour. If this was therefore falsely asserted by a defendant, it could be deemed to be an attack on the complainant's character and therefore open this gateway to admit the suspect/defendants relevant bad character material into evidence.

The court must not adduce evidence of the defendant's bad character under this gateway where it appears that the admission of it would have such an adverse effect on the fairness of the proceedings that the court ought not to admit it.

A defendant makes an attack on another person's character if:

- they adduce evidence attacking the other person's character
- they ask questions in cross-examination that are intended to elicit such evidence or are likely to do so, or
- evidence is given of an imputation about the other person made by the defendant on being questioned under caution before charge, about the offence with which they are charged, or on being charged with the offence, or officially informed they might be prosecuted for it

If the relevant piece of bad character evidence can pass through one or more of the gateways, then it will be admissible in court, but the court still has a discretion to exclude evidence, even if it passes through one of the gateways. The court must not adduce evidence of the defendant's bad character under gateways D and G where it appears that the admission of it would have such an adverse effect on the fairness of the proceedings that the court ought not to admit it (section 101(3)).

Section 78 of the Police and Criminal Evidence Act 1984 may also be used to exclude any evidence (not just bad character) which would have such an adverse effect on the fairness of the proceedings that the court ought not to admit it. This can be applied to bad character evidence. Evidence including bad character evidence could also be excluded by the court using common law powers of discretion where it considers the prejudicial effect of the evidence would outweigh its probative value.

When gathering investigative material in relation to a suspect's bad character, investigators should consider exploring a wide range of sources. These might include:

- details of relevant previous convictions
- acquittals for similar offences
- allegations of a similar nature to the offence under investigation
- previous disciplinary hearings
- relevant information and intelligence that may have been recorded but not actioned

These suggestions are not exhaustive, and efforts should be made to identify all reasonable lines of enquiry into potential sources of bad character material.

Obtaining admissible bad character material may not always be as straightforward as face value suggests. Police records are only as good as the information inputted into them and experience has shown that information such as modus operandi (MO) detail is not always recorded as accurately or as comprehensively as it could be.

Depending on the efficiency of the organisation's archiving process, original documents associated with computer records might be difficult to locate. These could include, for example, victim and witness statements and interview records.

Once located, victim and witness statements may be found to be incomplete and not contain the relevant information required. This could be for various reasons including perhaps because the necessary questions were not asked by the investigator when the statement was obtained, or the information was not revealed by the victim or witness, or because its relevance was not recognised at this time.

It may be necessary to recontact a previous victim in a previous case, which is possible when investigating a current allegation of rape or sexual assault. Any proposed contact must be meticulously planned and consider the impact it may have on the victim or witness. Their personal and domestic circumstances may have changed since their complaint was dealt with. They may have new life partners who are unaware of the history because the victim does not want them to know.

The person may be dissatisfied with the outcome of any court hearing or critical of the way a previous investigation was handled. They may have lost trust and confidence in the police ability to investigate and the wider criminal justice process due to their experience. The need for developing a sensitive approach, including how the initial contact is to be conducted cannot be overemphasised, not least because of the potential to reopen memories of a traumatic event which has a negative effect on the individual.

It is good practice to seek assistance from an interview adviser at as early a stage as possible to assist with developing an appropriate strategy. Intelligence will need to be gathered on previous victims to identify their current circumstances and lifestyle. This should inform the most appropriate method of approach and initial contact, including the location, the time and what information is to be provided.

If a direct approach must be made, a contingency should be considered to use a cover story in the first instance. This could be used if the previous victim is not alone at home, or a caller arrives during the contact. The reasons for the visit and the nature of the bad character enquiries enquiry should only be revealed to the victim when it has been established it is safe to do so.

A credible cover story for the initial contact would be for the investigator to say they were conducting enquiries in the area in relation to a minor crime or an anti-social behaviour matter. Any crime or incident used ought to be of a minor nature so as not to raise alarm or anxiety. If such a cover story is deployed, neighbouring residences and nearby premises should also be visited on the same pretext to add authenticity.

Depending on the circumstances it is possible that a victim of a previous offence may need interviewing further in relation to the bad character enquiry. An interview adviser should be involved in the planning to assist with setting the objectives for the interview, the method of recording, the timing and location of the interview and any pre- and post-interview welfare considerations following a needs assessment for the witness.

Important considerations should also focus on developing the most appropriate questions to trigger and support the witness account. This includes how the interviewers should deal with any new or previously unrevealed information from the witness. It is important to establish the provenance of any new information and its integrity to satisfy a future decision maker as to its relevance and reliability for use in evidence. Depending on the circumstances of the case this could include establishing what, if anything, the witness knows about the current offence under investigation.

The victim or witness must be given sufficient suitable information for them to provide informed consent to be interviewed. This includes making them fully aware that it may be necessary for them to provide future witness testimony in court.

Any initial recontact is likely to be unexpected and may come as a shock to the victim. They may have difficulty processing what they are told due to various emotions, so they should be given time to make their decision if they wish.

KEY POINT

Although a victim may be a victim of a previous offence, they are never really a previous victim. The offence could be as real to them today as it was on the day that it was committed. Any victim being recontacted regarding a bad character enquiry should be treated with the same sensitivity and consideration as if they were the victim of the current investigation.

10.7.6 The propensity to offend

The propensity to offend relates to any investigative material that can be adduced as admissible evidence in court, that goes towards showing the defendants inclination to commit an offence similar to the one(s) with which they are charged. Subject to the discretion of the court, such evidence can be admitted as relevant to the question of the defendant's guilt. It may also be relevant to whether or not the defendant is lying.

A defendant's propensity to commit offences of the kind with which they are charged could be proved by evidence that the defendant has been convicted in the past of an offence of the same description or category. An offence is of the same description where the statement of the offence in an indictment or charge would be in the same terms.

An offence is also of the same description if it belongs to the same category of offences prescribed by an order made by the Secretary of State for the purposes of section 103(2) of the Criminal Justice Act 2003. So far, the only two categories that have been prescribed are the 'theft category', which includes all of the main offences under the Theft Act 1968 and the 'sexual offences category'.

Offences committed outside England and Wales are admissible through this gateway, provided they would constitute an offence of the same category if committed in England or Wales. This is an important consideration and line of enquiry when gathering bad character material in relation to suspects who are foreign nationals.

Whether or not a conviction can establish a propensity to commit similar offences depends on the nature of the conviction, its age and its interrelation with the present offence. The greater the similarity the greater the chance of establishing a propensity to commit that type of crime. The accurate identification of similarities between the offenders modus operandi including the offender's behaviour when committing the offence is an important consideration when evaluating the investigative material gathered.

Propensity may also be established through the evidence of other previous convictions that are not of the same category or description as the ones(s) the subject of the present charge or investigation. A defendant's propensity for other reprehensible behaviour might be established by using evidence of misconduct that is:

- the subject of another count on the indictment
- misconduct for which the defendant has never been prosecuted
- misconduct for which the defendant was prosecuted but acquitted, or
- misconduct not amounting to the commission of an offence

10.7.7 The propensity to be untruthful

It is important to note that in the context of bad character evidence, 'untruthful' is not the same as 'dishonest'. For example, committing or being convicted of a dishonesty offence such as theft does not automatically equate to being untruthful. Previous convictions for dishonesty offences or otherwise are only likely to capable of demonstrating a propensity to be untruthful where:

- the truthfulness of the defendant is an issue in the current case and in the previous case
- the defendant gave an account which the jury must have disbelieved (because the defendant was convicted), or
- the manner in which the offence was committed demonstrates a propensity for untruthfulness. This could include, for example, dishonesty offences such as deception, fraud and making false representations which involved deceit, lying and untruthfulness as part of their commission by the defendant

KEY POINT

In rape investigations, a police supervisor will only take no further action and not refer a case to the CPS if the Full Code or the Threshold tests are not met (see Chapter 13) *and* the case cannot be strengthened by further investigation, or early CPS advice, *or* the decision does not require the assessment of a complex evidential or legal issue. In practice this means that a police decision to not take any further action only applies to cases that clearly cannot meet the evidential standard because all reasonable lines of enquiry have been exhausted and there is no prospect of further enquiries or evidence strengthening the case sufficiently to eventually meet either the Full Code Test or the Threshold Test.

10.8 **Child Sexual Exploitation (CSE)**

Child sexual exploitation (CSE) is a form of child abuse involving children and young people receiving something in exchange for sexual activity. Victims can be male or female and from a range of ethnic origins. Perpetrators are not restricted to a particular ethnic group and there have been offences committed all over the country (Department for Education 2011).

The National Child Sexual Exploitation Action Plan (College of Policing 2014) aims to reduce the gap between the threat of CSE and the capability of the police to deal with it. It has seven key themes:

- public confidence and awareness
- protecting, supporting and safeguarding victims and managing risk
- effective investigations and bringing offenders to justice
- prepare, prevent, protect and pursue (the 4 P's)
- intelligence and performance monitoring
- police leadership
- learning and development for police leaders and front-line staff

The 4 Ps

Prepare—providing strong leadership, effective systems whilst working with partners to tackle CSE

Prevent—raising awareness of CSE amongst young people, parents, carers and potential perpetrators to prevent incident/repeat incidents

Protect—safeguarding vulnerable young people and supporting victims and those professionals who seek to reduce instances of CSE

Pursue—disrupting, arresting and prosecuting CSE offenders, ensuring a victim centred approach at all times

Local Safeguarding Children's Boards (LSCBs) are responsible for ensuring appropriate local procedures are in place to tackle CSE. All front-line practitioners must be aware of their local procedures and their own areas of responsibility within them. LSCBs and frontline practitioners should ensure that safeguarding actions promote the welfare of children and young people and focus on the needs of the child.

10.8.1 Risk factors and warning signs—victims

There are several warning signs and risk factors to be aware of when dealing with victims of CSE. These potential indicators are not exhaustive and further information is available in a government publication entitled 'What to do if you suspect a child is being sexually exploited' and also in the College of Policing APP.

Checklist

- Staying out later than expected
- Missing overnight and longer
- Drug and alcohol misuse
- Sexually transmitted infections, requesting contraception and terminations
- Missing from education
- Unexplained money, gifts, etc
- Transient to professionals

10.8.2 Management of CSE victims

Victims of CSE need to be managed through a multi-agency approach to protect them from further harm and identify and prosecute offenders. They may be challenging to deal with and uncooperative with the police and other agencies. This is mainly because they do not necessarily perceive themselves to be victims.

Checklist—Management of victims

- Prioritise safeguarding risks for immediate/urgent action
- Views of the child considered where appropriate
- Address any specific needs and diversity factors
- Disruption tactics around victim and perpetrator
- Contingency plan for a missing child

- Disruption tactics around victim and suspects
- Identified actions to manage and reduce risk

10.8.3 Child sexual exploitation offenders

The majority of CSE offenders are males whose ages vary from school age to elderly. However, women and victims of CSE themselves can also be groomed to recruit and coerce other victims into exploitation. CSE offenders groom their victims and manipulate them. The power and control exerted by the offender is intended to increase the dependence of the victim on them as the exploitative relationship develops. This type of exploitation can include:

- inappropriate relationships
- boyfriend model
- peer-on-peer exploitation
- groups and gangs associated with CSE
- organised network of sexual exploitation or trafficking

Investigators should be aware that offenders may come from within the victim's family and therefore victims should only be returned home when it is safe to do so.

10.8.4 Risk factors and warning signs—offenders

There are several indicators and warning signs that investigators ought to be aware of when dealing with CSE. However, these are not exhaustive:

- previous sexual abuse arrests, relevant convictions and non-convictions
- harboring juveniles during the daytime and overnight
- providing juveniles with alcohol or drugs
- previous Child Abduction Notices issued
- peers involved in CSE

- lives alone/living alone after previous marriage
- social media contact with juveniles

10.8.5 Managing CSE offenders

Managing CSE offenders should follow the Integrated Offender Management process. This involves the police and other agencies conducting home visits with the offender, intelligence briefings for police and utilising Child Abduction Notices, civil orders, human trafficking legislation as well as proactive and covert tactics.

10.9 Missing Person Enquiries

Anyone whose whereabouts cannot be established will be considered as missing until located and their wellbeing or otherwise confirmed (College of Policing 2019).

The majority of missing persons are quickly located or return unharmed of their own accord. Some cases do not require any police action, such as relatives losing contact where referral to other support agencies is the most appropriate action. Other missing people are never located, and in a small number of cases they are the victims of serious crime, including murder.

It cannot be overemphasised that some missing person reports can and do escalate into major investigations and critical incidents. In a number of cases the initial response to a missing person report has led to criticism of the police handling of the case. Criticisms have included failure to recognise or identify vulnerability from the characteristics of the missing person or their circumstances, incorrect assessment of any risk to them and inadequate early searches and intelligence gathering. In some high-profile cases the missing person was found deceased and secreted in their own home days after the initial report and after an initial search of the address had been conducted by the police.

KEY POINT

If in any doubt, the worst possible scenario must be considered to ensure investigative opportunities are fully exploited and nothing is missed during the early stages of a missing person enquiry. Time is critical; statistics show most murders occur quite soon after a person goes missing, particularly children and young persons.[4]

A missing person investigation begins on first notification to the police. Accurate information must be obtained about the circumstances, including any known reasons for the disappearance, which informs the risk assessment and determines the scale and immediacy of the response.

Reports are graded as high, medium, low or no apparent risk based on risk factors including:

- information that the person is likely to self-harm or attempt suicide
- whether the person is suspected to be the victim of a crime in action, such as abduction
- vulnerability due to age, infirmity or any other factor
- any inclement weather which would seriously increase the risk to health, particularly concerning children or elderly people
- whether the missing person needs essential medication or treatment not readily available to them
- the presence of any physical illness, disability or mental health problems
- the missing persons ability or inability to interact safely with others, or in an unknown environment
- involvement in a criminal, violent, homophobic and/or racist incident or confrontation immediately prior to disappearance
- they are victims of ongoing bullying or harassment

[4] CATCHEM database. CATCHEM stands for 'Centralised Analytical Team Collating Homicide Expertise and Management', a dataset maintained by the National Crime Agency (NCA).

- where the person has disappeared AND suffered or was exposed to harm
- any behaviour that is out of character or departure from their normal patterns (this can often be a strong indicator of risk)
- lack of any legitimate reason to go missing
- indications that preparations for absence have been made
- the intentions of the missing person when they were last seen are known and they have not completed them, for example going to work and failing to arrive there
- any family and/or relationship problems
- any recent history of family conflict including abuse
- victim or perpetrator of domestic abuse
- victim or perpetrator of domestic abuse
- on a child protection register
- drugs or alcohol dependency
- links to serious criminality or OCG activity
- work, school, college, university or relationship problems
- employment, financial or other depression problems
- any local concerns or community issues
- any other factor(s) which would influence the risk assessment

The risk levels as described in the College of Policing Missing Persons APP are:

1. **No apparent risk (absent)**—in which there is no apparent risk of harm to the public or the missing person. For absences assessed as having no apparent risk, the actions to locate the subject and/or gather further information should be agreed with the informant. The latest time to review the risk assessment should be set.
2. **Low risk**—where the risk of harm to the subject or the public is assessed as possible but minimal. Proportionate enquiries should be conducted to ensure the individual has not come to harm. In these circumstances, in addition to recording information on the PNC, the person reporting should be advised that,

following these proportionate basic enquiries, unless circumstances change, further active enquiries are unlikely to be conducted unless new or changed information revises the assessment.

3. **Medium risk**—where the risk of harm to the missing person or the public is assessed as likely but not serious. These cases require an active and measured response by the police and other agencies to trace the subject and support the person reporting, including the missing person's family.
4. **High risk**—where the risk of serious harm to the subject or the public is assessed as very likely. In these cases the risk posed could be immediate. There may be substantial grounds for believing the subject is in danger because of their own vulnerability, or the public are in danger. High-risk cases almost always require the immediate deployment of police resources and should lead to the appointment of an investigating officer (IO) and possibly a Senior Investigating Officer (PIP3) and a police search adviser (PolSA). Action may be delayed in exceptional circumstances, such as searching water or forested areas during the hours of darkness.

A member of the senior management team must be involved in examining the initial response and lines of enquiry and the approval of appropriate staffing levels and other resources. There should be close contact with outside agencies, and children's services must be notified immediately if the person is under 18. The Missing Persons Bureau should also be notified without undue delay. Appropriate family support should be put in place and a media strategy developed.

KEY POINT

All missing person reports should be continually reviewed as risk can increase or decrease as circumstances change and time passes. High-risk cases must be quickly identified and brought to the attention of supervisors and senior investigators (if believed suspicious) as soon as practicable.

To formulate an appropriate response, it is important to establish why the missing person is not where they are expected to be. Generally, people are missing for one of four reasons:

1. They are lost and temporarily disorientated, for example they do not know where they are but want to be found.
2. They have control over their decisions and are voluntarily missing, having decided on a course of action, such as they wish to leave home or commit suicide.
3. They are missing due to accident, injury or illness, for example someone who has wandered off due to a medical condition like dementia.
4. They are missing against their will or may be under the influence of a third party, such as sexual exploitation, an abduction or murder victim.

A priority line of enquiry is establishing and exploring the circumstances of the last sighting. This includes the location and time, which needs to be corroborated if possible, plus the relationship to the missing person of the person reporting or witnessing the last sighting.

The demeanor and the intentions of the missing person at that time are important factors to develop and they will inform the risk assessment and identify relevant lines of enquiry to be prioritised. Questions to be asked and answered include, for example:

- Was the missing person in a location that they could be expected to be or was this an unusual or unfamiliar location?
- Were they behaving out of character?
- What were their intentions?
- What direction were they heading in?
- Was the direction of travel consistent with their intentions if this is known?
- Were they on foot or did they have access to transport?
- Did they arrive at any intended destination?

- Were they intending to catch a train, a bus or take a taxi?
- Did they have anything with them?
- Were they accompanied by anyone else?
- Why might they have gone missing?

These questions are not exhaustive and the answers to each should generate further questions and enquiries.

The witness to the last sighting might not be the same person who reported the person as missing. Accurate background information should be established, such as possession and use of mobile phones or other communications devices, possession of bank/payment cards and cash and any essential medication required. It is important to consider whether the person reporting the person missing has a motive for providing false or misleading information. Experience has shown that people are sometimes reported as missing to cover up a crime.

10.9.1 Missing person searches

Thorough and systematic searches are a necessary element of missing person investigations. These include ensuring a comprehensive search is made of the person's home, the immediate surrounding area and any other relevant locations, such as the place they were last seen.

The objective of this search is to locate the missing person, including ensuring they have not returned to, or been hidden in their home. Searches also need to locate any material which might assist the enquiry, such as items that have been taken by the missing person (phones, money, payment cards, medication, etc) or left behind, including a letter or suicide note.

Checklist—Searches

Phase 1—a routine search of the missing person's home and immediate area

Phase 2—a hasty but thorough search based on the most likely circumstances of the disappearance, responding to early information gathered and likely to include the last known location of the missing person

Phase 3—an intelligence led scenario-based search of likely locations. This should be led by a PolSA using trained search teams and any other assets considered necessary. A high level of assurance that the missing person is not present is required at the conclusion of the search.

KEY POINTS

- Search levels increase according to the identified vulnerability and concerns for the missing person (high risk factors). Advice should be sought at the earliest opportunity from an in-force PoLSA plus, if required for complex searches, the NCA National Search Adviser who can provide advice including use of technical and specialist search equipment.
- The last known location should always be searched, and areas can be widened to include locations where a missing person has previously been found.

10.9.2 Lines of enquiry

Depending on the circumstances of the disappearance, after reviewing the initial action taken, some suggested lines of enquiry, in no order of priority, include:

- conduct searches, including places of possible concealment at the missing persons home address
- obtain a full description of the person and confirm its accuracy before any media release
- H2H enquiries in the vicinity of the persons home address

- trace and interview (T/I) the last person to see the person alive (always to be treated with appropriate caution and professional scepticism)
- investigate and confirm the circumstances of the last sighting, including the time, location and direction of travel
- validate any reported sightings to avoid following false sightings and trails (these may be made with good intent following media appeals)
- formulate a 'sightings policy' stating how such reports are to be dealt with and managed, including the accuracy of descriptions, considering whether the person reporting knows the missing person and evaluating anything said or observed
- H2H enquiries in the area of the last sighting
- passive and communications data opportunities, including mobile phone location services, financial transactions, use of social media sites
- CCTV recovery and analysis from the vicinity of the persons home address
- CCTV recovery and analysis in the vicinity of the last sighting
- CCTV and recovery and analysis from any routes known or believed to have been taken
- T/I witnesses to the persons movements
- T/I friends and associates
- produce a timeline of the persons movements (include confirmed and unconfirmed sightings)
- identify places habitually frequented
- education establishment
- place of employment/education/social clubs
- other places of interest to the missing person
- obtain biometric samples such as DNA, fingerprint and dental records depending on the circumstances of the case and the length of time missing
- establish if there is a reason to go missing such as threatened suicide, financial or domestic difficulties, bullying at school or through social media

- establish if the disappearance is out of character
- establish if preparations for absence from home have been made by taking clothing (obtain description), bag/carrier (obtain description), money/bank cards, cheque books, mobile phone and charger (obtain number and supplier), medication, personal possessions, passport, laptop/tablet
- victimology information, identifying friends, associates, places frequented, habits/routines, access to transport, relationships, places habitually used for hobbies/interests, drinking, eating and sleeping. Shopping and spending (including using loyalty cards), banking/finances, social media usage, medical conditions and medication used
- if previously reported missing, enquiries at locations previously found
- locations with a previous or emotional attachment, such as cemeteries where loved ones are interned, holiday locations and other familiar areas
- significant events/anniversaries possibly linked to the date of disappearance
- any useful information in diaries, computers, data storage devices, phones, social media accounts, receipts, letters, travel documents, etc.
- checks with establishments such as hospitals, doctors, welfare agencies, hotels/guest houses, transport companies, financial institutions.[5]
- communications data enquiries including last calls made to/from the missing person's home address and specialist location services (access will be influenced by the risk grading)
- telephone billing and subscriber information for the missing person and their associates
- text or leave a message on the missing person's phone to make contact if they are safe and well

[5] The NCA Major Crime Investigative Support team has a matrix to use as an aide-memoire for conducting these types of enquiries, aka a 'proof of life' template.

- circulations:
  - PNC
  - PNC marker on vehicles owned or used by the missing person
  - PNC audits for checks by others on the missing person
  - Special Circulation Bulletin within force and to other forces
  - Interpol/Europol if believed abroad
  - media appeals (local/regional/national including social media sites)
- Notifications:
  - UK Missing Persons Bureau (IMPORTANT and MANDATORY)
  - Missing People Charity (formerly the National Missing Persons Hotline).

When located, missing persons should always be interviewed to establish whether they have been a victim or committed any crime before or whilst missing, where and by whom they have been harbored and any information which may lead to their early discovery should they disappear again. Intelligence records including COMPACT, and the National Missing Persons Bureau should be updated, and relevant support put in place to avoid a reoccurrence.

KEY POINTS

- When an adult missing person is located, their whereabouts must not be disclosed to others against their wishes. Some people are reported missing to the police so they can be located for reasons that are not in their best interest such as fleeing honour-based violence/abuse. If consent is not provided, the person reporting should be informed that the subject has been located and reassured concerning their wellbeing.
- Be mindful of child sexual exploitation (CSE) involving young vulnerable missing persons, especially those who frequently go missing from care placements and who may be the target of sexual predators and systematic or organised abuse.

- The UK Missing Persons Bureau (MPB) must be contacted and notified. They provide a range of services including coordinating enquiries and cross-matching with other unidentified persons. They act as the centre for the exchange of information between forces and organisations, including provision of general advice, guidance and support (<http://www.missingpersons.police.uk>).

10.9.3 **Other agencies**

Young people in care and other people such as the elderly and people with mental health problems or learning difficulties are likely to be vulnerable when missing from their residential settings. Local police-force protocols concerning multi-agency responsibilities, including adopting a problem-solving approach in these circumstances should be researched.

The police are entitled to expect parents and carers, including staff acting in a parenting role in care homes, to accept normal parenting responsibilities and undertake reasonable actions to try and establish the whereabouts of the individual.

Individuals whose whereabouts are known, including children in care who are absent without authorisation, will not be considered as missing but may require other police activity to ensure their welfare. Local safeguarding procedures should be consulted to ensure an appropriate response (College of Policing 2019 and Department of Education 2014).

Safeguarding and promoting the welfare of children and protecting them from risk is a key duty on local authorities and requires effective joint working. Additional guidance is contained in the *Statutory Guidance on Children who Run Away or go Missing from Home or Care* (Department of Education 2014) which is addressed to Children's Services, Local Safeguarding Children's Boards (LSCB) and other organisations providing services for children and families, including the police, health and education practitioners and the voluntary sector. In this guidance a child is also a person who has not yet reached their 18th birthday but expands the police definition of a missing person with the following:

Young runaway—a child who has run away from their home or care placement or feels they have been forced or lured to leave.

Missing child—a child reported as missing to the police by their family or carers.

Missing from care—a looked after child who is not at their placement or the place they are expected to be (eg school) and their whereabouts are not known.

Away from placement without authorisation–a looked after child whose whereabouts are known but who is not at their placement or place they are expected to be, and the carer has concerns or the incident has been notified to the local authority or the police.

A 'looked after child' is a child who is looked after by the local authority by reason of a care order or being accommodated under the Children Act 1989 (section 20). The local authority that is responsible for a looked after child's care and planning is the 'responsible local authority'.

A 'host local authority' is the local authority in which a looked after child is placed when they are placed outside the responsible local authority's area. Furthermore, the Children's Act 2013 (section 13) requires local authorities and other named statutory partners to make arrangements to ensure that their functions are discharged with a view to safeguarding and promoting the welfare of children, including planning to prevent children from going missing and to protect them when they do.

The local authority and the police should work together to risk assess cases of children missing from home or care and analyse data for patterns that indicate particular concerns and risks. It is beyond the capacity of this handbook to describe all the local arrangements for police areas in the United Kingdom, which differ between forces. Investigators are therefore advised to research their own local Runaway and Missing from Home and Care (RMFHC) protocols, particularly as young runaways may be at higher risk of being or becoming victims of child sexual exploitation, involvement with gangs, county lines drugs distribution or other criminal activity. Repeatedly going missing should not be considered to be a normal pattern of behaviour.

The response set out in the RMFCH protocol should be put into action as soon as a child is reported missing. Regarding risk assessment, the police will prioritise all incidents of children categorised as 'missing' from home or care as medium or high risk. Where a child is classed as 'absent' the details will be recorded by the police and a review time and any ongoing actions agreed with the child's family, carer or responsible local authority.

A missing child incident would be prioritised as high risk where:

- the risk posed is immediate and there are substantial grounds for believing that the child is in danger through their own vulnerability
- the child may have been the victim of a serious crime
- the risk posed is immediate and there are substantial grounds for believing that the public is in danger

KEY POINT

Any risk assessment must be kept under review and revised for any changes in circumstances during the course of the investigation. Any emerging or developing information should be brought to the attention of a supervisor as soon as possible, and immediately if the risk is deemed to be high.

10.10 Honour-based Violence/Abuse and Forced Marriage

The terms 'honour crime', 'honour-based violence' and abuse (HBV/A) or 'izzat' (Arabic for honour) are generic terms for crimes, where the victim is punished by their family or community for bringing shame or dishonour on them by transgressing perceived correct codes of behaviour. Such offences are prosecuted under the relevant law, such as assault, false imprisonment, kidnap and murder.

A forced marriage is when one or both spouses do not consent, and duress is involved to force the victim into the marriage; this may involve physical, psychological, sexual and emotional abuse which continues after the marriage.

Forced marriage can occur within the United Kingdom or by taking the victim abroad, often not knowing in advance that they are to be married. Once outside the United Kingdom, they may find it impossible to return and be unable to communicate with others.

All agencies encountering victims of forced marriage and HBV must follow the 'one chance' rule, meaning they may only have one chance to speak to the victim and thus only have one opportunity to save their life.

Reports of forced marriage should only be handled by officers qualified to deal with such cases through experience and specialist training. Police forces have their own protocols including multi-agency working, but any investigator could find themselves in a situation where they receive an initial report of forced marriage/HBV.

In these circumstances it is essential to remember the 'one chance' rule and take immediate action, including gathering the information in the checklist suggested in this section, and contacting a supervisor according to local force protocols for specialist resources and senior investigative oversight.

The safety and welfare of the person under threat takes priority, and confidentiality must be maintained with only necessary personnel informed. The family of the person under threat or a person acting on their behalf (possibly innocently) may attempt to locate them, including reporting the victim as a missing person or the perpetrator of a crime. No information should be supplied, and any incident logs should have restricted access.

Protective measures include removing the victim to a place of safety, or, in the case of a child, taking them into police protection. High-risk cases may be managed by a Multi-Agency Risk Assessment Conference (MARAC) or by Multi-Agency Public Protection Arrangements (MAPPA) with only essential personnel involved. The Forced Marriage Unit at the Foreign and Commonwealth Office is an important source of advice and should be contacted and obtaining a Forced Marriage Protection Order considered.

Checklist—HBV information to be gathered

- Details of the person making the report and their relationship with the individual under threat
- Details of the person under threat including:
  - date of report
  - name
  - nationality (including any dual nationality which has implications for consular assistance abroad)
  - age
  - date and place of birth
  - passport information, including ascertaining if they have two passports and which one they will be travelling on
  - school
  - employment
  - full details of the allegation
  - name and address of parents or those with parental responsibility
  - National Insurance number
  - driving licence number
  - distinguishing features
  - recent photograph and any other identifying documents
- A list of trusted friends and family and their contact details
- A code word to authenticate future contacts

- A way of establishing discreet future contact that will not put the person at risk of harm
- Background information, including any involvement with adult or children's social care, doctors or other health services
- Addresses of the extended family in the United Kingdom and any known phone numbers
- Details of any threats, abuse or other hostile action against the person, whether reported by the victim or a third party
- The nature of the risk level (eg pregnancy, if they have a secret boyfriend/girlfriend or if they are already married)
- Any other family members that are at risk of forced marriage, or if there is a history of forced marriage and abuse
- Visually recorded interview (vulnerable/intimidated witnesses)
- Voluntary DNA sample and fingerprints if the individual is going abroad imminently and this cannot be avoided

Obtain where known:

- a photocopy of their passport and encourage them to keep details of the number and place and date of issue
- any address they may be staying overseas
- potential spouse's name
- Name of potential spouse's father
- Date of proposed wedding
- Addresses of the extended family overseas and any known phone numbers
- Information that only the victim would be aware of (to corroborate their identity if later interviewed at the British Embassy/High Commission and prevent a similar person being produced pretending to be them)
- Details of any travel plans and people likely to accompany them

- Name and address of close relatives remaining in the UK
- A safe means of contact, for example a mobile phone that will function overseas and be kept hidden
- Advise them to take emergency cash, in local currency and also hard currency (pounds, dollars, euros) for use in the country of destination if problems arise
- If reported by a third party, their details in case the person contacts them from overseas, or on their return
- Details from the person under threat of a trusted friend/advocate in the UK who they can maintain contact with and who can be approached by the police if they do not return
- The estimated return date with request that the person under threat makes contact without fail on their return
- A written statement from the person explaining they want the police, adult/children's social care, a teacher or third party to act on their behalf if they do not return by a certain date
- Provide contact details of the department and person handling the case (with advice to avoid discovery of the information)
- Supply the address and contact number for the nearest British Embassy/High Commission
- Encourage them to memorise at least one telephone number and email address, preferably the British Embassy/High Commission if they are a British national
- Explain the implications of dual nationality, which limits consular assistance
- If they are not a British national, encourage contact with the Forced Marriage Unit
- Contact any identified friend/advocate and obtain a statement of their support before the person departs
- Take contact details with them of a person they can trust in the country of destination

- Provide a copy of the Forced Marriage Unit's leaflet 'Forced Marriage Abroad' and advise them to contact the Forced Marriage Unit

KEY POINTS

- There is a difference between forced marriage and arranged marriage, as the latter implies there is consent of both parties and involves choice.
- There is no specific criminal offence of forced marriage, although at the time of writing this is under government consideration.

10.11 Modern Slavery and Exploitation

This section seeks to only to provide a short overview of modern slavery and exploitation, and the investigation of associated offences. These crimes will almost certainly involve serious organised crime group activity in their commission.

Modern slavery and trafficking is where a person is taken from one area of a country to another area, or they have crossed national borders. Trafficked people, when they arrive at their destination, are exploited by having their means of escape removed, including the confiscation of any identification documents, such as their passport. This makes such a victim become dependent on the trafficker, and they are exploited, for example sexually (perhaps in massage parlours and brothels), agricultural labour, manufacturing, construction, car wash operations, nail bars, domestic servitude and other forms of exploitation. This exploitation may take place in plain sight under the veneer of being a legitimate business.

The investigative response requires team working and wider consideration such as victim safeguarding, financial investigation, multi-agency working, information sharing, cross border and international cooperation and protected tactics that are not for publication.

All police forces now have investigators who have been trained on how to plan and develop investigative strategies to respond to modern slavery. Additional information is also accessible for authorised users in the College of Policing>Major Investigation and Public Protection>Modern Slavery>APP knowledge hub.

Slavery and trafficking require a multi-agency response regarding safeguarding and investigation. This includes the role of the Single Competent Authority and the National Referral Mechanism (NRM). The NRM is a single framework for reports of modern slavery and is centred on a multi-agency approach to identifying victims and referring them to appropriate support.

10.11.1 The statutory defence for child victims of trafficking and slavery

Section 45 of the Modern Slavery Act 2015 came into force on 31 July 2015 and provides a statutory defence for victims of child trafficking and slavery who are compelled to commit criminal offences.

To potentially avail themselves of a section 45 defence, the child has to be under 18 years old when they committed the act that constitutes the offence they are accused of. They must also have done this act as a direct consequence of being, or having been, a victim of slavery or a victim of relevant exploitation. A reasonable person in the same situation as the person and having the person's relevant characteristics would also have done that act.

In cases where the police or the court have reasonable grounds to believe a person is a victim of trafficking and their age is uncertain, but they may be under 18 years old, the court *must* presume they are a child.

The section 45 defence reflects an international principle of non-prosecution of trafficked children. It is consistent with the UK's obligation under the Council of Europe Convention on Action against Trafficked Human Beings 2005 and the EU Directive on Trafficking.

KEY POINTS

- Schedule 4 of the Modern Slavery Act 2015 lists 140 serious offences which are exempt from the statutory defence under section 45. These excluded offences include murder, kidnap, false imprisonment, certain firearms offences, various serious offences against the person and many others that are too numerous to mention here. Investigators should consult Schedule 4 to establish if they are dealing with a qualifying offence before deciding on any action to be taken concerning a potential section 45 defence.
- Offences subject to a section 45 defence include theft (pick pocketing), offences relating to prostitution, cultivation of cannabis and immigration offences. A section 45 defence cannot be applied to offences committed before 31 July 2015.
- Where an offence is not specifically covered by the section 45 defence, the CPS should still consider whether it is in the public interest to prosecute, taking account of the Director of Public Prosecution's (DPP) guidance on modern slavery cases.

If a person joins an illegal organisation or a similar group of people with criminal objectives and coercive methods and they voluntarily expose or submit themselves to illegal compulsion, they cannot rely on a section 45 defence.[6]

Where a potential section 45 defence is an issue in a criminal case, investigators should conduct enquiries to identify if the suspect is a credible potential victim of trafficking and/or slavery. This ought to include whether

[6] *R v Fitzpatrick* [1977] NILR 20.

the person has previously claimed to be a victim and has raised the section 45 defence before.

The onus is on the police (and prosecutors, the court and the defence) to identify indicators of trafficking regardless of whether or not a suspect makes any disclosure that they are a potential victim and whether or not they make any admissions concerning the offence under investigation.

10.12 **County Lines Investigations**

The term 'county lines' relates to the supply of drugs from major cities and towns into the smaller towns and villages and the less densely populated areas of the country. By using this method, organised criminal networks and gangs *export* illegal drugs into the *importing* areas.

County lines are likely to use or exploit vulnerable young people and vulnerable adults to facilitate the movement, storage and supply of drugs and/or money. It is not uncommon for criminals from the exporting area to move into an importing area and take over the homes of vulnerable people who are incapable of resisting them. This person's home is then used as a base to deal or store drugs in a practice known as 'cuckooing'. In the beginning this relationship is likely to appear innocuous but any vulnerability is subsequently exploited through coercion, the offer of rewards, intimidation or threatened and actual violence including sexual violence.

Central to a county line operation is the use of mobile phones and the movement of illegal drugs. A dedicated phone number known as a 'deal line' is used by buyers in the importing area to contact dealers in the exporting area to facilitate the supply of drugs.

The capture of mobile phones and analysing the data obtained from them is one of the primary objectives of a county lines investigation. In practice this can be challenging for investigators due to the prevalence of frequently changed 'burner' phones, swapping SIM cards in mobile devices and challenges of attributing phone use to specific individuals located in different police force areas.

Collaboration between police forces is essential to successfully dismantle a county lines network rather than just pursuing local investigative opportunities in isolation. This involves developing a joint intelligence strategy including effective information sharing and organising co-ordinated action.

Contact should be made with the National County Lines Coordination Centre (NCLCC) in accordance with local policy. This may be through a force single point of contact or the intelligence unit. The NCLCC are responsible for liaising with police forces with the aim of maximising all opportunities to identify, investigate and disrupt county lines.

Ultimately, partnership and multi-agency working should be considered to address any longer-term vulnerability and safeguarding issues that may be identified during the investigation. Such a broader problem-solving approach in the importing force area is important to prevent another gang or criminal group filling the void and setting up another county lines network.

Checklist

- Intelligence development to identify the presence of outsiders with no apparent family, work or social connections to the importing area.
- Identify any links between local vulnerable young people and vulnerable adults in the importing area associating with apparent outsiders
- Consider local missing children debriefs to assess possible county lines involvement
- Develop intelligence packages, including subject profiles of all relevant individuals
- Conduct PND checks and develop a joint strategy with other police forces involved in the network.

Include the exporting force and any other police area on the route between the exporting and importing force.

- Establish any travel patterns of identified individuals
- Identify potential transport routes between the exporting area and the importing area
- Identify potential transport hubs being used such as railway and bus stations in both the exporting and importing force area
- Identify any passive data opportunities in transport locations. For example, CCTV on trains and buses and in and around the transport hub.
- Consider the potential reactive and proactive investigative opportunities available through passive data sources.
- Engage with intelligence and source handling units regarding CHIS tasking to obtain the number(s) of any mobile phone 'deal lines'.
- Request analytical support to establish the pattern of use to convert intelligence from mobile device data to evidence.
- Consider obtaining and analysing reverse billing
- Identify points of sale for mobile phones, SIM cards and pay as you go top ups and develop any investigative opportunities.
- Identify the residence of possible 'cuckooing' victims and consider the viability of covert evidence gathering tactics

Other offences could be considered in addition to the drug supply offences, for example these could potentially include offences against the person and sexual offences.

Depending on the circumstances it may also be appropriate to use legislation available under the Modern Slavery Act 2015 for any exploitation aspect of county lines offending, such as holding someone in slavery, servitude, or forced compulsory labour.

10.13 Criminal Use of Firearms

Many incidents involving firearms can be investigated using standard major investigation principles, for example domestic murder and armed robbery. All reports of the suspected or potential criminal use of firearms must be investigated. However, additional issues arise for certain types of 'gun crime', including so-called 'bad on bad' shootings. These may be linked to territorial disputes and drugs, perhaps involving power, status and respect in a gang culture. In extreme cases the investigation might involve shooting a selected target that has been meticulously planned and executed. This could be the result of engaging an external contractor or otherwise.

Difficulties encountered often include offences not being reported; late or third party reporting when forensic material has already been disposed of by the offender(s); victims and witnesses refusing to cooperate through fear of repercussions; criminals' knowledge of conventional police investigation techniques enabling them to take forensic countermeasures; the increased use of communications technology to organise shootings; and the mobility of criminals who may travel to other parts of the country to carry out attacks.

Covert policing techniques can be considered as part of the reactive investigation strategy. However, to protect their sensitivity and future effectiveness, these tactics are not revealed in this handbook and this section only provides general overt suggestions.

Often, in advance of shootings, warning signals are available, including heightened tension in communities from disputes between drug dealers, the release from prison of notorious gang members or an overt act of disrespect. If these signals are identified and properly assessed using the National Intelligence Model (NIM), firearms incidents can be prevented, possibly by issuing a threat to life (aka TTL or an Osman) warning.

KEY POINTS

- The link between the criminal use of firearms and the supply of drugs is often evident, and an effective strategy to tackle 'gun crime' may depend on an effective police response to drug dealing and territorial control.
- Some larger forces have specialist units investigating gun and gang crime. It is recommended that advice is obtained from them on best practice.
- In firearm discharges, stray bullets can and do travel much further than a target or victim location. Proposed search areas for bullet heads may need to be significantly extended when deciding on cordon parameters.

Different scenarios likely to be encountered with the criminal use of firearms include:

- gunshots heard but no evidence to substantiate a firearms discharge
- gunshots fired with evidence of a firearms discharge (no bullets or cartridge casings)
- gunshots fired but no victim or offender (cartridges, bullets or casings recovered)
- gunshots fired with an identified victim but no offender
- gunshots fired with a victim and suspect (no weapon)
- persons reported with injuries that are gunshot wounds, for example by doctors and medics, including ones that are accidentally self-inflicted such as when firearms are activated when concealed in clothing or when being demonstrated or tested
- a suspect with a weapon (with or without a victim)
- recovery of weapons or ammunition
- weapons trafficking

Checklist—Firearms incidents

- Gather as much information as possible from the source of the report

- Resources deployed are based on the initial risk assessment with preservation of life a priority
- Obtain advice from a firearm's tactical adviser
- If the offence is in progress, instigate procedures for authorities, firearms silver command and control, risk assessment and intelligence capabilities
- Scene risk assessment to be conducted by attending officers
- Identify, secure and protect scene(s):
  - victim
  - suspect
  - weapon and ammunition (considering safety and security)
  - location
  - hospital (victim may be in hospital and still under threat from suspects/gangs)
- Forensic recovery of evidence including a weapon and ammunition:
  - any firearm or suspected firearm must be recovered by a trained officer to certify it has been made safe; weapons must be secured whilst maintaining their evidential integrity; details of the precise procedures followed should be recorded
  - identify and evidence whether the firearm was loaded or unloaded, and what position the cylinder and barrel (if revolver) was in
  - exhibit each weapon, component part and item of ammunition, stating where they were found
  - photograph firearms and component parts alongside a scale to indicate dimensions and include copies of photographs with the case file
- Forensic opportunities to be fully exploited, fingerprints, DNA, firearms discharge residue (FDR):
  - fingerprint examination
  - DNA recovery
  - Quasar testing
  - medical examination of suspects for gunshot injuries and marks around the hands for weapon recoil marks and bruises

- examination of suspects' external skin and recovery of clothing for FDR (including pockets and waistbands)
- establishing compatibility of the firearm with any ammunition recovered

- Weapon identification
- Submit samples for forensic examination by a Forensic Service Provider (FSP) and the National Ballistics Intelligence Service (NABIS), considering fast track submission in urgent cases for comparison analysis
- Identify witnesses at an early stage and arrange for their care and safety
- Interview witnesses, consider video recording as witnesses to specified gun and knife offences are automatically categorised as intimidated under section 17(5) of the Youth Justice Criminal Evidence Act 1999 (YJCEA) as inserted by the Coroners and Justice Act 2009 unless they want to opt out (see Chapter 8)
- Fast track identification of the victim and provisions made for their safety, including any further attempts on their life
- Develop a full intelligence package/profile on the victim
- Interview the victim including a hostile/reluctant victim/witness strategy (video recording)
- Fast track identification of suspects
- Prepare suspect profile
- Suspect management strategy (sterility and avoidance of cross-contamination is essential, especially when swabbing for FDR on external bodily surfaces and seizing clothing)
- Set intelligence requirements including passive data/social network opportunities
- Community Impact Assessment
- Media management strategy
- Hot debrief of all officers involved

- Adopt a positive prosecution strategy; consider evidence-based prosecution without the cooperation of hostile victims or witnesses
- Incident finalisation code (firearms) to be completed on incident logging systems
- Arrange intelligence support to the investigation and management of incoming information including a single point of contact (SPoC) for firearms intelligence
- Analyse the potential significance of the report, unless it is proved to be false or malicious, including future risk analysis and predictive intelligence capability (repercussions/reprisals)
- Identify if any recovered firearm is involved in a series of incidents and linked to others via NABIS
- Establish the weapon/ammunition profile (forensic history/ballistics comparison) including mandatory national data sharing
- Further information and guidance are available in *Investigators Checklist* (National Ballistics Intelligence Service 2015) which is cross-referred to in the *Major Investigation and Public Protection, Gun Crime APP* (College of Policing).

10.14 Cyber Crime and Cyber Investigations

The fast-changing nature of cyber criminality means this is only an introduction to a continually increasing demand on police resources. Internet users now undertake a greater amount of financial activity online, from making purchases from numerous sources including auction sites, to completing banking transactions and other functions including opening accounts, applying for loans and investments and paying bills.

It is apparent that fraud is significantly under reported as many individuals do not inform Action Fraud and their losses are reimbursed by their financial services provider. It is known that 'card not present' crime involving the online fraudulent use of bank/credit card information is not fully included in industry reports.

In addition to widespread use of social media, the internet is also used for specific social and relationship activity as demonstrated by the proliferation of online dating sites. Investigators should familiarise themselves with their force protocols in relation to allocating and investigating cyber offences. The nature of some traditional crime types has been transformed in terms of scale and the extent of reach by using computers and other communications technology for offending such as:

- fraudulent financial transactions
- sexual offending
- harassment and threatening behaviour
- commercial damage and disorder

10.14.1 Definition and national response

Cybercrime is using any computer network for crime and is divided into three categories:

1. 'Pure online' crimes where a digital system is the target as well as the means of attack. These include attacks on computer systems to disrupt IT infrastructure and stealing data over a network using malware (the purpose of the data theft is usually to enable further crime).
2. 'Existing' crimes that have been transformed in scale or form by use of the internet. The growth of the internet has allowed these crimes to be carried out on an industrial scale
3. Use of the internet to facilitate drug dealing, people struggling and other transnational types of crime.

The National Fraud Intelligence Bureau (NFIB) sits alongside Action Fraud within the City of London Police, who are the national policing lead for fraud. The NFIB takes all Action Fraud reports and assesses the millions of reports of fraud and cyber-crime to identify series of offences and serial offenders, organised crime groups and established as well as new and emerging crime types. The NFIB receives reports from:

- individuals and small businesses reporting to Action Fraud by phone or online either directly, or via the police
- fraud data obtained from industry and the public sector, including banking, telecommunications and government departments
- various intelligence sources including but not limited to, national and international police crime/intelligence systems

10.14.2 Glossary of terms and crime comparisons

Traditional crimes	Cybercrimes
Burglary Breaking into a building with intent to steal	**Hacking** Computer or network intrusion providing unauthorised access
Deceptive callers Criminals telephoning victims and asking or persuading them to provide their financial and/or personal identification information	**Phishing** A high-tech scam that frequently uses unsolicited messages to deceive people into disclosing their financial and/or personal identification information
Extortion Illegal use of force or one's professional position or powers to obtain property, funds or patronage	**Internet extortion** Hacking into and controlling various industry databases (or the threat of) and promising to release control back to the company or organisation if funds are received or some other demand satisfied

Traditional crimes	Cybercrimes
Fraud Deceit, trickery, sharp practice or breach of confidence perpetrated for profit or to gain an unfair or a dishonest advantage	**Internet fraud** A broad category of fraudulent schemes that use one or more components of the internet to defraud prospective victims, conduct fraudulent transactions or transmit fraudulent transactions to financial institutions or other parties
Identity theft Impersonating or presenting oneself as another to gain access, information or a dishonest advantage	**Identity theft** The wrongful obtaining and use of another person's identity information in some way that involves fraud or deception, typically for economic gain
Child exploitation Criminal victimisation of minors for indecent purposes such as pornography and sexual abuse	**Child exploitation** Using computers and networks to make it easier to criminally victimise minors

Some common terms used in cybercrime investigation include:

- **Denial of Service Attach (DOS)**—designed to overwhelm a targeted website to the point of it crashing or becoming inaccessible. A successful DOS attack can disable any entity relying on their online presence by rendering their website virtually useless.
- **Distribution Denial of Service Attack (DDOS)**—more devastating than a DOS attack launched from a single system. A DDOS uses other systems (without them even knowing), flooding the target server with a speed and volume that is exponentially magnified.
- **Malware**—a malicious program that causes damage. It includes viruses, Trojans, worms, time bombs, logic bombs or anything else intended to cause damage upon the execution of the payload.
- **Phishing**—a form of social engineering conducted in electronic form, usually by email, with the purpose of

gathering sensitive information. Often these communications look genuine and appear to originate from a legitimate source like a social networking site, a well-known entity such as PayPal or eBay or a bank. They have links directing to a very convincing looking site which asks to verify personal account information. When logging in to verify information on the bogus site, the provision of the information is sufficient for it to be gathered and used in cybercrime.

- **Social engineering**—to deceive someone for the purpose of acquiring sensitive and personal information, like credit card details or usernames and passwords. For example, a call purporting to be from IT services informing of new password and username guidelines being implemented by the company which asks for the target to reveal theirs so they can ensure they meet the requirements of the new guidelines. The only way to ensure not becoming a victim of social engineering is to never provide personal and sensitive information to anyone unless absolutely sure of their identity and this is confirmed.
- **Spyware**—software designed to gather information about a user's computer use without their knowledge. Sometimes spyware is just used to track a user's internet surfing habits for advertising purposes to match their interests with relevant advertising. Spyware can also scan computer files and keystrokes, create pop-up ads, change a homepage and/or direct the user to pre-chosen websites. Often spyware is bundled with free software like screen savers, emoticons and social networking programs.

No single piece of legislation deals with cybercrime; there is legislation dealing with the end result of the use of a computer network for criminal activity such as the Fraud Act 2006 and legislation dealing with computer misuse (particularly hacking), malicious communications and data protection including under the Malicious Communications Act 1998, the Computer Misuse Act 1990 and the Data Protection Act 1998 and 2018.

This area of investigation will continue to evolve and needs the support of in force and external specialists in cybercrime teams and financial investigation.

10.15 Terrorism and Extremism

Terrorism is the use or threat of action (including outside the United Kingdom) where:

1. it involves serious violence against a person, serious damage to property, endangers a person's life (other than the person committing the action), creates serious risk to the health and safety or the public or a section or the public, or is designed to seriously interfere with or seriously disrupt an electronic system.
2. it is designed to influence the government or an international governmental organisation or to intimidate the public or a section of the public.
3. it is made for the purpose of advancing a political, religious or ideological cause.[7]

The diverse nature of terrorism includes individuals and groups affiliated to or inspired by international terrorist organisations such Al-Qaeda (AQ), Islamic State, Dissident Irish Republicans (DIR) in Northern Ireland to extreme right wing (XRW) activity in the United Kingdom.

Terrorists can operate in organised cells receiving instructions from others in a hierarchy; they could be individuals, or a group inspired by an ideology but not directed by a core leadership, or they might operate individually as 'lone wolves'.

The challenge of investigating terrorism is different to other types of crime; due to its global reach the investigation could have international dimensions and multiple

[7] Terrorism Act 2000, section 1.

centres of simultaneous activity at locations throughout the United Kingdom spanning several police force areas.

Investigations are generally a fusion of covert and overt activity with clearly defined command and coordination structures operated on a strictly 'need to know' basis to prevent compromise.

Terrorism powers including arrest, detention and search are different to powers under the Police and Criminal Evidence Act 1984 (PACE) and are not generally familiar to police personnel outside of the counter-terrorism (CT) investigation structure.

Countering terrorism and extremism is not the sole responsibility of investigators working in the specialist counter-terrorism policing command in the Metropolitan Police and the regional units. All police staff have a role to play through developing community intelligence and remaining vigilant whilst conducting their day-to-day activities and reporting suspicious activity.

Planned terrorism investigations are conducted by specialist officers, but any investigator could identify intelligence or become involved in the initial stages of an unplanned spontaneous incident, for example through discovery whilst conducting other enquiries, such as searching premises, vehicles or people for unconnected matters.

All investigators should be aware of suspicious activity which could transpire to be terrorist reconnaissance and attack planning of potential targets, fundraising, acquiring storage facilities or purchasing vehicles, chemicals and components to construct an improvised explosive device (IED).

Recent years have also seen marauding terrorist attacks involving knives and vehicles driven into crowded places whose acquisition and use should not be excluded when considering possible links to terrorism.

This section is only intended to raise awareness amongst all investigators that terrorists do reside in our communities and operate throughout the United Kingdom. History has proved that intelligence opportunities are available, and investigators in whatever capacity should always remain vigilant.

KEY POINT

Any officer suspecting terrorist activity should immediately contact their Force Special Branch/Counter Terrorist Unit no matter how insignificant they feel the information may be. It could be an important link that prevents an attack.

10.16 European and International Enquiries

Increased freedom of movement throughout the Europe together with illegal entry into the United Kingdom by asylum seekers and economic migrants from outside the European Union (EU), means it is not unusual to conduct enquiries with an international dimension. This could range from conducting additional checks when dealing with foreign nationals, such as obtaining details of convictions in international jurisdictions, to initiating enquiries to be conducted abroad, or disrupting criminality and supporting transnational investigations and immigration enforcement.

Police force Intelligence Bureaus have International Liaison Officers (ILO) who should be consulted for advice and guidance, including access to restricted intelligence opportunities that are not for publication in this handbook. An International Crime Coordination Centre (ICCC) has been established to support and advise UK policing on the use of international instruments and alternative arrangements following the UK exit from the EU. The contact details for the ICCC are available through the College of Policing International Investigation APP (College of Policing 2019) but a local ILO should be contacted in the first instance.

Situations likely to be regularly encountered by investigators are summarised in this section for basic guidance and awareness.

10.16.1 Foreign National Offenders

A Foreign National Offender (FNO) is 'a person known or suspected to be involved in criminality who cannot be confirmed as a British citizen at birth'. Mandatory checks to be conducted to assess the risk posed by an FNO and to assist with identifying the most appropriate tactical option with Immigration Enforcement include:

- Immigration Enforcement National Command and Control Unit (IENCCU). Slower time requests for foreign nationals of interest in criminal investigations should be submitted by email using the IENCCU proforma and are answered within 24 hours. Other arrangements are available for fast time immigration status checks outside the custody environment.
- PNC and PND checks which may contain details needed for ACRO and other checks. Consider #VF on addresses.
- ACRO criminal records office foreign national conviction check. ACRO is a national police unit responsible for exchanging criminal conviction information between the UK and other countries. ACRO also has delegated responsibility for managing the UK Criminal Record Information System (UK-CRIS) with EU member states. They also exchange conviction information via Interpol with a number of other countries outside the EU. It may not be possible to conduct ACRO checks for asylum seekers and refugees if such checks would require disclosing information to foreign national authorities which the subject claims to fear.
- I-24/7 Interpol check. This provides an immediate response under certain circumstances, but a IENCCU check needs to be conducted first.

Additional checks for consideration include:

- SIENA/Europol Check. This is Europol's secure system for transferring information and checks can be made for nominals, vehicles, etc for matters involving serious and organised crime.
- Interpol check for wider data sharing, including fingerprint checking and tasking requests to other countries.

KEY POINTS

- Investigators should not try to conduct these international checks themselves and should always contact their local intranet, force point of contact or Interpol Liaison Officer for guidance on international enquiries.
- It is the responsibility if the officer in the case to obtain the convictions of FNO's and ensure these are included in the case file.

10.16.2 Arrest and custody procedures

When a foreign national is in custody, in addition to the usual procedures that are conducted, checks should be taken to confirm their identity and status. The information obtained may identify a risk they could potentially present to others or themselves and inform their risk assessment regarding detention, bail or release. They may, for example, have previously committed offences against vulnerable people or be vulnerable themselves.

Checklist

- Ensure the subjects fingerprints are checked on Livescan. This also checks against the immigration database and an identification will be returned if the person is of interest to immigration, which should be pursued. Only subjects who have interacted with Immigration Enforcement will have their fingerprints on the system.

- Once the Livescan check has been completed, for real time immigration status the IENCCU should be contacted and provided with the subjects:
  - o full name
  - o any alias details
  - o date of birth
  - o nationality
  - o Livescan results (if the Livescan results are not available, IENCCU checks can still be completed)
- Obtain and seize any identity documents such as a passport, identity card, driving licence or birth certificate.
- Request previous foreign convictions via ACRO. Different countries have different minimum information requirements for requests.
- Request Interpol I-24/7 check. This will provide an instant result and could identify if the person is wanted or missing in another country or the subject of a warning (green) notice.
- Serve an IM3 immigration deportation liability notice at the point of charge on FNO's over 17 who have been charged with an imprisonable offence.

10.16.3 International Letters of Request (ILOR)

The United Kingdom is a signatory to a number of international treaties and conventions which provide the legal framework for mutual legal assistance overseas and govern the exchange of evidence between the United Kingdom and other countries both inside and outside the EU. Police forces cannot initiate enquires in an overseas jurisdiction without the necessary permissions.

An International Letter of Request (ILOR) is a written request from one judicial authority to another requesting enquiries to obtain evidential material from jurisdictions outside the United Kingdom which cannot be completed on a police-to-police basis. The judicial authority for England and Wales is the CPS.

If it appears that an offence has been committed or there are reasonable grounds for so believing, and proceedings/investigation have been instigated, any judge or justice of the peace in England or Wales may issue an ILOR on the application of a prosecuting authority (or, where proceedings have been instituted, a person charged in those proceedings).

A designated prosecuting authority itself (including CPS) may issue an ILOR if it appears that an offence has been committed, or there are reasonable grounds for so believing and proceedings/investigation have begun.

The CPS will advise on mutual legal assistance, including which countries and states will accept an ILOR, the procedure for making requests, plus any grounds for refusing assistance and restrictions on the use to which the assistance may be put.

An ILOR contains an outline of the case, the evidence requested and any legislation that needs to be adhered to, ensuring it is admissible in the requesting state's proceedings. It must contain specific information on the assistance required.

Although there are no hard and fast rules on when or when not to use an ILOR, they are generally used to obtain evidence or data which is not in the public domain, or to conduct enquiries which require coercive powers. Examples include taking statements, seizing evidence, searching premises, surveillance, and covert operations, obtaining information from closed databases, banking information, company records, ISP and email content, and transfer of consenting persons in custody to give evidence in criminal proceedings. Requests for gathering intelligence as opposed to obtaining evidence should not be made in an ILOR.

The police draft the ILOR for scrutiny and finalisation by the CPS who, in making the request for assistance, are exercising a statutory power and stating the evidence requested is required for use in the proceedings or investigation. This is not a 'rubber stamping' exercise as it is the prosecutor's request, not the police.

KEY POINTS

- The CPS should be approached as soon as it is known that evidential enquiries will be required abroad. ILORs require considerable care to draft and although there are measures in place to transmit them abroad in cases of urgency, they can take some time to execute. An ILOR is a legal document and failure to comply with its requirements could lead to legal challenge, including the admissibility of any evidence obtained.
- If it is necessary for UK police officers to travel abroad on enquiries, they do so at the invitation and with prior permission from the relevant state. They do not have any more power than a citizen of the country they are visiting, and in the majority of cases will be assisting and cannot initiate action themselves in the foreign jurisdiction.
- Investigators may also be required to gather evidence in the United Kingdom on behalf of a requesting nation via an ILOR.

10.16.4 Interpol circulation notices

Interpol notices are international requests for cooperation or alerts which allow police in member countries to share crime related information. These are shared on the Interpol database and are visible to all Interpol member state. They are accessed through I-24/7I checks. International circulations must be submitted through the force International Liaison Officer whose advice should be sought regarding the relevant notice, summarised below. Further information and a full list of notices is available on the Interpol website:

Checklist

- **Red Notice**—seeks the arrest or provisional arrest of persons wanted for prosecution or to serve a sentence. It is a request for law enforcement worldwide to locate and provisionally arrest a person pending extradition, surrender or similar legal action.

- **Yellow Notice**—issued to help locate missing persons, often minors, or to help identify people who are unable to identify themselves.
- **Green Notice**—provides details of criminals who are not currently wanted but are of international significance and may be of interest to law enforcement agencies in member countries or are likely to commit offences affecting several countries.
- **Blue Notice**—collects additional information about a person's identity or activities in relation to crime, for example unidentified offenders.
- **Black Notice**—provides details of unidentified bodies or deceased persons who may have used a false identity.

10.17 Non-recent/Historical Investigations

Investigations into past offences are now usually referred to as 'non-recent' investigations rather than the previously used label of 'historical' investigations. This is to recognise that for the victims of many serious crimes the impact for them can remain over many years up to the present day and the incident is therefore never historic for them.

The investigation of non-recent offences is currently more prevalent than ever. Contemporary high-profile examples include but are not limited to:

- Operation Hydrant—a national policing operation to manage and coordinate police forces' response to investigating non-recent child sexual abuse in institutional settings or abuse alleged to have been perpetrated by persons of public prominence.
- The Independent Inquiry into Child Sexual Abuse—a statutory inquiry instigated because of serious concerns

that some organisations had failed and were continuing to fail to protect children from sexual abuse.

- Operation Resolve—the criminal investigation into the causes of the 1989 Hillsborough football stadium disaster.
- The Infected Blood Inquiry—an independent public statutory inquiry established to examine the circumstances in which men, women and children treated by health services in the United Kingdom were given infected blood.
- Operation Midland—conducted between 2014 and 2016 in response to allegations from Carl Beech of non-recent sexual abuse committed by prominent individuals. This investigation was subsequently discredited and heavily criticised for automatically believing Beech's allegations without adequate further investigation.

There are many other examples of non-recent investigations where forensic led cold case reviews of murders and serious sexual offences have resulted in successful prosecutions, and this section only seeks to provide a brief overview.

The conventional principles of investigation continue to apply to non-recent investigations but there are some additional issues for investigators to consider. Non-recent investigations could be forensically led due to developing scientific techniques that were not previously available to examine forensic material from the original investigation. In such cases the forensic material will likely have been retained and archived by the Forensic Science Service since the previous report and investigation.

Alternatively, an investigation could be instigated following a contemporary report of a non-recent offence but there are no forensic opportunities available because the crime was not reported near to the time it was committed. In these cases, the investigation and any subsequent prosecution will need to rely on the complainant and witness accounts and any relevant documents from the time of the offence.

An ideal scenario for a forensic led non-recent investigation is where the context of any contact trace material provides compelling evidence to support a prosecution, for example the suspect's DNA is on a vaginal swab taken from the victim of a stranger rape. In these circumstances, enquiries need to establish the integrity of the exhibits handling in the case including the continuity of movements and the storage arrangements.

Depending on the time that has elapsed since the original investigation this might not be straightforward to establish. A good source to start with is the submission forms that accompanied the items to be examined to the forensic service provider. In non-recent cases this is almost always the Forensic Science Service which was closed in 2012 due to austerity measures following the worldwide financial crisis of 2008.

Depending on the completeness of the submissions document bundle and records it may be necessary to obtain further witness statements from officers and staff involved in the chain of continuity. It is possible with the passage of time that this is not possible because some of the people involved are now deceased. In this case the authenticity of the original records needs to be established to enable it to be submitted and admitted into evidence as a contemporaneous document, and to prepare for a hearsay application to the court.

The importance of witness evidence in non-recent investigations where no forensic opportunities are available to connect a suspect to the crime cannot be understated. The accuracy, reliability and credibility of the witness testimony in these circumstances is crucial.

Obtaining a victim or witness account when they are recalling events that happened a long time ago requires careful planning and execution. Engaging with an interview adviser at an early stage to assist with developing a witness strategy is strongly recommended.

It should be self-evident that the nearer to the time of the event to be recalled that a witness account is obtained, generally the more accurate and reliable the information is likely to be. This is accepted by the courts when they consider and grant permission for witnesses to refresh their memories from any accounts they made at the time. An early issue to consider is therefore to establish whether the witness has provided a previous account at the time of the incident or during the intervening time period.

The victim or witness will need supporting throughout the process including when they provide their account, starting with a victim needs assessment. Their questioning needs to be sensitive, including diplomatically establishing their motivation for reporting the offence at this time. The evolution of the witness account is an important element, including whether they have discussed this with anyone else or whether they have revealed and described the incident before, perhaps during therapy or to relatives or friends for example.

If the victim's account is one of several other complainants in the same investigation, additional thought needs to be given to informing the victim about the other allegation(s). Being aware that they are not the sole complainant could assist a victim to decide on whether they want to engage with the investigation and support a prosecution. It is acceptable in general terms to inform a victim that other complaints have been made against a suspect; however, to protect the integrity of any subsequent account and prevent it being contaminated, it is important not to provide details about any such other allegations.

Similarly, an investigative area that ought to be covered during the victim's interview is whether they have discussed their account with any other victims or witnesses as this has the potential to contaminate and influence these.

Efforts need to be made to corroborate the account where possible, including identifying, locating and reviewing any documents and records that were made at the time. These could, for example, include medical records and local authority and social services files which contain information about the complaint and the complainant. The potential disclosure implications need considering from the outset regarding third party material such as records of therapy which may need disclosing to the defence if a prosecution ensues. At all stages, the victim needs to be informed about what is happening along with the reasons, to enable them to provide their informed consent.

Exploring the context of events at the time when the alleged offence was committed requires an investigative mindset and nothing should be assumed or accepted at face value. As an example, when investigating religious orders who may have been responsible for various care facilities, difficulties could be encountered establishing the names and the correct identity of the persons involved. Nuns, for example, are given religious names which were sometimes changed, and the records from the time for these names could be incomplete or might not exist at all. Enquiries must therefore ensure that the correct identity of the persons they are investigating is accurately established. It is useful practice to obtain photographs of victims, witnesses and suspects that depict how they looked at the time of the alleged offence.

The interview under caution of any suspects also requires careful consideration and planning. The approach needs to mitigate any potential prejudice a suspect might claim by being expected to answer questions about events from perhaps years in the past. It is likely that any consideration for an adverse inference to be drawn from a suspect's silence will be strongly resisted with an argument that they could not reasonably be expected to reliably answer questions about events from so long ago. From a suspect's perspective, the risk is that misremembering an event in response to a question could be construed as a lie.

References

College of Policing (2021) Authorised Professional Practice (APP) available at <https://www.college.police.uk/app> accessed 22 September 2022

College of Policing (2021) Authorised Professional Practice (APP) available at <https://www.college.police.uk/app/major-investigation-public-protection/gun-crime> accessed 15 February 2022

College of Policing (2021) Authorised Professional Practice (APP) available at <https://www.college.police.uk/app/major-investigation-and-public-protection/modern-slavery> accessed 15 February 2022

College of Policing (2019) Authorised Professional Practice (APP) available at <https://www.college.police.uk/app/investigation/international/international> accessed 10 January 2022

College of Policing (2019) Authorised Professional Practice (APP) available at <https://college.police.uk/app/major-investigation-and-public-protection/missing-persons/missing persons> accessed on 15 February 2022

College of Policing (2014) National Child Exploitation Action Plan

CPS (2018) *A Guide to 'Reasonable Line of Enquiry' and Communications Evidence*

Department of Education (2014) *Statutory Guidance on Children who Run Away or go Missing from Home or Care*

Department for Education (2011) *Tackling Child Sexual Exploitation Action Plan* (HM Government)

National Ballistics Intelligence Service (2015) Investigators Checklist

NCIS (2000) *National Intelligence Model*

NPIA (2009) *Volume Crime Management Model*

Chapter 11

Investigating Sudden and Unexplained Deaths

11.1 Introduction

Deaths that occur outside medical settings and unexpectedly are often referred to as 'sudden and unexplained deaths'. They all require some form of investigation even though the death may not be suspicious or associated with criminality. Most deaths occur from natural causes, and the role of the investigator is to confirm that no criminal offences have been committed, particularly homicide.

Where there is potentially third party involvement, which might be indicated due to the nature and type of any visible injuries and/or other information available, the incident must be treated as suspicious. Most police forces have specialist units for investigating murder and suspicious or unexplained deaths (some working under collaboration agreements with neighbouring forces) where the investigation is led by a Senior Investigating Officer (PIP3) who is a Detective Chief Inspector or Detective Superintendent depending on the homicide classification of the incident.

Not all homicides are straightforward to identify; however, people who are deceased aren't able to offer any verbal explanation, so caution and an investigative mindset are required. Mistakes in the initial investigation of a murder can prove costly and affect

Blackstone's Crime Investigators' Handbook. Steve Hibbitt and Gary Shaw, Oxford University Press. © Oxford University Press 2023.
DOI: 10.1093/oso/9780192867896.003.0011

the chances of success. The investigation relies heavily upon accurate initial assessments and recognition by attending officers and following a methodical process. Therefore, crime investigators need to acquire a good level of understanding, professional knowledge and expertise in preparation for when they might be called upon to attend or deal with a sudden and unexplained death.

It would be extremely difficult to condense all the necessary information and guidance into one chapter, so the aim in this handbook is to outline the basic knowledge and skills required. Sections on suicides, child deaths, deaths in the workplace, deaths in care settings and deaths in prison have also been included. These require considerations in addition to the standard investigative activity and can prove complex and challenging to deal with.

Should further information be required on any of the topics covered, there are dedicated manuals and practical guides that contain more detailed content, such as the *Major Crime Investigation Manual* (NPCC 2021) and Cook, 2019.

11.2 Types of Death Investigation

An outline of the various routes a death investigation could follow is outlined in Figure 11.1, accepting they may switch from one to another if the circumstances change. For example, with a coroner's sudden death investigation, if it transpires during a post-mortem examination that a homicide has occurred due to the discovery of previously unseen injuries or the results of toxicology analysis or other factors, then the coroner's investigation will cease and a murder enquiry will commence.

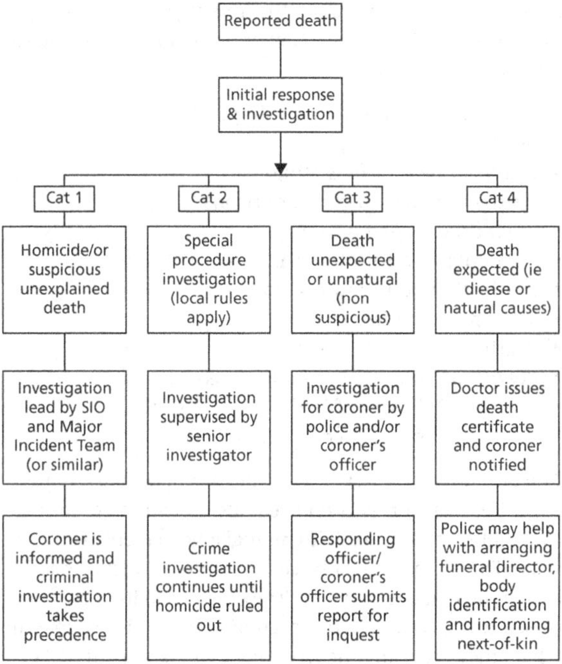

Figure 11.1 Death investigation process map

11.3 Special Procedure Investigations

Category 2 in Figure 11.1 shows what are sometimes termed 'special procedure investigations'. Some forces deem that certain types of unexpected deaths require a higher level of response and investigation (see column 2). This may include the early notification and involvement of a more senior detective such as a Detective Inspector. They will be expected to assume early responsibility for supervising and conducting the investigation. These types of deaths, which require a higher level of response and investigation, could include:

- deaths of any person under 18 years of age
- deaths in a workplace
- deaths in healthcare settings
- deaths in police custody or prisons
- illicit drug-related deaths
- accidental deaths (other than road collisions)
- deaths that occur out-of-doors
- suspected suicides
- deaths of vulnerable persons
- deaths of prominent or famous people
- deaths in Ministry of Defence establishments
- deaths that become critical incidents

The aim of the process is to ensure a proportionately thorough investigation is conducted and to eliminate mistakes by establishing any possible criminal involvement at an early stage. These types of deaths are often more difficult to judge and prone to more suspicion. They require an increased level of scrutiny because of the circumstances and locations in which they occur and the types of individuals involved. Such cases could attract public and media interest and therefore carry with them a higher degree of reputational risk.

KEY POINT

If an investigator considers that an enquiry into a sudden death that they are attending at or dealing with would benefit from the input and advice of a more senior detective, either in person or via a communications link, then they should not hesitate to contact one.

11.4 Post-mortem Examinations

The post-mortem process in most cases helps to determine the cause of death and confirm the type of investigation to be conducted. Post mortem means 'after death' and is the examination of a body to determine the cause of death.

There are two types of post mortems: those conducted on behalf of the coroner in hospital-based mortuaries by a general pathologist; and those conducted on behalf of the police by a Home Office registered pathologist, often referred to as forensic post-mortems. Determining whether it is necessary to conduct a post mortem and if so the type of examination to be conducted is usually the coroner's decision. If, for example, a patient dies of an illness or disease that has been recently treated by a medical practitioner prior to death, then the doctor who was treating them can certify the cause of death to satisfy the requirements of a coroner. If, however, a medically qualified person is not able to certify the cause of death, then a general post mortem must be conducted. If there are grounds for suspicion that any third party caused or contributed to the death, a general post mortem will be insufficient, and a forensic post mortem should be conducted.

The police can make a request to the coroner for a forensic post mortem to be conducted because the circumstances are suspicious or cannot be ascertained. A forensic post mortem advances the investigation by gathering wider forensic material, including contact trace evidence as well as establishing the pathological cause of death and the mechanism involved. Although the pathology procedures are similar, a forensic post mortem is far more rigorous and intrusive with an emphasis on collecting evidence as well as determining cause of death. A forensic post mortem will usually link to and be relevant to the wider forensic strategy for the investigation and they are more time consuming. If a criminal prosecution ensues, it is likely that the pathologist's evidence will be examined and scrutinised in the Crown Court.

Forensic post mortems are usually authorised through consultation and agreement between a senior detective/ Senior Investigating Officer (SIO) and the coroner. If the death is classified as a category 1 (homicide or suspicious) there is nearly always a need for forensic post mortem; category 2 and category 3 are discretionary and could be forensic or general; and for a category 4 death a post mortem may not be necessary at all.

11.5 Role of the Forensic Pathologist

Forensic Pathologists used to be known as 'Home Office pathologists' because they were registered with the Home Office. This term has since been replaced by Consultant Home Office Registered Forensic Pathologist. However, many judges, juries and lay people probably still know and understand the previous terminology.

A Forensic Pathologist is a medically qualified doctor who is an expert in identifying the patterns of natural disease and unnatural trauma in the human body, and they use their skill and knowledge to assist investigations and the legal process. The Forensic Pathologist is essentially a medical adviser and potential expert witness. Whilst maintaining the professional integrity and impartiality of the Forensic Pathology role, the police and the pathologist work as a team.

The investigation into a suspicious death has two separate components. The role of the coroner is to identify the deceased and establish a cause of death, whereas the role of the police is to establish if a criminal offence has occurred and investigate. The Forensic Pathologist is involved in both and is acting under the authority of, and on behalf of, the coroner, but they provide evidence, advice and guidance to the police to assist with the criminal investigation.

KEY POINTS

- Forensic Pathologists can usually only be authorised and requested by a senior detective/SIO in consultation with coroners. Individual police force policies will direct the level of authority required for a request.

- Pathologists prefer to visit the scene and view the body and surroundings in context of possible.
- If unsure about a cause of death or whether it is suspicious a safe option is to forensically remove the body for forensic post-mortem examination while keeping the scene protected and sterile. If the examination then finds the death to be a homicide, the scene is still intact.

11.6 **Cause and Manner of Death**

Two terms that need to be understood so they are not confused are 'cause of death' (COD) and 'manner of death' (MOD). A medical COD is the pathological condition which causes the death; whereas the MOD is the mechanism, instrument, physical agent or other means used to cause it. This is an important distinction to make because, for example, the medical cause of death could be a head injury, and the manner of death might be repeated punching or kicking, or perhaps blunt force trauma caused by being struck with a weapon. These are just illustrative examples as there are numerous possibilities for the manner of causing a death, and establishing the MOD is one of the primary objectives for conducting a forensic post-mortem.

The manner of death is generally divided into five categories:

1. Natural death (natural cause or disease)
2. Accidental death (unintentional or inadvertent actions)
3. Suicide
4. Homicide
5. Unascertained or unknown (cannot be determined with reasonable certainty)

Medical cause of death and evidential interpretation as to manner of death play a crucial role in coroners' verdicts and criminal proceedings. If, for example, a person falls down a flight of stairs, the cause of death may be determined at post mortem as a severe not survivable head injury, whereas determining the manner of death would have to be informed and assisted by the police investigation. The result could point to either an accidental fall or the deceased being pushed by a third party (deliberately or otherwise). To establish the manner of death, a combination of police investigation and pathological findings is required to complete the evidential evaluation.

Two other terms that are often misunderstood and used incorrectly are 'certified death' and 'pronounced life extinct'. Before a post mortem is conducted there must be a formal pronouncement that life is extinct by a doctor or other qualified medical professional such as a paramedic. This usually occurs at the location the body is discovered and before it is moved to a mortuary. Certifying a death takes place once the cause of death has been established and after the post-mortem examination has been conducted if one is required. The cause of death is recorded in the post-mortem report and on the death certificate when issued, hence 'certifying'. This is not the same as pronouncing life extinct, and these terms should be used correctly to avoid confusion.

11.7 Briefing the Pathologist

Good practice is to provide a written briefing document to the pathologist before any forensic post-mortem examination is conducted. This should be factual and include where known:

- name of the deceased
- age and date of birth
- date and time life was pronounced extinct
- date and time the deceased was last seen or otherwise confirmed to be alive

- location the body was discovered
- weather conditions if outdoors or the internal conditions if inside
- how the deceased was discovered and the circumstances of the discovery
- any first aid administered or any other medical intervention already conducted
- any medical equipment etc left *in situ* on the deceased
- progress of the initial investigation
- photographs, images and visual recordings of the scene, including the deceased *in situ*
- any provisional hypotheses with the reasons behind these
- summary of the medical history of the deceased
- medical records of the deceased

Providing a written briefing document assists the pathologist to formulate their approach to the post-mortem examination. It also provides a permanent record of the information provided to the pathologist for future scrutiny if required. It is a document that is potentially relevant material under the Criminal Procedure and Investigations Act 1996 (CPIA) and disclosable to the defence if the approach to the post mortem and/or the results of the examination become a matter in issue during a prosecution and trial. The SIO or an officer in the case with the necessary knowledge should be present to answer any questions from the pathologist and make a note of these. A copy of the pathologists briefing document should also be provided to the Coroners Officer.

11.8 Sudden Deaths—Initial Actions

Investigators and other police officers who receive notification of a death must ensure comprehensive information is obtained and relevant questions are asked ('5WH'—see Chapter 3). Any potential for obtaining relevant information and securing evidence and wider investigative material needs to be quickly recognised and all factual details accurately recorded.

Response officers who attend sudden deaths must first check whether there is the slightest indication of signs of life, in which case first aid should be attempted and medical assistance summoned. People can and do appear dead when their life signs are barely visible, for example in hypothermia cases. The police are not medical experts and must always consult and defer to those who are. Sometimes life may have already been pronounced extinct or is obvious due to heavy decomposition, skeletisation, vital body parts missing or when submerged in water. In any case, conducting enquiries to confirm or establish the identity of the deceased should begin quickly and be closely followed by an investigation into how the death occurred.

KEY POINTS

- The first task is always to confirm death and check whether any necessary medical assistance has been given. Preservation of life is an overriding priority.
- Clear instructions need to be provided to those who report finding a deceased person so that potential evidence is preserved pending the arrival of initial response officers.
- Attending officers should only take action that may be necessary to preserve life. The scene, including the deceased, should be preserved as far as possible when conducting any necessary actions.
- It should be considered that in many cases the person reporting the death has been the person who was responsible for causing it.

11.9 Pronouncing Life Extinct

As outlined earlier, only qualified medical experts can formally certify a clinical cause of death. Medical doctors, pathologists or qualified paramedics can officially pronounce that 'life is extinct'. The precise time and date and by whom death is pronounced is a relevant piece of information and it is a time that is used as a starting point for setting the relevant investigative time parameters. Accurately establishing and confirming the last time the deceased person was seen, or was otherwise known to be alive, along with the time that life was pronounced extinct, will establish the relevant time parameters for investigating when the death might have occurred.

Some movement of or interference with a deceased at a scene may be necessary to administer first aid, to check for signs of life and to pronounce life extinct. This may involve attaching monitoring devices, surgical dressings, medical equipment including defibrillators or physically moving a body. This activity may interfere with or contaminate the subsequent collection of forensic material and evidence and could leave extra marks and traces on the body that need to be accounted for. Defibrillators, for example, leave heavy bruising on the chest area.

It is therefore important to debrief medical practitioners who have been involved in the initial response and to establish exactly what they did ensuring this information is included in the briefing to the pathologist. An account should be obtained of:

- who the person(s) was who administered medical treatment
- what their initial assessments and findings were
- what treatment, equipment, dressings or drugs were used and why
- what equipment, packaging or dressings they left at the scene
- what actions they took and what if anything was found on, noticed, moved or removed from the body or surroundings in which it was discovered
- who pronounced life extinct
- what precise time death was certified pronounced

- what notes, details, sketches or photographs were made/taken
- who they saw or spoke to or what they were told
- what is known about the deceased's medical history and their doctor's details
- what else was seen or heard that might be of use to the investigation

KEY POINT

Medical professionals may be asked for their opinion as to what may have caused a death based on their knowledge, experience and assessment of the circumstances. They may have noticed something that gave them cause for concern or suspicion. Though never conclusive, their opinion might help provide an early indication as to what may have been the COD and MOD. They should not be encouraged to begin examining the body after life is pronounced extinct as this could interfere with the collection of forensic material and examinations required later.

11.10 **Initial Investigation**

Implementing correct procedures by methodically preserving and examining a potential crime scene and body is always the safest option. The principle of 'if in doubt, think murder' applies.

With anything other than a Category 4 death (natural causes and expected due to disease or old age) where there is sufficient doubt or insufficient information, this rule MUST APPLY until the cause and manner of death are established. Once a decision has been made to treat a death as suspicious then the scene(s) should be identified, secured and protected, leaving the body undisturbed. A senior supervisory detective should be summoned to assume control of the investigation. The responsibility for continuing the investigation then transfers to that person. Relevant specialists and experts, such as a Forensic Pathologist and Crime Scene Investigators/Managers (CSI/CSM), forensic specialists and photographers can also be summoned. The investigation status and resources required will be escalated until such time criminal involvement can be ruled out.

11.11 Scene and Body Assessment

If a cause of death is uncertain, depending on local policy, a careful assessment of the scene where the death has occurred should be conducted applying an investigative mindset. Wherever possible, this assessment should only be conducted in conjunction with a competent CSI.

This assessment may include a brief examination of the body to check for obvious wounds, injuries or signs of recent trauma. Provided it appears safe to do so and protective clothing is worn, this should be limited to a visual inspection of exposed areas of the body such as the head, face, neck and forearms. The protective clothing to be worn should include gloves and a mask as a minimum. Any touching, moving or disturbance of a body should be kept to an absolute minimum and a body SHOULD NEVER BE TURNED OVER or subjected to any other movement that might cause bodily fluids to be released and cause contamination such as from the nose or mouth.

Visual inspections can never be conclusive but are useful to look for signs or indicators of death by unnatural causes. This will not eliminate or confirm the possibility of homicide, as only a Forensic Pathologist at a post mortem can establish that. Some causes of death, for example suffocation, poisoning, lethal drugs injection or internal bruising and bleeding caused by blows from a fist or blunt instrument, are difficult to detect on external examination even in a mortuary setting.

11.12 Scene Management

As much information as possible needs to be appropriately gathered from the scene(s) and the surrounding area, remembering what a 'scene' might include (see Chapter 5). Many of the actions required are common to the procedures followed at any crime scene and it is the crime investigator's role to ensure those procedures are applied and that they are applied correctly.

Once a death is considered to be suspicious, certain prescribed procedures apply with the scene(s) being secured so there is no risk of interference. Indoor scenes are easier to identify, secure and protect (ISP), whereas outdoor scenes tend to be more difficult. CSIs will help in advising on protecting scenes, taking visual recordings and still photography before anything is moved or touched, helping secure a common approach path (CAP) and using stepping plates to secure a route around the body and preserving forensic material and potential evidence.

Rough sketches can be made to note the position of a body relative to its surroundings and context regarding objects such as furniture, possible weapons, damaged items, footwear imprints (visible and invisible) and bloodstains and markings in bloodstains. This assists to answer the 'where' and 'how' questions (5WH) in relation to the manner of death. The position of the body in the context of the surroundings helps to assess whether it has been moved before (ante) or after (post) death. Information may be gained from the distribution of blood in relation to the position of the body for example, which may indicate blows and the use of a weapon or drag marks.

Bodies at hospitals, such as on arrival at accident and emergency departments, require other considerations when preserving evidence; both for the body and anything that may come from it but been removed such as clothing or possessions. It is advisable to quickly locate the whereabouts (in the hospital) of the body and any associated possessions. Even in a hospital or other medical facility, a body must be treated as a crime scene. Once medical treatment has finished and life pronounced extinct, hospital staff become less involved with a deceased's body, so arrangements need to be made in conjunction with a CSI to secure and protect it in a body bag for transportation to a mortuary. Grieving relatives and friends may add further complications, depending on the circumstances of the death and religious or cultural considerations.

KEY POINT

A deceased's body is a crime scene and a valuable source of potential evidence in any death investigation.

11.13 Gathering and Analysing Information

The investigator's role is to conduct enquiries and investigate where, when, how and why a person died, and in a criminal investigation who was responsible. Making effective use of the 5WH questions together with an investigative mindset provides a structured approach to seeking, analysing and recording information. A list of possible questions can be raised relatively quickly, and information gaps identified.

Checklist—5WH questions

- Who is the deceased?
- Who found the body? What is their relationship to the deceased? What is their background and character? How, why and when did they discover the deceased? What have they said in their initial account?
- What is the connection of the deceased to the location where the body was discovered?

- What is the connection of the person who discovered the deceased to the location where the body was discovered?
- Who pronounced life extinct, at what time, where and when?
- What medical treatment or first aid (if any) has already been given, why and who by?
- Where is the body now?
- Who is with the body?
- What arrangements are in place for preserving and securing the scene(s)?
- What appears to have happened?
- Where has death taken place? What signs are there of the deceased having been or died elsewhere such as mud on their clothing, drag or scuff marks, blood trails?
- When did the death taken place? What dated articles are lying around such as mail, newspapers in the house or behind the front door, or other items such as shopping including foodstuffs that can be dated?
- What is noticeable at the scene, such as signs of theft, traces of a disturbance, forced entry or insecurity, missing items, indicators of a clean-up, blood distribution corresponding to the position of the body?
- What significant items of property are present or missing such as personal items, wallet, purse, mobile phone, cash, medical items/aids?
- How long has the person been dead for?
- What are the reasonable hypotheses as to cause and manner of death?
- How and why did death occur?
- What clues, information and wider investigative material are available?
- Where does the deceased live?
- When was the deceased last seen alive, who by, where and under what circumstances?

- Who does the deceased live with? Where are they now? What do they know or say about the death? What background information can they provide?
- Who are their next of kin? When were they told? What were they told and who by? Where are they now? What support have they been given?
- Who is/are the deceased's partner, close friends or associates?
- What is the deceased's family tree?
- What are the deceased's social habits and routines?
- What are the deceased's employment, professional habits and routines?
- What is the deceased's medical history?
- Why was the body not found sooner?
- What was the deceased doing before they died?
- What is known about their last movements, moods, problems and behaviour?
- What could be a motive for them having been attacked or murdered?
- What evidence suggests anything other than a natural or accidental death occurred?
- What recent activities or events might be linked to their death?
- What other information is available?
- Who has informed the coroner and what have they been told?
- Who else has been informed or requested?
- What enquiries have been conducted?

11.14 Identification of the Deceased

Identifying the deceased quickly is necessary and important, not only to advance the investigation, but also for the next of kin to be informed as soon as possible.

Checking for personal possessions such as identification documents, bank cards and mobile phones and seeking information from those who might know them can assist with early identification. This is important, as failure to do so could cause unnecessary distress to the deceased's close family and relatives and unsettle their relationship and cooperation with the police investigation. Informing the next of kin before any news of the death or the incident under investigation breaks on digital news sites or social media sources can be particularly challenging.

Continuity of a body when being transferred to a mortuary is necessary, and upon arrival the deceased needs to be identified to the mortuary staff and/or pathologist. This duty is performed before a formal identification, viewing or post-mortem examination takes place. The continuity is usually conducted by an officer accompanying the body to the mortuary so as to provide evidence of the handover to the mortuary staff. Some forces may have arrangements agreed with the local coroner for attaching identity bracelets to the deceased. Funeral directors are usually involved in the process of transporting bodies to and from mortuaries. This is a normal procedure as they have the appropriate experience and the most suitable vehicles and equipment for the purpose (and it is more dignified).

Police identification is made by officers or police staff who have observed the body at the scene, whereas personal identification is performed by a relative of the deceased or a person who knew them well. In practice, the personal identification is conducted at a mortuary in a suitable viewing room once the external examination of the deceased has been completed and all of the necessary external swabs and samples have been obtained.

The formal identification process is a statutory responsibility for coroners and is necessary to prove who the deceased was, which is an inquest requirement. Visual identification may not always be possible because of injuries sustained or decomposition of the body. The coroner will decide on a process that is acceptable to them to establish or confirm the identity of a deceased, and there are a number of alternative methods.

Checklist—Methods of body identification

- Biological samples (DNA from blood or biochemistry, toxicology)
- Samples from frequently used personal items such as a toothbrush or hairbrush to compare with a profile obtained from the body. This may produce a match where a search of a DNA prolife from a body has been searched against the NDNAD without success
- Finger and palm prints
- External physical characteristics such as marks, scars and tattoos
- Odontology (teeth, gums, contents of oral cavity)
- Internal organs and soft tissue such as caused by surgical operations or modification
- Facial reconstruction, facial image analysis, artist's impression
- Radiological imaging (for use in osteology, odontology and facial reconstruction)
- Identification on surgical implants such as knees and hips
- Osteology (study of the human skeleton which is a sub-discipline of anthropology)
- Computed tomography (CT scans for two-and three-dimensional imaging)
- Personal effects (identification documents, bank cards, jewellery, watches, spectacles, wallets, phones, keys, clothing, etc.)
- Podiatry (using foot analysis for diseases, walking gait, abnormalities and deformities etc)
- Environmental information including specialist examinations to identify the likely environment within which a person lived. Examples include stable isotope fingerprinting, pollen, soil and botanical samples to identify a geographic region, or diatoms in water to do the same

- Missing Persons Bureau assistance to identify possible matches
- Media appeals

11.15 Families and Relatives

Establishing and managing effective family liaison is important throughout an investigation into a death, particularly in homicide or suspicious cases. The police have a duty to communicate effectively and inclusively with a bereaved family (McGarry and Smith 2011). One of the most significant relationships the police must develop is the one with bereaved families, relatives and close friends of a deceased person. This requires professionalism and sensitivity during what is a very distressing and upsetting time and one which they will never forget. High standards of service delivery are expected and if the police/family relationship breaks down it is likely to take a long time to recover.

A priority is to identify the deceased and notify their next of kin and relatives promptly to establish an early trusting relationship with them. There are many methods and sources of communication such as social media sites through which they can find out for themselves, so investigators must try to stay one step ahead of digital communication methods that may relay information about a person's death.

When a deceased's identity is known or suspected, an option is for the next of kin to be informed that a body of a person *matching or similar to the description* of their relative or spouse etc has been found. This might be necessary in some missing person cases, especially if the body is not readily identifiable. Although this is not an ideal situation, it is preferable to not telling the family anything and them finding out via a non-police source such as the mainstream or social media. In these circumstances it will be necessary to ensure caveats are communicated to tactfully manage their expectations.

Families and relatives need information which must be given to them as long as it does not undermine or interfere with the investigation. Families themselves are also an important *source* of information, such as about the deceased's antecedent history and background, lifestyle, habits and routines for what is often termed 'victimology' enquiries. Depending on the needs of the investigation this might also include providing information to build a digital profile of the deceased. This 'digital victimology' could provide many investigative opportunities including identifying friends and associates, communications profiles and patterns, including the last person(s) contacted and when, location data material, metadata to identify the location photographs were taken and internet searches.

KEY POINTS

- Providing inaccurate information must be avoided. It is better to explain why details cannot be provided rather than having to make corrections later. Explaining why it is necessary to withhold information is preferable to giving no/misinformation that leads to a loss of trust and confidence.
- **Never delay** in informing the next of kin and family if there is a strong indication of who the deceased is. Often this can be provisionally established quickly by carefully checking personal possessions such as a wallet, purse, phone or information received.

11.16 Identification of the Family

A deceased's family has to be considered in the broadest sense and generally includes spouses and partners (of whatever sex), parents, guardians, children, siblings, members of the extended family and any others with whom they may have had a direct and close relationship. Ideally a suitable single point of contact in the bereaved family should be identified to receive and facilitate passing on information to the others. This can, however, become complicated, when it involves fractured families, split marriages, ex-partners and children dispersed across geographic locations. Sensitive diversity issues may need to be considered such as gay, lesbian, bisexual or transgender characteristics or membership of a faith group or community which the family members may not be aware of. Communication and contact need to be managed tactfully so as not to exclude anyone with a legitimate close relationship and thus cause friction or animosity by being perceived to show favour to one or the other.

11.17 **Role of a Family Liaison Officer**

In homicide and suspicious death cases, trained specialist Family Liaison Officers (FLOs) are usually deployed. It is useful for all investigators to be aware of what this role entails, as some of the same working principles can be adopted and used in other types of death investigations where FLO's are not formally deployed. This might include, for example, when managing or dealing with an unexplained or sudden death that has yet to be designated as suspicious or declared to be a 'special procedure' investigation.

The primary role of an FLO is as an *investigator* (PIP2) who contributes to achieving the overall aim and objectives of the inquiry (ACPO/NPIA 2008). FLOs are specially trained to facilitate the day-to-day communication and management of the interaction between the investigation and bereaved families. The role also includes ensuring the family receive appropriate practical support, but they are not bereavement counsellors.

Checklist—Role of an FLO

- Provide families with updates on the investigation with as much detail as appropriate depending on the circumstances. The information should be as full as possible whilst recognising that sometimes it may be necessary for operational reasons to withhold certain information
- Provide reassurance that the investigation is being conducted diligently and expeditiously
- Provide or facilitate practical support
- Consider any threats or concerns for the family's safety and welfare
- Assist in arranging and escorting the family to conduct the identification of the deceased
- Deal with requests for organ donations
- Gather antecedent information and evidence of identification
- Gather 'victimology' type information
- Offer information and advice re supporting agencies
- Monitor the relationship between the family and the police investigation
- Deal with requests or complaints from the family
- Establish liaison with the coroner and make arrangements for the release of the body or body parts seized under the Human Tissue Act 2004 (HTA)
- Consider funeral arrangements and any police attendance or other involvement such as sending flowers and/or messages
- Liaise with the family regarding media matters and shield them from unwarranted or unwanted media intrusion
- Manage the exit strategy ensuring the police requirements under the Code of Practice for Victims of Crime are fulfilled (after an FLO deployment ends the case officer usually continues and maintains family contact)

11.18 Faith, Culture and Diversity

A deceased, their family and friends may be part of any number of nationalities, cultural groups or faiths, or have no faith at all. Assumptions should not be made about any beliefs, preferences or lifestyle choices and any bias avoided. It is advisable to develop knowledge about cultural beliefs and any diversity matters which might need considering and managing sensitively and tactfully when dealing with deaths.

People's differences, beliefs and individual requirements must be considered, although the nature of some types of deaths may mean it is not always feasible for any wishes to be met in the early stages of an investigation. The need for quick, practical action, such as informing a family of the death, may need to take precedence over what the investigator perceives (rightly or wrongly) to be possible cultural preferences, including the characteristics of the officers involved. As the investigation progresses, however, it may be more likely that any cultural preferences or requirements can be accommodated, and specific arrangements made.

A range of local resources and advisers are usually available to provide advice and offer support to ensure the most appropriate course of action is taken. Local race and diversity units, for example, can be consulted and they may make use of contacts and networks of key representatives and advisers. A local police force policy may be available containing details of procedures for guidance.

11.19 Victimology Enquiries

The often-used phrase *'Find out how a victim lived, and you'll find out how they died'* refers to those important clues that are available and can be identified when enquiring into the background of a deceased person. An objective is to seek and obtain as much detail about a deceased as possible, which is a process often referred to as 'victimology'. This involves seeking personal and sometimes intrusive information and often requires careful and tactful management. It can entail a thorough search of the victim's belongings and/or room, house, etc to look for any information and wider investigative material that is relevant to the investigation. This also includes developing a digital profile of the deceased, which involves the intrusive examination of their communications devices and the potential collateral intrusion for family members and friends and associates that this involves. The reasons for this activity need to be carefully explained to a deceased's family and relatives, informing them how it can provide valuable leads and identify lines of enquiry.

Researching a deceased's background and lifestyle is a strategy that features in the list of main lines of enquiry (MLOE). Obtaining these details, if unknown, should be a 'fast track' or high priority (HP) action. It is an unfortunate consequence of a murder or suspicious or unexplained death inquiry that investigators must delve through someone's personal life to seek clues. These enquiries often generate productive leads however, by piecing together the deceased's final movements, habits, lifestyle, digital activity, family tree and associates, etc.

Checklist—'Victimology' information

- Full name(s), address(es), description (including recent videos or photographs), social background, education, qualifications, specialist skills, character, personality, likes and dislikes, drug use, habits or other vices, secrets, sexual orientation and preferences
- Attitude to risk-taking
- Lifestyle, employment, habits, social activities, hobbies and interests

- Vehicle details, means of transport used and with access to
- Premises, or businesses used or linked to
- Places and locations frequented
- Previous convictions, criminal intelligence, reports/ complaints of crime made, previous incidents of note connected with
- Involvement in any precursor events, incidents or activities
- Financial information, investments, spending habits and patterns and locations (including online)
- Close associates and relationships, current, intended, and previous romantic or sexual relationships and partners, use of dating sites
- Routines, daily activities, places visited, people they encountered and when, last known movements, when last seen and what they said and their mood
- Personal possessions, phones, diaries, secure storage places, digital devices, laptops, tablets, computers, locations where money and expensive items are kept, who had access to their belongings, any missing items
- Medical details and history, details of doctor (GP), any illnesses, level of fitness, physical and mental health, surgery and operations, prescribed medicines, deformities, allergies, unusual marks or scars, tattoos, piercings, dental history and details of dentist
- Any vulnerabilities or disabilities
- Any specific information, such as if female, had they been pregnant or had a termination
- Communications profile from social media and digital device usage, itemised phone billing, computer usage (gaming) websites visited or access to any other passive data sources or devices, social media contacts, etc.

11.20 Categories of Murder

The ACPO official categories of murder are useful to know. These tend to relate more to command and control and resourcing than decision making, but nonetheless have been widely adopted and are regularly used in police major crime terminology.

Category A+	A homicide or other major investigation where public concern and the associated response to media intervention are such that 'normal' staffing levels are not adequate to keep pace with the investigation.
Category A	A homicide or other major investigation which is of grave public concern or where vulnerable members of the public are at risk; where the identity of the offender/s is/are not apparent, or the investigation and the securing of evidence requires significant resource allocation.
Category B+	A homicide or other major investigation where the identity of the offender(s) is not apparent, the continued risk to the public is low or unknown, and the investigation or securing of evidence requires additional force resourcing or other considerations, due to added complexities or aggravating factors.
Category B	A homicide or other major investigation where the identity of the offender(s) is not apparent, the continued risk to the public is low, and the investigation or securing of evidence can be achieved within normal resourcing arrangements.
Category C+	A homicide or other major investigation where the identity of the offender(s) is known from the outset and the investigation or securing evidence can be achieved easily, but may require additional force resourcing or other considerations, due to added complexities or aggravating factors.
Category C	A homicide or other major investigation where the identity of the offender(s) is apparent from the outset and the investigation and/or securing of evidence can easily be achieved.

NPCC, 2021

11.21 Suicide Deaths

Committing suicide is not a crime per se but assisting someone to commit suicide is. Some homicides are disguised and staged to appear as suicide, or the suicide is attributed to some form of assistance, threats, bullying or harassment, which could be in person or online. There have been many cases where murders have been committed and disguised to look like suicide, which is why these types of deaths need a cautious approach. Apparent facts presented must not be taken at face value and must always be rigorously evaluated. The investigator's mindset should be no different for suicide than in any other death investigation and **if in doubt think murder.**

The final determination of whether a death is a suicide can only be made by a coroner aided by pathology and the results of the police investigation. Evidence will be obtained from the scene of the death and inquiries into the time period leading up to the death to establish the circumstances, including the deceased's state of mind and any contributory factors. The post-mortem examination of the body should establish the cause of death but also eliminate any possible third party involvement such as the presence of defence marks or wounds on the hands and arms.

The cause and manner of death in many apparent suicides is reasonably straightforward to ascertain, such as asphyxiation through hanging or a *single* gunshot wound to the head. Investigators always need to consider other possibilities and explanations however, as the manner of death might be more difficult to conclusively establish. For example, whether a deceased person has deliberately jumped from a balcony or rooftop intending to kill themselves, or whether they accidentally slipped and fell or were pushed by an unidentified person and did not jump or slip; or whether a deceased person has been strangled by a ligature and then hoisted up to look like a suicidal hanging. In such a case the deceased will likely have two rope lines around their neck, and the offender, who could possibly also be the person reporting, may have rope marks/abrasions/cuts on their hands.

Although it is well established that there are links between mental disorders and suicide, in particular depression and alcohol abuse, there is also a high incidence of suicides which happen impulsively in moments of crisis where an individual's ability to deal with the stresses of life breaks down, for example financial problems, a relationship break down or suffering chronic persistent pain or perhaps a serious potentially fatal illness.

Any determination of suicide must be based on linked a series of factors that eliminate homicide, accident, third party involvement or natural causes. To assist, investigators can apply three basic considerations that help establish the manner of death:

Checklist—Three suicide considerations

1. Proximity to the body of the weapon or means of causing death. How close was this?
2. Injuries or fatal wounds that appear self-inflicted AND could have feasibly and practically been inflicted by the deceased.
3. The existence of a motive and/or evidence of intent on the part of the deceased to take their own life.

Motive and intent can be established by examining the movements, activities and behaviour of a deceased in the period leading up to their death. For example, their sourcing of a ligature such as a rope and fixings to hang themselves, purchasing flammable materials to set themselves on fire, purchasing hose pipe and tape to asphyxiate in a vehicle through carbon monoxide poisoning, visiting buildings or bridges from which to jump to their deaths, obtaining excessive amounts of medication such as sleeping tablets, telling others of their intent, researching suicide websites, writing and leaving notes, a history of previous failed attempts, significant changes in behaviour, excessive use of drink or drugs, severe depression and mood swings. The World Health Organisation (2019) report that, amongst populations, there are at least 20 attempts for every suicide. Several studies have also identified that the deceased in completed suicides were significantly more likely to have encountered severe employment difficulties and financial stress with insufficient economic and social support.

There are several possible motives in suicide cases:

- Depression
- Drug abuse
- Alcohol problems
- Relationship/domestic problems
- Frustration
- Fear/anger/resentment
- Hostility
- Guilt (eg of a crime)
- Terminal illness
- Illness in the family
- Severe emotional crisis
- Psychological problems
- Physical deterioration
- Loss of a loved one
- Death of a child
- Financial problems
- Teenage/adolescence problems
- Loss of employment
- Despair and general inability to cope

11.21.1 Suicide notes

Leaving a suicide note is a strong indication of a person's intent to take their own life, as long as the note is genuine. It needs to be **confirmed** that any suicide notes were actually written by the deceased and that they were written voluntarily. Any note should be recovered in a manner to preserve forensic evidence, including DNA and fingerprints. Past samples of handwriting from the deceased should be collected for comparison by experts who can compare not just handwriting but the comparative writing style and grammar.

There is the possibility that sometimes notes and letters written by the deceased and the means of committing suicide may be removed or destroyed before police attendance. Every suicide is a tragedy for a family, and investigators should be mindful of family members who in some cases remove or conceal evidence because they have trouble accepting that their relative or loved one has taken their own life. Close family members may be experiencing feelings of shame or even guilt that their behaviour and actions may have inadvertently contributed to the death. It has also been known for relatives of people who have committed suicide to falsely accuse the police of a cover-up or conducting a poor investigation and request a formal review with the intention of influencing or changing a coroner's finding.

Diaries, letters, text messages, digital communications and social media data sources and other similar material can be examined for material that may corroborate information in a suicide note. Any stated or inferred intention of a person to take their own life and sudden and strange precursor activities are important investigative information.

Recovered articles and material can help contribute to compiling a 'psychological autopsy' of the deceased. This is a collaborative procedure involving law enforcement and mental health experts who attempt to determine the state of mind of a person prior to their death.

11.21.2 False reports of suicide

Some people commit a murder and try and stage it to appear as a genuine suicide, then feel duty bound and compelled to report the death due to their alleged finding of the body and/or relationship to the victim, for example a spouse, lover, relative or close friend. What this person says and does can be useful investigative information and potential admissible evidence to prove or disprove their honesty and truthfulness. This emphasises the importance of obtaining the full contents of any report or emergency call to the emergency services (police, ambulance), which should be carefully scrutinised for the precise wording and detail using a recording and transcript (if available) of the exact words spoken. Studies have shown that mistakes are often made by offenders in how they report such deaths including how they behave. Indications of guilt might come from their words, language, intonation and general behaviour that can be recognised.[1] It must be noted, however, that taken on their own these indicators may give rise to suspicion but are unlikely to be conclusive evidence.

11.22 **Child Deaths**

Depending on the circumstances, child deaths are generally investigated by specialist officers from homicide/major investigation teams or departments, such as family and public protection or protecting vulnerable people (names vary between police forces). These investigations broadly fall into one of three groups:

- natural non-suspicious, including sudden infant death syndrome, natural or medical causes where there are no concerning factors
- suspicious child deaths that may feature criminal offences other than the four homicide offences below, such as child neglect
- homicide offences of murder, manslaughter, infanticide and familial homicide

Most child deaths are not suspicious and sadly many are cause by accidents, natural causes and medical conditions (FSID 2009). It is recognised that different parties and agencies may use different terminology but for clarity and for the purpose of this handbook, the following descriptions are contained in *Sudden Unexpected Death in Infancy and Childhood: Multi-agency*

[1] Further details and advice can be obtained from the NCA Major Crime Investigative Support team.

Guidelines for Care and Investigation' (Royal College of Pathologists 2016).

11.22.1 SUDI/SUDC (Sudden Unexpected Death in Infancy/Childhood)

This term encompasses all cases in which there is death, or a collapse leading to death, of a child that would not have been reasonably expected to occur 24 hours previously and in whom no pre-existing medical cause of death is apparent. This is a descriptive term used at the point of presentation and will include deaths for which a cause is ultimately found and those that remain unexplained following investigation. This means that while many of these guidelines may be applied if required, they are not necessarily intended to be applied in cases with a previously diagnosed medical condition where a cause of death can be certified (a category 4 death). The guidelines are intended to be used for infants but may be applied to older children in appropriate circumstances.

A SUDI is a term used to facilitate use with other agencies for infants up to 24 months old. A SUDC relates to a child over 24 months and under 18 years old.

11.22.2 Sudden Infant Death Syndrome (SIDS)

This refers to the sudden and unexpected death of an infant under 12 months old, with the onset of the lethal episode occurring apparently during normal sleep, which remains unexplained after a thorough investigation including performance of a complete post-mortem examination and review of the circumstances of death and the clinical history.

11.22.3 SUDI unexplained

This is the preferred term for use in cases in which there is no clear cause of death and there are no features to suggest unnatural death or inflicted injury, but in which the circumstances do not fit the criterial for SIDS. An example would be a death in which the history, scene or circumstances suggest a high likelihood of asphyxia but in which positive evidence of accidental asphyxia is lacking.

11.22.4 Undetermined pending further investigation

This term might be used by pathologists to provide a preliminary report to the coroner following the initial post-mortem examination if no cause of death can be initially identified and there are no features to suggest unnatural death.

11.22.5 Unascertained

This is a legal term often used by coroners, pathologists and others involved with death investigation where the medical cause of death has not been determined to the appropriate legal standard, which is usually the balance of probabilities.

11.22.6 Investigative approach

SUDI/SUDC investigations should never be considered straightforward. It is essential to maintain an investigative mindset and search for the truth, which may not be readily apparent or straightforward to ascertain. Investigators are in the difficult position of providing care and support to families and persons connected with the child, whilst simultaneously sensitively preserving and obtaining evidence as to the cause of the death, which in extreme cases could identify the parents as suspects (Marshall 2012)

KEY POINT

Five common principles pertinent to child deaths, especially when having contact with family members are:

1. Being caring and sensitive particularly to those who are grieving.
2. An inter-agency response, including working together and sharing information.
3. Keeping an open mind and adopting a balanced approach.
4. Ensuring a proportionate response to the circumstances.
5. Preservation of all potential evidence.

Working Together to Safeguard Children (Department of Education 2015), (often referred to as 'Working Together'), is a guide to inter-agency working to safeguard and promote the welfare of children in accordance with the Children Acts of 1989 and 2004. It contains statutory guidance, which is underpinned by the Children's Act 2004 (section 16) relating to the child death review process and serious case reviews of certain child deaths.

Investigations into childhood death involve professionals from different agencies with distinct roles to perform. They work together to share information and professional knowledge to establish how and why a child died, including seeking to answer the four key questions:

1. Why did the child die?
2. What was the cause of the death and the circumstances?
3. Are there any criminal offences disclosed?
4. If a criminal offence is identified, who was/were responsible for committing those offences?

The linked processes of child death review have been compulsory since 1 April 2008 and operate across England but are coordinated on a local geographical basis within the Local Safeguarding Children Board (LSCB) and Child Death Overview Panel (CDOP). There are similar processes in Wales, Scotland and Northern Ireland.

The term 'child' encompasses children and young people up to the age of 18 years but excludes 'babies who are still born and planned terminations of pregnancy carried out within the law'.

'Working Together' states that an appropriate balance should be drawn between the forensic and medical requirements and the families' need for support. Families should be treated with sensitivity, discretion and respect at all times and professionals should approach their enquiries with an open mind, but in all cases enquiries should:

- seek to understand the reasons for the child's death
- address the possible needs of other children in the household
- consider the needs of all family members
- identify any lessons learnt about how best to safeguard and promote children's welfare in the future

11.22.7 Joint agency response and the Child Death Overview Panel

There are two categories of rapid response and CDOP processes.

11.22.7.1 Joint agency response

This is a coordinated multi-agency response of police investigator, on call health professional and duty social worker to a sudden unexpected death, which should be triggered if a child's death:

- is or could be due to external causes
- is sudden and there is no immediately apparent cause (including SUDI/SUDC)
- occurs in custody or where the child was detained under the Mental Health Act
- where the initial circumstances raise any suspicions that the birth may not have been natural
- in the case of a stillbirth where no healthcare professional was in attendance

It is intended that a joint agency response takes place as soon as possible after the unexpected death of a child or young person. It is aimed at establishing the cause of death, safeguarding other siblings, coordinating support for families and gathering information for the Child Death Overview Panel (CDOP).

A rapid response meeting involves a multi-agency collaboration of professionals with attendees determined on a case-by-case basis chaired by a designated paediatrician. Many of these professionals will have contributed to the actual rapid response itself, more often than not at the hospital. Consideration is given to a joint home or location of death visit by the police and paediatrician or other healthcare professional within 24 hours.

11.22.7.2 Child Death Overview Panel (CDOP)

This is a sub-committee of the Local Safeguarding Children's Board (LSCB) whose function is to review all child deaths in their area against national criteria to inform local strategic planning on how best to safeguard and promote the welfare of children. The process is a paper-based review, parents do not attend the CDOP meeting and all cases are anonymised prior to discussion. The CDOP reviews all child deaths, but the rapid response process only relates to sudden and unexpected deaths.

KEY POINT

The police are statutory partners with the LSCB and have a duty to safeguard children so must take 'Working Together to Safeguard Children' into account and only depart from it if they have clear reasons.

Investigations into child deaths where factors arouse suspicion are police led and require detailed investigation into the circumstances. Such enquiries are particularly challenging where there is no direct evidence or grounds to suspect a specific criminal act, but there are factors that raise the possibility that a criminal act may have contributed to the death and thereby merit more detailed investigation of the circumstances.

Investigations into SUDI/SUDC will usually be undertaken by investigators in family protection/child abuse units supervised by a Detective Inspector. Investigations involving suspicious child death or homicide, including causing or allowing the death of a child or vulnerable difficulties adult under section 5 of the Domestic Violence, Crime and Victims Act 2004 (child under 16) should be led by an SIO (PIP3).

The presence of the following factors *may* raise levels of concern regarding whether or not a death is suspicious. Their presence is not conclusive proof of a criminal act but may justify a more detailed investigation when seen in the context of a particular set of circumstances.

Checklist—Factors that could increase suspicion

- History of domestic abuse, including violence towards children
- Accounts and behaviour from those caring for the dead child that are inconsistent with the physical findings, and may vary or alter on questioning
- Mental health issues within the family or parent/carers
- History of hospital or GP visits when symptoms ascribed to the child cannot be verified by independent observation or investigation. Numerous visits to different hospitals/medical practices may occur
- History of alcohol/drug abuse or a criminal record for the parent/carer
- Deaths of children over the age of one year (these are commonly more suspicious than those less than a year old)
- The child or the family are known to Social Services and children in the family may be on a child protection plan, at risk, or recent events or intelligence suggest this should be the case
- The child comes from a family in which a previous child has died unexpectedly
- There was an inappropriate delay in seeking medical help

Suspicious physical findings include:

- Bruising in a baby too young to be independently mobile, multiple bruises, bruises in unusual sites, such as behind the ears or on the trunk/abdomen, or bruises of obviously different ages without a clear plausible explanation of how they occurred
- Petechiae or retinal hemorrhaging, for example in the eyeballs (a sign of shaking)
- Blood on the face (pink frothy blood is often found in non-suspicious deaths but thicker blood warrants further investigation)
- The child has been dead longer than stated
- Fractures identified from a radiological skeletal survey prior to post mortem
- Evidence of bleeding over the surface of the brain, between two of the membranes that surround the brain (subdural hemorrhage), bleeding into the inside surface of the back of the eye (retinal hemorrhage) and brain swelling identified by diagnostic imaging before autopsy
- Identification of prescription or recreational drugs (other than those used in attempted resuscitation) in samples taken for toxicological analysis

Also, to be considered if relevant:

- Home environment/conditions
- Stressors, for example financial difficulties/debt or relationship problems
- Mode of death, position of child, its surroundings and general condition
- Family dynamics
- Strange interaction between the parents/their demeanour or behaviour
- A foreign body in the upper airway
- Suicide attempt
- Comments made (verbal/text/written)
- Prior unusual or unexplained illnesses
- Apparent life-threatening event (ALTE)
- Signs of neglect, such as impaired growth and development, inadequate hygiene, lack of food.

- Previous physical abuse
- Previous neglect

Whilst the 'five building block principles' (see Chapter 4) continue to underpin the investigation process, a child death investigation contains considerations that are different to that of an adult homicide and may impact on the investigation:

- The initial circumstances may show no obvious cause of death or be immediately apparent, even after the post-mortem examination. It may take some time to establish if death was caused by a crime or natural causes
- The vulnerability and small size of very young children makes it possible to obscure the cause of death and the circumstances
- Sensitive management is required due to the extremely emotional nature of child death and the uncertainty in establishing the cause of death and circumstances
- Investigators require specialist knowledge
- Specialist post-mortem procedures, including using a pediatric pathologist, are required
- Considerations that would not arise in adult cases, but which have a significant impact on the parents, such as holding their deceased child and being allowed time and access to the body to say goodbye
- Forensic opportunities that are of limited value when a family member is responsible for the death, such as contact trace material
- Risk to other siblings and safeguarding issues if the child is unlawfully killed or suspected to have been unlawfully killed by a parent or carer
- Multi-agency response with possible issues concerning conflicting priorities, information sharing and communication
- Suspects within the family which present challenges for family liaison

- Reliance on experts, particularly medical experts, where there are limited witnesses to the circumstances surrounding the death
- Criminal offences relating solely to children
- Faith and child-rearing practices
- Parallel proceedings in the Criminal and Family Courts which may create issues in relation to disclosure in a criminal trial and access to siblings who may be witnesses
- Media reporting

11.23 **Work-Related Deaths**

A work-related death is a fatality from an incident arising out of, or in connection with work. It is also where the victim suffers injuries in such an incident which are so serious that there is a clear indication, according to medical opinion, of a strong likelihood of death. Such deaths are investigated in accordance with the Work-related Death Protocol (National Committee for Work Related Death 2016).

This is an important definition to understand because applying it to the circumstances of the death will determine who will conduct the investigation. Incidents that have not resulted in death or are not anticipated to become fatal are investigated by the Health and Safety Executive (HSE).

The source of a medical opinion on the likelihood of death occurring should be considered in a broad context providing the person is appropriately qualified. For example, a paramedic at the scene of a death in a factory that has resulted from a work activity, such as operating machinery or performing another work function, would be suitably qualified to make this assessment. This is important for investigators because the golden hour principles will apply and scene preservation and evidence gathering needs to commence quickly.

KEY POINT

For a death to be classed as a work-related death it must have involved an activity connected with work. Deaths from natural cases in a workplace, such as a heart attack, for example, would not be due to a work activity. Although police attendance may be required such a death would not fall within the protocol.

Signatory organisations to the Work-related Death Protocol are the:

- Health and Safety Executive (HSE)
- Association of Chief Police Officers (ACPO)
- British Transport Police (BTP)
- Local Government Association
- Welsh Local Government Association
- Crown Prosecution Service (CPS)
- Office of Rail Regulation (ORR)
- Maritime and Coastguard Agency (MCA)
- Chief Fire Officers Association (CFOA)

Depending on the circumstances, other investigation and enforcement agencies who could be involved in the response and the investigation include:

- Local Authorities (LA)
- The Care Quality Commission (CQC)
- Fire and Rescue Authorities (FRA)
- Maritime and Coastguard Agencies (MCA)
- Office of Rail and Road (ORR)
- Office for Nuclear Regulation (ONR)
- Medicines and Healthcare Products Regulatory Authority (MHPRA)
- Environment Agency (EA)
- Civil Aviation Authority (CAA)
- Trading Standards
- Department of Business, Innovation and Skills (DBIS)
- Marine Accident Investigation Branch (MAIB)
- Rail Accident Investigation Branch (RAIB)
- Air Accident Investigation Branch (AIB).

Identifying the relevant partner agency, and their responsibilities, priorities, evidence gathering techniques and powers, is a management decision. Other agencies may have powers that are different to the police and in some cases even exceed police powers. For example, in certain circumstances the HSE, MAIB, RAIB and AIB can compel interviewees to answer questions and produce documents. This is because these agencies have responsibilities for preventing future similar incidents and the information may be required as a matter of urgency to inform these decisions. An extreme example would be whether it is necessary to close down similar premises due to a recurring manufacturing fault involving the same equipment, or even grounding a fleet of aircraft due to a potential fault.

There are significant managerial level decisions to be taken when the Work-related Death Protocol is engaged. These could include developing and producing a memorandum of understanding and formal arrangements for working with the HSE and other agencies. This includes arrangements for working together, information sharing, who is responsible for the investigative decision making and dealing with any primacy issues. For this reason and the seriousness of any death investigation, police forces have attendance policies which usually require the attendance of a Detective Inspector.

Upon initial attendance the circumstances of the death are likely to be unclear. The HSE needs to be contacted to deploy an investigator to the scene. Immediate attendance may not always be possible particularly outside of normal office hours and at weekends. Attending officers, including investigators, should adopt standard crime scene preservation methods.

11.23.1 Offences to be considered

A significant consideration for the officer in charge of the police investigation is to establish what type of offence is being investigated. This decision will determine the resources required and the investigative approach to be adopted. At this stage the principal consideration will be whether there is suspicion of:

- corporate manslaughter
- gross negligence manslaughter, and/or
- principle health and safety offence

In many cases it will not be obvious what offence may have been committed by the circumstances alone and an initial investigation will be necessary to establish this. In accordance with the Work-related Death Protocol, an investigation into either of the manslaughter offences will be conducted by the police, supported by the HSE.

If there is no suspicion of manslaughter the investigation will be conducted by the HSE, and apart from transferring the investigative material gathered up until that point, the police will not be involved further.

11.23.2 Strategic considerations

Some of the initial management considerations include:

- establishing if there is any suspicion of corporate manslaughter
- establishing if there is any suspicion of individual gross negligence manslaughter
- securing investigative material and evidence of any regulatory offences
- identifying what investigative material could have evidential value, should consider securing material in relation to the workplace/company systems and processes, computer and documentary records, staff training records, material relating to any similar non-fatal incidents (near misses), accident reporting records, etc
- difficulties dealing with staff may be encountered due to their conflicting interest with their employer which could lead to loss of earnings
- any links to modern slavery should be considered at locations such as recycling centres (batteries, catalytic converters) or other locations were there are apparent

dangerous working conditions and the use of migrant labour and a lack of record keeping is apparent
- obtaining investigative material from companies whose offices are abroad
- may need early liaison with Major Incident Team Senior Investigating Officer (SIO)—be careful not to take on more than you can deal with without at least seeking advice
- FLO deployment or deploying a suitable officer with the skills of an FLO
- delivering death messages for deceased workers with families abroad
- embassy liaison
- coroners' liaison
- investigative strategy
- case management
- informing the duty/on call SIO if manslaughter is suspected

11.23.3 Duties of attending officers

Mainstream investigators below Detective Inspector level should ensure they understand the requirements placed on the first officer attending the scene of a work-related death. It is likely that initial attendance will be by uniformed officers who may be unaware of these responsibilities themselves, who will require support. The basic principles to attending any other suspicious or unexplained death should be followed, including:

- identify scene(s)
- ascertain the location of the fatality (the body will need to be treated as a separate scene if removed).
- perform an initial risk assessment. This may require careful consideration as the location of the body may be in a hazardous or difficult to reach environment
- inform supervision
- set and secure the initial parameters of scene(s)
- inform coroner

- commence a written record/scene log
- request CSI attendance
- establish who pronounced life extinct
- identify witnesses
- enquire whether the employer (or other responsible person) has contacted the police or relevant enforcement agency

Due to the locations in which work-related deaths might occur, specific hazards may be encountered. These need identifying to establish whether they contributed to the cause of death, and to inform the risk assessment for the scene.

11.23.4 Additional duties of a first officer—domestic gas incidents

- Which gas appliances were switched on when the deceased was found?
- If gas flames were seen, were they a yellow colour? (a correctly adjusted gas burner produces a blue flame, sometimes with a yellow core)
- Was there any ventilation (open windows, doors, etc) to the room where the victim(s) were found?
- Are there any substantial sooty stains above or around any gas appliance in the property?
- Did any of the emergency service personnel suffer illness (typically headaches, nausea) while attending the property?
- Are there any other people still in the property who might be at risk if the gas appliances are used again?
- Is the property rented?
- When and by whom were the gas appliances certified?
- Inform the National Gas Emergency Service (0800 111 999)

11.23.5 Additional duties of a first officer—work-related road death incidents

- Attend and deal with the incident in accordance with force policy and procedures.

- In accordance with the Road Death Investigation Manual a Supervisory Traffic Officer must attend.
- HSE will need to be contacted and may wish to attend the scene if the road death involves:
    - o exposure to a dangerous substance being conveyed by road
    - o loading or unloading of an article or substance (not passengers) onto or off a vehicle
    - o where works vehicles and where workers (not on vehicles) are engaged in specific work activity (other than travelling), such as hedge cutting, construction, demolition, alteration, repair or maintenance activities on or alongside public roads and vehicles connected with work premises manoeuvring out of, but in proximity of, those work premises
    - o the Office of Rail and Road, the British Transport Police and the Rail Accident Investigation Branch will need to be contacted and may wish to attend the scene if the road death involves an accident involving a railway, a tramway or other system of guided transport

11.23.6 Additional duties of a first officer—railway incidents

- Ensure the safety of responding agencies by establishing close liaison with the infrastructure controller (normally Network Rail), in accordance with the Rail Incidents Code of Practice (Network Rail/ACPO).
- Liaise with the Rail Incident Officer (RIO) from the Infrastructure Controller (Normally Network Rail).
- Advise and request the attendance of BTP, ORR and RAIB.
- Preserve all equipment involved in the incident including rolling stock.
- Consider a screening breath test of relevant workers—consult with BTP by telephone if necessary.
- Consult with BTP, ORR and RAIB regarding preservation of offsite evidence (signal boxes etc).

- Consider securing all paperwork, including safety briefings, at offsite locations

11.23.7 Additional duties of a first officer—maritime incidents

- Inform/request the presence of MCA (Duty Enforcement Officer and Duty Surveyor)
- Inform/request the attendance of MAIB.
- Check the vessels nationality, and if non-UK, establish whether the incident within 12 miles of the coast?
- If the vessel is still at sea, check the port of destination and times of arrival and departure
- Liaise with MCA to:
  - o seek guidance on documents to be copied/seized
  - o administering breath tests as appropriate
  - o if applicable, secure Voyage the Data Recorder (VDR)

11.23.8 Fire incidents

- Ensure the cause of the fire is established; liaison between Fire and Rescue Service investigators, CSI and forensic scientists will be required.
- Ensure the standard of fire safety provisions to achieve compliance with the Fire Safety Order is established and documented.
- Ensure relevant evidence is gathered from attending firefighting crews, statements, video footage, etc.

11.23.9 Incidents involving a medical advice

- A medical device is used in the treatment of patients, the diagnosis of disease or to alleviate physical disabilities. All medical devices must be CE marked before they are placed on the market in the UK in accordance with Europe wide disabilities. Products that have a pharmacological action are normally regarded as medicines and, as such, are licensed through a different regulatory process. Consider informing the Medicines and Healthcare products Regulatory Agency (MHRA) if a medical device is implicated in a death that is under investigation.

These are initial investigators who find themselves attending the scene of a work-related death before a more senior detective arrives. Any further investigative activity should wait until further direction is given.

11.24 Summary

Checklist—General considerations: all sudden death investigations

- Before approaching a body or location consider any health and safety risks, for example dangerous environments, fires, unstable premises, or terrain, electric or gas appliances, live wires, diseases, body fluids, possibly loaded firearms, needles, insects, water, animals
- Check for signs of life and consider administering first aid/medical assistance unless death is obvious, such as the body is decomposed, skeletal remains or vital organs/body parts are missing
- Secure, preserve and prevent unnecessary contamination of the scene
- Confirm life has been pronounced extinct with the relevant time recorded and by whom
- Make a visual inspection of exposed body parts and avoid touching anything unless unavoidably necessary (record what has/has not been touched). Always wear protective gloves
- Make an accurate note of any obvious and visible marks or injuries

- Make an accurate note of the position of the body, state of the clothing worn or undress and anything else that could be relevant such as visible injuries, signs of blood, secure or insecure premises, broken or missing furniture or items, the room temperature, whether the lighting was on or off, whether the curtains were closed or open, medication lying around, drugs paraphernalia
- Note and preserve any physical evidence in the area such as a weapon, suicide note, mobile phone
- Establish if anyone witnessed the death
- Determine if there are any other potential crime scenes and take appropriate action
- Establish if anyone has touched or moved the body or any items prior to arrival including first responders, other police officers and staff, paramedics, medical examiners, family, friends, witnesses
- Establish details of the person finding the body and the last person to see the deceased alive
- Make enquiries to establish the identity of the deceased and next of kin details
- Establish what enquiries have been made to contact the next of kin. If there is some degree of certainty as to who the deceased is, the next of kin can be tactfully informed who the deceased *might be* without delay. This is provisional until the deceased has been formally identified
- Make enquiries into the background and last known movements of the deceased, including their medical history and GP details
- Assess or confirm what type of death investigation process is required
- Consider what additional resources are needed
- Ensure the coroner has been informed of the death and has been liaised with
- Keep any bereaved parties informed of the progress of the investigation
- Accurately record all relevant detail and information available

- Consider that suicides can be staged to cover up murders
- Child deaths require a different approach, more sensitive handling, and a multi-agency approach to the investigation>
- Make a record of actions and decisions taken with the underpinning reasons
- In all sudden death investigations keep an <open mind, apply an investigative mindset and **if in doubt think murder**

References

ACPO/NPIA (2008) *Family Liaison Officer Guidance Manual*

Cook T (2019) *Blackstone's Senior Investigating Officers' Handbook* (5th edn, OUP)

Foundation for the Study of Infant Death (FSID)(2009), fact sheet available at <http://www.fsid.org.uk> accessed 21 November 2021

Department for Education (2015) *Working Together to Safeguard Children. A guide to inter-agency working to safeguard and promote the welfare of children*

Marshall D (2012) *Effective Investigation of Child Homicide and Suspicious Deaths* (OUP)

NPCC (2021) *Major Crime Investigation Manual*

McGarry D and Smith K (2011) *Police Family Liaison* (OUP)

Royal College of Pathologists (2016) Sudden Unexpected Death in Infancy and Childhood: Multi-agency Guidelines for Care and Investigation

National Liaison Committee for the Work Related Deaths Protocol (2016) *Work Related Deaths: A Protocol for Liaison*

Chapter 12

Proactive Investigation and Preventative Measures

12.1 Introduction

In reactive investigations the police respond to reports of crimes that have already been committed. Initial reports are taken and responded to, then further investigations are conducted.

In proactive investigations the police initiate action against some kind of continuing criminal activity; this could be targeting suspected offenders or targeting a particular type of crime where the offenders are unidentified.

Proactive investigation is not confined to covert operations, such as surveillance. A range of overt proactive options to prevent, detect and disrupt crime are available, including activities like executing search warrants, high visibility patrols, road checks and exercising stop and search powers.

Other proactive preventative options include consulting and working with specialists in covert operations, confiscation of criminal property, dealing with threats to life (TTL), managing dangerous offenders through Multi-Agency Public Protection Arrangements (MAPPA) and using options from the various prevention orders and injunctions that are available for certain types of crime.

Complex investigations may require an integrated approach and use every available technique at some stage.

Blackstone's Crime Investigators' Handbook. Steve Hibbitt and Gary Shaw, Oxford University Press. © Oxford University Press 2023.
DOI: 10.1093/oso/9780192867896.003.0012

The National Intelligence Model (NIM) recognises three levels of criminality:

- Level 1—local crime issues that can be managed within a Basic Command Unit (BCU)
- Level 2—cross-border issues where organised criminality affects more than one BCU and potentially crosses boundaries into neighbouring forces
- Level 3—serious and organised crime operating on a national or international level

These NIM levels influence the tasking and coordination process, including the deployment of local, regional and national specialist assets in targeted operations. This does not mean proactive techniques are the sole preserve of specialists, but it does mean investigators will face competing demands for resources when submitting applications at whatever NIM level.

Investigating crime is not a 'one size fits all' or 'tick box' activity and creative problem solving is to be encouraged (see also Chapter 3), including the properly managed use of proactive techniques.

This chapter aims to provide mainstream investigators with an overview of considerations, but it is not exhaustive.

12.2 Covert Investigation

Covert operations can be used as a stand-alone tactic or to complement conventional lines of enquiry depending on the needs of the investigation, for example developing intelligence to potentially convert into evidence where overt techniques cannot or are unlikely to achieve the required objective. In simple terms, overt investigation gathers evidence that implicates suspects and covert investigation obtains evidence of suspects implicating themselves.

Some covert tactics such as the use of vehicle, foot and technical surveillance, static observation points and covert human intelligence sources (CHIS) are generally known, and some even more sensitive techniques have been revealed in television documentaries.

Preservation of tactics is essential to ensure their future effectiveness and minimise the risk of compromise and possible harm to those involved. Knowledge of certain methods is restricted even within police circles, and it is not appropriate to mention these in this handbook. Investigators encountering or involved in covert operations at whatever level must strictly adhere to the 'need to know' (as opposed to 'nice to know') principle, including amongst their colleagues.

Due to the intrusion on Article 8 of the European Convention on Human Rights (ECHR), the right to respect for private and family life, covert investigation at whatever NIM level must be authorised and will be closely scrutinised. The evidence obtained is often compelling, so defence tactics at trial may seek its exclusion by questioning the integrity of the process and challenging police adherence to the procedures involved. This includes not just the authorisation of the activity and the actions of operatives but compliance with the disclosure obligations under the Criminal Procedure and Investigations Act 1996 (CPIA).

Balancing a defendant's right to a fair trial alongside the management of sensitive material is challenging and may necessitate a Public Interest Immunity (PII) hearing to prevent certain information being disclosed to the defence. Early consultation with the Crown Prosecution Service (CPS) is essential.

The principal legislation governing covert investigation can be summarised in two parts:

- The Police Act 1997, Part III, which empowers authorities to interfere with private property in circumstances which would otherwise be trespassing. This may be

necessary to facilitate actions under the Regulation of Investigatory Powers Act 2000 (RIPA 2000)
- RIPA 2000, which empowers investigators to use specific methods to acquire evidence without the subject of the investigation being aware.

The basic covert methods of investigation under RIPA are:

- Interception of communications (not discussed in this chapter due to the sensitivity of this tactic)
- Directed surveillance

12.3 Authorisation

All covert investigation methods must be authorised before their use. Generally, the higher the level of intrusion sought, the higher the level of authority is required, which is balanced against the increased seriousness of the crime.

Police forces have individual protocols for authorisation covert activity which involve either a central or a designated on-call Authorising Officer (AO). Investigators should familiarise themselves with their local arrangements.

The authority levels are broadly summarised in the table below: contingencies in cases of urgency are strictly controlled to avoid abuse of the system and applicants and AOs must be members of the same organisation, for example the same police force.

Method	Authority level
Interception of communication	• Home Secretary
Intrusive surveillance	• Chief Officer of Police subject to prior approval of the Chief Surveillance Commissioner. The authorisation period is for three months unless renewed. • Designated deputies (Deputy Chief Constable/ Assistant Chief Constable (DCC/ACC)) if urgent provisions apply. The authorisation period is 72 hours in such cases.

Method	Authority level
Directed surveillance	• Superintendent who can authorise a period of three months unless renewed (72 hours if authorised orally unless renewed). • Inspector if urgency provisions apply. The authorisation period in such cases is 72 hours unless renewed by a Superintendent.
CHIS	• Assistant Chief Constable (ACC) for juvenile CHIS. The authorisation period is one month in such cases. CHIS under 16 years of age are prevented from providing information on an adult with parental responsibility for them. • Superintendent for adult CHIS. The authorisation period for such cases is 12 months (72 hours if authorised orally unless renewed). • Inspector for adult CHIS if urgent provisions apply. The authorisation period in such cases is 72 hours unless renewed by a Superintendent.

12.4 **Surveillance**

Surveillance is only covert when it is conducted in a manner calculated to ensure the subject is unaware it is taking place and is defined by RIPA 2000, section 48(2) as including:

- monitoring, observing or listening to persons, their movements, their conversations or other activities or communications
- recording anything monitored, observed or listened to in the course of surveillance
- surveillance by or with the assistance of a surveillance device

KEY POINTS

Not construed as surveillance, includes:

- any conduct of CHIS for obtaining or recording any information which is disclosed in their presence, whether a surveillance device is used or not

- the use of CHIS for obtaining or recording information
- entry onto or interference with property or with wireless telegraphy which would be unlawful unless it was authorised property interference under Part III of the Police Act 1997 (as amended by RIPA 2000)

12.4.1 Directed surveillance

Directed surveillance is the lowest level of intrusion within the framework of covert methods and can be authorised for the purpose of preventing or detecting crime, preventing disorder or to apprehend a suspected offender: RIPA 2000, sections 28(3), 81(2) and 81(5). Directed surveillance is also permitted:

- in the interests of national security
- In the interests of the economic wellbeing of the United Kingdom
- in the interests of public safety
- for the purpose of protecting public health
- for the purpose of assessing or collecting certain fiscal levies

Outside the police service these additional statutory reasons are restricted to specific agencies and are not generally available, which may need taking into consideration if planning joint operations, such as with Trading Standards for example.

Directed surveillance is:

- covert but not intrusive
- undertaken for the purpose of a specific operation or investigation
- will or is likely to obtain private information about any person, not just the subject of the operation
- does not include observations conducted in immediate response to spontaneous events

If an officer on routine duties, for example, witnesses an offence, and whilst in pursuit of the suspect conceals themselves to watch where they go, this would not be directed surveillance, as the officer's actions are in immediate response to a spontaneous event and are not pre-planned.

Private information is defined by RIPA 2000, section 26(10) as any information relating to a person's private or family life or personal relationships with others.

Directed surveillance can be conducted anywhere except:

- inside any premises at the time being used as a residence, no matter how temporary, including hotel accommodation, tents, caravans, a prison cell or even railway arches.
- in any vehicle which is primarily used as a private vehicle, either by the owner or a person having the right to use it. Note that this does not include taxis
- outside such premises or vehicles if conducted by remote technical means such as using a long-range microphone which enables events and conversations inside the residential premises and/or private vehicle(s) to be monitored from outside, and the product is of the same quality as would be obtained by devices or persons inside the premises or vehicle(s).

The fact that an individual is in a public location does not diminish their right to an expectation of privacy, and surveillance should only be conducted if authorised. This should be considered when using local authority CCTV cameras; although their presence to the public is known, a directed surveillance authority is required if they are used in a pre-planned operation.

Applicants and AOs must acknowledge any potential collateral intrusion into the privacy of third parties who may be present in the surveillance arena but are not subjects of the operation. It must be demonstrated that actions taken are proportionate and a necessary breach of the right to privacy, with measures used to minimise any collateral intrusion and its consequences.

12.4.2 Observation posts *(R v Johnson)*

An Observation Post (OP) is a position from which to observe, record and report activity at a given location or area; it must be staffed by a minimum of two specially trained operatives with the relevant RIPA 2000 authorisation, and arrangements to record, preserve and produce any evidence obtained including the use of surveillance logs.

To safeguard against the location of the OP being disclosed and exposed in court, which could put any occupants or persons connected to the premises at risk, certain requirements derived from the 1988 case of *R v Johnson*[1] must be followed:

- The police officer in charge of the observations should be a sergeant or above, responsible for issuing logs and equipment in accordance with the surveillance authority and briefing and debriefing the officers conducting the surveillance.
- This officer must be able to testify that prior to the observations commencing they visited all observation posts and ascertained from the occupier(s) of the premises their attitude towards the use being made of the premises, and the possibility that subsequent disclosure may lead to the identification of the premises and occupant(s).
- The officer in charge may inform the court of any difficulties encountered in a particular locality and of any problems obtaining assistance from the public.
- Immediately before any trial a Chief Inspector or above must visit the places used for observations and be able to testify that they ascertained:
    - o whether the occupant(s) was the same as when the observations took place
    - o their attitude to possible disclosure of the use made of the premises and any facts which could lead to the identification of the premises and occupants
- A statement of evidence must be submitted to the CPS outlining these points, and the officer may be required

[1] [1989] All ER 121.

to provide witness testimony if an application to exclude the evidence is made.

12.4.3 Intrusive surveillance

Intrusive surveillance by definition is more intrusive than directed surveillance, and as such can only be used for the investigation of serious crime with a higher level of authority.

Serious crime is defined by RIPA 2000, section 81(3) as:

- offences for which a person aged 21 years or over with no previous convictions could reasonably expect to be sentenced to three years imprisonment or more
- involves the use of violence
- results in substantial financial gain
- is engaged by a large number of people pursuing a common purpose

Intrusive surveillance is activity that intrudes on a person's private life, and is:

- covert
- carried out in relation to anything taking place within a residential premises or in any private vehicle
- involves the presence of an individual or any surveillance device on any residential premises or in any private vehicle or
- is carried out in relation to anything taking place on residential premises or in a private vehicle by means of any surveillance device that is not present on the premises or in the vehicle

12.5 Covert Human Intelligence Sources

The term CHIS covers undercover officers, test purchase officers and individuals formerly known as 'informers' or 'informants'. Nationally accredited training exists for undercover and test purchase officers, and NPCC guidance recommends that CHIS are only handled and managed by trained staff assigned to Dedicated Source Units (DSU). This is due to the high risk of retribution if the CHIS is compromised, the tradecraft required and operational security surrounding the dissemination and storage of sensitive material. There have also been occasions in the past where CHIS have been mishandled by officers, including allegations and cases of corruption and inappropriate relationships.

At the time of writing the Covert Human Intelligence Sources (Criminal Conduct) Act 2021 has received royal assent and is in the final stages before implementation. The Act will include provision for the authorisation of criminal conduct by a CHIS with strict conditions and safeguards. This was introduced to amend RIPA 2000 to allow undercover agents to commit criminal offences in the course of their duties in some strictly controlled circumstances, if properly authorised.

Section 26(8) of RIPA 2000 sets out the full definition of CHIS, which in essence is:

- A person who establishes or maintains a personal or other relationship with another person for the covert purpose of facilitating anything that:
  - covertly uses such a relationship to obtain information, or
  - to provide access to any information or to another person, or
  - covertly discloses information obtained by the use of such a relationship or as a consequence of the existence of such a relationship.

Before authorising CHIS activity, AOs must believe it is necessary:

- in the interests of national security
- for preventing or detecting crime or preventing disorder
- in the interests of the economic wellbeing of the United Kingdom

- in the interests of public safety
- for the purpose of protecting public health
- for assessing or collecting any tax, duty, levy or other imposition, contribution or charge payable to a government department
- for other purposes which may be specified by order of the Secretary of State

As with surveillance, most of the organisations empowered to deploy CHIS are limited to the statutory purposes of the prevention and detection of crime, and/or disorder.

Authorisation for the use and conduct of CHIS must be proportionate to what it is trying to achieve, and if a particular conduct is not recorded on the authority, it will not be authorised.

Potential dangers of using CHIS include possibly exposing and compromising a police operation by tasking them (they become a double agent), the CHIS deliberately supplying misinformation or receiving more information from the police than they supply, plus the instigation of crimes that would not otherwise be committed (an agent provocateur).

As they conduct their daily business, mainstream investigators should be alert to potential subjects for potential CHIS recruitment and make a referral to their DSU. On no account should they handle a CHIS themselves, which would be outside RIPA 2000 and therefore unlawful.

The issue of 'status drift 'often arises where, as part of their normal duties, investigators speak with someone who provides information about local criminals. This is community information and does not require a RIPA authority, but if the investigator then asks the person to find out more information this could be deemed as tasking them and require an authority.

The pertinent question to consider is whether the person has established or is maintaining a covert relationship to obtain and pass on the information; if there is any doubt at all, advice should be sought from the DSU or AO.

KEY POINTS

- CHIS authorisation is necessary in all circumstances where the CHIS uses or exploits a personal relationship to acquire information from another person which that person would regard as private.
- All individuals fitting the RIPA definition must be managed as CHIS. The Office of the Surveillance Commissioners (OSC) have expressed dissatisfaction over terms such as 'confidential source', 'confidential contact' and 'tasked witness', which seem to indicate an attempt to manage individuals outside of the regulated provisions.

12.6 Developing a Covert Strategy

The first stage in developing a covert/proactive strategy is to establish clear objectives about what is trying to be achieved. Only then can appropriate tactics be considered to fill the intelligence or evidence gaps.

The general principles of deploying covert techniques are that they must be lawful, appropriate, necessary, proportionate and auditable. The process can be time consuming, involving tasking and coordination, pre-application feasibility studies, detailed risk assessments, planning for contingencies (including any compromise and the consequences) and preparing and submitting applications.

Covert operations can be expensive both in monetary value and time and resources; there will inevitably be other competing demands and there should be a formal tasking through the NIM. Wherever possible, investigators should anticipate the need for covert activity early and identify relevant issues by asking themselves the following questions:

- What are the objectives to be achieved and how is this relevant to the investigation? For example:
  - o identify suspects
  - o identify subjects of interest
  - o locate a subject or item or place of interest
  - o obtain information about a subject
  - o collect evidence
  - o gather intelligence
  - o develop/update existing intelligence
  - o obtain evidence to support a conspiracy
  - o identify evidence of planning
  - o identify post-offence intelligence
  - o recover evidence
  - o recover weapon(s)
  - o identify a stronghold to locate property
  - o prevent commission of further offences or arrest
  - o control measure to minimise risk to the public
  - o identify associates
  - o obtain evidence of association
  - o identify addresses
  - o identify vehicles used
  - o identify locations of interest
  - o attribute mobile phone use
  - o attribute ATM use
  - o identify further/new lines of enquiry
  - o covertly obtain biometric material such as sources of DNA
  - o obtain lifestyle information
- Is the application based on reliable information/intelligence?
- Is the proposed action necessary and justified or can the material be obtained by other non-intrusive means?
- What is the least intrusive method of securing such evidence or information?
- What are the legal constraints?
  - o RIPA 2000
  - o Police Act 1997
  - o Human Rights Act 1998

  - ECHR—Articles 2, 6 and 8
  - CPIA 1996
- What is the timeframe for the operation or is there a unique window of opportunity that is available?
- Are sufficient trained and accredited staff available to properly conduct the operation?
- Is sufficient equipment and funding available?
- What are the risks to the organisation of deploying the tactics?
- What are the risks to the organisation's staff of deploying the tactics (including briefed and unbriefed personnel)?
- What are the risks to the public or specified third parties of deploying the tactics?
- What are the risks to the subject of the investigation?
- Will the methods breach ECHR Article 8(1)?
- Is there justification for doing so provided by ECHR Article 8(2)?
- What is the risk of collateral intrusion and how will this be managed?
- How will the covert methods be protected at trial?
- What advice should be sought?

It is only by asking and answering these questions that an authorisation can proceed and a tactical plan can be developed and implemented.

KEY POINT

Investigators considering covert tactics should seek advice from force surveillance specialists, Force Intelligence Bureau, Covert Authorities Bureau and Technical Support Units or externally from the NCA Covert Advice Team.

12.7 Asset Recovery

Financial investigation is not only a line of investigation to complement mainstream enquiries; it can also be used proactively to deter and disrupt all levels of criminality by using powers under the Proceeds of Crime Act 2002 (POCA).

Generally, POCA powers are under used due to a misconception that they only apply to high-level organised offending, but this is not the case; opportunities are available to target all levels of offending, including NIM level 1 locally based individuals.

POCA provides a framework to conduct financial investigations, restrain and confiscate assets, seize cash in excess of £1,000, seek its forfeiture and tackle money laundering. This prevents the funding of further criminal activity, ensures crime does not pay and removes negative role models from communities.

Confiscation is not restricted to drug dealers, so in addition to the primary objective of detecting and prosecuting the offence another objective should be set to conduct a 'criminal lifestyle' investigation to identify and trace offenders' criminal assets, particularly when dealing with acquisitive crime.

The 'criminal lifestyle' investigation questions a person's ability to account for their assets, in simple terms to establish if their expenditure exceeds their identified legitimate income and whether can it be accounted for apart from being the benefit of crime. Any assets that cannot legitimately be accounted for may be seized as proceeds of crime.

Confiscation powers may be triggered where the suspect has been:

1. convicted of drug trafficking, money laundering, directing terrorism, people trafficking, arms trafficking, counterfeiting, intellectual property offences (copyright/patent/trademarks), pimping, brothel keeping, blackmail, theft, fraud offences or aiding, abetting, attempting, conspiring or inciting any of these
2. charged with an offence or a series of offences committed over a period of at least six months where they

have obtained £ 5,000 from that offence or others taken into consideration at the same time

3. convicted of a combination of offences amounting to 'a course of criminal activity'. The suspect satisfies this final test if they have:
    (a) been convicted in the current proceedings of four or more offences of any description from which they have benefited
    (b) been convicted in the current proceedings of any one such offence and has other convictions for any such offences on at least two separate occasions in the past six years. In addition, the total benefits from the offences and/or any others taken into consideration by the court on the same occasion (or occasions) must not be less than £5,000.

The form MG17 is used to refer potential asset recovery cases to specialist financial investigators who should always be consulted along with the CPS to select charges to enable a court to find that the defendant had a 'criminal lifestyle' within section 75 of POCA 2002 and apply confiscation.

Lines of enquiry to consider may include searching premises to acquire evidence of conspicuous wealth to show 'living beyond their means', such as receipts, banking details, luxury goods, high value motor vehicles jewellery and watches.

The court may issue a confiscation order following the conviction of an offender who has benefited from criminal conduct. The court decides the value of the confiscation order based on the offences for which the defendant has been convicted and any others taken into consideration.

If the court determines a defendant has a 'criminal lifestyle' they assess their benefit from 'general criminal conduct'. This includes the specific conduct for which they have been convicted, but also their other criminal conduct at any time, all of which can be proved on the balance of probabilities.

The benefit can be calculated over a period of up to six years and can therefore be considerably more than the offence with which they are charged.

12.8 Money Laundering

Money laundering is where the proceeds of crime are converted into assets which appear to have a legitimate origin. Criminal property is property (not just money) that has been gained as a result of, or in connection with, criminal conduct (in other words the proceeds of crime), and the offender knows or suspects the property constitutes or represents this benefit. This includes cash but can also include other property, such as a car, house or an interest in land.

The three common money laundering offences are:

1. Concealing Criminal Property etc (section 327 of POCA) where an offence is committed when there are reasonable grounds to suspect any person is involved in concealing, disguising, converting, transferring criminal property or if they remove criminal property from the United Kingdom.

Disguising criminal property includes concealing or disguising its nature, source, location, disposition, movement, ownership or any rights connected with it. This means that a person who hides stolen goods (concealing) or puts false number plates on a stolen car (disguising) may be guilty of money laundering.

Property is obtained by a person if they obtain an interest in it; the prosecution needs to prove the person's knowledge from the circumstances in which they came into possession of the property, but it is not necessary to prove the identity of the person who committed the crime that gave rise to the creation of the criminal property.

Possession means having physical custody of the criminal property, but a defence is available if the person acquired, used or had possession of it for 'adequate consideration'. There is no distinction between the proceeds of a person's own crimes and crimes committed by others, but the alleged offender must know or suspect the property represents such benefit.

2. Arrangements (section 328 of POCA) where a person commits an offence if they enter into or become concerned in an arrangement which they know or suspect will facilitate (by whatever means) the acquisition, retention, use or control of criminal property by or on behalf of another person. This could cover a suspect allowing a third party to use their bank account for the transfer of cash.

3. Acquisition, use and possession (section 329 of POCA) where a person commits an offence if with the necessary knowledge or suspicion they acquire, use or possess criminal property.

KEY POINTS

- The relationship between money laundering offences and handling stolen goods often raises issues that require careful consideration by the police, the CPS and the courts in cases where the charge could be money laundering based on possession under section 329 of POCA or an offence of handling stolen goods.
- The Code for Crown Prosecutors and CPS Legal Guidance advises that a money laundering charge may be appropriate when either a defendant has possessed criminal proceeds in large amounts or in lesser amounts but repeatedly, and where assets are laundered for profit.
- In straightforward cases where 'A' has passed stolen goods to 'B', the appropriate charge will generally be handling stolen goods. Where there are aggravating factors, such as a significant attempt to transfer or conceal ill-gotten gains, money laundering could be considered as an additional charge.

Under Parts 2 and 8 of POCA, Accredited Financial Investigators (AFI) may obtain production orders, search and seizure warrants, account monitoring orders, customer information orders and restraint orders which are only available to support a confiscation or money laundering investigation. They can only be applied for by an AFI and require the signed authority of a Crown Court judge.

12.8.1 Production orders

A production order requires the specified person who appears to be in possession or control of confidential material, such as bank account information, to produce it to an appropriate officer.

12.8.2 Search and seizure warrants

Search and seizure warrants authorise an appropriate person to enter and search specified premises and to seize any material found which is likely to be of substantial value (whether or not by itself) to the investigation.

Search and seizure warrants may be obtained if a production order is not complied with, or it would not be appropriate to obtain a production order as it is not practicable to communicate with any person against whom the production order may be made.

12.8.3 Account monitoring orders

Account monitoring orders require a financial institution to provide account information on a specified account for a specified period not exceeding 90 days. The information is provided in a manner and at a time or times stated in the order.

12.8.4 Customer information orders

There is no single database in the United Kingdom that is guaranteed to provide a comprehensive list of all financial accounts an individual might hold. Customer information orders are used when there are reasonable grounds for suspecting that an individual is using financial accounts at various banks in an area and in different names for criminal purposes, for example money laundering.

An order allows a notice to be sent to those banks in the area to ascertain if that individual holds an account(s) under any of the names provided. If identified, the financial institution must provide sufficient account information for the investigator to obtain a production order.

12.8.5 Restraint orders

A restraint order prohibits a specified person dissipating any realisable assets held before they can be the subject of a confiscation order.

A restraint order should be anticipated and considered at an early stage of the criminal investigation. They will not be needed in all cases and there must be a real risk that without a restraint order, assets may be dissipated.

Only accredited financial investigators can apply for a restraint order, the decision to obtain one is taken in conjunction with the CPS and authorised by a Superintendent and they are applied for by the prosecutor before a conviction is obtained.

KEY POINT

Investigators should seek early advice and guidance from their Financial Investigation or Economic Crime Unit in accordance with local force policy on how this legislation can be exploited in support of an investigation.

12.9 Cash Seizure

Investigators can seize cash for its evidential value under the Police and Criminal Evidence Act 1984 (PACE) where the following conditions apply:

- they are lawfully searching a person or premises and find the cash

- under the authority of a warrant to search for cash as evidence of a particular crime
- a specific search for cash under a magistrate's authority issued under sections 289 and 290 of POCA

A further power exists to seize and detain cash with a view to forfeiture under sections 294 to 298 of POCA where a constable or customs officer finds £1,000 or more in any kind of currency, cheques, postal orders, bankers drafts or bonds and suspects that it has come from or is intended to be used to commit crime.

Prior written authority to search should be obtained from a magistrate; if this is impractical, approval can be given by an Inspector prior to the search, such as when the search is not preplanned; if this is also impractical, a search can be completed without authority and an Inspector informed afterwards, for example if there is a random find.

This is a civil procedure and does not require the suspect to be charged or convicted of a crime, and it can run in parallel with a criminal investigation.

In most cases, cash seizure, detention and forfeiture will be dealt with by an accredited Financial Investigator. However, there is always a possibility that mainstream investigators may start the process, such as when there is an unplanned discovery of large amounts of cash (remember this is not just money) when searching persons, vehicles or premises.

An officer may seize cash under the following conditions:

- their presence is lawful (there is no power of entry under POCA)
- there are reasonable grounds to suspect the cash is recoverable property (obtained by unlawful conduct), or is intended for use by any person in unlawful conduct
- there appears to be £ 1,000 or more

Depending on the surrounding circumstances of the cash find, a person's possession of £1,000 or more may or may not be suspicious, depending on any explanation given.

Cash seizure powers require some objective grounds and discretion may be required depending on the individual circumstances, particularly when considering the seizure of smaller amounts.

If a situation is encountered where several persons are together and each has an amount of cash, these amounts can be added together and if the total amounts to £1,000 or more the POCA provisions apply, for example four persons in a vehicle each with £500 in their possession.

Investigators should note:

- time the cash was first seen
- where it was found or concealed
- description of the cash

To establish ownership of the cash and whether it is 'recoverable property', the person found in possession of it should be asked to provide an explanation of its origins when deciding if there is reasonable cause to believe it is from crime or is to be used in crime. Relevant questions may include:

- How much cash is there?
- What types of notes or cheques are there?
- Who does it belong to?
- From what activities did the cash derive?
- How did it get there?
- Has the person touched or handled it?

When seizing cash it is advisable that:

- it is not counted (to prevent contaminating future drugs or other forensic examination) and the amount is estimated
- gloves are worn
- photographs are taken
- cash is double-bagged and sealed using clean tamper evident bags in the presence of the subject, and if possible, an entry signed in the officer's official notebook or other official record

- cash should not be removed from any wrapping, bag or container, but if this is absolutely necessary the receptacle should be seized in the same manner
- two officers are present throughout the procedure, and both sign the exhibit labels
- cash is lodged in a safe, a receipt is provided to the person as soon as possible and the search record completed

It is advisable to avoid:

- placing property on floors or other contaminated surfaces
- letting the person found in possession of the cash touch it
- handling the cash any more than is necessary
- using officers who have recently been in contact with drugs, explosives, firearms or other substances
- taking the cash into the custody suite to prevent contamination with drugs and other substances

12.9.1 Cash seizure forms

There are four forms investigators must consider:

1. First/Further Detention of Seized Cash (Form A). This is a legal document, and a copy must be served on each individual from whom the cash has been seized *prior to them being released from custody.*
2. POCA Receipt for Cash. This consists of two pages both to be signed by each individual and the officer serving. The top copy is forwarded to the Financial Investigator/cash seizure officer in accordance with local practice and the bottom copy is retained by the individual.
3. Court Notification. This provides details of the hearing for continued detention at the magistrates' court, including the date and time.
4. Disclaimer. If any individual disclaims any right to the seized cash, they should be asked to sign a disclaimer form to be supplied to the Economic Crime Unit/cash seizure officer.

The first three forms are mandatory, but the disclaimer is optional depending on the circumstances.

12.9.2 Financial interviews

If appropriate, financial questions should be incorporated into the main PACE interview, such as where the person has been arrested for money laundering.

Where the cash seizure does not form part of a criminal investigation, although there is no power of detention for the purpose of questioning, a separate voluntary financial interview not conducted under PACE is undertaken.

Financial interviews are not conducted under caution but are tape recorded; as cash seizure and forfeiture is a civil process, investigators should not direct questions towards the person's possible criminality.

As the cash is believed to be derived from crime, the interviewer is entitled to ask questions about its origins. The person found in possession may be legally represented (but there is no guarantee they will receive legal aid) and they are not obliged to answer the questions, however a court may draw inferences from a 'no comment' or silent response.

During the financial interview, in addition to questions concerning the origins of the cash, investigators should explore the person's legitimate income and financial situation, including their income, expenditure and assets. These questions are to establish if the person has more assets and expenditure than can be supported by any legitimate income. Investigators should consult their own force policy and procedures regarding financial interviews, which could be conducted using pro forma questionnaires, and, during office hours, by financial investigators.

A constable or customs officer must apply to a magistrates' court for a cash detention hearing which must be concluded within 48 hours of the officer first seizing the cash (not including Saturdays, Sundays, Christmas Day, Good Friday and bank holidays).

As this is a civil procedure, the CPS is not involved, and the application can be contested by other parties. If the hearing is not completed within the 48 hours the cash must be returned unless it is also being detained as evidence under section 19 or 22 of PACE.

Legally, any *police officer* can complete the paperwork and attend the magistrates' court for the cash detention hearing, but usual practice is for specialist officers to deal with this process. In most forces the Financial Investigation Unit provides this support, but in some areas appointed cash seizure officers are embedded within BCUs.

Investigators should contact the Financial Investigation Unit without delay following seizure to instigate the cash detention hearing. Contact outside office hours is usually by email subject to local procedure.

It is a legal requirement that the First Application for Continued Detention of Seized Cash (Form A) is served on the person found in possession of the cash and any other identified interested party. A copy must also be supplied to the court.

Form A informs the person that an application for further detention of the cash is to be made and where and when the hearing will take place.

Mainstream investigators may have to complete this initial process, particularly outside office hours when financial investigators may be unavailable. Investigators should ensure they have proof of service such as completing a witness statement or receipt.

A right of appeal against the detention of the cash is available and a notice is also served informing the person how they can reclaim the seized cash. The use and format of this form varies from force to force.

Normally specialist financial investigators arrange and progress the application, including completion and submission of the required documentation. For information purposes the process is briefly summarised as follows:

- Information in support of application for further detention is prepared including:
  - o grounds for the application
  - o detailed description of the circumstances

  - o enquiries already conducted (including information from any interviews)
  - o enquiries to be completed
- The cash should be deposited in a bank account at the earliest opportunity (complying with individual force policy) unless it is required in its original state as evidence in the case or it is to be submitted for drug testing or other forensic analysis.
- A Cash Detention Hearing within 48 hours of the cash first being seen.
- If the magistrate grants an order for continued detention a Form B is issued with a Notice to Affected Persons for the Order of Continued Detention (Form C).
- If the magistrate decides the cash is not to be forfeited, they may direct it be returned to any person.
- Investigate the origins of the cash within the three-month period.
- A further detention hearing must be held within three months and further applications may be made in three-monthly increments up to a total of two years.
- The magistrate may order the forfeiture of the cash or any part of it if satisfied that it is recoverable property or is intended for use in unlawful conduct based on the civil standard of proof.
- Once an application for forfeiture is made, cash cannot be released under any circumstance until the forfeiture proceedings are concluded.

KEY POINTS

- The powers under POCA complement the powers normally used under PACE for evidential purposes, for example section 19 for the seizure of items in evidence and section 22 for the retention of items for use in evidence.
- Advice should be sought from the financial investigation/economic crime unit when considering obtaining POCA search warrants. This is a specialist area where prior authority may be required; a prior authority does not include the power to enter premises.

12.10 Preventative Measures

12.10.1 Prolific and priority offenders

In 2002 the 'Narrowing the Justice Gap' programme first established the definition of a persistent offender as a person aged 18 years or older who has been convicted of six or more recordable offences in the previous 12 months. This definition has developed both nationally and locally, but continues to be based on the premise that, however defined, a large proportion of crime is committed by relatively few offenders.

In 2003 the national Persistent Offender Scheme was implemented with the aim to more effectively catch, bring to justice and rehabilitate this core group of prolific offenders who are responsible for a disproportionate amount of crime.

The scheme aimed to ensure that each criminal justice agency had an enhanced focus concerning Persistent and Priority Offenders (PPOs) at every stage of the process and was part of the Crime and Disorder Reduction Partnerships with a series of mandatory actions.

The national framework has three strands:

1. Prevent and Deter—has the overall objective of preventing those most at risk from becoming prolific offenders and focuses on the target groups of young offenders who are not yet prolific, older children and young persons at high risk of criminality, children who need early intervention programmes.
2. Catch and Convict—requires the criminal justice agencies to work together to ensure effective investigation, charging and prosecution of PPOs; specifically it refers to the timeframes within which offenders are brought to justice.
3. Rehabilitate and Resettle—presents PPOs with the opportunity to reform or face a swift return to court should

they reoffend or fail to comply with the conditions of court orders. This is supported by locally agreed and implemented rehabilitation plans which manage statutory and voluntary interventions to prevent reoffending.

From an investigator's perspective the identification of a person as a PPO means they may be under active supervision, being tracked and monitored or possibly prioritised for proactive targeting via the Tasking and Coordination Group under the NIM. A final stage is the removal of a PPO from the list of priority offenders because of their reduced risk to the community.

12.10.2 Multi-Agency Risk Assessment Conference (MARAC)

A Multi-Agency Risk Assessment Conference (MARAC) is a single meeting involving representatives of all agencies that have a role in a particular case. The aim is sharing information to increase the safety, health and wellbeing of victims and others by combining current risk information with an assessment of the victim's needs.

The MARAC process establishes whether the offender poses a significant risk to an identified individual or to the general community; it produces a multi-agency risk management plan for implementation which should provide professional support to all those at risk, thus reducing harm and repeat victimisation.

12.10.3 Multi-Agency Public Protection Arrangements (MAPPA)

Multi-Agency Public Protection Arrangements (MAPPA) is the process through which the police, probation and prison service, known as the responsible authority (RA) work together with other agencies to protect the public by managing the risks posed by violent and sexual offenders living in the community.

Three categories of offender are managed through MAPPA:

- registered sexual offenders required to notify details to the police under the terms of the Sexual Offences Act 2003
- violent offenders sentenced to 12 months or more in custody (or to detention in hospital) who are living in the community subject to probation supervision
- dangerous offenders who have committed a sexual or violent offence in the past and are considered to pose a risk of serious harm to the public

These offenders are managed within three MAPPA levels based on risk, but they can move up and down the levels:

- normal agency management applicable to most MAPPA offenders (Level 1)
- local inter-risk agency management for offenders assessed as high or very high risk of harm (Level 2)
- Multi-Agency Public Protection Panels (MAPPP) appropriate for the small number of offenders assessed as posing the highest risk of causing serious harm, or whose management is so problematic and unpredictable that they require oversight at a senior level and the commitment of exceptional resources (Level 3)

The MAPPA encourages cooperation from other authorities who, under section 325(3) of the Criminal Justice Act 2003, have a duty to cooperate with the RA. These include local authority social care, health, local authority housing, registered social landlords, Youth Offender Teams and Job Centres and local education authorities.

The structured process enables formal information sharing, which is lawful, necessary, proportionate, accountable and secure to formulate risk management plans for proactive multi-agency management of offenders, particularly on their release from prison, for example by securing suitable accommodation away from perceived risks and triggers to offending.

Details of all MAPPA nominals are held on the ViSOR[2] database along with another category called Potentially Dangerous Person (PDP), who are persons who have not been convicted or cautioned for any offence which would place them into one of the MAPPA categories, but whose behaviour gives reasonable grounds for believing there is a present likelihood of them committing an offence or offences that will cause serious harm.

Inclusion of a PDP on ViSOR requires a Superintendent's authority and should be considered by investigators when dealing with and submitting intelligence on persons who fall within the definition.

Police forces have their own systems and processes for managing sexual or violent offenders (MOSAVO). These could include management and monitoring by dedicated teams and officers, or operating in multi-agency safeguarding, or community safety hubs. Investigators are advised to familiarise themselves with their local arrangements.

12.11 Threats to Life (TTL/Osman) Warnings

The police have a positive obligation to preserve life under ECHR Article 2 (right to life), which is supported by case law. Any threat to someone's life that comes to notice through intelligence must be carefully considered. This includes any information which the police know or ought

[2] ViSOR is a UK-wide system used to store and share information and intelligence on those individuals who have been identified as posing a risk of serious harm to the public.

to have known concerning future activity where a person's life may be put in danger.

The basic principle is that if there is a *real and immediate threat* to the life (TTL) of a named individual, that person should be informed of the threat unless there is a justifiable reason for not doing so. Such a reason could include:

- causing serious risk to an identifiable third party by informing the victim
- protection of the life of the source of the intelligence
- likely pre-emptive attack/retribution, with serious risk of loss of life
- escalation of gang warfare with consequent serious risk to third parties
- test of a police source (CHIS)

The 'immediacy test' is decided by conducting an objective assessment of all the facts on the capability of carrying out the threat; this might include considering an escalation of a series of incidents which when considered together trigger the ECHR Article 2 obligations.

Police action to minimise a known threat to life will depend on the nature of the threat, the intent and capability of the perpetrator and the wishes of the individual concerned. Action should be determined on a case-by-case basis ranging from warning the person of the existence of the threat (often called Osman warnings), providing personal safety advice, implementing target hardening measures and temporary removal of the person from their home to proactive covert and intrusive tactics.

Another element of threat to human life warnings is what is often called a 'reverse Osman warning'. This relates to occasions where a warning is delivered to the alleged perpetrator indicating the police are aware of the threat and basically 'warning them off'. Again, this involves complex decision making, including protection of covert sources and tactics, and managing the consequences. Local force policy must always be complied with regarding authority levels and action required. Depending on the circumstances, a superintendent or the duty SIO may need informing as early as possible after the discovery of the threat to consider what further action is required and appropriate.

Failure to take appropriate measures (within the scope of police powers) could have catastrophic consequences for the subject of the threat and lead to litigation against the police. Such threats should be treated as a priority and potential critical incident. Operational decisions to manage threats to life can be complex, possibly involving the management of sensitive information (CHIS related) and covert tactics. Investigators should familiarise themselves with their own force 'threat to human life policies'. These include authority levels for issuing warnings, tactics to be considered (which are not appropriate for publication), delivering and documenting the warning, placing warning markers on intelligence databases and producing a documented audit of the threat to life risk management.

The principal current case law concerning threats to life is *Osman v UK*[3] and *Van Colle and others v CC of Hertfordshire Police*.[4]

12.12 Prevention Orders and Injunctions

To effectively prevent and deter future offending, investigations should not always be considered to be concluded upon conviction. Prevention orders and injunctions are available for some crime types for use in appropriate cases and these have the potential to significantly disrupt all levels of criminal activity and help to prevent further offending. The use of appropriate prevention orders and

[3] [1998] EHRR 101.
[4] [2008] UKHL 50.

injunctions are a significant tactic for investigators to consider in mainstream and specialist investigations.

12.12.1 Criminal Behaviour Orders

A Criminal Behaviour Order (CBO) is an order made in the magistrates' court, Crown Court or youth court aimed at preventing anti-social behaviour by a person who has been convicted of any other criminal offence (CPS 2016). They can be a useful tool for addressing hate crime and preventing its escalation, disrupting gang-related crime, and addressing the abuse of social media. In cases of domestic abuse, it is usually more appropriate to obtain a restraining order for a named individual rather than a CBO.

A CBO is made in addition to a sentence imposed by the court for a criminal offence (including a conditional discharge). It does not require a direct link between the criminal behaviour which led to the conviction and the anti-social behaviour which it aims to prevent. Breaching a CBO is a criminal offence in itself that can be punished by imprisonment and/or a fine. Other sanctions are also available in respect of secured or assured tenants that could lead to their eviction from a property.

The court needs to be satisfied beyond reasonable doubt that the offender has engaged in behaviour that caused or was likely to cause harassment, alarm or distress to any person, and it is considered that imposing a CBO would help to prevent the person engaging in such behaviour in the future. Examples of CBO conditions imposed on offenders by the courts to prevent anti-social behaviour have included, for example:

- approaching unknown persons to ask for money or alms within a specified area (begging)[5]
- consuming alcohol in a public place other than licensed premises[6]

[5] *Samuda* [2008] EWHC 205 (Admin).
[6] *Starling* [2005] EWCA Crim 2277.

- being drunk or consuming alcohol in any public place.[7]
- being in a state of drunkenness in any public place in England and Wales.[8]
- wearing any article of clothing with an attached hood in a specified public place, whether the hood is up or down[9] (a useful gang case restriction used to prevent causing fear)
- certain curfew restrictions
- being in possession of a can of spray paint in a public place[10] (to prevent future criminal damage).
- informing the local police of the name and address of any female (excluding family members) with whom he resides for a period or more than 14 days, whether consecutive or otherwise[11] (to prevent serial domestic abuse).
- driving any mechanically propelled vehicle on a public road in the United Kingdom without being the holder of a valid driving licence and certificate of insurance[12]
- carrying a mobile phone which is not registered to their own name[13] (to prevent drug dealers using unregistered pay as you go phones). This case also included non-association with other named individuals who had been arrested as part of the same police drugs operation
- congregating in a public place in a group of two or more persons in a manner causing or likely to cause any person to fear for their safety.[14]

These are not exhaustive examples by any means. When formulating suitable restrictions for a CBO application, investigators should consider the circumstances of the

[7] *Anthony* [2005] EWCA Crim 2055.
[8] *Blackwell* [2006] EWCA Crim 1671.
[9] *Boness* [2005] EWCA Crim 2395.
[10] *Boness* [2005] EWCA Crim 2395.
[11] *R v Maguire* [2019] EWCA 1193.
[12] *Hall* [2004] EWCA Crim 2671.
[13] *R v Dyer* [2010] EWCA Crim 2096.
[14] *Boness* [2005] EWCA Crim 2395.

individual case and the anti-social behaviour an application is trying to prevent. Proposed restrictions need to be precise and avoid wide-ranging vague requests to increase their chance of approval by the court.

A CBO can also include a positive requirement aimed at addressing the underlying cause of the person's anti-social behaviour. An example of this could be a requirement to attend an alcohol or drugs misuse programme amongst other available measures.

An order must specify the period of time in which it takes effect. For a CBO made for offender who has not attained the age of 18, the order must be for a fixed period of:

- not less than one year, and
- not more than three years

For a CBO made after the offender has reached the age of 18 years, the order period must be for:

- a fixed period of not less than two years, or
- an indefinite period, so that the order takes effect until further order

The courts do not order CBO's lightly and it is a matter of judgement for the court to decide whether making such an order would help prevent the offender engaging in anti-social behaviour. The mere fact that a person has a history of disobedience to court orders is a relevant consideration, but an application needs to consider and present evidence of the nature of the conduct, its frequency, duration and impact on victims or a community, the likelihood of repetition, previous convictions and responses to past sentences and anti-social behaviour interventions. If the offending is more serious, an application may still be appropriate even if the behaviour has not previously been repeated.

It is important to obtain and present evidence to the CPS and ultimately the court to support why a CBO would help to prevent future harassment, alarm or distress. An application for a CBO should be raised with the CPS as a possibility at the charging stage. In addition to considering the evidence to support a CBO application, the CPS will also need to decide whether an application to the court is in the public interest.

The actual criminal offence itself may be sufficient but investigators should always consider presenting prosecutors with additional evidence to prove the points required for the application. This could include for example:

- a CBO application form
- a witness statement from the lead officer which summarises the defendant's offending history
- evidence in support of the application
- the defendant's current prosecutor's Police National Computer (PNC) record
- victim personal statements, if necessary
- a community harm Statement, if necessary
- if an exclusion zone is proposed, a clear map of the suggested area. If the defendant lives near the proposed exclusion zone, their home address should be indicated on the map
- the views of the Youth Offending Team (YOT), who must be consulted if the defendant is under 18 years old

KEY POINTS

- The proceedings in which the defendant is convicted are criminal, but the proceedings for applying for a CBO are civil. This means that Part 1 of the Criminal Procedure and Investigation Act 1996 and the Attorney Generals Guidelines on Disclosure of Material in Criminal Proceedings do not apply to the CBO application.
- Special measures directions for vulnerable and intimidated witnesses, however, apply to CBO proceedings in the same way they apply to criminal proceedings in the Magistrates and Crown Court.
- In addition to the police, the local authority for a particular area can also apply for a CBO.

12.12.2 Knife Crime Prevention Orders

The Offensive Weapons Act 2019 includes provisions to help tackle knife crime, attacks using acids and other corrosive substances, and the misuse of firearms. This Act also includes Knife Crime Prevention Orders (KCPOs), which is a preventative civil order.

A KCPO may be made by any court dealing with the defendant on conviction so therefore includes a Crown Court, magistrates' court or youth court. The conditions that must be met for the court to issue a KCPO on conviction are set out in section 19 of the Act (Home Office 2021)

The courts also have the power to issue a KCPO without a conviction upon complaint by the police. A KCPO may be made in respect of any person who is over the age of 12. When the intended recipient is an adult, the application must be made to a magistrates' court. When the intended recipient is under 18 years old, the application is made to the youth court.

For the court to issue a KCPO on complaint, it must be satisfied that the defendant has on at least two occasions during the two years before an order is made (the relevant period) had a bladed article with them in a public place or on school or further education premises.

The court must consider it necessary to make the order to protect the public generally, or to protect particular persons (including the defendant) from risk of physical or psychological harm involving a bladed article, or to prevent the defendant from committing an offence involving a bladed article (CPS 2021).

The burden of proof for KCPO applications is the civil standard of the balance of probabilities rather than the criminal standard of being beyond reasonable doubt. A KCPO should be considered for individuals who are:

- charged with knife possession
- suspected of knife carrying on more than one occasion
- habitual knife carriers

A KCPO is intended to prevent individuals being drawn into (or further into) knife crime, knife possession and related serious violence. The intention is to provide preventive intervention to turn individuals away from violence rather than to be punitive. The range of positive outcomes and their availability varies between local areas and examples include:

- educational courses for both adults and under 18 year olds
- life skills programmes
- sporting participation such as membership of sports clubs or participation in group sports
- awareness raising courses
- targeted intervention programmes
- relationship counselling
- drug rehabilitation programmes
- anger management classes
- mentoring

The application process for a KCPO is likely to vary between police forces depending on their internal processes and structure. Investigators involved in knife crime investigation or related proactive activity are encouraged to research their local procedures.

Generally, applying for a KCPO other than on conviction follows a process of:

- identification of a subject for a KCPO
- preparation for the application, involving (this is not an exhaustive list):
  - o compilation of supporting evidence
  - o considering and deciding on appropriate requirements and prohibitions for the order
  - o engagement with the Youth Offending Team (for under 18 year olds)
  - o laying of the complaint with the court
  - o scheduling a hearing at the relevant magistrates'/ youth court for the local justice area
  - o provision for the cost of the hearing

- o completion of notice and application form
- o service of the summons and the application upon the defendant

An application for a KCPO may be made only by the relevant Chief Officer of Police, the Chief Constable of the British Transport Police (BTP) or the Chief Constable of the Ministry of Defence (MoD) Police. This authority can be delegated to a member of their force of any rank who can be police officers or police staff capable of making such an application. The applicant will present the application to the court based on the complaint laid with the court in accordance with court rules. In practical terms, local arrangements are likely to use an applicant from the force's legal services department or equivalent, due to their legal qualifications and court presentation experience.

The applicant must indicate who will be responsible for monitoring the subject's compliance with a KCPO's conditions. A plan should be prepared for the conduct of the monitoring as well as how to deal with breaches of conditions. The Youth Offending Team should be involved in the process if the application for the KCPO relates to a child.

Once a KCPO has been obtained, the order, along with the relevant PNC forms must be sent to the PNC Bureau as soon as practicable to be loaded onto the system. It must also be stored on any local system where a copy of all documents and a copy of the order can be saved.

A KCPO application upon conviction follows a different process because the subject is already appearing at court for a criminal matter. In these cases, the application is made by the CPS prosecutor. This will usually be on the recommendation of the police who should identify suitable cases and complete the 'Orders on Conviction' section on the form MG3 within the case file, along with the evidential bundle and consideration of the conditions requested.

The CPS will review the material provided to them by the police, including the material provided as part of the prosecution file for the relevant offence. They will decide whether or not to make an application for a KCPO in the event of conviction. The CPS review of the KCPO application is separate from their review of the evidence for the substantive charges. Proceeding with a KCPO application must be considered to be in the public interest.

As a minimum standard, the following should be provided in a file for the prosecutor/applicant. This material should also be provided to the defendant if it is intended to be presented to the court:

- a KCPO notification and application form
- a lead statement from the applicant or other officer/staff on a MG11 statement form. This should include a summary of the subject's offending history, background information and details of other information, such as intelligence reports or information from other agencies
- a PNC court print/record

In addition, the following may assist:

- statements (MG11) from officers, witnesses or other agencies
- other evidence such as CCTV, body worn video or forensics
- victim impact statements
- reports from the Youth Offending Team
- any material required to assist the court in determining the requirements or prohibitions; for example, maps to depict a prohibited area, or information regarding a particular activity

The evidence to be out before the court needs to be relevant and proportionate. This means it might not be necessary to use all of the material outlined in the previous section. The submission of statements containing hearsay evidence needs to comply with the hearsay rules under the Civil Evidence Act 1995 and the Magistrates Courts (Hearsay Evidence in Civil Proceedings) Rules 1999. This means a hearsay notice needs to be served at the same time as the notice of intention to apply for the KCPO, and in any case at least 21 days before the hearing date.

KEY POINT

It is important to note that rules of service for hearsay notices in civil proceedings are not identical to the rules of service in criminal proceedings. In particular, service by email is not permitted (Rule 6).

12.12.2.1 Breaching a Knife Crime Prevention Order

Breaching a KCPO without reasonable excuse is an offence that can be tried either in the magistrates' court or the Crown Court. The maximum sentence that can be imposed in a magistrates' court is six months imprisonment and/or a fine. The Crown Court can impose a maximum sentence of two years imprisonment and/or a fine. The full range of community sentences are available to both courts, and when sentencing defendants under 18 years old the court must have regard to the principle aim of the youth justice system, which is to prevent offending by children and the welfare of the child.

12.12.3 Injunctions against gang-related violence

A court may grant an injunction to prevent violence and drug dealing activity against a person aged 14 or over where it is satisfied on the balance of probabilities that:

- The person has engaged in, encouraged, or assisted gang related violence. This includes threats of violence and violence against property, or drug dealing activity including supply, importation or exportation of a controlled drug or psychoactive substance.
- An injunction is necessary to prevent the person from engaging in, encouraging, or assisting this conduct, or to protect them from gang-related violence or drug dealing activity.

KEY POINTS

- Hearings to decide whether a 'gang injunction' should be granted are not criminal trials and the evidence is satisfied on the balance of probabilities. This is the civil burden of proof rather than the criminal standard of beyond reasonable doubt. It is noteworthy, however, that the evidential standard for proving that a respondent has breached a condition of the injunction is beyond reasonable doubt.
- Police in the local authority can also apply for a gang injunction in a particular area. Gang injunctions should be based upon and supported by multi-agency partnership working.

Gang-related activity is that which occurs in the course of, or is otherwise related to, the activities of a group of *three or more people* which has characteristics enabling its members to be identified by others as a group. The individual who is subject to a gang injunction or whom against a gang injunction is sought is referred to as the 'respondent'. The police force or local authority applying for a gang injunction are referred to as the 'applicant'.

A gang injunction is a civil tool which allows the police or a local authority to apply to the County Court, the High Court or the youth court for an injunction against an individual respondent to prevent gang-related violence or drug dealing. It is intended to be used against members of violent street gangs and aims to:

- prevent the respondent from engaging in, encouraging or assisting gang-related violence or gang-related drug dealing activity
- protect the respondent from gang-related violence or gang-related drug dealing activity

KEY POINTS

- The statutory definition of gang-related violence under the Policing and Crime Act 2009 (as amended by the Serious Crime Act 2015) is intentionally wide ranging and broad. This is because the nature of gang-related violence varies significantly between areas and is therefore not easily captured by a single definition. The definition can therefore be used in response to the different types of gangs encountered in different areas. All applications must focus on gang-related violence and gang-related drug dealing rather than acts of anti-social behaviour or acquisitive crime.

- If there is sufficient evidence available and it is in the public interest to do so, those engaged in gang-related violence and/or gang-related drug dealing should be prosecuted under the criminal law. However, there may be occasions where criminal proceedings have not yet been brought and applying for a gang injunction may be an appropriate response. Close and regular contact with the CPS is essential.

Police forces and local authorities are required by the Policing and Crime Act 2009 to have regard for the *Statutory Guidance, Injunctions to Prevent Gang-Related Violence and Gang Related Drug Dealing* (HM Government 2016). This publication was laid before parliament under section 47(4) of the 2009 Act and contains guidance which is too extensive to reproduce in this handbook, which only outlines some of the main considerations from an investigation perspective.

The statutory guidance should be considered compulsory reading for any investigator contemplating seeking a gang injunction. It contains guidance on how to build a case, drafting and filing applications and how to approach follow up enforcement. It is important for applicants to have a sound understanding of the gang problem in their local area so as to satisfy the court that the respondent had been involved in gang-related violence. This should be informed by intelligence from the community and local partners.

Specific principles need to be considered for respondents between 14 and 17 years of age regarding their safeguarding and welfare. Similarly, there are additional considerations regarding female gang-member respondents.

Youth Offending Teams are a statutory consultation partner as they have comprehensive assessment tools, including managing risk and vulnerability. To ensure parental/family support and increase the chances of a successful intervention, where appropriate applicants should work closely with the young person's family from the earliest possible stage.

12.12.3.1 Admissible evidence

A wide range of evidence may be used by applicants to support an application, for example:

- direct evidence from witnesses (witness statements)
- hearsay evidence from community members and/or police officers
- documentary evidence
- statements from professional witnesses such as council officials, health professionals or other experts
- photographic, video or CCTV evidence, screen captures of gang members internet pages
- previous relevant arrests or convictions
- items seized during searches, such as clothing which identifies a respondent with a particular gang, evidence of communication with other gang members and evidence of drug dealing

Witnesses may be afraid to provide witness statements due to the fear of reprisals, and the risk of intimidation in gang-related cases is high. The admissibility of professional witness and hearsay evidence is intended to alleviate this problem as it enables a statement to be made on behalf of a witness who does not want to provide testimony themselves. However, the court may give less weight to hearsay evidence than it would to direct evidence.

KEY POINT

When presenting hearsay evidence to the court, applicants need to ensure they have undertaken a security risk assessment and implemented any necessary security measures.

Applicants may apply for any reasonable prohibition or requirement to be included in the injunction, provided it does not conflict with the respondent's religious beliefs, or interfere with the times, if any, that the respondent normally works or attends any educational establishment. It is good practice to consider:

- Does the evidence show that the prohibitions and requirements are necessary to prevent gang-related violence or gang-related drug dealing, or protect the respondent from gang-related violence or gang-related drug dealing?
- Are they targeted at the needs and behaviour of this particular respondent?
- Are they enforceable?
- Are they clear, concise and easy for the respondent and partners to understand?
- Do they have any implications for the respondent's human rights?
- Will they have the effect of protecting and reassuring the public?

The duration of each prohibition should be determined by the unique circumstances of each case and there is no minimum duration for any injunction or any of the conditions contained in it. No prohibition or requirement can be ordered to last more than two years however, and the court must order the applicant and the respondent to attend a review hearing within the last four weeks of the one-year period.

Examples and suggested prohibitions to consider include, but are not limited to:

- Non-association in public with named gang members. Difficulties may arise justifying to the court and enforcing such a prohibition if the respondent is closely related to the named gang members or is required to be in their presence.
- Prohibition on visiting or travelling through a particular area or areas. Applicants should demonstrate that such

a restriction is proportionate and enforceable, for example by not excluding a respondent from the entire area in which they live, work, study or worship.
- Prohibition of being in charge of a particular species of animal, or from being in a particular place with a particular species of animal. This is aimed at dangerous dogs and other animals that could be used to intimidate others, incite fear or commit acts of violence.
- Restricting the use of the internet and other technologies. This is aimed at posting videos to encourage gang-related violence that promote the gang, or threatens rival gangs, or perhaps uploading details of gang meetings on social networking sites. For such a prohibition the applicant will have to satisfy the court that such a restriction is proportionate and can be monitored.

An application may also apply for any reasonable requirement, such as requiring the respondent to:

- notify the applicant of the respondent's address and of any change of address
- be at a particular place between certain times on specified days
- present themselves to a particular person at a place where they are required to be between certain times on particular days
- participate in particular activities between particular times on particular days

No application can require a respondent to be in any particular place for more than eight hours in any one day. Also, as far as practically possible, any requirements should avoid any conflict between the respondent's religious beliefs and any interference with the times (if any) that they normally work or attend an educational establishment.

12.12.3.2 Power of arrest

The court can attach a power of arrest to any injunction, prohibition or requirement, with the exception of any requirement that the respondent participates in a particular activity. This is because when framing the Crime and Disorder Act 2009 it was not considered proportionate to have an automatic power of arrest for not attending mentoring sessions or other particular activities. In such circumstances it is more appropriate for the applicant to apply for a warrant under section 44 of the 2009 Act or to commence proceedings for breaching the injunction.

12.12.4 Serious Violence Prevention Orders

At the time of writing this handbook the introduction of Serious Violence Reduction Orders (SVROs) is in progress as a result of the Police, Crime, Sentencing and Courts Bill 2021. For precision, it would be premature to include specific detail about SVPOs until they have been finalised in law. The consultation process has been completed and further information is available in the publication *Consultation on Serious Violence Reduction Orders, Summary of Consultation Responses and Conclusion* (Home Office 2021).

12.12.5 Domestic Violence Protection Notices

The Crime and Security Act 2010 (section 24) introduced Domestic Violence Protection Notices (DVPNs). These can be used to provide short-term protection for victims of domestic abuse (DA) and assist with early intervention following a domestic incident. A DVPN is a civil notice that provides short-term protection to a victim when positive action is required. In some circumstances an arrest might not have been made, or an arrest could have been made but the investigation needs to continue and is therefore in progress, or the situation could be that a decision to caution the perpetrator of the abuse has been made, or no further action is being taken so suitable bail conditions cannot be applied.

A DVPN is effectively a non-molestation and eviction notice which can be issued to a perpetrator by police officers attending a DA incident. Such a notice becomes effective from the time it is issued. It is important that investigators of DA incidents always seek to identify and charge the substantive offence and do not rely on a DVPN as a substitute for effective investigation and prosecution.

KEY POINT

The use of a DVPN is intended to fill the gap before any prosecution is initiated and aims to provide temporary respite to victims from their abuser. This can allow time for referral to support services and enable a victim to seek help and to plan and make practical arrangements to leave the abusive relationship. This covers the time period when often a victim is at most risk from an abuser.

The criteria for issuing a DVPN are that the alleged perpetrator is aged 18 or over, and an authorising officer who is not below the rank of superintendent has reasonable grounds for believing that violence has been used or threatened towards the victim and/or an associated person and issuing a DVPN is necessary to protect the person.

Before issuing a DVPN the authorising officer must take reasonable steps to establish and consider:

- the welfare of any person under the age of 18 whose interests the officer considers relevant to the issuing the DVPN (whether or not that person is an associated person)
- the opinion of the person whose protection the DVPN would be issued for regarding issuing such a notice
- any representations made by the person who would be subject to the DVPN regarding its issue
- the opinion of any other associated person regarding issuing a DVPN if any are involved

An associated person is a person who is associated with the alleged perpetrator within the meaning of section 62 of the Family Law Act 1996. In summary this includes relationships such as:

- they are married or have been married
- they are cohabitants or former cohabitants
- they live, or have lived, in the same household other than one of them being a tenant, lodger, boarder or the other's employee
- they are relatives
- they have agreed to marry one another (whether or not that agreement has been terminated)
- in relation to any child, they are a parent or have parental responsibility

If authorised a DVPN must state:

- the grounds on which it has been issued
- that a constable may arrest a person without warrant if they have reasonable grounds to believe the person is in breach of the DVPN
- that an application for a Domestic Violence Protection Order (DVPO) will be heard within 48 hours of the time of service of the DVPN and a notice of the hearing will be given to the person
- that in effect the DVPN continues until that application has been determined
- the provision that a magistrate's court may include in a DVPO

A DVPN must be in writing and be served personally by a constable who must ask the person for an address for the purpose of giving notice of the DVPO application hearing.

12.12.6 Domestic Violence Protection Orders

An application for a Domestic Violence Protection Order (DVPO) must be made by way of complaint to a magistrate's court no later than 48 hours after the DVPN was served (excluding Christmas Day, Good Friday, any Sunday and certain other bank holidays).

The court may make a DVPO if they are satisfied that on the balance of probabilities the person has been violent towards, or has threatened violence towards, an associated person. Plus, the court thinks that making the DVPO is necessary to protect that person from violence or a threat of violence by the associated person.

Before making a DVPO the court must, in particular, consider:

- the welfare of any person under the age of 18 whose interests the court considers relevant to the making of the DVPO (whether or not that person is an associated person)
- any opinion the court is made aware of about the opinion of the person for whose protection the DVPO would be made and the opinion of any other associated person who lives in the premises to which the provision of the DVPO would relate.

KEY POINT

A court has the power to make a DVPO even if the victim does not consent to the making of such an order.

A DVPO must contain a provision to prohibit the person from molesting the victim for whose protection the order is made. These provisions may be expressed in general terms or refer to particular acts or to both, for example:

- to prohibit the person from evicting or excluding from the premises the victim for whose protection the DVPO is made
- to prohibit the person from entering the premises
- to require the person to leave the premises
- to prohibit the person from coming within a specified distance from the premises

A DVPO must state the period for which it is in force, which is no fewer than 14 days beginning with the day it is made, and no more than 28 days beginning with that day. A person arrested for breaching a DVPO must be held in custody and brought before a magistrate's court within 24 hours of the time of their arrest. If the matter is not disposed of when the person is brought before the court they may be remanded in custody.

12.12.7 Sexual Harm Prevention Orders

From 8 March 2015, Sexual Harm Prevention Orders (SHPO) replaced the previous Sexual Offence Prevention Order (SOPO). Section 103 of the Sexual Offences Act 2003 deals with SHPOs. However, an SHPO can be ordered for offenders whose convictions pre-date the commencement of the 2003 Act.

An SHPO is available to be imposed in both magistrates' courts and the Crown Court when a defendant appears in relation to an offence in Schedule 3 or Schedule 5 of the Sexual Offences Act 2003. A CPS prosecutor may make an application for an SHPO in these circumstances and the court may impose an order if they are satisfied that an SHPO is necessary for the purposes of protecting the public (or any particular members of the public) from sexual harm from the defendant.

Schedule 3 offences are most of the substantive sexual offences, such as rape and indecent images of children. Some offences have specific conditions on when an SHPO can be consulted so the relevant schedule of offences should be consulted.

Schedule 5 contains a range of generally violent offences, such as murder, inflicting grievous bodily harm and child cruelty, but theft and harassment are also included.

A second route to obtaining an SHPO is available where a Chief Officer of Police or the Director General of the National Crime Agency applies by complaint to a magistrates' court. In these circumstances applications are made by a CPS prosecutor.

12.12.7.1 sexual harm test

The implementation of SHPOs lowers the bar from the previous 'serious sexual harm' to just 'sexual harm'.

Section 103B of the Sexual Offences Act 2003 defines this as:

> 'sexual harm' from a person means physical or psychological harm caused—
> (a) by the person committing one or more offences listed in Schedule 3,
> (b) or (in the context of harm outside the United Kingdom) by the person doing, outside the United Kingdom, anything which would constitute an offence listed in Schedule 3 if done in any part of the United Kingdom;

12.12.7.2 Prohibitions

An SHPO can only impose conditions that are necessary for protecting the public from sexual harm from the defendant and the court may consider the following questions:

1. Would an order minimise the risk of harm to the public or to any particular members of the public?
2. Is it proportionate?
3. Can it be policed effectively?

Prohibitions can be wide ranging but can only include negative prohibition; there is no power to impose any positive obligations on a defendant that require them to do something. The terms of an order need to be specific, focused and balanced to the exact requirements of the case. Requests for blanket conditions are likely to be challenged as disproportionate and unnecessary.[15]

Some common examples of prohibitions that could be considered depending on the specific requirements of the case and the harm to be prevented could include:

- no contact with children to prevent contact offences (it is essential to include an exemption for incidental contact such as is inherent in everyday life)
- not to undertake certain forms of employment

[15] *R v Smith and others* [2011] EWCA Crim 1772.

- not to work or volunteer in any place where persons under 18 will be present.
- not to engage in certain activities on the internet
- no foreign travel for a fixed period of not more than five years (this can be extended for up to five years on each application)
- not to enter or frequent certain areas where children may be present, including in the vicinity of schools, children's playgrounds and parks for example
- not to partake in certain leisure activities, such as visiting a public swimming pool
- not to be in a certain area or place (this is usually a ban from the address where the offence or incident occurred)

The Court of Appeal has emphasised the need for the terms of any SHPO to be effective, clear, realistic, proportionate and tailored to the facts.[16] When considering the previous approach involving blanket bans on internet access the Court stated that such a prohibition would not be appropriate except in the most exceptional cases. It was recognised that developments in technology and changes to everyday living as a result called for an adapted and targeted approach, particularly in relation to risk management software, cloud storage and encryption.

Prohibitions should be aimed at the deliberate installation of software other than that which is intrinsic to the operation of the device. Some suggested prohibitions regarding computer and communications devices include (but are not limited to):

- using any device capable of accessing the internet unless::
  - o the person who is the subject of the SHPO notifies the police ViSOR/MOSAVO team within three days of the acquisition of any such device
  - o the device has the capacity to retain and display the history of internet use

[16] *R v Parsons and another* [2017] EWCA Crim 2163.

- o the person does not delete such history from the device
- o the person makes the device available on request for inspection by a police officer or police staff employee, and they allow such a person to install risk management monitoring software if they so choose

This prohibition would not apply to a computer at the person's place of work, Job Centre Plus, Public Library, educational establishment, or other such place on the condition that the person notifies the police ViSOR/MOSAVO officer within three days of them commencing use of such a computer.

- o interfering with or bypassing the normal running of any such computer monitoring software
- o using or activating any function of any software which prevents a computer or device from retaining and/or displaying the history of internet use, for example using 'incognito' mode or private browsing
- o using any cloud or similar remote storage media capable of storing digital images (other than that which is intrinsic to the operation of the device) unless, within three days of the creation of an account for such storage, they notify the police of that activity, and provide access to such storage on request for inspection by a police officer or police staff employee
- o possessing any device capable of storing digital images such as a USB stick or external hard drive unless they make it available on request for inspection by a police officer or police staff employee
- o installing any encryption or wiping software on any device other than that which is intrinsic to the operation of the device

- having contact of any kind with any person they know or believe to be under the age of 18, whether directly or

indirectly via social media, or Skype or a similar method of communication in any way, other than:
- o inadvertent contact which was not reasonably avoidable in the course of lawful daily life, or
- o with the supervision of an adult who has knowledge of the persons convictions and is approved in advance by social services

Breach of an SHPO is triable either way and the maximum penalty for conviction on indictment in the Crown Court is imprisonment for a term not exceeding five years. It is the responsibility of the CPS to prosecute a breach of an SHPO irrespective of how the order was first made.

12.12.7.3 Sex offender notification rules

Under the Sexual Offences Act 2003 (sections 80 to 102), the sex offender notification rules automatically follow upon conviction for most sexual offences. The notification requirements range from two years in cases involving a caution, to an indefinite period if the sentence is imprisonment for 30 months or more.

KEY POINT

Notification provisions and SHPOs are different entities. An SHPO has to be applied for and ordered by the court and is not automatically applied, which is the case for notification requirements.

12.12.8 Sexual Risk Orders

On 8 March 2015, Sexual Risk Orders (SROs) replaced the previous Risk of Sexual Harm Orders. Section 122A of the Sexual Offences Act 2003 deals with SROs. These are civil orders that can be applied for by the Chief Officer of Police or the Director General of the National Crime Agency by way of complaint to a magistrates' court.

An SRO is generally made against a person who has not been convicted or cautioned for an offence. The court must be satisfied that as a result of an act of a sexual nature, there is reasonable cause to believe it is necessary to make an order to protect the public or any particular members of the public from harm from the defendant, or generally protecting children or vulnerable adults in the United Kingdom. An order can also apply to protecting any particular children or vulnerable adults who are abroad.

An SRO has effect for a fixed period of not less than two years or until a further order is made. It is a criminal offence for a person to breach an SRO and this would be prosecuted by the CPS. The maximum penalty for conviction on indictment is imprisonment for a term not exceeding five years.

12.12.9 Serious Crime Prevention Orders

A Serious Crime Prevention Order (SCPO) is a civil order intended to prevent or deter serious crime. Such an order enables a court to impose additional restrictions on serious offenders which can then be monitored to ensure compliance. Applying for and obtaining a SCPO can be an effective tactic to manage the current and future behaviour of serious and organised criminals. Many of these offenders are lifetime career criminals, and the imposition of a SCPO is designed to restrict and disrupt them engaging in further criminal activity and prevent reoffending.

Breaching a SCPO is a criminal offence which can be punished by up to five years imprisonment and an unlimited fine. Wide-ranging restrictions can be imposed provided they can be shown to be justified, necessary and proportionate to the circumstances of the case. They can include restrictions on:

- associating and communicating with criminals
- communications devices such as mobile phones
- financial, property and business dealings and conducting specific types of business bank accounts
- working arrangements

- the premises they are allowed to use and for what purpose
- geographic and travel restrictions both within the United Kingdom and abroad

An order can also require a person to answer questions or provide information or documents specified in the order. It is essential that any conditions are enforceable and are necessary and proportionate.

Application for a SCPO is made to the Crown Court if a person has been convicted of a serious offence or to the High Court as a standalone application if the person has been involved in serious crime. A serious offence includes an extensive list which in the particular circumstances the court considers sufficiently serious to be treated as such for the purposes of an SCPO application. This list of offences is set out under the following 15 headings:

- drug trafficking
- slavery
- people trafficking
- firearms offences
- prostitution and child sex
- armed robbery
- money laundering
- fraud
- blackmail
- computer misuse
- counterfeiting
- bribery
- organised crime
- offences in relation to public revenue
- environment

For applications in the High Court, the judge must be satisfied that the person has been involved in serious crime, whether in England and Wales or elsewhere, in that:

- they have committed a serious offence in England and Wales

- they have facilitated the commission by another of a serious offence in England and Wales, or
- their conduct was likely to facilitate the commission by themselves or another of a serious offence in England and Wales, whether or not such an offence was committed

The court must ignore any act which the person can show was reasonable in the circumstances, and subject to that, also ignore their intentions or any other aspect of their mental state at the time. In effect, this means that a person could successfully argue that they should not be made subject of a SCPO because their conduct as alleged by the prosecution was reasonable in the circumstances.

A SCPO should not be used as an alternative to prosecution. An application should generally only be made following a conviction for a serious offence where there are reasonable grounds to believe that an order would protect the public, or in the case of a High Court application where the evidence available does not provide a realistic prospect of conviction after applying the threshold test or would not be in the public interest. It should usually be in the public interest to prosecute a person for such serious crimes and in such circumstances investigators and prosecutors should keep the possibility of bringing a prosecution under review.

Applying for a SCPO must be seen as a serious step due to potentially imposing significant conditions that affect the rights of the individual or organisation concerned. It ought to be self-evident that close consultation with the CPS will be required throughout the process.

12.12.10 **Travel Restriction Orders**

The aim of a Travel Restriction Order (TRO) is to reduce re-offending by restricting the movements of convicted drug traffickers. A TRO can be imposed on any offender convicted of a drug trafficking offence and sentenced to four years or more imprisonment, regardless of their nationality.

UK passport holders may be required to surrender their passport to the court; this includes those with dual nationality.

A TRO has a maximum length of two years and comes into effect upon the release of the offender from prison. The penalty for breaching such an order is up to five years imprisonment and/or a fine.

12.12.11 Slavery and Trafficking Prevention Orders

A Slavery and Trafficking Prevention Order (STPO) is a civil order which is dealt with under Part 2 of the Modern Slavery Act 2015. STPOs are aimed at defendants who, in respect of a slavery or human trafficking offence, including an equivalent offence abroad, are convicted, cautioned, receive a reprimand or final warning, found not guilty by reason of insanity or are found by the court to have committed the act charged but are not fit to plead or stand trial due to being under a disability (eg insanity). An STPO is a preventative measure intended to deter unlawful and harmful activity (Home Office 2017).

In granting such an order, the court has the power to impose a wide range of restrictions on an individual which will depend on the nature of the case. The court will only make an order if it is satisfied that the behaviour giving rise to the behaviour took place and considers it necessary to impose an STPO to protect a person or persons from harm caused by the commission of slavery and human trafficking offences. Harm can include psychological harm as well as physical harm.

Breach of an order without reasonable excuse is a criminal offence which can be tried summarily or on indictment. The maximum penalty on indictment for breaching an STPO is five years imprisonment.

12.12.11.1 STPOs on conviction

It is not necessary to make an application to the court on conviction although the court may ask that the pre-sentence report considers the suitability of an STPO on a non-prejudicial basis. The prosecutor may also invite the court to consider making an order in appropriate cases. The evidence presented at the trial (or hearing in the event of a guilty plea) is likely to be an important factor in the court's decision together with the defendant's previous convictions. The assessment of risk contained in the pre-sentence report is also a key influence.

12.12.11.2 STPO on application

The police, National Crime Agency, Immigration Service and the Gangmasters and Labour Abuse Authority can apply for an STPO when an offender is behaving in a way that suggests they might commit a slavery or human trafficking offence.

To make a successful application it must be demonstrated to the court that the defendant is a 'relevant offender' meaning they have been convicted, cautioned, received a reprimand or final warning, been found not guilty by reason of insanity or been found to have done the act charged but were under a disability, and since becoming a relevant offender (the date of their conviction) the defendant has acted in such a way that there is a risk they may commit a slavery or human trafficking offence. An order needs to be necessary to protect the public, or any member of the public in the United Kingdom, from harm likely to occur from the commission of the offence.

KEY POINT

An STPO on application ought to be considered in situations where a relevant offender was not subject to an order following conviction but there is a risk that they are continuing to commit human trafficking and slavery offences and pose a risk to others.

12.12.12 Slavery and Trafficking Risk Orders

Slavery and Trafficking Risk Orders (STROs) are civil orders that are also dealt with under Part 2 of the Modern Slavery Act 2015. They were introduced with the intention of restricting the activities of a person who has not been convicted, cautioned etc of a slavery or human trafficking offence but are thought to pose a risk of harm in that they will commit such an offence.

An STRO could be considered where there is an investigation into a slavery or human trafficking offence, and it is needed to protect victims who remain at risk from a person who has not been convicted. The court must be satisfied that making an order is necessary to protect a named or potential person from the risk of physical or psychological harm if the offence was committed. This enables action to be taken to protect the public notwithstanding the lack of a conviction.

The STRO is a preventative measure and is not intended to be a substitute for a prosecution when sufficient evidence is available to pursue an offence. The court may impose a wide range of restrictions if they are deemed necessary to protect the public from harm. This includes a defendant providing their address and any subsequent changes to this. The minimum duration of an STRO is two years.

12.12.13 STPO and STRO prohibitions

The prohibitions in an STPO and an STRO need to be tailored to deal with the circumstances of the individual case. It will ultimately be for the court to decide what provisions are necessary, but examples could include (but this is not exhaustive):

- advertising for staff
- recruiting staff
- employing staff

- being a gangmaster
- working with vulnerable people
- working with children
- residing with specified children/vulnerable people
- organising transport for other people
- organising accommodation for other people
- travelling to specified countries
- directly or indirectly contacting/recruiting specific people either personally or by electronic means
- holding a licence to act as a sponsor for visa applications
- going to a specific place, for example where a victim resides

It is sensible to seek CPS advice regarding the wording of the prohibitions in any application as they are responsible for prosecuting any breaches of the order.

12.12.14 Forced Marriage Protection Order

It is a criminal offence under the Anti-social Behaviour, Crime and Policing Act 2014 to force someone to marry in England and Wales and can result in a prison sentence of up to seven years. Forced marriage is also a criminal offence in Northern Ireland but under separate legislation. It also includes:

- taking someone overseas to force them to marry, whether or not the forced marriage takes place
- marrying someone who lacks mental capacity to consent to the marriage whether they are pressured or not

A forced marriage is a marriage that takes place without the full and free consent of both parties. Force can include emotional pressure, threats and psychological abuse as well as physical force. Forced marriage should not be confused with an arranged marriage where the couple involved have the free will and choice whether to accept or decline the marriage.

A Forced Marriage Protection Order (FMPO) is unique to each case and contains legally binding conditions and directions. An order is intended to help a person who is being forced into a marriage or who is already in a forced marriage.

An application for a FMPO can be made at the same time as a police investigation or other criminal proceedings. Applications can be made by the person who is to be protected by the order, a relevant third party or any other person with the permission of the court.

It is rare that mainstream investigators will be involved with applying for an FMPO, so the process is not explored further for the purpose of this handbook. If further guidance is required, the local Protecting Vulnerable Persons Unit (or the host force equivalent) should be consulted. Advice is also available from the Forced Marriage Unit, which is a joint unit of the Foreign, Commonwealth and Development Office and the Home Office.

KEY POINT

In appropriate cases when investigating any of the offences that could potentially trigger an application for a relevant prevention order, the evidential requirements for any application should be considered for inclusion in the overall investigative strategy. This includes gathering additional wider investigative material that is not necessarily required or relevant for the primary investigation.

References

CPS (2016) *Criminal Behaviour Orders (CBO's) on Conviction: A Guide for the Police – Preparing CBO Applications*

Garside R (2004) *Crime, persistent offenders and the justice gap* (Crime and Society Foundation)

HM Government (2016) *Statutory Guidance: Injunctions to Prevent Gang-Related Violence and Gang Related Drug Dealing, Revised Guidance*

Home Office (2017) *Guidance on Slavery and Trafficking Prevention Orders and Trafficking Risk Orders Under Part 2 of the Modern Slavery Act 2015*
Home Office (2021) *Knife Crime Prevention Orders (KCPO's) Practitioners Guidance*
Home Office (2021) *Consultation on Serious Violence Reduction Orders, Summary of Consultation Responses and Conclusion*
NCIS (2000) *National Intelligence Model*

Chapter 13

Case Management and Disclosure

13.1 Introduction

Once a suspect has been charged, or a prosecution is otherwise initiated, such as by requisition, the case is far from over for the investigator. Further additional requirements need careful consideration and management before and during any court hearing. Generally, the Crown Prosecution Service (CPS) has the responsibility for prosecuting cases, and investigators need to work collaboratively with the CPS prosecutors to ensure the case is prosecuted effectively and to achieve the best results (Moreno and Hughes 2008).

This chapter sets out particular areas that need considering during the case management phase of the investigation. Investigators require a good working knowledge of the processes and procedures that come before a defendant appears at court. Matters such as knowing about threshold tests and charging policies, dealing with specific evidential points, powers to give cautions, national file standards and last but not least the importance of giving and presenting evidence all come under the general scope of case management. Alongside court procedures, they become highly relevant and important responsibilities for a lead crime investigator. Mistakes and poor practice in this phase of the investigative process can work against any chances of mounting a successful prosecution.

Blackstone's Crime Investigators' Handbook. Steve Hibbitt and Gary Shaw, Oxford University Press. © Oxford University Press 2023.
DOI: 10.1093/oso/9780192867896.003.0013

13.2 Responsibilities of Police and Prosecutors

The responsibilities for the police are:

- ensuring that cases appropriate for out-of-court disposal are identified at an early stage and appropriately dealt with
- conducting an evidential evaluation to assess whether a case has met the evidential Threshold Test for referral to the CPS
- referring serious cases, such as those involving death, rape or serious sexual offences for early advice
- prosecution file building and submission in accordance with national file standards
- addressing any CPS action plans and conducting further enquiries as required
- submitting further reports and additional investigative and evidential material within the timescales required
- considering and addressing any further investigation required following receipt of a defence case statement
- ensuring disclosure responsibilities under the Criminal Procedure and Investigations Act 1996 (CPIA) are carried out effectively and subject to ongoing review
- finalising cases that do not meet the evidential threshold test for referral to the CPS in which no further action can be taken.
- ensuring that national crime recording standards have been adhered to and any relevant material has been preserved and archived pending possible future developments in forensic science

Prosecutors are responsible for:

- making charging decisions and providing advice
- deciding whether it is appropriate to apply the Threshold Test
- recording decisions on forms MG3 and MG3a

- ensuring pre-charge action plans only require the gathering of necessary evidence with agreed timescales for completion of any work
- ensuring cases appropriate for out-of-court disposal are identified prior to charge, and in police-charged cases, prior to the first hearing

13.3 Operational Arrangements

The police undertake investigations and should pursue all relevant lines of enquiry. Investigative material should be secured including anything that could undermine a prosecution case or assist the defence. This material also requires investigation and should be referred to in any investigative or charging advice requested from the CPS.

The police initially decide whether there is sufficient evidence to charge by assessing the investigative material to identify what would be admissible evidence in a court and supports the points to prove the offence. This determines whether the Threshold Test has been met before proceeding to charging or referring the case to a CPS prosecutor for decision.

If the appropriate test cannot be met and the case cannot be strengthened by more investigation, the police will take no further action.

KEY POINT

Where the police proceed to charge, the following will have been assessed:

- evidence that supports the prosecution
- justification in treating the case as an anticipated guilty plea suitable for sentencing in the magistrates' court (where applicable)
- reason(s) why the public interest requires prosecution rather than any other disposal

13.4 Referred Cases

When cases are referred to the CPS for a decision, the Custody Officer will determine whether the suspect should remain in custody or be released on bail to facilitate the referral.

The prosecutor, when making charging decisions, will assess the evidential material that supports the points to prove. They will also consider the impact of any investigative material that has the potential to undermine a prosecution, or which would assist the defence. The prosecutor will identify and suggest how to rectify evidential deficiencies and identify those cases that cannot be strengthened by further investigation or where prosecution is not in the public interest.

13.5 Early Investigative Advice

CPS prosecutors make the decision to charge and provide early investigative advice (EIA) in serious, sensitive or complex cases. Specific cases involving death, rape or other serious sexual assault should always be referred by a police supervisor to a local area prosecutor at as early a stage as possible if it appears that continuing investigation will provide evidence upon which a charging decision could be made.

Cases may also be referred to the CPS for early advice to develop a joint prosecution strategy. This is where a case would benefit from CPS expert advice regarding the evidential requirements for the points to prove or other elements of the offence, including any necessary corroborative or supporting evidence. Early investigative advice should also identify any additional enquiries or actions to be undertaken by the police.

As the name suggests, cases referred to the CPS for early investigative advice will be at a preliminary stage of the investigation. This means that the Full Code Test will not be met at that time as all the evidence will not be available. A police supervisor must believe that the investigation will eventually obtain evidential material that meets the Full Code Test and in practice this means evaluating the available investigative material to assess whether:

- there are any further lines of enquiry to pursue, and/or
- the evidential strength of the case can be improved which would make it possible to meet either the Full Code Test of the Threshold Test
- CPS advice would benefit the investigation on matters such as legal aspects of the case, the course of the investigation or gathering further evidence which would be admissible in court. This may involve particular consideration in cases involving vulnerable victims

KEY POINTS

- Early investigative advice takes place, where practical, within 24 hours when a suspect is being detained in custody or within seven days if they are released on bail.
- Seeking early investigative advice from a prosecutor does not negate the investigator's responsibility to identify and pursue relevant lines of enquiry.
- The decision to refer a case for early investigative advice is made by a police supervisor.
- Cases involving vulnerable victims may benefit from EIA.

13.6 Full Code Test

The Full Code Test has two stages:

1. the evidential stage
2. the public interest stage.

Police decision makers should identify cases where the evidential Full Code Test cannot be met. Such cases should not be charged or referred to CPS prosecutors unless the evidential threshold test has been met and a charging decision is required and is justified.

13.7 Evidential Stage

Prosecutors must be satisfied there is sufficient evidence to provide *a realistic prospect of conviction* for each suspect on each charge. They must consider the potential defence case and how it is likely to affect the prospect of conviction. A case which does not pass the evidential stage cannot proceed, no matter how serious or sensitive it may be.

A realistic prospect of conviction is an objective test based solely on the prosecutor's assessment of the evidence that would be admissible in a court, including any information available about the defence that may have been put forward by the suspect. Under consideration is whether an objective, impartial and reasonable jury or a bench of magistrates, or a judge hearing a case alone, properly directed and acting in accordance with the law, would be more likely than not to convict the defendant of the charge on the alleged facts. This is a different test to the one that the criminal courts themselves must apply; a jury may only convict if they are sure the defendant is guilty *beyond reasonable doubt.*

Prosecutors, when deciding on evidential sufficiency, must consider whether the evidence on which they are basing their decision is reliable and credible and that it can be presented to a court. In many cases the reliability and credibility of the evidence does not cause concern, but there will also be cases where the evidence may not be as strong as it first appears to be, or it is undermined by other material obtained during the investigation. Increasingly, CPS prosecutors require disclosure to be completed at the time they make a prosecution decision so they can consider any impact this may have.

13.8 **Public Interest Stage**

In 1951, Sir Hartley Shawcross, the then Attorney General, made what is considered to be a classic statement on public interest which has been endorsed by Attorneys General ever since:

> It has never been the rule in this country—I hope it never will be—that suspected criminal offences must automatically be the subject of prosecution.

He added that there should be a prosecution:

> wherever it appears that the offence or the circumstances of its commission is, or are of such a character that a prosecution in respect thereof is required in the public interest.[1]

If a CPS prosecutor decides there is sufficient evidence to justify a prosecution or to offer an out-of-court disposal, they must go on to consider whether a prosecution is required in the public interest. Unless the public interest factors against a prosecution outweigh those in favour of one, a prosecution will usually proceed.

The prosecutor might also be satisfied that the public interest may be properly served by offering an offender the opportunity to have the matter dealt with by an out-of-court disposal. The more serious the offence or the offender's record of criminal behaviour, the more likely it is that the public interest will require a prosecution.

Although there may be public interest considerations tending against prosecution in a particular case, prosecutors should nevertheless consider whether a prosecution should be pursued, and those factors put before a court for

[1] House of Commons Debates, Volume 483, 29 January 1951.

consideration when sentencing. Each case must be considered on its own facts and merits.

13.9 Threshold Test

Prosecutors will apply the Full Code Test unless, at the time of making their decision, not all of the available evidence has been obtained, but the suspect presents a substantial risk if released on bail. In such cases, the Threshold Test may be applied to a charging decision for a suspect who may be justifiably detained in custody to allow evidence to be gathered for the Full Code Test if:

1. there is insufficient evidence currently available to apply the evidential stage of the Full Code Test
2. there are reasonable grounds for believing that further evidence will become available within a reasonable time
3. the seriousness or the circumstances of the case justifies making an immediate charging decision
4. there are continuing substantial grounds to object to bail in accordance with the Bail Act 1976 and in all the circumstances of the case an application to withhold bail may be properly made.

Where any of these four conditions are not met, the Threshold Test cannot be applied, and the suspect cannot be charged. Such cases must be referred back to the Custody Officer to determine whether the person may continue to be detained or released under investigation, or on bail, with or without conditions.

13.10 Reasonable Suspicion

The prosecutor must be satisfied that there is at least a reasonable suspicion that the person to be charged has committed the offence. In determining whether reasonable suspicion exists, they must consider the evidence which is currently available. This could include, for example, witness statements, CCTV recordings and other material or information, provided the prosecutor is satisfied that:

- it is relevant
- it is capable of being put into an admissible evidential format for presentation in court
- it would be used in the case

If this part of the Threshold Test is satisfied, the prosecutor may proceed to the second part of the Threshold Test.

13.11 **Realistic Prospect of Conviction**

The prosecutor must be satisfied that there are reasonable grounds for believing that the continuing investigation will provide further evidence, within a reasonable time, so that when taken together, all of the evidence would be capable of establishing a realistic prospect of conviction in accordance with the Full Code Test. Any further evidence must be identifiable and not merely speculative, and in reaching a decision under this second part of the Threshold Test, the prosecutor must consider:

- the nature, extent and admissibility of any likely further evidence and its impact on the case
- the charges that all the evidence will support
- the reasons why the evidence is not already available
- the time required to obtain the further evidence and whether any consequential delay is reasonable in all the circumstances

If both parts of the Threshold Test are satisfied, the prosecutor applies the public interest stage of the Full Code Test based on the information available at that time.

KEY POINTS

- Investigators need to be properly prepared when approaching a CPS prosecutor for a Threshold Test decision. They should present factual information and be prepared to discuss matters such as:
- The nature of any anticipated additional investigative material to be relied on, including its evidential value in the context of a prosecution case. This could include the results of forensic examinations, expert evidence and reports, witnesses who are currently unavailable, the examination of digital devises and analysis of the results. These examples are not exhaustive.
- The timescales for obtaining the results, which must be realistic, accurate and if possible, confirmed in writing by any service provider. The dates of any fast track forensic submissions already made or the date that material is to be submitted to a Forensic Service Provider should be included. It will be unlikely that a persuasive argument can be made for the CPS decision if the investigation is not proceeding with as much urgency as possible.
- Whether there is any reason to suspect that the results of further enquiries might not be as anticipated, including the potential of undermining a Threshold Test decision.
- The reasons why the material is not currently available and the steps that have been taken so far to obtain it.
- Making a Threshold Test decision involves a CPS prosecutor accurately assessing the evidential value of investigative material to be obtained on which they are basing their decision. This is a significant decision for them and causes significant challenges and issues for a prosecution if either the anticipated material is not obtained as anticipated, or it does not have the anticipated evidential value, or it unexpectedly undermines the prosecution case. In a worst-case scenario this could lead to future discontinuance of proceedings with potential consequences if a defendant has been remanded in custody.
- Investigators need to make the strongest and most reliable case for their request without relying on just the seriousness of the offence, or providing imprecise or vague information, or perhaps even resorting to wishful thinking or emotion. The CPS prosecutor must be objective and cannot take any of these into account.

13.12 Reviewing the Threshold Test

A decision to charge using the Threshold Test must be kept under review. The evidence must be regularly assessed to ensure that the charge is still appropriate and that continued objection to the granting of bail is justified. The Full Code Test must be applied as soon as reasonably practicable and in any event before any applicable custody time limit or extended custody time limit expires.

KEY POINTS

- The Threshold Test may NOT be used to charge a summary only offence that does not carry imprisonment.
- Where it is used by the police to charge an imprisonable summary only offence, the reason will be recorded on the form MG6 and provided to the CPS with the case file for the first hearing.

13.13 Diversion from Prosecution

The police should consider at an early stage whether a case can be dealt with out of court. The appropriateness of such an outcome will depend on:

- the seriousness of offence
- the consequences of the offending behaviour
- the antecedents of offender
- the likely outcome at court, particularly when there may only be a nominal penalty

KEY POINT

Where an out-of-court disposal is considered, the views of the victim should be obtained and considered wherever possible.

When the police consider that a conditional caution is an appropriate disposal, the case must be referred to a CPS prosecutor. This requires completing and submitting a form MG5 Case Summary which also contains any proposed conditions and the offender's previous convictions.

13.13.1 Conditional cautions

A conditional caution is a statutory development of the non-statutory simple caution, and the basic criterion for its use is that the offender is aged 18 or over, they have made admissions to the offence and in the opinion of the CPS there is sufficient evidence to charge the offender.

This scheme is aimed at cases when public interest might be met more effectively by offenders carrying out specific conditions of the caution rather than being prosecuted. The conditions applied to the caution must help to rehabilitate the offender and/or ensure that the offender makes reparation for the effects of their offending on the victim or the community.

The CPS is responsible for deciding whether to offer an offender a conditional caution, which must meet the Full Code Test. Prosecutors will offer a conditional caution where it is proportionate to the seriousness and the consequences of the offending and where the conditions offered meet the aims of rehabilitation, reparation or punishment within the terms of the Criminal Justice Act 2003.

Prosecutors must follow the Code of Practice and the DPP's Guidance on Conditional Cautioning when deciding whether to offer such a caution to an offender. They may offer a conditional caution where, taking account of the views of the victim, it is considered to be in the interests of the suspect, the victim or the community to do so.

A conditional caution is not a criminal conviction, but it does form part of an offender's criminal record and may be cited in court during any subsequent proceedings. It may also be considered by prosecutors if the person reoffends.

The offer of a conditional caution, which is accepted and complied with, takes the place of a prosecution. If the offer is refused or the suspect does not make the required admission of guilt to the person who seeks to administer the conditional caution, a prosecution must follow for the offence.

If the terms of the conditional caution are not complied with, the prosecutor will reconsider the public interest factor and decide whether to prosecute the offender; usually a prosecution should be brought for the original offence.

13.13.2 Simple cautions

A simple caution can be issued by the police in cases where an admission is made by the offender and consideration has been given to the seriousness of the offence. A simple caution has no conditions attached to it. In exceptional cases, prosecutors (not the police) can authorise the offer of a simple caution to an offender for indictable only offences (only triable in the Crown Court).

In all other cases, prosecutors may direct that a simple caution is offered in accordance with CPS and Home Office Guidance or suggest an alternative, for example issuing a Penalty Notice for Disorder. Issuing a penalty notice is, however, a decision for the police.

In any case where a prosecutor authorises or directs that a simple caution be offered by the police, they must be satisfied that the Full Code Test is met, and a clear admission of guilt has been made by the offender.

Accepting a simple caution or other out-of-court disposal which is complied with takes the place of a prosecution. If the offer of a simple caution is refused, a prosecution must follow for the original offence. If any other out-of-court disposal is not accepted, prosecutors will apply the Full Code Test upon receipt of the case and decide whether to prosecute the offender.

13.14 **Police Charging Decisions**

The police can decide to charge a summary only offence without referral to the CPS, irrespective of plea, for example criminal damage when the value of loss or damage is less than £5,000. The police can decide to charge an offence that can be heard either way (at a magistrate or a crown court) where a guilty plea is anticipated and the offence is suitable for sentencing in a magistrates' court, provided it is not:

- a case requiring the consent of the Director of Public Prosecutions (DPP) or Law Officer to prosecute
- a case involving death
- connected with terrorist activity or official secrets
- classified as hate crime or domestic violence/abuse under CPS policies
- an offence of violent disorder or affray
- grievous bodily harm or wounding or actual bodily harm
- a sexual offence committed by or upon a person under 18 years
- an offence under the Licensing Act 2003

13.15 **CPS Charging Decisions**

In addition to the offences listed in the previous section, only CPS prosecutors can make charging decisions for:

- indictable only offences
- either way offences that are not suitable for sentencing in a magistrates' court
- Cases where a guilty plea is not anticipated

In cases where any of the offences under consideration for charging includes one which must be referred to the CPS, then all of the offences under consideration should be referred to a prosecutor, even they are ones that the police could normally charge.

13.16 Anticipated Guilty Plea

A guilty plea may be anticipated where either:

- the suspect has made a clear and unambiguous admission to the offence, and they have not said anything that could be used as a defence
- no admission has been made but the suspect has not denied the offence or indicated it will be contested, and the commission of the offence and the identification of the offender can be established by reliable evidence, or the suspect can clearly be seen committing the offence on a good quality visual recording

13.17 Simple Caution for Indictable Only Offences

Any offence which can only be tried on indictment (in a crown court), but which a police decision maker considers suitable to be dealt with by a simple caution, MUST be referred to a CPS prosecutor who will decide whether there is a realistic prospect of conviction on the evidence available and whether disposal by a simple caution is in the public interest.

A prosecutor will only confirm that this is an acceptable outcome in exceptional circumstances. A careful record of the rationale for such a decision must be made on the form MG3.

13.18 Police Charging—Prosecutor Authority Unobtainable

There may be times when it is not possible to obtain a prosecutor's authority to charge a suspect before their relevant detention time expires. In such instances an inspector may authorise charging an offence where the continued detention of the suspect is justified after charge. This power is only to be used in exceptional circumstances, so investigators should anticipate detention time limits under the Police and Criminal Evidence Act 1984 (PACE) and seek charging decisions in good time.

The police may apply the Threshold Test when charging under this provision, and any cases charged in this manner must be referred to a prosecutor as soon as possible following charge, and not later than the time proposed for the first court appearance.

The CPS will review all police-charged cases prior to a first court appearance. Cases will only proceed when all the appropriate tests have been met and the public interest has been considered, including whether an out-of-court disposal would be more appropriate.

13.19 Management Review of Charging Decisions and Actions

The police will carry out the recommendations of a prosecutor unless the case is escalated for management review. There may however be occasions when police or prosecutors disagree over decisions made or the proposed action following a referral. In such cases these matters can be escalated to the first line of management to review the disputed decision(s) as soon as possible. First line management is:

- a Detective Chief Inspector
- a District Crown Prosecutor

If this review cannot resolve the issue(s) the case should be escalated and referred to:

- a Basic Command Unit (BCU) commander
- a Chief Crown Prosecutor

13.20 Information Required for Investigative Advice or Charging Decisions

The police will provide the prosecutor with the material and evidence which is available at that time, and which is relevant to the aspect of the case on which guidance is sought. In more complex cases this should be by way of a case report or form MG3. The decision of the prosecutor will be set out in an MG3 and include an action plan of matters to address with an agreed date for completion.

Where a case is referred for a charging decision, the police will compile a pre-charge report comprising:

- a Form MG3 (a summary of facts may be provided on an MG5) which contains the views of the Investigating Officer on any issues on which the decision of the prosecutor is sought
- key evidence in the case, such as witness statements, relevant exhibits, CCTV and forensic reports that establish the elements of the offence to be proved
- a PNC record of the suspect and any previous convictions of key prosecution witnesses
- any material that may undermine the prosecution case or assist the defence

In cases where the suspect has made a full admission during an interview under caution, the specific admissions will be included in the case summary.

Where an investigator considers there is no evidential value from an interview ('no comment' made or the questions answered have no evidential value) then no record of interview is required.

To ensure a speedy and responsive charging service, referral arrangements for all but the most serious and complex cases can be made over the telephone. The police will submit pre-charge reports and key evidence across the electronic exchange by direct input or secure email. The police will then consult with a CPS prosecutor by telephone. During weekday office hours (9 am to 5 pm) calls should route to the local CPS group; outside office hours referral is to CPS Direct.

13.21 'Face-to-Face' Consultations

A 'face-to-face' meeting (including by remote means) between the investigator and a prosecutor handling the case must be authorised by CPS supervision and will normally only take place in the following circumstances:

- any case involving death
- rape and serious sexual offences
- child abuse
- large-scale or long-term fraud
- cases with substantial or complex video or audio key evidence
- cases expected to take longer than 90 minutes' consultation
- any other cases agreed locally with CPS

Sometimes it is beneficial to have specialists present at face-to-face meetings to assist with the interpretation of evidence such as forensic or communications data

13.22 Written Advice Files

Advice files should only be submitted in exceptional circumstances, such as:

- lengthy achieving best evidence (ABE) witness interviews
- complex/lengthy documentary exhibits to consider

Arrangements to submit such files should be made through the CPS Group Charging Manager.

13.23 Evidence Admissible in Court

A criminal investigation will gather investigative material which may or may not be evidence that is admissible in a court. Investigative material is valuable because it may support, develop or identify lines of enquiry. It can take many forms, such as witness accounts, interviews under caution, forensic material, audio/visual material, digital material, communications data, objects and items recovered, documents and intelligence and information. None of this is necessarily evidence.

Evidence in court must be relevant to either a fact in issue or a collateral fact and tend to prove or disprove its existence or absence. If it is relevant and not subject to any exclusionary rule the material may be admissible evidence depending on the circumstances of the individual case.[2] An item of evidence is considered to be relevant if it renders the fact to be proved *more probable than it would be without that evidence.* An item of evidence therefore is relevant provided it has probative value, however little this may be.[3]

Direct (or original) evidence concerns matters that were personally perceived by a witness, which if believed would be sufficient to prove a fact in issue without further evidence or the need for inference. In straightforward parlance this is what a witness personally saw, heard, felt, smelt or otherwise experienced.

Testimonial evidence is the oral evidence of statements made in court by a witness (witness testimony).

Real evidence is evidence which may be inspected by the fact finders, or a trier of facts and includes, for example, material such as images, objects, computer records and documents. These are not exhaustive examples and

[2] *R v Guney* (1998) 2 Cr App R 242, 265.

[3] *R v Harz* (1967) AC 760, 785.

documents constitute the majority of real evidence. In criminal cases, the Criminal Justice Act 2003 (section 133) provides that where a statement in a document is admissible in evidence in criminal proceedings the statement may be proved by producing either:

- the document
- whether or not the document exists, a copy of the document or of the material part of it, authenticated in whatever way the court may approve

Circumstantial evidence (as distinct from direct evidence) is evidence from which a fact in issue may be inferred. In other words, it is evidence of a relevant fact as opposed to evidence of a fact.[4] An example of circumstantial evidence could be the presence of an accused's fingerprints on an object which was found at the scene of a crime. Another example could be the presence of an accused at the scene of a crime between the relevant time parameters for the offence being committed. This would be circumstantial evidence of the opportunity to commit the offence. Similarly, the post-offence conduct of a defendant could be circumstantial evidence although on its own this would not be direct evidence of them committing the offence. Likewise, the bad character of a defendant would also be circumstantial evidence if admitted by the court.

Saying that evidence is circumstantial does not diminish its value compared to other evidence in a case when its relevance to the whole circumstances is considered. However, circumstantial evidence should be approached with caution, as described by the appeal court in the case of a *Teper v R*[5] where it ruled that:

> Circumstantial evidence may sometimes be conclusive, but it must always be narrowly examined, if only because evidence

[4] *R v Taylor* (1928) 21 Cr App R 20, 21.
[5] (1952) AC 480, 489.

> of this kind may be fabricated to cast suspicion on another ... It is also necessary before drawing the inference of the accused's guilt from circumstantial evidence to be sure that there are no other co-existing circumstances which would weaken or destroy any inference.

Hearsay evidence is testimony from a witness giving evidence about statements that they say someone else has said. In other words, this is what a witness describes someone else saying. Hearsay evidence is not the best evidence because of the inherent danger of its unreliability due to the accuracy of the witness recalling the words spoken and that the demeanour of the person who originally spoke the words cannot be assessed or challenged in cross-examination.

In criminal proceedings, the hearsay provisions are contained in the Criminal Justice Act 2003 but are too extensive to cover in a handbook of this nature.

KEY POINTS

- The admissibility of evidence in court includes relevant legislation, criminal procedure rules, case law and statutory instruments which are voluminous and complex. They are the subject of routine legal examination, scrutiny and argument in all courts by experienced and highly qualified legal professionals, including solicitors, barristers and judges.
- Investigators are strongly advised to familiarise themselves with at least the rudiments of the Criminal Procedure Rules because these rarely feature in any detail in current police training.
- Investigators should always gather a wide range of investigative material and not make judgements or assessments at that stage about evidential admissibility, which could be complex. Relevance and admissibility are decisions for the CPS and arguments for lawyers in court.

13.24 National File Standards

The National File Standard, which includes the Better Case Management streamlined process, provides a staged and proportionate approach to the preparation of prosecution files. It specifies material required for first hearings and identifies how file preparation should continue through the life of a case.

13.24.1 Anticipated guilty plea cases

1A—Pre-charge report	1B—Post-charge national file standard
For charging decision to police supervisor or CPS prosecutor	First court hearing
Must include: • MG3—report to prosecutor • MG3a—further report to prosecutor • PNC record of suspect and key prosecution witnesses' previous convictions • Any material that may undermine the prosecution case or assist the defence • Disclosure schedules are NOT required at this stage	**Must include in addition to pre-charge report:** • MG4—charge sheet • MG5—police report • MG9—list of witnesses • MG10—witness availability
If applicable include: • MG11's—key witness statements or Record of Video Interview (ROVI) if the interview was visually recorded • MGDD A/B drink drive forms • Other key evidence: CCTV (a copy only when it is the sole evidence to be relied upon) • Other relevant material: domestic abuse/hate crime, incident reports, etc	**If applicable include:** • MG2—special Measures assessment • MG4A/B/C—bail, variation of bail and surety forms • MG7—remand application • MG8—breach of bail conditions • MG11s—all key witness statements or ROVI if the interview was visually recorded • MG15—interview record (only to be compiled in serious and complex cases) • MG17—Proceeds of Crime Act (POCA) review • MG18—Offences taken not consideration (TIC)

13.24.2 Anticipated *NOT* guilty plea cases

2A—Pre-charge report	2B—Post-charge national file standard
For charging decision to police supervisor or CPS prosecutor	First court hearing
Must include: • MG3—report to prosecutor • MG3a—further report to prosecutor • MG11s—key witness statements or ROVI if the interview was visually recorded • PNC records of suspect and key prosecution witnesses' previous convictions • Any material that may undermine the prosecution case or assist the defence • Disclosure schedules are NOT required at this stage •	**Must include in addition to pre-charge report:** • MG4—charge sheet • MG5—police report • MG9—list of witnesses • MG10—witness availability • MG11s—all key witness statements or ROVI if the interview was visually recorded
If applicable include: • MGDDA/B drink drive forms • Other key evidence: CCTV (copy only when it is the sole evidence to be relied upon) • Other relevant material: domestic abuse/hate crime incident reports, etc.	**If applicable include:** • MG2—special measures assessment • MG4A/B/C—bail, variation of bail and surety forms • MG4D and E—postal requisition forms • MG6A—record of pre-interview briefing • MG6B—police officer/staff disciplinary record • MG6C—police schedule of non-sensitive unused material • MG6D—police schedule of sensitive unused material • MG6E—disclosure officers report

2A—Pre-charge report	2B—Post-charge national file standard
	• MG7—remand in custody application • MG8—breach of bail conditions • MG9—witness list • MG10—witness non-availability • MG11—witness statements • MG12—exhibits list • MG13—application for order(s) on conviction • MG15—interview record (only to be compiled in serious and complex cases) • MG16—Evidence of bad character and/or dangerous offender information • MG17—POCA review • MG18—offences taken into consideration (TIC) • MG19—compensation claim

13.24.3 Contested and indictable only cases

3A—Upgraded file

Magistrates' court trial or committal or sending to Crown Court for trial

In addition to the post-charge national file standard, the file must include:

- MG6C—schedule of non-sensitive unused material
- MG6D—schedule of sensitive material
- MG6E—disclosure officer's report

If applicable include:

- MG2—special measures assessment
- MG6B—police officers' disciplinary record
- MG11—other relevant key witnesses
- MG12—exhibits list
- MG15—interview record (only to be supplied when relied upon and a summary on an MG5 is considered insufficient for trial)
- MG19—compensation form plus supporting documents
- MG21/21A—forensic submissions

Plus, for Crown Court trial:

- MG11—all statements including corroboration, continuity etc.
- MG15—interview record

13.25 Case Building Evidential Points

13.25.1 Identification evidence

Where a suspect's identity is disputed, sufficient evidence to prove this is an evidential requirement of the prosecution case. Although a suspect maintaining silence during an interview does not challenge involvement in an offence, it does necessarily remove the need for proper identification by the investigation when this is not admitted.

Each case needs to be considered on its own merits. The strength of witness testimony or CCTV evidence regarding the identification of an offender when considered against their silence or no comment replies will assist with deciding whether identity procedures are necessary.

The risk of a witness making an honest but mistaken visual identification of a suspect is well established. When conducting witness interviews, investigators should ensure that the elements of the ADVOKATE mnemonic (see Chapter 8), commonly known as the Turnbull points[6] are covered, as these are required for the court to assess the quality and reliability of a witness identification.

Additional enquiries may also be required at the location where the witness made their identification to establish if the circumstances were as they described.

When a jury are considering the testimony of a witness who purports to be able to identify a defendant, it is necessary for the trial judge to give them a Turnbull warning about the identification points. This does not apply where the witness evidence in question is *description* evidence rather than *identification* evidence. An example of this situation would be where a witness can describe an offender's clothes but expressly states they would not be able to recognise the person wearing them. On this point, the Court of Appeal stated in the case of R v Gayle[7] that there is a:

[6] *R v Turnbull and Camelo* (1976) 3 All ER 54.

[7] *R v Gayle* (1999) 2 Cr App R 130, 135.

> … qualitative difference between identification evidence and what the judge (in the original trial) called 'evidence of description'. The special need for caution before conviction on identification evidence is because, as experience has often shown, it is possible for an honest witness to make a mistaken identification. But the danger of an honest witness being mistaken as to distinctive clothing, or the general description of the person he saw are minimal. So, the jury can concentrate on the honesty of the witness in the normal way.

For the same reasons therefore, under Code D of PACE 1984, the police are not under a duty to hold a formal identification procedure unless:

- an eyewitness has identified a suspect, or purported to have identified them
- there is an eyewitness available who expresses an ability to identify the suspect
- there is a reasonable chance of an eyewitness being able to identify the suspect

Investigators in consultation with prosecutors should ensure that identity procedures as required by Code D of PACE are conducted when they are necessary and justified. Full reasons for considering and requesting identification procedures should be recorded on the form MG3 including details of the issues in dispute.

13.25.2 Cases involving the forensic identification of a suspect

Where cases involve the forensic identification of a person, such as comparison of DNA, fingerprint or other forensic material, confirmation of the identification by an expert's witness testimony, accompanied by other supporting evidence, is sufficient to meet the threshold test for charging purposes, and for the initial magistrates' court appearance.

Preliminary information regarding fingerprints must include the location they were found and their position. Details of other lifts taken, whether they have been identified and, if so, whether that person has been eliminated from the investigation should also be included. A comprehensive evidential statement (as opposed to a preliminary abridged report) is only required if the matter proceeds to trial and aspects of the preliminary report are challenged by the defence.

13.25.3 Cases involving identification of controlled substances

In offences where a controlled substance has been identified by using a drug testing kit (or in the case of cannabis by an experienced trained identification officer), further scientific evidence is usually only required in straightforward possession cases if the identification is challenged. The equipment used should be mentioned in the case summary.

13.25.4 Dealing with medical evidence

In most cases involving minor assaults, such as common assault or assault occasioning actual bodily harm (AOABH), which are suitable for sentencing in the magistrates' court, evidence of a medical practitioner is not usually required. A medical statement will be required in cases of AOABH where the injuries can only be proved through the interpretation of medical records or X-rays by a medical practitioner, and the defendant did not accept the nature and extent of the injuries caused when interviewed under caution.

Reliable eyewitness evidence or good quality photographs or a body worn video recording accompanied by a description of the injuries can suffice for other summary hearing assault cases. However, if the victim has sought medical attention, this must be brought to the attention of the prosecutor.

13.26 Summaries of Audio/Visually Recorded Material

Generally, when making charging decisions, there is no substitute for the prosecutor viewing recordings such as CCTV, body worn video (BWV) or photographs. The prosecutor may consider accepting an accurate summary of what can be seen on the recording if viewing is not practicable, perhaps due to technical limitations, providing:

- the summary is a factual account provided by an officer who has viewed the recorded material
- the images displayed are of sufficient quality to clearly identify the suspect
- where practicable the material was shown to the suspect during interview and their response recorded

The prosecutor must then exercise judgement, considering:

- Does the recorded material provide a continuous account of the alleged offence, taking into account any witness statements provided?
- Is the recorded material consistent with other available evidence?
- Has the suspect put forward a defence which requires interpretation of the recorded material?
- Has the suspect put forward a defence including actions that are not referred to in the summary?

A summary will not be accepted by the prosecutor if they conclude that they must view the material before making a decision. A summary should be provided in report form on the form MG3 or on a separate report attached to it and should contain:

- a clear factual account of what can be observed
- the actions of the suspect
- the actions of others present

- clear descriptions of the suspect, including their clothing
- a clear reference point for the start and end of the relevant parts
- an indication of other parts of the recorded material that have been viewed

13.27 Prepared Statements During Interviews Under Caution

Prepared statements produced by suspects during an interview under caution should be referred to in the case summary (MG5). A copy should be retained and listed as unused material for the purposes of cross-examination in court should an alternative explanation be offered during trial.[8] The content of any prepared statement should also be included in the record of the interview under caution and should be assessed for any potential to draw adverse inferences.

13.28 Evidence of Bad Character

Investigating and presenting the bad character evidence of a suspect or defendant is a relevant line of enquiry that should be considered for all investigations. In some cases this could be the difference between a suspect being charged with an offence or a defendant being convicted. A more detailed discussion regarding evidence of bad character is included in Chapter 10 in the context of rape and serious sexual offences so is not repeated here. It is also outlined in Chapter 9 regarding managing suspects.

[8] Dealing with prepared statements during interview is described in Chapter 9.

13.29 Youth Offenders

In all cases involving youths[9] prosecutors must consider that the United Kingdom is a signatory to the United Nations 1989 Convention on the Rights of the Child, and the United Nations 1985 Standard Minimum Rules for the Administration of Juvenile Justice. They must have regard to the principal aim of the youth justice system, which is to prevent offending by children and young people and must consider the interests of the youth when deciding whether it is in the public interest to prosecute. Prosecutors, however, should not avoid a decision to prosecute simply because of the suspect's age. The seriousness of the offence or the youth's past behaviour are relevant.

Cases involving youths are usually only referred to the CPS if the person has already received a reprimand and final warning (these are the same as simple cautions, just using different terminology). The public interest will usually require a prosecution in such cases because the commission of a further offence may indicate that these previous disposals have been ineffective in preventing reoffending.

13.30 Reconsidering a Prosecution Decision

Occasionally, particularly in serious cases, there are special reasons that permit the CPS to revisit and overturn a decision not to prosecute, or having dealt with the case by an out-of-court disposal, allow the restart of a prosecution. These reasons include:

- rare cases where a review of the original decision not to prosecute concludes it was wrong, and to maintain

[9] For the purposes of the criminal law a youth is a person under 18 years of age.

confidence in the criminal justice system, a prosecution should be brought despite the earlier decision

- cases which are stopped so that more evidence, which is likely to become available in the fairly near future, can be collected and prepared. In these cases, the prosecutor will tell the defendant that the prosecution may be restarted
- cases involving a death in which a review following the findings of a coroner's inquest concludes that a prosecution ought to be brought, notwithstanding any earlier decision not to prosecute

There may also be exceptional cases where, following an acquittal for certain serious offences, a prosecutor may, based on new and compelling evidence, and with the written consent of the DPP, apply to the Court of Appeal for an order quashing the acquittal and requiring the defendant to be retried. These are often referred to as double jeopardy prosecutions.

13.31 **Prosecution/CPS Appeals**

The CPS may consider exercising a right of appeal, which is available when it is believed the court has made a wrong legal decision. The prosecution has limited rights of appeal and can consider appealing court decisions in the following circumstances:

- immediately, in serious cases where magistrates grant bail and it is considered the defendant should be remanded in custody pending reconsideration of the bail decision by a Crown Court judge
- within 24 hours, with the approval of a Chief Crown Prosecutor or Head of the relevant Headquarters Division (CPS), where a judge stops a case before a jury is allowed to consider the evidence. This is so the decision can be reconsidered by the Court of Appeal as soon as possible

- in a limited range of cases, where a sentence is considered to be unduly lenient, the Attorney General can be requested to refer the sentence to the Court of Appeal. Members of the public, victims and their families can also submit cases which they consider to have unduly lenient sentences for consideration of appeal by the Attorney General using an online process. Strict time periods apply to such appeals.

Other forms of appeal may be considered where it is believed the court has not followed procedure correctly, may have made a decision that is very seriously wrong or the law needs clarifying by a higher court.

If a defendant appeals against a decision of the court, the CPS instructs an advocate to represent them or assist the court, except in appeals against sentence in the Court of Appeal when the CPS could appear itself if there is a compelling reason to do so.

A Court of Appeal decision may be appealed further by the CPS if the Court of Appeal upon request certifies there is a point of law which is of general public importance in the case that should be decided by the Supreme Court. The CPS should keep victims informed of the progress of any appeal (often facilitated with the investigator) and explain the effect of the court's decision to them.

13.32 Managing Disclosure

It is a fundamental principle of the legal system that every accused person has a right to a fair trial. The disclosure process secures the right to a fair trial and in criminal investigations is a responsibility under the Criminal Procedure and Investigations Act 1996 (CPIA), as amended by the Criminal Justice Act 2003.

Statutory requirements are set out in the Code of Practice under Part II of the Act and the CPIA Codes of Practice were revised in 2020. An updated set of Attorney

Generals Guidelines for investigators, prosecutors and defence practitioners also came into force on 31 December 2020 (AG6).

Despite the CPIA and the corresponding disclosure obligations being in place for some 25 years, some police investigations continue to experience difficulties managing disclosure effectively. Errors have been made concerning disclosure leading to potential miscarriages of justice and cases being dismissed, including in several high-profile prosecutions.

It is evident that managing the prevalence and sheer volume of digital and communications data which is routinely generated by contemporary investigations is causing difficulty in the context of disclosure. This has proved particularly challenging with investigations into sexual offences.

Identifying, recovering and analysing the communications records on victims' mobile phones is often a relevant line of enquiry, particularly where consent to the sexual act is the matter in issue between the parties. Despite the sensitivities involved, the police are duty bound under CPIA to address and investigate this depending on the circumstances of the individual case.

The current challenges are reflected in the number of initiatives and updated guidance and policy that has been published since 2018, including:

- *Joint National Disclosure Improvement Plan* (CPS 2018)
- *A Review of the Efficiency and Effectiveness of Disclosure in the Criminal Justice System* (Attorney General's Office 2018)
- *Disclosure Manual* (CPS 2018)
- *Criminal Procedure Investigations Act Codes of Practice* (Ministry of Justice 2020)
- *Attorney Generals Guidelines on Disclosure* (Attorney General's Office 2020)

The CPIA applies to criminal investigations in England and Wales conducted by police officers, which began on or after the day that the Act came into effect on 1 April 1997. Investigations that commenced before this date fall under the previous Common Law Disclosure Rules, which is important because it could apply to cold case historical or non-recent investigations that are re-opened for further investigation. The further investigation could be instigated due to scientific developments or new information that opens new lines of enquiry which lead to a prosecution or consideration of a prosecution. Nevertheless, technically, the investigation commenced before 1 April 1997.

The process of managing disclosure differs between police forces. Some forces have criminal justice units or file build teams which deal with disclosure in all cases freeing investigators to concentrate on other duties. In other forces, individual officers manage their own disclosure without assistance from dedicated teams. Major Investigation Teams tend to have specialist disclosure officers embedded in them.

No matter how disclosure is managed in their respective police force or organisation, all investigators are advised to ensure they are fully conversant with their disclosure responsibilities and procedures. The code of practice states that as soon as a criminal investigation starts the following roles should be designated:

- Investigator
- Officer in Charge of the Investigation
- Disclosure Officer

An investigator is any police officer (or staff) involved in the conduct of a criminal investigation. All investigators have a responsibility for carrying out the duties imposed on them under the code. These are:

- to pursue ALL reasonable lines of enquiry, whether these point towards or away from a suspect
- to record information and retain records of information and other material

The officer in charge of an investigation is the police officer responsible for directing a criminal investigation. They are also responsible for ensuring that proper procedures are in place for recording information and retaining records of information and other material in the investigation.

The Disclosure Officer is the person responsible for examining material retained by the police during the investigation; revealing material to the prosecutor during the investigation and any criminal proceedings resulting from it and certifying that they have done this; and disclosing material to the accused at the request of the prosecutor. The prosecutor is the authority responsible for the conduct, on behalf of the Crown, of criminal proceedings resulting from a specific criminal investigation.

Material takes on its normal meaning as far as investigation is concerned and is material of any kind, including information and objects, which is obtained during a criminal investigation. This includes not only material coming into the possession of the investigator (such as documents seized while searching premises) but also material generated and produced by the investigation (such as interview plans and notes).

Material may be *relevant to an investigation* if it appears to an investigator, or to the officer in charge of an investigation, or to the disclosure officer, that it has some bearing on any offence under investigation or any person being investigated, or on the surrounding circumstances of the case, unless it is incapable of having any impact on the case. When assessing and reviewing material cognizance needs to be taken on whether the material is 'non sensitive' or 'sensitive'.

A fair trial does not require consideration of material that is not relevant, and the disclosure regime does not require irrelevant material to be obtained or reviewed.

KEY POINTS

- The most basic approach to managing criminal disclosure uses the four R's principle of retain, record, review and reveal.

Retain
Record
Review
Reveal

- It is important that all investigators adopt a thinking approach and consider the disclosure responsibilities from the outset of the investigation. It is generally more difficult to back track disclosure if it is left to the charging phase or when it seems likely that a suspect might be prosecuted.
- Adopting a thinking approach to disclosure from the beginning of the investigation, particularly in high volume and complex cases greatly assists managing the process. The disclosure function is not merely a scheduling exercise, it requires judgement and careful consideration. This is required to identify the issues in the case and to develop a proper understanding of the material. It includes considering on an individual basis, what is relevant and meets the disclosure test from the wider investigative material that has been obtained.
- The Code for Crown Prosecutors (CPS 2018) now states that in certain cases disclosure will be required to have been completed for a charging decision to be made. Such requirements for investigations are becoming increasingly frequent.

The process of 'revealing 'the existence of relevant unused material to the CPS is managed by using a series of standardised MG forms.

13.32.1 None—sensitive schedule (MG6C)

This is basically the default schedule for most cases, and it should contain the descriptions of all relevant material in the case unless that material is sensitive in which case it should be scheduled on a form MG6D.

If an item contains sensitive personal information such as names, addresses and telephone numbers but would otherwise be non-sensitive, the personal details can be redacted. A note should be made on the items entry that the material has been edited to omit sensitive information.

The MGC schedule will be copied by the CPS and supplied to the defence. The descriptions of the material on an MG6C need to be accurate and contain sufficient detail to enable a properly informed review of the item to take place.

13.32.2 **Sensitive material schedule (MG6D)**

The MG6D schedule should only contain material deemed to be sensitive by which it is not in the public interest to disclose it to the defence. The disclosure officer must be able to show that disclosing this material would give rise to 'a real risk of serious prejudice to an important public interest'. Each item must be considered and justified on its own merits.

The three most significant public interests that might apply to police investigations are:

- the ability of law enforcement agencies to fight crime by the use of covert surveillance tactics and techniques (CHIS) and undercover operations etc
- the protection of secret methods of detecting and fighting crime
- the willingness of citizens, agencies, commercial institutions, communications service suppliers, etc to provide information to the authorities in circumstances where there may be some legitimate expectation of confidentiality

The default position is that material is non-sensitive unless the disclosure officer decides that it fulfils one or more of the criteria that requires it to be deemed as sensitive.

This decision needs to be made at an early stage to ensure that the material is listed on the correct schedule. Wrongly scheduling sensitive material on a non-sensitive form MG6C is a serious error and must be avoided. Such a mistake could have significant consequences because unlike the MG6D, the MG6C is supplied to the defence who would then be aware of the presence of sensitive material.

Some material, especially documents, may contain a mixture of non-sensitive and sensitive material which adds another layer of complexity. It may be that careful redaction is required, which will need to be justified, or perhaps a lengthy document dealt with as a series of pieces of separate items of material to properly manage the sensitive and non-sensitive aspects.

A situation frequently encountered is where material that would not otherwise be treated as sensitive, such as incident logs, officers' notes and recordings of interviews, contains personal sensitive information such as a witness's address, place of work or phone number. For non-sensitive material such as this, which contains personal information, if the decision is that it falls to be disclosed because it could undermine the prosecution case or assist the defence, the sensitive personal information can be redacted. The fact that personal information has been redacted should be reflected on the items description on the relevant disclosure schedule.

13.32.3 Highly sensitive material/CHIS material (MG6D)

Mainstream investigators are unlikely to be required to perform the disclosure function for highly sensitive and CHIS material, which for all intents and purposes is a type of sensitive material. For information, highly sensitive information is that which, should it be compromised, would lead directly to loss of life or threaten national security.

The procedure for dealing with CHIS material and whether it is to be treated as highly sensitive or sensitive can vary between police forces. If this situation arises, investigators should ensure they adhere to their local policies and procedure.

13.32.4 Disclosure Officers Report (MG6E)

Entries on an MG6E should have already appeared in either the MG6C or the MG6D schedules. The Disclosure Officers Report (MG6E) refers to this material because in the view of the disclosure officer it could either undermine the prosecution case or assist the defence. The reasons for this assessment are explained on the form and the record is cross-referenced to the item number as recorded on the MG6C or the MG6D, which contains the description of the material.

The form MG6E is not supplied to the defence, and the material referred to in it should be copied and provided to the CPS. This includes anything that could cast doubt on the reliability of a confession or the reliability of a witness. This also includes anything which has been provided by an accused that amounts to an explanation for the offence. It is more likely, however, that any explanation from an accused will form part of the prosecution case, so would be evidence and not unused material.

Behind what, on the surface, appears to be a relatively straightforward process are several potentially difficult decisions that need to be made, including what constitutes a reasonable line of enquiry and what material is relevant for example, which will depend on the specific circumstances of the case.

Relevant lines of enquiry should be documented and explained by the lead investigator in a decision log or policy entry. The requirement of the CPIA includes keeping a record of the conduct of the investigation, so maintaining decision logs is important.

A full log of disclosure decisions and the reasons for those decisions must be kept on file and made available to the prosecution team. This requirement is fulfilled through proper completion of the forms MG6C, MG6D and MG6E.

13.32.5 Investigation Management Document

Following the revised CPIA Codes of Practice 2020 and the updated Attorney Generals Guidelines on Disclosure 2020, since 31 January 2020 there has also been a requirement to complete an Investigation Management Document. In effect, this is a decision log in which a variety of information is recorded that is relevant to disclosure. It includes, for example, parameters on searching and reviewing mobile communications devices, amongst other matters.

It is essential that all investigators apply a thinking approach to determine what the relevant issues in the specific case are, and these decisions are carefully documented using the MG6C, MG6D and MG6E forms together with the Investigation Management Document. There needs to be an accurate audit trail of the decisions taken which contains sufficient detail to enable others involved in the process to fulfil their disclosure responsibilities.

Any prosecutor must be able to see and understand previous disclosure decisions before carrying out their continuous review. Investigators and prosecutors have a professional responsibility to do all they can to facilitate proper disclosure. This requirement could identify some further reasonable lines of enquiry, including pursuing enquiries that may lead away from a suspect.

The challenge is to anticipate what might be reasonable and relevant, particularly if the suspect themselves has not provided any information at that stage, for example if they decline to answer questions during their interview under caution.

13.32.6 Disclosure Management Document

The production of a Disclosure Management Document (DMD) is mandatory for serious and complex cases. This document is prepared by the CPS, and it describes the process by which disclosure in the case is being managed. It is likely that in some cases the CPS will ask for assistance from the police investigator and/or the Disclosure Officer to assist with preparing the DMD.

13.32.7 Disclosure test

The CPS will supply the defence with a copy of the MG6 which contains the descriptions of non-sensitive material. This does not fulfil the prosecution's disclosure responsibilities and does not count as disclosure; it basically reveals the existence of the material. Assessing the material for anything which falls to be disclosed to the defence is the most significant element of the process and requires careful consideration.

At this stage, the decision will be based on the description of the material recorded on the relevant MG6C or MG6D schedule. The importance of descriptions on schedules being accurate and containing sufficient detail on which to inform a prosecution and defence decision cannot be overemphasised.

At this stage, it does not matter whether the material is non-sensitive, sensitive or highly sensitive. The only concern is whether the material falls to be disclosed (provided) to the defence and is identified to the CPS using a disclosure officers report (MG6E). No actual material will be supplied to the defence as this is a decision for the CPS reviewing lawyer.

Whilst all decisions taken during the disclosure management process are important, this is perhaps the most significant. Failure to disclose material that the defence are entitled to receive continues to be a recurring issue; it is central to virtually all case law regarding disclosure.

The disclosure test was amended in 2005 by the Criminal Justice Act 2003. A single disclosure test was created by merging what was previously termed as 'primary disclosure' (material undermining the prosecution case) and 'secondary disclosure' (assists the defence).

The challenge of applying this test to the unused material obtained during the investigation is remaining objective when critically evaluating any weaknesses in the prosecution case. It is necessary to adopt a defence attitude and critically review the material with an unbiased mindset to successfully perform the function.

A 'thinking approach' is required in which each case is dealt with on its own merits with its own considerations. The process is not about listing material on schedules; these are essentially the means to perform the function. The key function is conducting the relevancy test. The following are some examples to consider (but this is not an exhaustive list):

- any material casting doubt upon the accuracy of any prosecution evidence
- any material which may point to another person, whether charged or not having involvement in the commission of the offence
- any material which may cast doubt upon the reliability of a confession
- any material which might go to the credibility of a prosecution witness
- any material that might support a defence that is either raised by the defence or is apparent from the prosecution papers
- any material which may have a bearing on the admissibility of any prosecution evidence

13.32.8 **Public interest immunity**

In principle, Public Interest Immunity (PII) is where in certain circumstances it is in the greater public interest that material, which is required to be disclosed in law, is nevertheless not disclosed to the defence. In these circumstances a PII application is made by the CPS to a judge who will decide whether there is a greater public good (interest) not to disclose.

A PII application is rarely encountered by mainstream investigators so is not expanded upon for the purpose of this handbook. The decision to make such an application will be taken by a senior CPS lawyer and a Detective Chief Inspector or a designated Detective Inspector but there are regional variations on this policy.

It is a common misconception that, in any case involving sensitive material a PII application is made to protect it. This is not the case, as a PII consideration only arises when sensitive material falls to be disclosed because it meets the relevancy test. In such a situation, if disclosure cannot be facilitated in any other way without disclosing the actual material, a judge will resolve the issue of whether there is a public interest conflict. In the worst-case scenario this could involve a decision whether to discontinue the case.

13.32.9 Attorney Generals Guidelines 2020

The Attorney Generals Guidelines 2020 replaced the existing Attorney Generals Guidelines on Disclosure that were issued in 2013 and the Supplementary Guidelines on Digital Material that were also issued in 2013. The current guidelines contain five important principles for regarding the disclosure process with judicial oversight:

- **Investigators**—pursue all reasonable lines of enquiry and keep a record of all material relevant to the case, including that which will not be used as evidence in the prosecution case. Investigators prepare disclosure schedules for review by the prosecution. Investigators must be fair and objective and must work together with prosecutors to ensure that disclosure obligations are met. They should be familiar with the CPIA Code of practice.
- **Prosecution**—engage with the investigators and advise on reasonable lines of enquiry. Ensure investigators provide disclosure schedules and review them. Apply the test for disclosure set out in CPIA 1996.
- **Defence**—engage with the prosecution (including pre-charge where appropriate). Serve a defence statement setting out the nature of the defence and request

any material which could reasonably assist their case. Participate in the process for completing a disclosure management document.

- **Prosecution advocates**—review schedules and disclosed material, advise the prosecution where advice is sought and at any rate where deficiencies in disclosure is apparent.
- **Ongoing evaluation**—disclosure is subject to continuous review throughout the lifetime of a case. All parties should reassess as new information or material becomes available and the case progresses.

13.33 Examining Digital Communications Devices

It is now well established that digital communications devices feature to a greater or lesser extent in most criminal investigations. The data storage capacity in such devices goes beyond what could have been envisaged when the CPIA 1996 was drafted.

Mobile devices differ between manufacturers and models, and operating systems and their capabilities change and develop over relatively short periods of time. Material on these devices includes communications data, internet uses, photographs, video, access to various social media platforms and cloud-based storage.

Data can be deleted but may still be recoverable depending on the device and the technical capability of the examination. When the privacy and collateral intrusion issues of examining a device are added to the volume of data and technical issues including encryption and servers located abroad, the decisions around managing extraction from a digital device and the disclosure process are significant.

The CPS guidance *Disclosure—A Guide to 'Reasonable Lines of Enquiry' and Communications Evidence* (2018), acknowledges that it is not possible to obtain and examine every artefact or item of digital evidence from a device for analysis in every situation. There are constraints to the extent and depth of an examination in the circumstances of each case. It is critical that the investigator and the prosecutor are aware of the investigative and evidential opportunities that a digital device may offer.

Equally relevant is understanding the limitations and boundaries of an examination. This includes the implications of deciding to use one method of examination over another if further work is required in the future. Technical capabilities and capacity vary across police forces, but essentially there are three levels of data extraction of mobile devices:

- **Level 1**—using digital forensic kiosks for configured local extraction.

This self-service equipment is based within police premises. Individual force policy will determine the level of authorisation required but this is usually at inspector level. Officers who operate the equipment need to be trained and competent to follow the equipment's preconfigured workflow.

A Level 1 mobile device examination provides a 'logical' extraction of live data that is readily available on the device. This is likely to be the data that would be seen if the device was switched on and could be browsed through. A logical extraction will extract the live data that is supported by the extraction software. This can vary depending on the handset, the operating system and the types of applications. It will not usually extract deleted material and might not extract all of the data present.

- **Level 2**—logical and physical extraction using digital forensic hubs, laboratories or forensic service providers.

This can be either a logical extraction conducted in a laboratory rather than a digital forensic kiosk or a physical extraction using laboratory tools. Physical downloads can recover data from the memory chip of the device.

Depending on the nature of the device, the operating system, the applications and whether they are supported by extraction software, a physical download can extract deleted material.

- **Level 3**—specialist extractions and examinations by central digital forensics laboratories or forensic service providers.

These use expert and bespoke methods to tackle complex examinations or damaged devices.

When developing a digital strategy, investigators should avoid using terms such as 'full extraction', or 'full download'. Decisions on the requirements of the examination need to be focused and precise with clearly defined parameters to prevent the instructions and agreed methods being misinterpreted (this is discussed further in Chapter 10).

13.34 **Principles for Investigation and Disclosure**

Communications between suspects, complainants, witnesses and others can be important investigative and evidential material. The relevance of the communication for investigation and disclosure purposes will depend on how its context is be applied to the circumstances of the matter under investigation. This includes considering any communication that is relevant to a matter in issue between the defence and the prosecution.

Developing a line of enquiry for digital communications is not confined to simply identifying the content of messages on a digital device, albeit this could be important. The objectives and parameters of the examination should in the first instance be developed to support what the line of enquiry is seeking to prove through examination of the device (including considering the 'for and away' rule).

An investigative mindset should be applied and the 5WH questions asked. The following questions are not exhaustive and are only illustrative of the type of questions to consider when developing a strategy for examining a digital communications device:

- Who was communicating with who?
- What was the investigative context of the outgoing communication?
  - o suspect to another identified suspect?
  - o suspect to an unidentified suspect?
  - o suspect to a witness?
  - o suspect to a victim?
  - o suspect to another identified person who is known, and who is relevant to the investigation?
  - o suspect to another identified person who is known, but is not apparently relevant to the investigation?
  - o suspect to an unidentified person who is relevant to the investigation?
  - o suspect to an unidentified person who is apparently not relevant to the investigation?
  - o suspect to another unidentified person who is relevant to the investigation?
  - o victim to another identified victim?
  - o victim to an unidentified potential victim?
  - o victim to an identified witness?
  - o victim to a potential unidentified witness?
  - o witness who known to the investigation to a suspect?
  - o witness who is unknown to a suspect?
  - o witness to a victim?
  - o witness to another identified witness?
  - o witness to a potential witness who is unidentified?
- Who initiated the communication?
- What time was the communication?
- What is the relevance of this time to the time parameters under investigation?
- What was the content of the communication?
- Were any images included in the communication?

- Was the offence or matter under investigation included in the content of the communication
- Were there any follow up messages as a result of this communication?
- Who was the next person to be communicated with (they could potentially be more significant than later contact)?
- Can the device and the communication be attributed to the individual concerned?

It is the investigator's decision to determine what devices to examine and the extent of the examination to be conducted. This could include text messages, WhatsApp and similar messaging platforms, call data, emails and social media communications such as Facebook, Instagram and Tik Tok.

Examination of mobile devices is not a requirement as a matter of course in every case. There will be cases where it is not necessary for the police to examine the media devices of a complainant or others. For example, it is unlikely to be necessary and justified in an opportunist stranger sexual assault where the victim has no previous knowledge of the offender.

The March 2015 edition of the Code of Practice issued under the CPIA (section 23(1)) sets out the position, which is useful when formulating and documenting such decisions. In particular, paragraph 3.4 states:

> In conducting an investigation, the investigator should pursue all reasonable lines of enquiry, whether these point towards or away from the suspect. What is reasonable in each case will depend on the circumstances. For example, where material is held on computer, it is a matter for the investigator to decide which material on the computer it is reasonable to inquire into, and in what manner.

In cases such as rape and sexual assaults (but equally other offences), where the parties involved are known to each other, particularly if this is only for a short period of time, a Level 1 search could be considered. This would arguably be justified and proportionate where there is no objective reason to consider that their communications will be important to the investigation, but nevertheless there is the possibility that they could be relevant. In these circumstances a Level 1 examination is a reasonable first stage. If relevant material is found or the examination reveals another reason to justify a more detailed examination, this could be considered.

Furthermore, evaluating the wider investigative material gathered or generated by the investigation has the potential to identify the necessity for a deeper examination of a device. This could include, for example, accounts obtained from witness or suspect interviews which indicate the use of the device. Reviewing CCTV recordings could identify a suspect, victim, witness or other person using a phone in circumstances which are not consistent with their accounts or the product of a Level 1 search. This might be an indication that messages have been deleted from the device and therefore be justification for a deeper search.

A post-charge necessity to further examine a device would be if the content of a defence statement from an accused indicated that a further or deeper examination of a device was required. In this situation, the CPIA 'for or away' rule applies, and the further investigation should be conducted.

In these circumstances it is likely the accused has failed to account for any relevant material when they were interviewed before charge. If an account or explanation had been provided the examination should already have been conducted. In this situation the potential for developing an application for an adverse inference direction in court should not be overlooked.

It is prudent to retain a complainant's phone until the accused has been interviewed under caution and has been given the opportunity to comment on the allegation. Regardless of whether the suspect answered questions during interview or whether they did not, their use of mobile devices during the relevant timeframes for the investigation should have been explored.

The precautionary retention of a complainant's phone will depend on the circumstances of the case. There may be cases where delaying the return of a phone would be disproportionate, but this consideration should be approached with caution. The benefit of doubt ought to favour retaining the phone until a more informed decision can be made about the necessity to retain and examine it further.

KEY POINT

The decision to retain a phone and the impact of this on the phone's owner should not be underestimated, particularly when the person is a victim or witness in the case. People's phones contain information and contact information that is essential to conducting their lives and business.

Investigations will also be encountered where it is necessary to conduct a Level 2 or a Level 3 examination of a mobile device from the outset. It is likely that this level of search will be required in all cases where electronic means are used to commit the offence, for example possession of indecent images or communicating with a child for a sexual purpose.

Similarly a Level 2 or Level 3 examination will also be necessary where the issue of consent to any sexual activity is a relevant issue between the complainant and the accused. Beyond any issue about consent, there will also be a case for deeper examination where the credibility of the complainant or reliability of the complaint is put in issue from the outset and in circumstances which necessitate a detailed examination of the complainant's phone. This information will be required before a decision can be made whether the case meets the threshold requirements for potential prosecution. If the police decision maker believes the Threshold Test has been met, the CPS will require this information before making a prosecution decision.

The decision on the level of examination should be taken on a case-by-case basis by evaluating the wider investigative material. This would include where the necessary grounds for exploring the history of contact between a complainant and accused, has been obtained from their interviews. Developing this further, it may also be necessary to investigate any contact either of the parties has made with others.

The level of intrusion for the owner of the device is potentially extensive and requires careful consideration and management, particularly when it concerns the device of a victim or a witness. It has been reported by some victims that the intrusive examination of their phone felt like another violation, which has been likened to a digital strip search.

For most people, their mobile devices are essential for conducting everyday life and business. In addition to communications data and social networking, they contain contact names and numbers, diaries and appointments, banking and financial access and perhaps authentication and secondary security applications which are needed to access cloud-based sites. This is particularly important when a device is used for business as the person may be unable to function effectively without it. Investigators should make every effort to explain the necessity for the examination where one is to be conducted, and the parameters.

KEY POINT

It may be necessary to provide a victim of domestic abuse with an alternative temporary mobile phone whilst their device is being examined. This is to mitigate the person being put at additional risk by the investigation by being left without the means to communicate in an emergency should they need to.

13.35 Analysis and Evaluation of Material

The investigator needs to set parameters for examining the product of the download obtained from a mobile device.

This is a requirement in an Investigation Management Document (IMD) but in any case should be documented in the investigative strategy and associated decision logs.

Due to the volume of data that can be contained in a digital device it will be necessary to identify and set the relevant time parameters for analysis within the recovered material. This timeframe needs to be informed by the facts of the individual case and might consider, for example, the date the complainant and the suspect met and include up until the point of arrest of the accused, and the recovery of the phones by the police.

A wider timeframe could be considered depending on the circumstances of the first contact between the complainant and the suspect. If the meeting was initiated online, perhaps through mutual use of a dating site, the relevant parameters could justifiably be expanded. This would take account of any potentially predatory behaviour by the suspect before the current allegation, and perhaps establish a pattern of behaviour and other offending.

As with all communication material, the investigator must be able to explain the approach to the examination to the defence and justify the actions in court if called upon to do so. This includes explaining what might not have been done and the reasons why, as well as explaining what examination was conducted.

What represents a reasonable line of enquiry is an investigative matter for the police, but the Attorney Generals Guidelines (2020) encourages early dialogue with the defence. This includes pre-charge engagement where the defence may be invited to suggest further lines of enquiry. Depending on the matter in issue, this could include requesting the examination, or further examination of a mobile device.

The Attorney Generals Guidelines (2020) provides assistance on what may amount to a reasonable line of enquiry. CPS prosecutors should help investigators when deciding what a reasonable line of enquiry is, but this does not absolve investigators of their responsibilities in this area. Ideally the police and the prosecutor should agree.

As has always been the position, if the investigation identifies communications material which supports the prosecution case it will form part of the case papers as evidential material. In all bail cases, the prosecutor must be able to assess the potential impact of communication material before making a charging decision.

From a case management and disclosure perspective, investigators are required to provide any material that undermines the prosecution case or assists the defence prior to charge and this includes communications evidence. Prosecutors should not make a charging decision until this has been provided. Inevitably this will lead to delays in prosecution decisions being made, particularly if a Level 2 or Level 3 examination is involved.

In the interim period before a prosecution threshold decision is made, it will be necessary to identify and consider any safeguarding issues. Risk assessments will need to be completed and any mitigating measures and tactics implemented for this period for suspects released under investigation or on bail. Risk assessments should be continually reviewed but will definitely need detailed reconsideration when the results of the digital device examination are known and can be assessed.

Any safeguarding, risk assessment and mitigation measures should consider the risk the suspect presents to:

- the victim
- any other identified individual
- any individual relevant to the investigation but whose identity is not known
- the public at large
- the suspect themselves, particularly for investigations involving possession or distribution of indecent images. Depending on the suspect involved and their family and relationship dynamics, they could involve an elevated risk of potential suicide.

Similarly, safeguarding implications should also be considered for complainants who could be impacted by the results of the digital device examination. This is particularly important if no prosecution is pursued as a result of the examination because material recovered from their device is considered to undermine a potential prosecution case.

References

Attorney General's Office (2018) *A Review of the Efficiency and Effectiveness of Disclosure in the Criminal Justice System* (HM Government)

Attorney General's Office (2020) *Attorney Generals Guidelines on Disclosure* (HM Government)

CPS (2018) *Code for Crown Prosecutors* (HM Government)

Ministry of Justice (2020) *Criminal Procedure and Investigations Act Codes of Practice* (HM Government)

Attorney Generals Office (2018) *Disclosure Manual* (HM Government)

CPS (2018) *Disclosure a Guide to 'Reasonable Lines of Enquiry' and Communications Evidence* (HM Government)

CPS, College of Policing, NPCC (2018) *Joint National Disclosure Improvement Plan* (HM Government)

Moreno Y and Hughes P (2008) *Effective Prosecution, Working in Partnership with the CPS* (OUP)

Chapter 14

Court Process and Giving Evidence

14.1 Introduction

Presenting evidence in court and giving witness testimony in the proceedings are usually the final elements of the case management phase of the investigation (Moreno and Hughes 2008). This is just as important as the earlier initial response and investigation phases and should be treated as such. Whilst recognising daily business continues for investigators, including responding to and investigating other crimes and incidents, it is nevertheless necessary to devote sufficient time to prepare for the impending court case.

Poor case presentation or a poor performance by an investigator when giving witness evidence in a court can be detrimental to the prosecution. The credibility of the investigator could be undermined or diminished in the eyes of the jury. The individual could suffer professional embarrassment and the organisation's reputation could be damaged. It should never be forgotten that poor performance lets down victims and could damage public confidence. Whilst it is acknowledged that investigators have multiple responsibilities and will likely be dealing with simultaneous investigations and enquiries, poor preparation leading to poor performance is rarely, if ever, treated sympathetically in court.

Blackstone's Crime Investigators' Handbook. Steve Hibbitt and Gary Shaw, Oxford University Press. © Oxford University Press 2023.
DOI: 10.1093/oso/9780192867896.003.0014

Investigators should present their evidence in a professional, confident, impartial and efficient manner. This helps to ensure that all of the good and extensive work conducted during the investigation up to this point is not undone.

KEY POINTS

- Investigators are encouraged to familiarise themselves with the rules of evidence for both the criminal and the coroners' courts. These rules are extensive and can be complex, and their interpretation is the subject of many legal arguments presented by lawyers in the various courts.
- When evaluating the potential evidential value of material gathered and generated during an investigation, a lack of knowledge is likely to impact on the effectiveness of an investigator's decision making. Investigators who do not have at least a basic knowledge of the rules of evidence for whatever type of court hearing they apply to are likely to find themselves at a disadvantage. There are differences in the rules for criminal and coronial investigations.
- As a starting point from which to develop knowledge, the relevant legislation to consider is the Criminal Procedure Rules and Practice Directions 2020, which consolidates the Criminal Procedure Rules 2015 and subsequent amendments.
- For inquests, the starting point to consider is the Coroners (Inquests) Rules 2013 and the Coroners and Justice Act 2009, which is up to date with all changes known to be in force on or before 29 October 2009. It should be noted that there are other changes which may be implemented in future.

14.2 Court Proceedings for Criminal Investigations

14.2.1 Summary offences

Summary offences are lesser offences that are generally only heard in a magistrate's court. The maximum sentence that a magistrate can impose for a summary offence is six months imprisonment. In January 2022, however, this was extended to 12 months as a temporary measure to try and address the backlog of cases awaiting a hearing as a consequence of the COVID 19 coronavirus pandemic.

In some limited circumstances, a summary offence may be heard in the Crown Court, for example where it is committed to the Crown Court for sentencing under the Power of Criminal Courts (Sentencing) Act 2000. This is because, for some convictions the magistrates do not believe their sentencing powers would be an adequate disposal.

A summary offence may also be tried in the crown court when it is to be heard on the back of an indictable or either way offence.

14.2.2 Either way offences

Crimes, which in ordinary circumstances can be tried in either the magistrates' court or the Crown Court are known as 'either way' offences. In accordance with the Magistrates Court Act 1980 (section 22), some 'either way' offences must be tried in the magistrates' court if the value involved makes them liable to be tried as summary offences.

14.2.3 Indictable offences

The more serious offences are 'indictable only' offences and these can only be tried in the Crown Court. The Crime and Disorder Act 1998 abolished the previous 'committal proceedings' for indictable only offences. Defendants appearing before a magistrates' court for the first time, charged with an indictable only offence, must therefore be sent immediately to the Crown Court.

14.2.4 Mode of trial hearing

In England and Wales, if a defendant pleads not guilty or they decline to state or enter a plea in relation to an 'either way' offence, a mode of trial hearing takes place. This decides if a case is to be heard in the magistrates' court or the Crown Court.

14.2.5 Guilty pleas

If a defendant pleads guilty to the offences charged, the case can be dealt with in the magistrates' court unless the sentence might require imposing more than six months imprisonment, or a total of more than 12 months imprisonment if more than one offence is involved. In such circumstances the defendant will be committed to the Crown Court for sentencing.

14.2.6 Not guilty pleas

When a defendant enters a plea of not guilty, the magistrates will consider the seriousness of the offence, the recommendations made by the prosecutor and the defence plus the defendants previous convictions, to decide on the mode of trial.

14.2.7 The indictment

In England and Wales the reviewing lawyer is responsible for preparing the draft indictment. In serious and complex cases however, counsel for the prosecution may be instructed to assist with this. An indictment must contain one or more counts which describe the offence in ordinary language and identifies the legislation it comes under. The particulars of the alleged conduct must make it clear what the prosecution alleges. Multiple counts must be numbered consecutively.

14.2.8 Plea and Trial Preparation Hearings

The Plea and Trial Preparation Hearing (PTPH) and the related procedures were introduced for all cases sent to the

Crown Court after 5 January 2016. They provide a single national process to be used in all Crown Courts. A PTPH takes place after the preliminary hearing and is usually held within 28 days of the case being sent to the Crown Court unless the resident judge orders otherwise.

By the time of the PTPH, the prosecution will have provided available information about the case and should have obtained the availability and non-availability information from the likely prosecution witnesses. At this time all of the information might not be available, for example the results of forensic examinations could be outstanding. If this is the case, it is important that the court is furnished with accurate timescales for the completion of these outstanding prosecution matters.

In all but the most complex cases this should be sufficient to enable the court to deal with the case management effectively. For more complex matters a Further Case Management Hearing (FCMH) may be necessary.

As part of the process, the CPS have to serve a disclosure management document (DMD) on the court in advance of the PTPH (Attorney General's Office 2020). The purpose of this is to clarify the prosecution's approach to disclosure, for example which search terms have been used when examining material from a digital device and the reasons for this. It is therefore essential that investigators ensure the CPS are supplied with the required information. This is intended to narrow the areas that are in dispute between the prosecution and the defence.

The PTPH presupposes that the prosecution and the defence will have communicated with eachother before the hearing and will continue to do so afterwards. This is in accordance with the duty of engagement required under Part 3 of the Criminal Procedure Rules.

The defendant should be arraigned at a PTPH unless there is good reason not to do so. Arraignment means the calling or bringing of a person before a court to answer a criminal charge. If a defendant pleads guilty, they should be sentenced on the day if possible, but delay may be necessary to enable the preparation of any pre-sentence reports if they have not previously been ordered and completed.

In the event of a defendant pleading not guilty, the court will:

- set the trial date
- identify the issues for trial so far as is possible at that stage
- consider the witness requirements that can be determined at that stage
- establish a timetable for the necessary pre-trial preparation and give appropriate direction to ensure an effective trial
- make provision for any FCMH that may be required at a time when it can be of maximum effectiveness.

Engagement between the parties to the case seeks to ensure that the elements of case management are achieved. An FCMH will only be needed in complex cases if the parties indicate that there is an issue that is preventing the arraignment of a defendant. In such situations, the court will issue directions to the parties involved. Examples might include ruling on a defence application to dismiss the case, or deciding about a defendants fitness to enter a plea in answer to the indictment where there is doubt about this.

14.2.9 **Digital Case System**

The documents relied upon in criminal cases will be loaded onto the Digital Case System (DCS) by the CPS on behalf of the prosecution and the other parties involved in relation to the defence. This includes material such as the indictment, witness statements, paper exhibits, the defence statement(s), applications made to the court and written directions and orders. The DCS is a court system and is not accessible to the police.

14.3 Direct Evidence and Circumstantial Evidence

The testimony of a witness regarding matters they personally saw, heard, felt, smelt, perceived or otherwise experienced constitutes *direct* evidence, which should it be believed, the testimony would be sufficient to prove a fact in issue without the need for further evidence or inference (Choo T 2018).

Evidence is *circumstantial* if it is evidence from which a fact in issue may be inferred. Types of circumstantial evidence could include, for example:

- circumstantial evidence of the opportunity to commit a crime, such as the presence of an accused person at the scene of a crime during the relevant time
- fingerprints and biological samples found at a location, including the scene of a crime which matches to the accused. These include forensic material linking the accused to objects (moveable or fixed) at a location or scene
- the post-offence conduct of an accused, which in certain circumstances may provide circumstantial evidence of their culpability for the crime. Examples could include fleeing from a crime scene or concealing items used in the commission of an offence or obtained as a result of committing the crime
- in the right circumstances, motive may also constitute relevant circumstantial evidence, such as previous acts or words of the accused to show they entertained malice towards a victim

14.4 Testimonial Evidence and Real Evidence

Testimonial evidence is oral evidence, so the testimony of a witness consists of their oral statements made in court.

Real evidence is not oral testimony, and it is evidence that can be inspected by the fact finders in court. Some examples to demonstrate real evidence include objects such as weapons, clothing, documents, photographs, CCTV and other material. Real evidence is diverse and could even include an out-of-court jury visit to a crime scene.

14.5 Hearsay Evidence

The hearsay provisions under the Criminal Justice Act 2003 which came into force on 4 April 2005 can be complex. Hearsay evidence is evidence of an out-of-court statement that is being adduced in court as evidence of a matter stated in the statement. Previously there was a common law rule that rendered hearsay evidence inadmissible in court unless it fell under certain exceptions to the rule.

The general rule against the admissibility of hearsay evidence continues due to its perceived reliability. To be allowed in evidence, an application will be required for consent under the narrow parameters defined in the Criminal Justice Act 2003.

14.6 Investigators' Pre-court Preparation

If required to give evidence during criminal procedures, investigators should prepare for a court appearance by reading the case file including all relevant statements and documents and particularly their own evidence. This assists to refresh the memory and reinstate a detailed knowledge of the case and contextualise the potential issues. It is likely that several months will have elapsed since the initial investigation so regardless of other priorities this preparation is essential.[1]

Investigators are not expert witnesses and will only be required to give evidence about matters they personally experienced or were involved in such as seizing exhibits and interviewing suspects and witnesses. Depending on the matter in issue between the prosecution and the defence, it is possible that an investigator could be required to provide witness testimony about the conduct of the investigation.

KEY POINTS

- Ensure that all the required exhibits are available at court.
- Ensure any unused material that may be required during the hearing if the defence make a successful request to the prosecutor, or an application is made to the judge is available at court.
- At court, maintain security of all exhibits and material and do not leave any unattended or in a public area
- Investigators need to ensure they are in possession of all notes or other records they may require when giving evidence. These must have been previously scheduled as either exhibits or unused material depending on the circumstances of the case.
- Do not assume that anyone else will be dealing with the points above unless this has been discussed and confirmed in advance.

14.6.1 Physical preparation

Taken at face value the following points seem straightforward and obvious. If adhered to and added to the pre-court

[1] At the time of writing in 2022, the COVID 19 pandemic has led to a backlog of court cases, which will extend the waiting time for trials considerably.

preparation, they will contribute to the professional provision of evidence.

KEY POINTS

- Arrive in plenty of time.
- Familiarise yourself with the location of the specific court, its surroundings and the witness box.
- Report to the court usher and the prosecutor.
- Do not speak to the defendant or their legal representative(s) without CPS approval.
- Always portray a professional appearance, even when out of the courtroom. Defence teams may try to spot inappropriate comments and unprofessional behaviour to discredit the police handling of the case.
- Be careful when liaising with or speaking to victims and witnesses at court who may be giving evidence in the case themselves. This could be construed as coaching and potentially an abuse of process, particularly when investigators are due to give evidence themselves.

14.7 **Taking the Oath**

When an investigator takes their place in the witness box, they will be asked by the usher whether they wish to take the oath or affirm. Deciding in advance which is preferred is advised; and even if known, it is advisable to READ from the card provided as it helps to settle any nerves and build confidence and composure.

When giving the oath or affirmation breathe slowly and be relaxed. It is important to appear professional and confident, even if feeling slightly nervous or perhaps apprehensive.

KEY POINT

Oath

I swear by almighty god that the evidence I shall give shall be the truth, the whole truth and nothing but the truth.

Affirmation

I do solemnly, sincerely and truly declare and affirm that the evidence I shall give shall be the truth, the whole truth and nothing but the truth.

Different oaths and religious books are available to support whatever faith the witness follows.

14.8 Golden Triangle

When in court it is an unnatural situation in which questions are asked by one person (generally the prosecution or defence lawyer/barrister but sometimes the magistrate/judge) but the witness directs the answers to a different set of people (magistrates/jury) and not the questioner. This is known as the 'golden triangle of communication' and is illustrated in Figures 14.1 (in the magistrates' court) and 14.2 in the Crown Court.

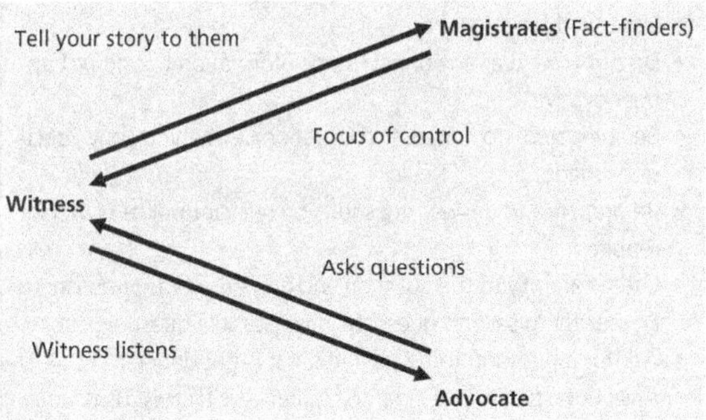

Figure 14.1 Magistrates' court

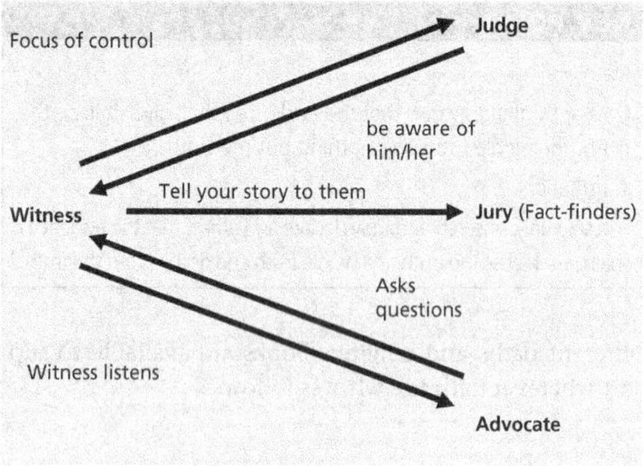

Figure 14.2 Crown Court

KEY POINTS

- Acoustics in court may be poor so project the voice.
- Slow down the pace of delivery so important points are not missed.
- Answers and explanations provided in court are for the benefit of the jury. The use of police jargon should be avoided.
- Keep answers straightforward and appropriately concise unless asked for a fuller answer.
- Do not volunteer any unnecessary information but do not appear evasive.
- Be prepared to discuss the rationale behind any decisions made.
- Be prepared to answer questions on relevant police powers if required.
- Listen carefully to the question and only answer that question. Do not try to second guess the next possible question.
- Ask for a question to be repeated if it is not understood.
- Answer factually; investigators' evidence is facts NOT assumptions and only expert witnesses can give evidence of their opinion.

- Request permission from the judge/magistrate to consult any relevant notes or records if this would help to answer the question.
- If reading a transcript of an interview be aware of intonation, do not be monotone and boring.
- Maintain eye contact with the fact finders and the jury.
- Know how to address the court correctly; show appropriate respect but try not to overuse the titles.
- If the answer to a question is not known, then say so.
- Consider the answer and THINK before speaking.
- Straightforwardness and integrity make for a credible witness; honesty is the only policy.

For the purpose of this handbook these considerations have been applied in the context of a magistrates' court or Crown Court, but they are equally relevant to a coroner's inquest or other tribunal or hearing.

References

Attorney General's Office (2020) *Attorney Generals Guidelines on Disclosure*

Choo AL-T (2018) *Evidence* (6th edn, OUP)

Moreno Y and Hughes P (2008) *Blackstone's Effective Prosecution, Working in Partnership with the CPS* (OUP)

Appendix

Checklist: 50 Initial Considerations for Crime Investigators

1. Obtain and review the incident log.
2. Identify the scene of the incident along with any additional scenes and other relevant locations.
3. Identify the person currently in charge at the scene(s) and make contact. Check and confirm decisions already made and the actions taken.
4. Ensure appropriate steps have been or are being taken to preserve identified scenes.
5. Identify the type of incident/offence and apply any local procedures (rape, missing person, suspicious–unexplained death, critical incident, major incident etc).
6. Take control and assume responsibility for the investigation if it is within your area of responsibility (record the time and update the incident log).
7. Attend the scene as soon as possible. If unable to attend record the reasons why this is not possible.
8. Assess the health and safety and welfare considerations for all staff and others involved including yourself. Identify and implement any necessary mitigation measures.
9. Identify, secure, protect (ISP) and sequentially number all scenes, for example attack sites, incident location, victim(s), arrested suspect(s), vehicles, weapons, deposition sites for weapons and other property etc.
10. Review cordons already in place and revise these if necessary. Ensure a scene log is commenced and

cordon officers are briefed regarding the requirements. Prevent cross-contamination between victims, scenes, witnesses and suspects.

11. Consider the digital scene and its preservation, including attending officers and emergency services, turning off wi-fi enabled devices to prevent contamination.
12. Identify rendezvous points and common approach paths and communicate these to all staff and others involved.
13. Make a record of the environmental conditions, including the weather, lighting/visibility.
14. Victim(s)—identify their location, personal details, injuries, medical attention received or required and other welfare considerations.
15. Victim(s)—appropriately obtain and record an initial account.
16. Victim(s)—forensic considerations including informed consent for obtaining forensic samples, recovery of clothing, mobile phones/devices and other investigative material.
17. Victim(s)—develop a wider interview strategy to expand on any initial account, including their categorisation, the method of recording, appropriate questioning to recall the event and the relevant background and victimology information.
18. Identify any safeguarding measures required.
19. Identify and interview the person(s) who reported the incident to the police.
20. Debrief the initial responders including other emergency services (out of the hearing of witnesses, friends, relatives and members of the public).
21. Collate any statements, notes, exhibits and wider investigative material already obtained. Maintain continuity and consider disclosure implications from the beginning.
22. Establish facts and information that are currently known or not known. Identify any information gaps

to be addressed and facts to be established (using the 5WH questions).

23. Identify location parameters and prioritise and co-ordinate all activities at the scene(s), for example scene examination, search, house-to-house (H2H) enquiries, CCTV identification and recovery.
24. Identify and review any fast track actions already initiated and monitor their progress. Commence a numbered list of actions raised and allocated.
25. Depending on the seriousness of the incident/offence implement the force escalation policy if necessary, for example inform the Force Incident Manager, duty detective inspector or on-call Senior Investigating Officer using local protocols for major and critical incidents.
26. Assess the need for and request any additional personnel required. Upon their arrival further brief attending staff on their roles and responsibilities.
27. Identify and request any specialist resources and equipment required, for example Crime Scene Investigator, scene tent, Forensic Medical Examiner, Police Search Adviser, Digital Media Investigator and scent dogs.
28. Conduct or arrange fast track H2H enquiries within line of sight/hearing of scene(s).
29. Conduct fast track searches including routes taken by suspects to and from the scene(s).
30. Identify CCTV opportunities and recovery along routes taken by suspects to and from the scene(s).
31. Develop early hypotheses about what may have happened, including where, when, who was involved and why. Set objectives and establish the timeframe(s) for the investigation including during, before and after the event.
32. Geography—survey the area/location, check environmental surroundings and local community impact in the context of offence, scene(s) and manage any disruption caused.

33. Decide on the main lines of enquiry and plan and prioritise the investigative strategies to progress these.
34. Other agencies—where relevant, notify the fire service, adult and child social care, HM Coroner, Health and Safety at Work Executive and any other agencies with joint investigation responsibilities.
35. Develop a CCTV recovery and viewing strategy, including prioritising any locations covered by CCTV which suspects(s) must have crossed on route to, and away from, the scene(s) as well as the primary scene(s) itself.
36. If necessary and proportionate develop a wider managed search strategy, considering forensic, physical, premises, open air, vehicles, water, etc.
37. If necessary and proportionate develop a managed H2H strategy including producing a bespoke questionnaire.
38. Develop a witnesses strategy including identifying and locating, obtaining first accounts, first descriptions of suspect(s), categorisation for interview (significant, vulnerable or intimidated), witness needs assessment and welfare, obtaining informed consent, conducting the interview, special measures, interview supporters and intermediaries if required.
39. Develop a suspect(s) strategy including identification, obtaining and circulating descriptions, locating, risk assessment, arrest planning, forensic recovery, detention management and interviews under caution.
40. Intelligence requirements—research victim(s), suspect(s), relevant location(s), using closed and open sources.
41. Other passive data opportunities, including Automatic Number Plate Recognition (ANPR), digital and communications devices and dashboard cameras.
42. Obtain recordings and accurate transcripts of related calls/messages (eg 999/101). Debrief the call takers/ resource despatchers if necessary.

43. Data communication collection, including mobile phones, social media use, images, photos and videos on devices.
44. Digital media investigation—identify and exploit digital opportunities at scenes and other relevant locations to establish wireless contact between devices.
45. Exhibits—accurately record handling processes, preservation of continuity and integrity and storage in appropriate conditions. Consider using a dedicated Exhibits Officer for larger scale investigations.
46. Identify linked or precursor incidents, research previous or linked incident logs, local knowledge and intelligence sources. Consider linked series and crime pattern analysis if appropriate.
47. Communications strategy—provide updates via the internal force briefing and debriefing process, other relevant team members, key personnel, supervisors, senior officers. Produce current situation reports, media holding statements and brief other relevant external agencies as required.
48. Provide regular updates to victims, families, witnesses and communities concerned.
49. Consider, plan and implement further safeguarding and/or crime prevention measures.
50. Record decisions taken and their reasons/rationale, including the time, the situation and information available at that time, the options available, actions taken or not taken and resources required and available.

Index

All references are to section numbers. Boxes, checklists, figures and tables are indicated by a b, c, f, and t following the section number.

Index

Index